Contents

Foreword vii
Preface viii
About the Authors xi

Part One — Preview

I
A Brief History of Philippine Mass Communication 1
From Spanish times to the present
Crispin C. Maslog

Part Two — Overview

II
Introduction to Communication 43
Definition of communication terms
Crispin C. Maslog

III
Communication and Society 57
Roles and importance of mass communication in society
Crispin C. Maslog

IV
The Role of Communication in a Crisis 69
The role of mass communication in the Philippine Revolution of 1986
Crispin C. Maslog

V
A People Power-Media Coalition 103
An analysis of the role played by mass media in harnessing of people power
Florangel Rosario-Braid

VI
Mass Media and Values 109
The role of mass media in the formation of values
Fr. Cornelio Lagerwey, M.S.C.

VII
Development Communication Today 113
Update on the new discipline of development communication
Nora C. Quebral

VIII
Development Journalism: An Update 125
Update on a new type of Third World journalism
Juan F. Jamias

Part Three — Print Media Today

Introduction to Print Media

IX
Manila's Metropolitan Press 139
Profile and analysis of metropolitan newspapers, magazines and journals
Domini T. Suarez

X
The Community Press 159
Profile and analysis of Philippine community newspapers
Crispin C. Maslog

XI
Book Publishing Industry 165
Profile and analysis of Philippine book publishing
Pacifico N. Aprieto

XII
Komiks in the Philippines 181
The role of comics, profile af the Philippine comics industry
Noel Bejo, SVD

PHILIPPINE COMMUNICATION: AN INTRODUCTION

Crispin C. Maslog

Foreword by
Senator Orlando Mercado

With chapters contributed by Adlai J. Amor & Alexander G. Amor, Pacifico N. Aprieto, Delia R. Barcelona & Virgilio M. Gaje, Noel Bejo, SVD, Florangel Rosario-Braid, Elizabeth L. Diaz, Lutgarda R. Elvinia & Ramon R. Osorio, Gloria D. Feliciano & Cesar M. Mercado, Ibarra M. Gonzales, Juan F. Jamias, Fr. Cornelio Lagerwey, MSC, Amiel Leonardia, Raul T. Panares, Josefina S. Patron, Jose L. Pavia, Nora C. Quebral, Ernesto I. Songco, Domini T. Suarez, Nicanor G. Tiongson and Victor T. Valbuena.

This book is dedicated to the Filipino communication student, recently freed from the Marcosian manipulation of Philippine mass media, but who still needs to be liberated from Western communication myths.

Copyright 1988
by Philippine Association of Communication Educators

All rights reserved.

Reprint editions, as per agreement with PACE,
by New Day Publishers
P. O. Box 167, 1100 Quezon City
Tel. No. 99-80-46

ISBN 971-110-061-4

First Impression by PACE, 1988
Second Impression by NDP, August 1988

A PACE Publication

Part Four — Electronic Media Today

XIII
Fundamentals of Radio Broadcasting 199
Profile and analysis of the radio profession and industry in the Philippines
Ernesto I. Songco

XIV
Broadcast Media at the Crossroads 211
The roles of Philippine radio and television, analsyis of the problems of the broadcast media
Raul T. Pañares

XV
Towards a Public Broadcasting System for the Philippines 229
A proposal for an alternative broadcasting system for the country
Elizabeth L. Diaz

XVI
Fundamentals of Film 241
Profile of Filipino movies and the movie profession and industry
Amiel Leonardia

XVII
Film Making: Problems and Prospects 253
Analysis of issues and problems of the Philippine movie industry
Nicanor G. Tiongson

Part Five — Small Media

XVIII
Folk Media and Development 273
The role of folk media in development communication
Victor T. Valbuena

XIX
Traditional Media 283
Description of most common traditional media in the Philippines
Josefina S. Patron

XX
Group Media 293
Description and analysis of the re-discovered communication media--group media
Ibarra M. Gonzales

Part Six — Adjuncts of Media

XXI
Advertising Today: Profile and Problems 307
Profile and analysis of the Philippine advertising profession and industry
Lutgarda R. Elvinia and Ramon R. Osorio

XXII
Government Information As Propaganda: The Past 325
Historical profile and analysis of the Marcos dictatorship's propaganda machine
Jose L. Pavia

XXIII
Government Information as Development Communication: The Present 337
Profile of the Aquino government's information thrust
Delia R. Barcelona and Virgilio M. Gaje

XXIV
News Agencies 345
Profile of news agency work in the Philippines
Adlai J. Amor and Alexander G. Amor

XXV
Communication Research 355
The status of communication research in the country today
Gloria D. Feliciano and Cesar M. Mercado

XXVI
Communication Education: An Overview 369
The status of communication education in the country today
Crispin C. Maslog

FOREWORD

We, Filipino mass communicators and communication educators, are a strange lot. We love to communicate orally but not in writing, We in broadcast media, especially, talk and talk but do not write. We communication teachers, also, talk a lot to our students but write very little. Especially books. Even our brothers in the print media have shown very little evidence of scholarly writing that is timeless as well as timely.

So over the years we have been using Western textbooks in our schools. Even our mass communicators have been reading mostly American or English books in communication. And so Western cultural imperialism has extended even to our mass media.

It comes as a pleasant surprise, therefore, that a friend and colleague in communication education, Dr. Crispin C. Maslog, has come out with this book, *Philippine Communication: An Introduction.* The book comes at a very opportune time, when we are reassessing the role of communication in our society and when people are protesting against Western inroads into our educational system. The author deserves our congratulations.

As a member of the board of directors of the Philippine Association of Communication Educators (PACE) many years ago, I remember how we talked fervently about the need for Filipino textbooks in communication. And I remember how no one did anything about it. Until now.

Philippine Communication: An Introduction is a comprehensive book that covers practically all aspects of the field of communication in the Philippines. And the names of the contributors to this book, both practitioners and educators, are practically a who's who in communication in the Philippines. It is scholarly yet simply written for the beginning student in communication. In short, it will make an excellent textbook for the Filipino student in communication.

As a mass communicator and communication educator, not to mention now as a politician, I am very pleased to welcome the arrival of this book and to endorse it wholeheartedly. Not only to communication students and their professors but also to practitioners and politicians. Politicians will understand journalists better after reading it. For that matter the entire Filipino reading public will benefit by this book that illuminates the central role of communication in our modern society.

Senator Orlando Mercado

PREFACE

To paraphrase a philosopher, this book is an idea whose time has come. Like most ideas, this one took a long time coming. It was conceptualized as early as the mid-seventies when the first book of its kind, *Philippine Mass Media in Perspective,* by Gloria D. Feliciano and Crispulo J. Icban, was almost a decade old and getting outdated.

Over the years after that, at seminars, workshops and conferences attended by Philippine communication educators, talk would inevitably wander into the area of locally authored textbooks in communication. Everyone would wax eloquent over the need for indigenous instructional materials, which are not only more relevant but less expensive for our Filipino students.

But almost always, the heated discussions would be followed by freezing inaction. Invariably the excuse was no time. There were a few exceptions, to be sure, but for the first course in communication for our Filipino students, only one, a book of readings, has been put together since the Feliciano-Icban book.

So we continued to nurture the idea of a textbook, or main reference, written especially for the Introduction to Communication course. We sought help from various quarters to translate this idea into reality.

The first assistance came in 1980-81, a faculty development grant from Silliman University, where we used to teach. The grant was given to some faculty members of Silliman's School of Communication then, to do research and write the first chapters for this book.

We did Chapter I (A Brief History of Philippine Mass Communication), Chapter II (Introduction to Communication) and Chapter III (Communication and Society). Our colleagues at the time, Amiel Leonardia, Ernesto I. Songco and Alexander G. Amor, wrote what is now Chapter XIII (Fundamentals of Radio Broadcasting), Chapter XVI (Fundamentals of Film), and Chapter XXIV (News Agencies).

In 1982-83, we were granted a sabbatical leave by Silliman University to complete the research and writing for the book at the Department of Development Communication, University of the Philippines Los Baños. It was while on sabbatical at UPLB that this author was able to get help in 1985-86 from The Asia Foundation for research and conference on "The Role of Communication in the Philippines After the Revolution." By that time, we had been elected president of the Philippine Association of Communication Educators (PACE), under whose auspices the conference was held in June 1986.

The Asia Foundation also provided funds for the publication of ten papers coming out of the conference, which now form Chapter IV (The Role of Communication in a Crisis), Chapter V (A People Power-Media Coalition), Chapter VI (Mass Media and Values), Chapter VII (Development Communication Today), Chapter IX (Manila's Metropolitan Press), Chapter XIV (Broadcast Media at the Crossroads), Chapter XV (Towards a Public Broadcasting System for the Philippines), Chapter XVII (Film Making: Problems and Prospects, Chapter XXI (Advertising Today: Profile and Problems), and Chapter XXII (Government Information as Propaganda: The Past).

After the chapters written by the Silliman communication faculty and the contributors to the PACE conference were put together, however, we saw gaps still to be filled if this book was going to serve as an adequate textbook or reference for Introduction to Communication. So we solicited contributions from communication teachers and scholars, who responded admirably to the call for service to the cause of communication education. Their contributions resulted in the following: Chapter VIII (Development Journalism: An Update), Chapter XI (Book Publishing Industry), Chapter XII (Komiks in the Philippines), Chapter XVIII (Folk Media and Development), Chapter XIX (Traditional Media), Chapter XX (Group Media), Chapter XXIII (Government Information as Development Communication: The Present), and Chapter XXV (Communication Research: A Status Analysis). And then we contributed two final chapters – Chapter X (The Community Press) and Chapter XXVI (Communication Education: An Overview).

Finally, 26 chapters were assembled, which we feel cover almost all the aspects of communication in the Philippines that the beginning Filipino student in communication needs to know, or has time to cover in a semestral course. This book is meant to be an introduction to communication for the first or second year Filipino student who even until now is being fed Western concepts and facts on communication in our schools.

Philippine Communication: An Introduction is more than just a book of readings, a collection of published materials. Its chapters were written especially for this book and with the needs of the introductory course especially in mind. We can say therefore that this is the second book in the Philippines of its kind, meant to update the Feliciano-Icban book.

Now that the chapters were assembled, the next major problem was editing. We needed time for it. We asked and were granted a writing leave (with no teaching duties) for one semester by the Department of Development Communication, UPLB, where we are now permanently situated. And so after years of planning, toil and tears, this book.

To paraphrase a world statesman this time, never has a single book owed so much to so many: to the writers of 20 of the 26 chapters; to Silliman University and the Department of Development Communication at UP Los Baños for the sabbatical leaves to write this book; to Mr. Roberto J. Panteñila, who ably assisted us in editing the manuscript; to The Asia Foundation for funding its publication; to the Philippine Association of Communication Educators under whose auspices this book is published; to the typists, typesetters, proofreaders and artists too numerous to mention by name but who worked equally long and hard on the production of this book; and finally to my wife, Florita, and children, Edgar and Juliet, who by staying out of the way gave me time and quiet, unwavering support in completing a seemingly endless task.

To all of them, this writer expresses his profound thanks. Because of them, what was once an idea is now a reality.

CRISPIN C. MASLOG

About the Authors

Adlai J. Amor is director, Philippine Press Institute; deputy executive director, Depthnews Asia; and training director, Press Foundation of Asia. He has an M.S. in journalism from Columbia University.

Alexander G. Amor, the father of Adlai Amor, is assistant professor, School of Communication, Silliman University. He was a former correspondent of the Philippine News Service and subsequently of the Philippines News Agency. He is also a practicing lawyer.

Pacifico N. Aprieto is author of six books, the latest of which is the book of short essays, *Things You Don't Read in the Papers* (Adriana Printing, 1986). He has free-lanced for various newspapers, written fiction and taught journalism in the U.P. Institute of Mass Communication. A graduate of U.P., he was the lone Asia Foundation Felllow in advanced science reporting at the Columbia University Graduate School of Journalism in New York in 1965. He writes a weekly column in the *Philippine Starweek*. He managed the Philippine Textbook Project from 1976 to 1986.

Delia R. Barcelona is associate professor and graduate program coordinator of the University of the Philippines, Institute of Mass Communication and concurrently Deputy Director for Research of the Philippine Information Agency. She holds a doctorate in sociology from the University of Chicago.

Noel Bejo, SVD, is a priest of the Society of the Divine Word. He is a second year theologian at Divine Word Seminary in Tagaytay City. He holds an M.A. in philosophy.

Florangel Rosario-Braid is executive dean, Asian Institute of Journalism. She is also president of *Philippine Daily Inquirer* and of the Philippine Communication Society. She was former member of the 1986 Constitutional Commission. She holds a Ph.D. in communication from Syracuse University.

Elizabeth L. Diaz is associate professor of broadcasting communication, Institute of Mass Communication, University of the Philippines. She has a master's degree in communication from Stanford University.

Lutgarda R. Elvinia is research and publications management officer, and faculty member, Communication Arts Department, Maryknoll College Foundation, Quezon City. She has been teaching advertising courses.

Gloria D. Feliciano was for two decades dean of the Institute of Mass Communication, University of the Philippines in Diliman, Quezon City. After she retired in 1986, she founded her own research agency. She has a Ph.D. in communication from Wisconsin University.

Virgilio M. Gaje is acting division chief for data bank of the Philippine Information Agency. He has been with the government information service since 1977, when he joined the then Ministry of Information as Media Specialist II. He is a graduate of journalism from the University of the Philippines, Institute of Mass Communication.

Fr. Ibarra M. Gonzales, S.J., is an assistant professor of the Department of Communication, Ateneo de Manila University. He finished his MA in Communication Research at the UPIMC, 1980 and Ph.D. in communication theories and research at the University of Southern California, Los Angeles, in 1986.

Juan F. Jamias is professor, Institute of Development Communication, University of the Philippines Los Baños. He was also former chairman of the Department of Development Communication. He has edited *Readings in Development Communication* (1977), and has just finished the manuscript for another book, *Writing for Development,* which will be published early in 1988 by UP Los Baños. He got his Ph.D. in communication from the University of Wisconsin.

Fr. Cornelio Lagerwey, MSC, is a Dutch missionary priest who came to the Philippines in 1955 and has since been pioneering in using media as social communication to serve people. He founded two communication institutes, the Social Communication Chevalier Center and the Communication Foundation for Asia (CFA).

Amiel Leonardia is playwright-in-residence, Speech and Drama Department, University of the Philippines, Diliman, Quezon City. He was former associate professor and chairman, Speech and Theater Arts Department, Silliman University.

Cesar M. Mercado is now on the staff of the United Nations Development Program (UNDP) in Bangkok, Thailand. He was former professor, Institute of Mass Communication, University of the Philippines, Diliman, Quezon City. He has a Ph.D. in communication from the University of Wisconsin.

Ramon R. Osorio is chairman, Communication Arts Department, Faculty of Arts and Letters, University of Santo Tomas and advertising executive of DYR–Alcantara, Manila. He has a master's degree in business administration and has been teaching advertising.

Josefina S. Patron was former director of planning and development, and director, VTR Cassette Project, National Media Production Center. Before that she was chairman of the Department of Communication, Ateneo de Manila University. She has a Ph.D. in communication.

Jose L. Pavia was former general manager, Philippines News Agency, and Unesco consultant on news agencies.

Raul T. Pañares is president of Radio Philippines Network Channel 9 and executive director of Kapisanan ng mga Brodkaster sa Pilipinas. He is at the same time broadcast consultant of Radio Mindanao Network. He has a master in business management degree from Ateneo de Manila University.

Nora C. Quebral is professor, Institute of Development Communication, University of the Philippines Los Baños. She was chairman of the Department of Development Communication for ten years until 1986, before it became an institute. She holds a Ph.D. in communication from the University of Wisconsin.

Ernesto I. Songco is executive director, Mass Media Commission of the National Council of Churches in the Philippines. He was former manager of radio station DYSR in Dumaguete City and taught broadcasting in the School of Communication, Silliman University, Dumaguete City.

Domini Torrevillas Suarez is a columnist of *Philippine Star*. She was former columnist of the defunct *Philippine Tribune* and editor of *Philippine Panorama* from 1981 to 1986. She has a master of science in journalism degree from Medill School of Journalism, Northwestern University, Illinois.

Nicanor G. Tiongson is artistic director of the Cultural Center of the Philippines. He is also associate professor and former chairman of the Department of Filipino and Philippine Literature, College of Arts and Letters, University of the Philippines, Diliman. He finished his Ph.D. in Philippine Studies at the University of the Philippines in 1979. He has written books on the *sinakulo*, the *komedya* and a contemporary *sarsuwela*. He has also edited an anthology of film criticism, *The Urian Anthology;* an anthology of essays, protest songs, poems, plays, film documentaries and visual arts: *The Politics of Culture: The Philippine Experience;* and *The Cultural Traditional Media of ASEAN.*

Victor T. Valbuena is senior programme specialist of the Asian Mass Communication Research Information Centre in Singapore. He is on leave as associate professor, Institute of Mass Communication, University of the Philippines. He has a Ph.D. in communication from Centro Escolar University.

Part One

Preview

To understand Philippine mass communication and other forms of communication at present, one has to go back to the past. This section, consisting of Chapter I, takes the reader back to our colonial past.

One will note that Philippine mass communication came with our colonizers. The Spaniards introduced printing and printed the first book in the Philippines, **Doctrina Christiana**, in 1593. They also published the first newspaper, **Del Superior Govierno**, in 1811. The Americans showed the first movies in the Philippines in 1897 and two Americans, Harry Brown and Albert Yearsly, produced the first two movies in the country (both about Jose Rizal) in 1912. Another American, Henry Hermann, started the first three 50-watt radio stations in Manila and Pasay in 1922. It was another American, Edmund Bullis, who set up the first advertising agency in the country, Philippine Publicity Service, in 1921. Again, the first television franchise in the country was granted to another American, James Lindberg. But a Filipino, Antonio Quirino, bought his company and earned the right to start the first TV station in the Philippines, DZAQ-TV, in 1953. No wonder then that our mass media are very much Westernized.

Chapter 1

A Brief History of Philippine Mass Communication

Crispin C. Maslog

To understand Philippine mass media at present, one has to look at them in the light of history. They have roots that go back quite a way to the country's colonial past. For example, the first book, *Doctrina Christiana*, was printed in the Philippines in 1593,[1] just a little over a century after John Gutenberg introduced printing with movable types in Europe, in 1425. Compare this with the fact that the first book was not printed in the United States until after 1638.[2]

The first Philippine newsletter, *Successos Felices* (Glad Tidings), the equivalent of the European broadsheets, was published in 1637, while the first American newsletter, Harris' *Public Occurrences, Both Foreign and Domestick*, was put out in 1690.

Although *Successos* could not be called the first Philippine newspaper, because there is no record of other issues after this first one, it is, nevertheless, a remarkable achievement. While the British corantos picked up the news freely from Dutch and German sources, the *Successos* was more of an original work, and not merely a compilation or a translation.[3] The first Filipino printer, Tomas Pinpin, who was responsible for putting out *Successos*, wrote about two major national events: a Spanish naval victory over the Dutch in Cavite and a military victory over Muslim Filipino rebels.

So, if we date the beginnings of mass communications to the invention of the printing press in 1425, it did not take long for mass communications to reach Philippine shores from Europe.

In 1521, the Portuguese explorer Ferdinand Magellan, sailing in the name of the Spanish Queen Isabela, discovered the Philippines for Europe. In all probability he brought with him the first European books, including a copy of the Bible, to the country. His chaplain and historian, Fr. Pigafetta, wrote a diary which has become a source book on early Philippine history.

The Spanish missionaries followed in succeeding waves of expeditions to the Philippines, bringing with them printing presses and other paraphernalia for converting Filipinos to Christianity. The first printing presses in the country were owned by the religious orders.

Inspite of their early beginnings, however, Philippine mass media did not advance as fast as those of other countries in Asia, like Japan, Hongkong and Singapore, for example. It seems that after that initial period of activity, the Philippine mass media went into hibernation for a more than a century, until the first real newspaper came out in 1811. Valenzuela, a Philippine journalism historian, estimates that between 1593 and the 19th century 541 books were printed in the Philippines.[4]

The history of Philippine mass communication may be divided into the Spanish Period from 1521 to 1900, the American Period from 1901 to 1946, the Post-War period from 1946 to 1972, and the Martial Law Period from 1972 to 1986.

There was a brief revolutionary period between 1890 and 1905 which overlapped with the end of the Spanish period and the start of the American period. There was also a brief period of four years - the World War II period - when the Japanese occupied the Philippines from 1941 to 1945. But technically the Philippines was still a colony of the United States at that time.

I. SPANISH PERIOD
1. Newspapers

Del Superior Govierno, started in 1811, was the first regularly issued publication in the Philippines, and while it did not function as a newspaper by modern standards, at least it was intended to be a newspaper. It carried news about the Spanish-American war, the proceedings of the Spanish Cortes,[5] and in general, news from the mother country for the benefit of the Spaniards in the Philippines. The Spanish occupation of the Philippines lasted from 1521 to 1900.

Although there were a number of important happenings in the Philippines during the early 1800s -- including volcanic eruptions and Filipino rebellions -- *Del Superior* carried only news from abroad, because the paper was meant for the Spanish elite. The paper was edited by the Spanish Governor-General himself, and therefore, it was more of a government organ than anything else.

After 15 issues, *Del Superior Govierno* stopped printing for the peculiar reason that there was no more news to print. In other words they had run out of European materials to reproduce.

According to one Philippine journalism historian, Armando Malay:

> It was a weekly newspaper issued by the office of the governor to inform the Peninsulars in Manila on the events of the homeland... probably not more than 100 copies were printed of the initial issue. Some were posted on the walls of the stone buildings. News was about the war between Napoleon's France versus Spain and England which were allies. Because of rumors to the effect that the war was going badly for Spain, the *Del Superior Govierno* was published by the Governor-General who reprinted the news about the war from English gazettes. *Del Superior Govierno* was banned by the Spanish Cortes which passed a law prohibiting the reprinting of accounts from foreign gazettes unless these had been previously approved by the home government. *Del Superior Govierno* ceased publication on February 7, 1812.[6]

The banning by the Spanish Cortes of the reprinting of news from foreign publications marked the first act of censorship in the Philippines.

The first daily newspaper was started in the Philippines in 1846. This was *La Esperanza* (Hope), which turned out to be a colorless and dull newspaper, in its attempt to avoid trouble with the censors. There was strict pre-publication censorship in the Philippines during this time. *La Esperanza* dealt mostly with non-controversial subjects in order to be on the safe side.

Of the dailies that followed *La Esperanza*, the best-edited during the Spanish period was *Diario de Manila*, which started publication in 1848. The paper had its own foreign correspondent in Spain and at one time spent P3,000 in one month for promotion because it was competing with another good daily at the time, *El Comercio*.[7] *Diario* was staffed by competent men headed by Felipe del Pan, who was considered by historians as the ablest journalist of his time.

With one exception, *Diario* lived the longest among many Philippine dailies established during the Spanish period -- 38 years.[8] This paper was suppressed by the Spanish Governor-General in 1898 because it allegedly incited the Filipinos against Spaniards. The worthiest rival of *Diario* was *El Comercio.*

Because of more efficient management, *El Comercio* became the most stable newspaper during its time. It had the biggest circulation and the longest life span of any paper during the Spanish regime, a total of 56 years.

El Comercio was at the peak of its success when U.S. Admiral Dewey sailed into Manila Bay on May 1, 1898 and brought about the downfall of the Spaniards in the Philippines. *El Comercio* subsequently lost all its provincial circulation and gradually declined during the American regime until it ceased publication in 1925.

Another paper that marked a milestone in the history of Philippine journalism was *La Opinion*, started in 1827. It marked the beginning of political journalism in the Philippines and perhaps it was the first opinion magazine in this country. While the other papers were afraid of the government censors, *La Opinion* was a fighter. It was the first paper that criticized the Spanish friars and campaigned for the ouster of the religious, including one archbishop from the Philippines.[9]

Among the mass media, it was the newspaper that first developed in the Philippines. It was only later that the magazines, such as we know them today, came into existence.

2. Magazines

The early magazines in the Philippines were not known as magazines, since this is a modern term. They were known either as weeklies, fortnightlies, monthlies, quarterlies, journals or reviews. These early publications specialized in particular fields, like commerce, industry, agriculture, the professions, religion, government, arts and letters.

One journalism researcher[10] has suggested that the history of magazine journalism in the Philippines started when the Royal Economic Society of the Friends of the Country published *Registro Mercantil de Manila* on January 20, 1824. This journal carried items on the products and commerce of the country and lasted eight years.

Another commercial journal was the *Precios Corientos* (Current Prices), which was the first publication in the country to use the English language. *Precios* started publishing on July 6, 1924, and used both Spanish and English.

Other early magazines were *La Ilustracion Filipinas* (first published in 1859), one of the first illustrated journals in the Philippines promoting culture, *El Trovador Filipino* (1874), considered the first of the intellectual journals, *El Bello Sexo* (1891), considered the first women's magazine in the country and *Patnubay ng Katoliko* (1890), the first publication entirely in Tagalog.

A number of magazines, which were coming out weekly starting in 1884, might perhaps be considered a special category. They were the satire magazines, which used personal allusions and sarcasm in poems, essays, short stories and literary pieces to hit the important public officials of the day. These satire magazines, the first of which was *La Semana Elegante* (1884), became popular because of their wit and their humor.

Colonial journalism during the Spanish period was marked by censorship by the state and the church and by financial instability. The papers were published in Spanish and therefore had limited circulation, reaching only the Spaniards in the Philippines and the Spanish-speaking Filipino elite.

While the journalists of the period possessed graceful literacy style, their news writing was faulty, opinion was injected into news stories and they lacked a sense of news values. By modern standards, therefore, the papers of the Spanish period were more literary organs than newspapers.

3. Revolutionary Press

A brief shining moment in the history of the Philippine mass media was the rise of the revolutionary press in the latter part of the Spanish rule in the Philippines and the early part of the American regime, approximately between 1890 and 1905. The Philippine Revolution of 1896 was directed against the Spaniards. After the Spaniards were beaten by combined Filipino and American forces, the Americans took over in 1898.

The most famous of these revolutionary papers was *La Solidaridad*, which first came out on February 19, 1889. It was published in Spain and in Spanish. It was read by the Filipino illustrados (elite) both in Spain and the Philippines. This revolutionary paper became the rallying point of the Filipino intellectual expatriates in Europe.

Its first editor was Graciano Lopez Jaena and among its contributors were some of the big names in Philippine history who became the revolutionary heroes of 1896. These were Jose Rizal, Marcelo H. del Pilar, Lopez Jaena and Mariano Ponce.

This paper was banned by the Spanish authorities in the Philippines but it was smuggled into the country and found its way into Filipino homes. Since this paper was in Spanish, however, it had a limited circulation. There was need for a paper in one of the dialects and this paper was provided by another revolutionary hero, Andres Bonifacio, and his friend, Emilio Jacinto. These two, who were leaders of the secret revolutionary society called the Katipunan, secretly put out *Kalayaan* on January 1, 1896. This paper was entirely in Tagalog and although only one issue came out, it was credited with having fanned the revolutionary fervor of the Filipinos. Before Andres Bonifacio and his revolutionary band could put out the second issue, however, the Spanish authorities discovered the location of their printing press and Bonifacio was forced to destroy the printing press before the Spanish authorities could move in.

There were other revolutionary papers, like *La Independencia*, founded on September 3, 1898. It was edited by another revolutionary hero, Antonio Luna. It became the mouthpiece of the Filipino rebels in the war against Spain and the Americans. Among its writers were Rafael Palma, Jose Palma, Leon Ma. Guerrero and Cecilio Apostol. This paper was finally suppressed by the American authorities.

The spirit of revolution fanned by *La Independencia* continued into the period of the American occupation in the pages of *El Renacimiento*. This was a very nationalistic paper founded by Don Edgardo Ocampo and edited by Teodoro M. Kalaw. It became famous in the early years of the American regime because it had an intellectual and aggressive staff.

Most of the papers that were founded during the American Period were published in English and were pro-American. Many Americans who had come over as soldiers, teachers and missionaries, started their own papers. *El Renacimiento* was outstanding among the papers of this period because of its critical attitude towards the Americans.

After the American civil government took over from the military in 1901, there was, theoretically, freedom of the press in the Philippines. In practice, however, such freedom was sorely limited. Although there was no prior censorship, the libel laws were so strict that it was very easy for any government official or private person to win a decision in court.

Perhaps this is best illustrated by the case of *El Renacimiento*, the fighting paper which was killed by a libel suit in 1908. The libel suit arose out of an editorial that the paper wrote, entitled "Aves de Rapina," which the U.S. Secretary of the Interior, Dean C. Worcester, thought was an attack against him. To quote the late Sen. Claro M. Recto:

> During the first decade of the century, freedom of the press was only true in the sense that there was no previous censorship, but the libel laws were so strictly enforced by the Courts, that to criticize a high government official, for instance, a member of the Cabinet, meant a stiff prison term and a sizeable fine, not to mention crippling civil damages. Teodoro Kalaw was sentenced to 12 months imprisonment and P3,000 fine, plus a judgment for moral and punitive damages in the amount of P25,000 for the publication of the editorial "Aves de Rapina" in *El Renacimiento*, written by Fidel A. Reyes, upon complaint of Secretary of the Interior Worcester. The latter was not mentioned in the article either by name, or by the title of his office, but was allowed to prove, by testimonial evidence, that it was he who was alluded to in the words "vampire," "vulture," and "owl." used in the allegedly offensive article. Worcester also succeeded in obtaining judgment from the Supreme Court against such persons as Galo Lichauco, Angel Jose, Mariano Cansipit, Felipe Barreto, and Manuel Palma, who for purely patriotic motives contributed some funds to the foundation of the newspaper, for the payment of P25,000 as indemnity. Even the names *El Renacimiento* and *Muling Pagsilang* went under the hammer and were awarded to Worcester. No prosecutor would file such information with our Courts today; nor would a court hand down a verdict of conviction in a similar case.[11]

II. AMERICAN OCCUPATION

The second period in the history of the Philippine press was the period of the American occupation, which started about 1900 when Americans gained complete control of Manila and most of the country.

1. Newspapers

The first English language daily in the Philippines was established in

1898, appropriately enough by an Englishman, Thomas Gowan. This was the first *Manila Times* in the Philippines. This original *Manila Times* existed only for 32 years. It changed hands many times until Alejandro Roces, Sr., the first newspaper chain owner in the Philippines, bought the paper in 1927. At the time that Roces bought the paper, he already owned *Taliba*, a Tagalog daily, *Vanguardia*, a Spanish daily and the *Manila Tribune*, an English daily. In 1930 Roces disbanded the *Times* because he saw no need for two English papers.

The oldest existing newspaper in the Philippines is the *Manila Bulletin* which started as a shipping journal in 1900. It was only in 1912 that this paper, founded by an American, Carson Taylor, widened its scope to include news of general interest. The *Bulletin* developed a reputation as the mouthpiece of the American community in the Philippines even after Philippine independence was granted in 1946 and as long as Taylor was its editor, publisher and owner.

When Hans Menzi bought the paper in 1957, he modernized the paper's format and gave the newspaper a Filipino orientation, while retaining its shipping and business pages.

The press during the early American period was dominated by pro-American newspapers, naturally enough. It was not until 1920 that a pro-Filipino newspaper was published -- the *Philippines Herald*. This nationalistic paper was founded at the instigation of Manuel L. Quezon, who became president of the Philippines later.

One of the early editors of the *Philippines Herald* was Carlos P. Romulo who later became president of the United Nations General Assembly and became famous in Philippine diplomacy.

2. Movies

The movies came to the Philippines also by way of the United States, as in the case of radio. One will notice also that newspapers and magazines came to the Philippines by way of the colonizing countries -- first Spain and then the United States.

The history of the Filipino film may be divided into three periods: the Period of the Silent Pictures from 1897 to 1929, the Talking Pictures Period from 1929 to 1970; and the Period of the New Cinema from 1971 to the present.[12]

The first period may be divided into three stages - the dominance of the documentary film, the rise of the feature film and the establishment of Filipino film companies.

The phase of the documentary film began on January 1, 1897 when six movies were exhibited for the first time on a 60-mm Gaumont Chronomatograph projector at the Salon Pertierra on the Escolta. It ran through the first decade of American rule, when American film makers like Joe

Rosenthal, Burton Holmes and Raymond Ackerman came to the Philippines to shoot local scenes and events. Produced for local consumption and for exhibition in America, some of the documentaries showed such events as the eruption of Taal Volcano in 1911, local bullfighting, gold mining in Paracale, and the fiesta at Obando. From Europe and America, came documentaries on Napoleon and the assassination of President McKinley. A pianist and/or a band played music to accompany these films. During this era, and through the short foreign films, the Filipino was slowly introduced to American culture.

The rise of the feature film started in 1912. The American Harry Brown produced and directed "La Vida de Rizal," based on a popular stage play by Edward Meyer Gross. The film used the actors of the Molina-Benito Company, a dramatic troupe managed by *sarsuwela* actress Titang Molina-Gross. Competing with this film was "El Fusilamiento de Rizal," which was produced by another American, Albert Yearsley. Both were box-office successes.

Soon after, Yearsley filmed the famous Severino Reyes *sarsuwela*, "Walang Sugat," using Reyes' own *sarsuwela* company. Brown and Gross, between them, produced eight other feature movies, which included "Gomez, Burgos and Zamora," "Nena la Boxeadora," "El Filibusterismo" and "Florante at Laura."

These films adapted stories already popular among Filipinos, like historical episodes, and stories from *sarsuwelas, awits* and novels. This phenomenon later became a tradition. Film producers would discover over and over again that familiarity with the subject motivates audiences to see its film version. Because it drew subject matter from popular culture, the Filipino film early in its life identified itself as a form of popular culture.

1919 ushered in the new phase dominated by the first Filipino film producers. In 1917, the brothers Jose and Jesus Nepomuceno founded the Malayan Movies, which sought to adapt the movie industry "to the conditions and tastes of the country" — obviously in reaction to foreign movies which were Americanizing Filipino tastes at that time. In 1919, Nepomuceno produced his first film, "Dalagang Bukid," the Ilagan-Ignacio *sarsuwela* hit and which starred the original stage stars, Atang de la Rama and Marceliano Ilagan. With its success, Nepomuceno went on to film "La Venganza de Don Silvestre" (1920), and later the "Noli Me Tangere" (1930).

Three other Filipinos ventured into film production: Vicente Salumbides who introduced new camera techniques from Hollywood in films like "Miracle of Love" (1925); Julian Manansala who dared produce movies on political and nationalist themes, like "Patria et Amore" (1929); and Carmen Concha, who used authentic costumes and props for her movies, like "Oriental Blood" (1930). Other Filipino producers were the Silos brothers (Cesar, Octavio, Manuel, and Augusto), Carlos Vander Tolosa, Jose Domingo Badilla, and Rafael Hernandez.

By this time, certain problems had cropped up.

First, Filipino capital tended to be small (Malayan Movies only had P100,000 to work with), so that Filipino films always compared unfavorably with Hollywood movies, which were now distributed widely and which were very popular with the middle and upper classes.

Second, the first movies got stage performers, whose exaggerated acting techniques were necessary for plays staged in big theaters and in plazas. But these techniques were "over-acting" in close-up, a film characteristic. The camera, like a person sitting in a theater orchestra, stood in one place. The stories were peopled by stereotyped characters (*bida* vs. *kontrabida*), had convoluted plots, and "correct" endings. Later, with the coming of sound, the films carried heavy rhetorical and didactic dialogue with kilometric antiquated words.

The second major period, that of the talking pictures, may be divided into three stages - by the rise of the big commercial film companies, the achievement of technological expertise, and the utter commercialization of the Filipino film.

With the advent of the talkies in 1929, George P. Musser soon produced the first Filipino talking picture, "Ang Asuwang." Produced in 1932, it was only partly a talkie. The talking pictures became very popular during this period that saw the beginnings of big Filipino film companies. Seeing the big business potential of film, these companies transformed filmmaking into a big industry. In 1936, the first of the big companies, Philippine Films, produced "Zamboanga" for local and international release. Soon after, other companies were founded: Excelsior and Sampaguita Pictures (1937); LVN Pictures (1938); and X'otic Films (1939). By 1941, the big companies had their own studio lots and production facilities and made three or four films at a time.

Significant developments may be observed during that era.

First is the rise of the star system. Following the Hollywood practice of building up stars, Filipino producers likewise contracted, trained, and promoted local movie personalities (many of them resembling American actors and actresses), who were Caucasian-looking and glamorous. These stars were cast in stereotype *bida* or *kontrabida* roles. *Bidas* were the likes of Rosa del Rosario, Elsa Oria and Norma Blancaflor, Leopoldo Salcedo, Fernando Poe, Sr. and Rogelio dela Rosa, while *kontrabidas* were Monang Carvajal, Ramon d'Salva and Oscar Keesee. Stars like them made local films very popular before the war.

A second development is the rise of the genre movies. Imitating Hollywood films, local movies now classed themselves into: the adventure or action movie, which featured an endless string of fights; the drama or melodrama, which squeezed the audience's tears through and which had convoluted plots centering on the oppression of the poor and the weak; the musical comedy, which entertained through lavish production numbers with songs and dances;

the comedy, whose slapstick humor revolved around cruel, practical jokes; and the historical film, which extolled the life of a hero or a historical event.

Between 1941 and 1945, most movie companies stopped production, and only one movie, "Tatlong Maria," was produced by the Japanese. Ironically, the war period affected Philippine movies most profoundly only after it was all over. After the war, the big companies reorganized themselves and, as may be expected, came out with pictures on the Filipino's war experiences. Typical war pictures were moneymakers like "Garrison 13" (1946) and "Campo O'Donnel" (1950).

The decade of the '50s has been described by many writers as the "Golden Age of the Filipino Film." The decade was "golden" in two ways: first, Filipino film makers seem to have gained more technological expertise in filmmaking; and second, the first award-giving bodies, the Maria Clara Awards of the Manila Times Publishing Company in 1950-1951, and the Filipino Academy of Movie Arts and Sciences (FAMAS) awards from 1952 onwards, were established during this decade. The awards helped a lot in upgrading the quality of Filipino films by calling attention to the works of directors like Gerardo de Leon ("Ifugao"), Lamberto Avellana ("Anak Dalita"), Gregorio Fernandez; and Ramon Estrella. But most of the films churned out by the Big Four during this period — Sampaguita, Lebran, LVN and Premiere Productions — still had the same stereotyped plots and characters of pre-war movies.

With the closing down of big studios in the '60s and with the proliferation of independent companies that cared for nothing but profit, the film industry sank into one of its lowest periods. The movies indulged its audiences in an orgy of escapism, pushing the star system to its limits (movies then made money because they had Nora Aunor). They dished out the same genre stories which imitated the latest trends in the West: 1) action-violence, showing karate or kung fu and an imitation of James Bond; 2) melodrama, which most often centered on love triangles; 3) musicals, which strung foreign and local songs together in implausible Cinderella-like stories; 4) the comedies, which were slow on wit and fast on slapstick and toilet humor; and in the late '60s, 5) the *bomba* or sex film, that had no other purpose but sexual titillation of its audience. By and large, this decade was marked by a deterioration of the artistic and technical standards achieved in the previous decades.

The birth and growth of the new cinema, from 1971 to the present, has to be understood in relation to socio-cultural conditions. First, the decade saw the development of film directors and actors who were familiar with the Italian neo-realists and surrealists, the French New Wave and the Japanese art films. Many had studied film abroad or in local universities. These film artists believed in film as art and entered the industry as "oddities." But they later gained the acceptance and respect of their colleagues and audiences.

Second, the decade witnessed the birth of a new social consciousness, which was the product of activism in the early 70's. The oppression and repression of Marcos' dictatorial regime grew. Freedom of expression was curtailed through a string of censors' bodies and the film artists were controlled through the government-controlled Film Academy of the Philippines. In the face of these, Filipino film artists could no longer remain indifferent or uninvolved.

The new cinema thus gave birth to what may be considered contemporary Filipino film classics: Ishmael Bernal's films on the middle class ("Pagdating sa Dulo," "Relasyon," "Broken Marriage"), Lino Brocka's works on the lower classes ("Maynila, Sa Mga Kuko ng Liwanag," "Jaguar," "Bayan Ko: Kapit sa Patalim"), Marilou Diaz-Abaya's films on the new generation ("Brutal '81," "Kisapmata," "Sister Stella L."), and Peque Gallaga's period films ("Oro, Plata, Mata," and "Virgin Forest").

Similarly, the short film has developed into a major form of cinematic expression. Cheaper and easier to create, these films may be considered feature films that are highly personal, like Raymond Red's "Kabaka" and "Ang Magpakailanman"; or documentary films, like Joe Cuaresma's "Sabungan." Since 1982, especially after the Aquino assassination, Asia Visions has used the documentary film to expose the abuses of the Marcos regime, in films like "The Arrogance of Power," "Signos" and "Lakbayan."

Finally, because of the regime's oppression, many politicized film artists banded together, to fight for their rights. In February 1983, Lino Brocka organized the first Free-the-Artist, Free-the-Media rally. He denounced the expansion of the powers of Marcos' Board of Review for Motion Pictures and Television (Board of Censors) and later pushed to oust censors chief, Maria Kalaw-Katigbak. In July 1983, the Free-the-Artist Movement became the Concerned Artists of the Philippines, the most militant artists group under the Marcos regime. In April 1986, Brocka spearheaded the founding of the Unyon ng mga Manggagawa ng Pelikulang Pilipino (MPP), whose hundred or so members are pledged to fight for the economic rights of film artists and technicians.

Viewed as a whole, the new cinema has contributed to the spread of more realistic and scientific mentality among the people through pictures like "Broken Marriage," "Brutal" and "Moral," and to the politicization of movie audiences through pictures like "Sister Stella L."

The artists of the new cinema have catalyzed the formation of protest organizations which, with other organizations, finally caused the regime's downfall.

After the February Revolt, President Aquino appointed Cirio H. Santiago to head a Task Force that would oversee and take charge of all film-related government agencies. These agencies include, among others, the Movie and Television Review and Classification Board (MTRCB), the Videogram Regulatory Board (VRB), the Film Development Foundation of the Philippine (FDFP, formerly the Experimental Cinema of the Philippines), the NMPC Color Laboratory, and the Film Archives. The Task Force, whose members include Brocka, Jose F. Lacaba, and Agustin Sotto, suggested in its first report the creation of a Film Commission. If the President creates a Film Commission, then the film industry can likely expect greater freedom.

3. Radio

The electronic media came much later than the print media to the Philippines, as in other parts of the world. Of the electronic media, radio came first to the Philippines -- as early as 1922, during the American regime -- only two years after the first American radio station was set up in Pittsburgh, Pennsylvania.[13]

The first Philippine radio stations were set up by an American, Henry Hermann, in June 1922. He organized three 50-watt radio stations in Manila and the neighboring city of Pasay.

In 1925 KZKZ stopped broadcasting and was replaced by KZRQ. Radio personalities who first featured in these stations were given much attention and publicity by Manila newspapers.

In 1927 J. Amado Araneta bought KZRM, the bigger station, and KZEG, the smaller one from its American owners. This was the start of a trend in later years "media monopoly," particularly "cross ownership" as we have come to know it at present, because Araneta also owned the DMHM newspapers. Both radio stations and newspapers were managed under the Far East Broadcasting Company, with Carlos P. Romulo as managing director.

In 1929, radio was introduced to the provinces, when station KZRC was set up in Cebu City by Radio Corporation of the Philippines.

Before World War II broke out, there were six commercial stations in the country: KZRM, KZRF, KZIB, KZEG, KZRH, all in Manila and KZRC, a short-lived relay station in Cebu City. A government station, KZND, was established so that the Civil Emergency Administration could keep the people posted on war events, and eventually, helped in preparing Filipinos for war.

The Radio Control Board, which allocates frequencies, examines applications and conducts inspections, was put up in 1931 to implement the Radio Control Law. It enabled the Secretary of Commerce and Industry to watch over the medium.

Most of these pre-World War II stations were owned by Americans and their announcing staff were mostly Americans. The language used, naturally, was English. The programming was mostly entertainment and newscasts. The radio stars then were celebrities, in much the same way that the movie stars of today in the Philippines are public idols.

Those prewar radio stations were owned by department stores which used them to advertise, first, the radio sets they were selling, and second, the general merchandise they were carrying in their stores.

When the Japanese occupied the Philippines in 1942, all radio stations were closed, except for KZRH, which was renamed PIAM and used by the Japanese for their broadcasts.

To force everyone to listen, the Japanese went to the extent of reconditioning radio sets to prevent the reception of short-wave broadcasts from the American stations. Filipinos, however, proved to be resourceful; with left-over radio equipment, they managed to operate underground and continue the resistance movement.

The war years created a hunger for news and information. Radio became the news and information medium. This was most pronounced in 1945 after the war when Congress enacted Commonwealth Act 729 on July 2, 1946 to give the President a four-year right to grant temporary permits to establish radio stations. The number of radio stations grew at a phenomenal rate from eight in 1945 to 22 in 1954.

In 1947, Congress passed another act stipulating that stations change their first call letters from "K" to "D" so as not to be confused with the American radio call letters. Hence, "DZ" now stand for Luzon-based radio stations, "DY" for those in the Visayas, and "DX" for Mindanao stations.

Radio came to being mainly as an entertainment medium. The quick acceptance of the medium by the public led local distributors to put up their own stations since they discovered it as good and profitable business.

4. Newspaper Chains

One significant development during the American regime was the start of the newspaper chain in the Philippines. The first Filipino newspaper chain owner was Alejandro Roces Sr., whose sons Joaquin "Chino" and Ramon were to inherit and expand his mass media empire.

The Roces chain was known as the TVT *(Taliba-Vanguardia-Tribune)*. It started in 1916 when Roces bought *La Vanguardia*, a Spanish daily, and *Taliba*, a Tagalog daily. At the time that Roces bought these two papers, he was new to the newspaper game and the two papers were not taken seriously by the readers. Roces pirated Romulo from the *Herald* and made him the first editor of the *Tribune*. Together they built the *Tribune* into one of the two leading papers during the American period.

The other leading English language newspaper at the time was the *Herald*, which was part of a rival newspaper chain -- the DMHM (*El Debate-Mabuhay-Herald-Monday Post*).

These two chains competed with each other up to the time of the outbreak of World War II in 1941.

The first publication to be called a magazine in the Philippines was the *Philippine Magazine*, which was established in 1904. It was started as a semi-government publication for public school teachers in the Philippines, and at first it was called the *Philippine Teacher*. It was only in 1905 that it was renamed the *Philippine Magazine* and in 1906 it went from government to a private company, the Philippine Education Company.

A significant development during the American period was the chain of magazines in the vernacular which was started by Ramon Roces, another son of Alejandro Roces Sr., in 1923 with the publication of *Liwayway* in Tagalog. Other vernacular magazines of Ramon Roces followed -- *Bisaya* for the East Visayan region in 1932, *Hiligaynon* for the West Visayan region in 1934, and *Bannawag* for the Ilocano region in the north in 1940. These vernacular magazines were similar in content, format and appeal. They were meant for readers in the rural areas. Their contents were mostly fiction, entertainment and how-to-do-it articles.

Another magazine was founded in 1907, floundered and was taken over by Robert McCullough Dick in 1908. Dick built the paper into the leading English language magazine before martial law in 1972 -- the *Philippines Free Press*. The *Free Press* built its reputation on its fearless crusades against government corruption. In the years before martial law it became a staunch nationalist.

During World War II the Philippine mass media were closed. Only *Liwayway* of the pre-war publications was allowed to publish during the Japanese Occupation from 1942 to 1945. Even then the paper was completely in the hands of the Japanese and was used for propaganda purposes.

5. Advertising

Another significant development during the American period was the introduction of advertising as a profession to the Philippines by Americans, although its beginnings as a form of mass communication date back to the Spanish period.

In the late 16th and 17th centuries, when the Spaniards had consolidated trade and industry in the Philippines, commerce flourished. Apart from word of mouth, news on the arrival of trading galleons from Mexico and of junks and other merchant vessels from Southeast Asia were on hand-painted bills displayed in markets or other public places. Small shops and trading posts at this time posted "anuncios" (or public announcements) outside their shops to announce goods for sale.[14]

In the 18th century, merchants started printing and distributing on a small scale handbills to call the attention of potential customers to their shops.

In the first decade of the 19th century, newspapers carried the first printed advertisements (also called "anuncios") with distinct features in layout as we know them today. These ads were for products, like perfume and cosmetics, and services in the elite commercial areas of Manila, such as Binondo and Escolta.

During the American occupation, the Filipinos had their first real taste of the American free enterprise system. As business and commerce prospered the need to advertise in order to introduce an idea or a product in the market was felt.

At first, advertising was prepared by one-man agencies. The 1920s saw the appearance of this type of agencies. Enterprising young men maintained contact with the producers/advertisers, wrote copy for them, presented the layout and artwork, and delivered the advertisements to the various newspapers and circulars for publication. These one-man agencies were the precursors of modern advertising agencies.

Among the earliest one-man advertising agencies in the 1920s were Americans like H. Edmund Bullis, who managed Philippine Publicity Service, Inc., Clifford Butler, Frank Minton, Hal Stone, Mason Anchor and Frank J. Herrier.

Herrier started out as head of the advertising department of Pacific Commercial Company, the nation's largest import house and the biggest advertiser at the time.

Herrier was apparently a whiz at advertising because he earned the sobriquet "Napoleon of Philippine Advertising." According to one writer, Herrier was "the Napoleon of many a big and successful advertising campaign. As adman and salesman, Herrier had no equal -- a genius in his chosen profession."[15]

Herrier later resigned from Pacific Commercial and became advertising manager of Roces' TVT newspaper chain at P20,000 a year, a big salary in those times. On the side he worked as a one-man advertising agency, writing copy and preparing layouts for a number of big companies, including San Miguel Brewery.

There was one Filipino who held his ground beside those American advertising pioneers in the Philippines -- Manuel Buenaventura, who was the first Filipino to handle advertising accounts.

The first advertising agency, the Philippine Publicity Service Inc., was set up and managed by Edmund Bullis in 1921.

Other advertising agencies soon followed: Philippine Advertising Bureau in 1929, founded by Florentino Garriz; Ros Chanco Advertising Agency in 1930; Philippine Agency Service Company founded by F. Theo Rogers, North W. Jenkins, and Frank J. Herrier; International Advertising Agency, founded by Pedro Escat and Ramon Zamora; S.S. Schier and Company; Braun and Rosedale, and Jean Bisson Enterprises, founded by a French artist by that name.

Bisson introduced something new which became a milestone in the history of advertising in the country. He started the use of illustrations in advertisements which had before this concentrated on copy writing. He soon cornered the art segment of Philippine advertising and started a trend.

Two Filipino names perhaps deserve special mention in connection with the history of Philippine advertising: Antonio Lagos and Pedro E. Teodoro.

Lagos was advertising manager of Hale Shoe Company, maker of Esco shoes which became famous during the 1920s. An aggressive advertising man, Lagos waged a battle of advertising against a competitor, Hike Shoe Company, whose advertising manager was an American, Frank Minton.

Lagos won the battle and made millions for Hale Shoe Company. Shortly after this Minton faded away and his shoe company folded up.

Pedro E. Teodoro might be considered the "dean" of Philippine advertising practitioners. He is one of the few practitioners now who got their start in the field before the last war.

Teodoro started as an advertising solicitor of the *Journal of Education* and then became advertising manager of Elizalde and Company. When the second World War ended, Teodoro and Fred Benitez organized in 1945 Philippine Promotions Bureau, later to become Philprom for short. Philprom was the first strictly Filipino advertising agency organized after the war and today is one of the top advertising agencies in the country.

Prominent advertisers of the time were the La Estrella Auto Palace, Ysmael and Co., J.P. Heilbronn and Co., the Pacific Commercial Co., Laget and Myers Tobacco Co., Caltex, Socony Vacuum Oil Co., Berg's Department Store, Heacock's, Times and Ideal movie theaters, the Philippine Manufacturing Co., Genato Commercial, Hale Shoes Co., and L.R. Aguinaldo's. San Miguel Corporation was known to have advertised its produce as early as 1896, being one of the first to use a slogan to publicize its products' excellence.

The use of radio as an advertising medium was at best experimental. There were then few radio sets in the country. In the late 1930s, however, when four major radio stations were already broadcasting, advertisers began using the new medium. But World War II broke out disrupting for more than three years the development of advertising.

Among the first advertising agencies to open after the war was the Commercial Advertising Agency founded by Gene Hubilla in 1945; the J. Walter Thompson Agency, locally represented by D.L. Brodt; the Philippine Promotions Bureau, founded in September 1945, and which is now known as Philprom; Pan Pacific Advertisers (1946); the Advertising Associates, originally established as an outdoor company before it branched out to print advertising; Grant Advertising (1948), now known as Bates-Alcantara; and the Gregorio Araneta Incorporated Advertising Agency Department, a house agency, that later became Ace Advertising. Ace Advertising merged with Compton Advertising in New York to become Ace-Compton.

The 1950s was an exciting and profitable decade for advertisers. Some of the top agencies were organized during this period. They include the Philippine Advertising Counsellors, Ideas Inc., Advertising and Marketing

Associates, Admakers-Dentsu, General Ads, Nation Ads, and Cathay Promotions. By this time, the marketing concept of advertising was already defined and established and was applied by multinational corporations in their sales and promotions. Large and ambitious advertising schemes were also carried out by the leading companies. Radio soap opera programs advertised Procter and Gamble products like Purico, Perla, and Mayon Cooking Oils. These soap operas were well listened to by housewives; so much so that P & G had them translated into the different languages for provincial listeners.

By 1948, there were 12 recognized advertising agencies and advertising began to shed off some of its American influence. But it was not until the 1960s that nationalism finally took over the advertising field. By this time, Tagalog became more widely used as a language of advertising. Filipino scenes were used and the Filipino psychology became a factor in framing the advertising message. Advertising also helped sell Philippine-made products to a nation which traditionally favored foreign brands.

The top 10 advertising agencies in 1973 with total billings of P141 million, were J. Walter Thompson, Ace Compton, Grant Advertising, Advertising and Marketing Associates, Inc., Philippine Advertising Counsellors, Philprom, McCann Erickson, Atlas Promotions and Marketing Corporation, J. Romero and Associates, and Ideas, Inc. in that order.

In 1974, there were two associations of advertising agencies with a total membership of 41 agencies.

The advent of television revolutionized advertising. The medium can effectively bring to life the advertisers' messages.

Advertising for television in the 1950s, however, was largely experimental. Not too many people owned a TV set.

In the 1960s, advertising in television developed rapidly and replaced radio in importance.

The following decade marked a drastic change in the country. Martial law was proclaimed, ushering in an era of uncertainty. The advertising industry grew by an average of 14.11 percent (the total gross media expenditures rose from P60 million in 1961 to 182.5 million in 1970 and 736.5 million in 1980, indicating a more than twelve-fold increase). But by the 1980s the economy had deteriorated and contracted.

Consequently, nearly 5,000 business firms closed shop from 1984 to 1985, including slightly less than 25 percent of all advertising agencies.

Marcos' fall in February 1986 transformed almost overnight the Philippine political and business climate from that of pessimism to optimism. This optimism spread also to the advertising industry itself.

III. POST WAR PERIOD

1. Newspapers

A number of newspapers sprang up right after the war. However, most of them were fly-by-night tabloids and lived short lives. Only a few of these postwar newspapers survived, among them the *Manila Chronicle*. The *Chronicle* was put up by a group of prewar newspapermen in 1945, but was sold a few years later to Don Eugenio Lopez, businessman and brother of Vice-President Fernando Lopez.

Meanwhile, the prewar newspapers were revived, including the *Manila Bulletin* and *Philippines Herald*. The *Tribune* was not. Joaquin Roces, who had taken over the newspaper business from his father, put up the new *Manila Times* in place of the *Tribune*. The Tagalog member of TVT (*Taliba*) was revived but the Spanish paper (*La Vanguardia*) was never reestablished. In its place, Roces put up an afternoon paper, the *Daily Mirror*, and together with the *Weekly Women's Magazine* (the leading women's magazine in the country before martial law), the Roces newspaper chain was reestablished.

Up to the time of martial law, the *Manila Times* led all the Philippine English language dailies in circulation, with an audience circulation of 250,000 copies daily. The *Manila Chronicle*, on the other hand, was building up a name as a paper of quality. Under its new editor, Rod Reyes, the *Chronicle* developed its interpretative reporting and perfected its offset process printing.

2. Television

Although television had its beginnings way back in the 1930s when the British, Russians and Americans were experimenting with it, it was not until the 1950s that it finally arrived in the Philippines.

Two Philippine universities were experimenting with television before it turned commercial. In February 1950 a professor and his students successfully demonstrated their homemade receiving set at the University of Santo Tomas. Two years later, Feati University opened an experimental television station.[16]

In 1953 commercial television came to the Philippines, when the very first station, DZAQ-TV Channel 3, was opened by Alto Broadcasting System in Manila. AQ in the station's call letters stood for Antonio Quirino, the owner of the station and brother of then President Elpidio Quirino.

The franchise to operate the first TV station was actually granted by Congress to Bolinao Broadcasting Corporation, which was owned by an American, James Lindberg. But Judge Antonio Quirino bought Bolinao Broadcasting in 1952 and thus earned the right to start the first TV station in the Philippines. Bolinao continued to operate radio stations.

By today's standards, DZAQ-TV Channel 3 in those days was crude. It started on a four-hour-a-day schedule (6-10 p.m.) and telecast only over a 50-mile radius. The prospects were dim for the future of television in the country at that time. There were mountains to overcome: there were no TV sets, there were no advertisers and production costs were high.

In 1957, the Chronicle Broadcasting Network which started with radio in 1956 and which was owned by the Lopez brothers, Fernando (vice president of the Philippines) and Eugenio (at that time one of the richest businessmen in the country), bought Alto Broadcasting Network. It opened another TV station, DZXL-TV Channel 9. ABS-CBN therefore became the first radio-TV network in the Philippines, operating the only two TV channels at the time.

By 1960, another company, Republic Broadcasting System, owned by Bob Stewart, a long-time American resident in the Philippines who started with radio in 1950, opened another TV station, DZBB-TV Channel 7.

The mountains of problems that plagued TV in the early days were still there. TV sets were expensive, the cheapest costing $600 (P2,400 at the exchange rate at that time). At that time the minimum daily wage was P4 a day. Local factories were later able to produce TV sets at half the price, but still beyond the means of the average income families. American-produced TV programs were expensive, but locally-produced programs cost even more-- in 1959, a half-hour local program cost P2,000 to produce. Philippine channels were asked to pay $125-$150 for a half-hour U.S. show, to be shown only once.

Despite these difficulties, however, it is surprising that television continued to grow in the Philippines in the late 1960s and early 1970s, leading to another problem: overcrowding. By 1966, only a little over ten years after television came to the Philippines, there were 18 privately-owned TV channels in the country, with a viewership of more than one million during the peak hours of 7 to 10 p.m. These channels were 2, 4, 5, 7, 9, 11, and 13, and the school-managed 14 (DZFU-TV of Feati University) in the Manila area; 3, 5, 7, and 13 in Cebu; 4 and 12 in Bacolod, 15 and 13 in Baguio and 6 in Dagupan.

The first provincial television station was Channel 3 in Cebu by ABS-CBN. With its two other provincial stations in Bacolod and Dagupan, ABS-CBN in 1968 became the largest radio-television network in the Philippines with five TV and 20 radio stations. In 1969, ABS-CBN made television history when it covered live the Apollo 11 moon shot, the landing of the first men on the moon -- in color.

3. Philippine Mass Media Before Martial Law

The Philippine mass media just before martial law was proclaimed on September 21, 1972 may be described broadly in the following terms:
- They were privately owned and pursued their objectives independently of government control;
- They were multi-lingual, but leadership was exercised by the English language press;
- They were Manila-centered and needed to be developed in the provinces;
- They were politically free but were controlled by big business; and
- They lacked ethics and professionalism.

a. Privately owned

All of the 21 daily newspapers and 100 or so community newspapers which came out weekly in the late 1960s were privately owned. All of the 16 leading magazines and an estimated 100 other magazines sold in the news stands were privately owned.

Of the 18 television stations in the country at that time, only one was government-owned. Of the 245 radio stations in the country, only half a dozen were owned by the government.

There was only one domestic news agency, the Philippine News Service, which was a cooperative of the Manila newspapers.

All of the 24 book publishers in the country were private entities. The government, however, had its printing arm in the Bureau of Printing.

The government had one weekly government paper, *Government Report*, which was scoffed at by the mass media people and by the elite.

There was no question that the mass media were almost entirely in private hands in the Philippines.

The government therefore, had to rely on other information channels which were non-media in nature – the government bureaucracy at various levels and in various departments, like agriculture, health, education, etc.

There was the National Media Production Center, which produced films, pamphlets and other audio-visual aids in the government information campaigns.

There was the Malacañang Press Office, which sent out the press releases and other features telling the story of government day after day.

As privately owned enterprises in a democratic capitalist society, the Philippine mass media saw their greatest role as watchdog on government. Hence, the adversarial relationship between the Philippine press and the government.

They also believed in the other traditional roles of the mass media in a democratic society: to inform the people and comment on issues so that the people may be more intelligent and active participants in government, to entertain and educate the people.

Educating people in a purposive manner, however, ranked lower than the other roles assumed by the mass media in the Philippines. That role was left mainly to the government.

The role of the Philippine mass media in national development was of a different kind. It was something pursued independently by the private press -- the less government intervention the better. The goals were set by the private press itself, not by the government.

b. Multi-lingual

Information in the Philippines is disseminated in many languages and dialects, with English and Tagalog as the main vehicles of communication.

This is because the Philippines is a nation that speaks 87 languages and dialects, although only five of these are spoken by the majority of the Filipinos. These five are English, Tagalog, Visayan, Ilocano and Bicolano. The average educated Filipino is bilingual, speaking usually English and one of the dialects.

It is interesting to note also that the Philippines was the only country in the world that used to have three official languages -- Spanish, English and Pilipino. Pilipino (based on Tagalog) was the national language. In the 1987 Constitution, Pilipino has been changed to Filipino.

The *Philippine Mass Media Directory* (1966) listed 1,193 print journalists in the country before martial law. Of this number 986 wrote in English and 116 wrote in the Philippine languages and dialects, mainly Pilipino.[17]

English had become, before martial law, the language of metropolitan journalism in the Philippines and opinion leadership was exercised by the six leading Manila dailies and the leading Philippine weekly, which were all published in English.

Of the 17 dailies that were published in Manila at the time, nine were in English, four in Chinese, two in Spanish and two in Tagalog.[18] The leading dailies, all published in English, were the *Manila Times, Manila Chronicle, Philippines Herald, Manila Bulletin,* the *Daily Mirror* and the *Manila Evening News.* The leading weekly magazines were the *Philippines Free Press* and the *Weekly Graphic.*

c. Manila-centered

The 17 dailies in Manila had a total estimated circulation of 985,674 in 1970.[19] Of this, however, 60 per cent, or 591,404 were circulated in the Greater Manila area where 8 per cent of the 37 million Filipinos at that time lived.

The 16 leading magazines in 1970 had a total estimated circulation of 970,000.[20] Of this number, about half went to the three million people living in the Greater Manila area. The other half went to the 34 million Filipinos in the provinces.

Of the 18 television stations in the country, seven, or almost half of the total, were located in the Greater Manila area.

If we consider the number of TV sets, the picture became even more focused on Manila. According to 1966 figures, there were 180,000 television sets in Manila, compared to 74,000 out in Cebu, Bacolod and Davao City. Outside these places, television was practically non-existent. Of course, television has grown since then, but the approximate proportion of set distribution in the 1970s was still 40 per cent in Manila and 0.5 to 3 per cent in the provinces.

Out of 732 theaters surveyed in 1969,[21] 121 were found to be in the Manila area. This meant that one out of seven theaters was in Manila, where one out of twelve Filipinos lived at that time.

Of all the mass media, only radio was perhaps more evenly diffused throughout the country. Yet, even this showed a greater concentration in the Manila area.

In 1966, radio was found in 88 per cent of the homes in the Greater Manila area, compared to 51 per cent of the homes in Luzon, 42 per cent in Mindanao, and 36 per cent in the Visayas.[22]

The community newspaper in the Philippines was also underdeveloped. Of the 100 or so weekly newspapers in the provinces at that time, probably only 40 were profitable. The rest were just breaking even.[23]

There was, in other words, a communications gap in the rural areas, where 34 million Filipinos lived in the early 1970s.

d. Press Freedom

The Philippine Constitutions of 1935 and 1973 guaranteed that "no law shall be passed abridging freedom of the speech and the press." This guarantee is reiterated in the 1987 Constitution.

Outwardly, the Philippine press (especially the Manila newspapers and magazines) appeared free before martial law was declared on September 21, 1972, because it could criticize government officials, including the president, bluntly. Some foreigners even thought that the Philippine press was too critical, too outspoken, and irresponsible.

Philippine and Austrian newsmen were the only journalists in the world whose sources of news were protected. Filipino journalists were also protected by the laws of libel and privilege. There was no prior censorship.

Anyone capable of using a typewriter could dish out a letter or put together a newspaper column that peddled opinion on everything under the sun.

The Philippine press enjoyed great political freedom in theory. In practice, however, such political freedom was limited.

A limitation on this press freedom in the Philippines was economic control -- by big business. Even if the Philippine press was politically free to a great extent, it was not truly free in the economic sense, because it was owned by vested interests.

Five families with vast business empires owned about 90 per cent of the country's mass media -- newspapers, magazines, radio and television. A look at Table 1 will show the extent of this monopolistic situation. Looking at radio alone, in 1967 there were a total of 203 stations in the country with a total wattage of 702 megawatts. Of this total, 24.6 percent was used to run 19 radio stations owned by one family -- the Lopez family.[24]

In the case of television, there were 15 stations in 1968, with a total wattage of 49,320 watts. Of this total, 40.6 percent was used to run the five stations owned by the same Lopez family.

Table 1. Chain Ownership of Philippine Mass Media in 1972

Owner & Business	Newspapers	Radio Stations (AM)	TV Stations
Don Eugenio Lopez Public utility (Meralco), Sugar, finance	Manila Chronicle Philippine Farms and Gardens	ABS-CBN (Alto Broadcasting System-Chronicle Broadcasting Network): 20 stations in Manila (6), Bacolod, Baguio, Cagayan de Oro, Cebu, Cotabato, Dagupan, Davao, Iligan, Iloilo, Laoag, Legaspi, Lucena Naga, Zamboanga	ABS-CBN: Channels 3, 9 Manila Channel 3 Cebu Channel 4 Bacolod Channel 10 Baguio
Andres Soriano, Jr. San Miguel Corporation, mining, lumber, textiles, fertilizers, paper industry, oil development, copper products, insurance, finance	Philippines Herald	RMN (Radio Mindanao Network): 8 stations in Manila, Baguio, Butuan, Cebu, Davao, Iligan, Cagayan de Oro (2)	IBC (Inter-Island Broadcasting Co.): Channel 13 Manila Channel 13 Davao Channel 13 Cebu
Manuel Elizalde Mining, insurance, shipping, import & export, steel and iron corporation, paints, oil, rope	Manila Evening News	MBC (Metropolitan Broadcasting Company): 8 stations in Manila (2), Cebu, Dagupan, Laoag, Legaspi, Roxas	MBC: Channel 7 Manila Channel 7 Cebu
Hans Menzi Mining, lumber, agricultural enterprises, school and office supplies and equipment finance	Manila Bulletin Liwayway, Hiligaynon, Bannawag, Bisaya		
Joaquin Roces	Manila Times, Daily Mirror, Taliba, Women's Magazine	ABC (Associated Broadcasting Company): 5 stations in Manila (3), Dagupan, Davao	ABC: Channel 5 Manila

The publisher of the *Philippines Herald,* in an interview with Lent,[25] said: "It is largely true that the newspapers in Manila push vested interests. I feel we need some mergers here. Maybe we need only two newspapers in the city but these four giants (Soriano, Lopez, Roces and Menzi) can't find any reason for getting together."

The former editor of the *Evening News*, in an interview also with Lent, said "Most newspapers here are extension of business empires. We are a country where, unfortunately, keeping a newspaper is a good defense weapon for big business."[26]

A top executive of Radio Mindanao Network and columnist of the *Herald*,[27] had declared in a speech:

> Big business can use their media for the promotion of special interests. Or negatively, they can hold back legitimate criticism for fear of antagonizing political allies... In the words of one exasperated publisher, 'We need our paper like some people need guns -- to protect ourselves!' Considering however that the business interests owning papers are also in other enterprises, it is not hard to see how they can be influenced or coerced into cooperating with the government.

This was, indeed, an undesirable situation.

e. Ethics and Professionalism

The Philippine mass media just before martial law were bombarded left and right with criticisms.

From one side, the government trained its guns on the members of the Fourth Estate, saying in so many words that they were irresponsible. They were irresponsible because all they did was carp and contribute to the building of negative attitude towards government and whatever it was doing for national development.

From the other side, there were the self-appointed critics of the mass media, both in and outside the Fourth Estate, who wrote self-confession articles, or inside stories, all relating how corrupt the mass media people were.

The most articulate and the most powerful critic of the Philippine press before martial law was no less than President Ferdinand Marcos himself. In his book, *Today's Revolution: Democracy*, published in 1971, President Marcos complained that the Philippine mass media were sensational, unfair, irresponsible, unethical and were used by their oligarch owners to serve their selfish political and economic interests. President Marcos said in his book:

> The permeation of oligarchic "values" is also managed through the control of the means of mass communication. It is no longer a secret that the displeasure of the oligarchs is communicated through radio and television commentaries and newspaper columns. The media have become the weapon of a special

class rather than serve as a public forum. The so-called "editorial prerogative" has been used to justify what is best described as "selective journalism."[28]

Marcos quoted samples of what he called irresponsible journalism from a column in the *Manila Chronicle*, owned by his arch enemy, Eugenio Lopez, Sr.

> Finally, Mr. Marcos, playing the favorite trick of every scoundrel, poses as a martyr and tells all of us that in spite of the constant attacks on his honest, hardworking and great person, he will allow the press its freedom and will not do anything to abridge freedom of speech.
>
> First of all, if Mr. Marcos feels he is that powerful and summons that much popular support, why doesn't he try putting an end to freedom of speech in his country?
>
> The answer to this question is obviously that even in his insufferable arrogance, Mr. Marcos realizes that the Filipinos value freedom of speech as much as they value life and if they did not surrender this to the succeeding Spanish, American and Japanese conquerors, they certainly will not surrender it to him.

The former president also quoted the *Philippines Free Press:*

> On the other hand, how can he bear being President -- and the most hated or despised man in the country? If we have to stand him, okay, but how could he stand himself? He'd smell. And if he smelt to the nation, how could he close his nose to the odor? One of the punishments of hell so vividly described in spiritual retreats, which aim at grace through terror, is the subjection of the damned to all the Gadawful smells that the fanatical imagination can conjure up. Marcos would smell to high heavens if he did not earn the respect of the people instead of their hatred and contempt...

It cannot be denied that there were many journalists in the country who were not above accepting bribe money, or even blackmailing people. Perhaps there were too many of them for the good of the Philippine press. It also cannot be denied that some owners were oligarchs who used their newspapers and other mass media units to serve their own interests.

But the cure for an abusive press is not repression. As it turned out the martial law that Marcos imposed on this irresponsible press did not cure the disease. It only made it worse.

One thing also that must be said in favor of the Philippine press at that time was that it was its most vocal critic. It admitted its sins, *mea culpa*. Furthermore, there were institutes and institutions trying to do something about the apparent lack of ethics and professionalism among the media men.

IV. MARTIAL LAW PERIOD

1. The Beginning

It did not come as a surprise therefore that when President Marcos decided to proclaim martial law (Proclamation 1081, signed September 21, 1972), the mass media were among the first to be brought to heel.

In Proclamation 1081, President Marcos said that one of the reasons he proclaimed martial law was because the lawless elements had been mounting massive propaganda assaults against the government through the:

publications, broadcasts and dissemination of deliberately slanted and overly exaggerated news stories and news commentaries as well as false, vile, foul and scurrilous statements, utterances, writings and pictures through the press-radio-television media and through leaflets, college campus newspapers and some newspapers published and still being published by these lawless elements.

In the same document, the President also claimed that the mass media were infiltrated and controlled by persons "who are sympathetic to the insurgents who consequently intensified their propaganda assault against the government and the military establishment of the government."

The very first presidential decree (issued on September 24, 1972) after the proclamation of martial law reorganized the government bureaucracy and created a Department of Public Information.

And the President's very first letter of instruction issued September 22, 1972, directed the Press Secretary and the Secretary of National Defense to "take over and control all communications media for the duration of the present national emergency."[29]

On the same day, however, that President Marcos ordered all mass media closed, he also authorized the continued operation of the government radio and television stations in Manila -- the Voice of the Philippines (operated by the National Media Production Center) and the stations of the Philippine Broadcasting Service. He also authorized the operation of two privately-owned mass media enterprises -- the four-month-old *Daily Express* (published by Juan Perez, but reportedly owned by Roberto Benedicto, a crony of Marcos) and the Kanlaon Broadcasting System (also owned by Benedicto), which later changed its name to Radio Philippines Network, because they had "not participated in the communist conspiracy" to overthrow the Philippine government. These mass media therefore could lay claim to the distinction that they were the only ones which were not closed by martial law.

The Far East Broadcasting System, owned and operated by Protestant missionaries in the Philippines, was allowed to resume operation on September 25.

On September 26 more newspapers and magazines were allowed to resume operations: the weekly magazines in the dialects -- *Liwayway, Bannawag, Hiligaynon* and *Bisaya* -- owned by Brig. Gen. Hans Menzi, former aide of President Marcos; the *Philippines Herald*, owned by Andres Soriano, Jr., owner of the biggest Philippine corporation, San Miguel Corporation; and Radio Mindanao Network-Interisland Broadcasting Company, affiliate companies of the *Herald*. However, the authorization to the *Herald* was rescinded at the last minute and the Soriano paper was not revived, reportedly because the government was sticking to its new policy of keeping mass media off the hands of big business and oligarchs.

All the leading premartial law metropolitan newspapers and magazines, except *Manila Bulletin*, were closed down permanently, including circulation-leader *Manila Times*, its sister publication in the afternoon, *Daily Mirror*, the anti-Marcos *Manila Chronicle*, the ultra-nationalistic *Philippines Free Press*, the *Graphic* and the *Nation*. The *Manila Bulletin* was revived on November 22, 1972, under a new name, *Bulletin Today*.

New metropolitan newspapers and magazines were established. The *Times Journal* spawned sister publications: the *Women's Journal* started in April, 1973; the *Manila Journal*, an international weekly launched May 23, 1973; and the *People's Journal*, the news magazine of the rural family, whose first issue came out in July, 1973.[30]

The *Daily Express*, taking advantage of the first few weeks of martial law when there were no other newspapers around, took the lead in circulation (within a few months the paper claimed a circulation of 300,000 daily, the biggest up to that time for a Philippine newspaper), volume of advertising, and in the number of sister publications that it gave rise to.

The sister publications that came out in succession before the martial law year was over were the *Evening Express* (October 9), *Pilipino Express* (October 21), *Express Week Magazine* (December 7), and *Express Sports* (December 23). The total circulation of all five publications was claimed to be 600,000.

September 21, 1972 was indeed a turning point in the history of Philippine mass media. For the first time in history, martial law was declared in the Philippines, and for the first time since the turn of the century, controls were imposed on Philippine mass media, which in recent decades had been one of the freest in the world.

When martial law was proclaimed, dozens of the top journalists in the country were picked up and brought to the stockades on charges of subversion. Among the big names who spent some time in jail were: Joaquin Roces, publisher of the *Manila Times*; Eugenio Lopez, Jr., publisher of the *Manila Chronicle*; his editor, Amando Doronila; Teodoro M. Locsin, Sr., editor of *Philippines Free Press*; Luis Mauricio, editor of *Graphic*; Max Soliven, top columnist of the *Manila Times*; Ernesto Granada, columnist of the *Manila Chronicle*; Napoleon Rama, staff writer of *Philippines Free Press*; and Juan L.

Mercado, joint chief executive of Press Foundation of Asia. They were eventually released, except Eugenio Lopez, Jr., who made a dramatic escape from the military stockade and slipped out to the United States.

Those of the pre-martial law journalists who were not put in jail fared only slightly better than their colleagues who were taken in: they had no more jobs, they did not know what to do, they were assailed with fears and doubts about their future, they were insecure, confused and bewildered.

The atmosphere in the journalistic world during those early days of martial law was one of unreality. The initial reaction of Filipino journalists was disbelief. They had heard whispered rumors a few months before that President Marcos was going to proclaim martial law, but they did not take the rumors seriously.

This generation of Filipino journalists was raised in the tradition of libertarianism brought over by the Americans when they occupied the Philippines at the turn of the century, and this generation could not believe that a Filipino president would suppress this cherished tradition of press freedom.

But it happened, and when it did, they were shocked and stunned. A few took to the hills or escaped abroad. But most decided to stay to mourn their lost freedom. After decades of unfettered freedom, these journalists had reason to mourn the sudden turn of events. One journalist summed up the feelings of Filipino journalists at the time when he told this author: "It was as if a whole world had crumbled -- and a new order has come to pass! That old world may never return!"[31]

Two years after martial law, most of the mass media practitioners rendered jobless when their newspapers, radio and television stations and other media agencies were closed down, had found new jobs in new mass media units or in other occupations and professions -- teaching, law, business, farming, poultry raising, grape raising, etcetera.

Those who had chosen to return to the journalistic field again under martial law, however, still had to regain their old self-confidence. The Philippine press in 1974 was a far cry from the free-wheeling, blustering, swaggering, unbridled, sometimes sensational, sometimes frantic, press of the pre-martial law days.

At the start of 1975, however, stories on graft and corruption in government, big time crimes and the Muslim problem in Mindanao, where Muslim rebels were fighting government forces, began to appear in the mass media. Even the trial of former senator Benigno Aquino, leader of the opposition during pre-martial law days, was reported in the press.

But while the news pages of the Manila newspapers were becoming more interesting, their editorial pages remained dull. The community press, on the other hand, still had not followed the lead of the Manila press: they were still colorless even in the news pages, contenting themselves with publishing government press releases and singing hallelujahs to the government.

2. Mass Media Controls

The early days of martial law saw the military being used to control the mass media. Upon orders of the civil authority in the person of President Marcos, the military padlocked the newspaper offices, news agencies and radio and television stations.

When some newspapers and stations were allowed to operate again, the military was utilized to do the prior censorship -- right in the newspaper offices and stations in the Greater Manila area.

In the provinces the newspapers and radio stations had to submit manuscripts and tapes to the local Philippine Constabulary (national police) commander before publication or airing. It was an entirely new experience for this generation of Filipino journalists and government officials.

The military censors were ultimately responsible to the Secretary of National Defense, Juan Ponce Enrile, and the Secretary of Public Information, Francisco S. Tatad. The two departments organized the Committee on Mass Media (CMM), with Tatad as chairman and Enrile as co-chairman. It was the committee that drew up the early guidelines for mass media.

On May 11, 1973, another presidential decree (No. 191) abolished the Mass Media Council and created the Media Advisory Council (MAC). The MAC was headed by the president of the National Press Club. Its vice-chairman was a recognized civic leader. Members were representatives (one each) from the Manila Overseas Press Club, from print media, from radio and from television, and "others as the President of the Philippines may designate." The vice chairman and all members of MAC were appointed by the President.

Meanwhile, because of administrative difficulties in absorbing an older, bigger and well-established agency into a new department, the NMPC was taken away from Department of Public Information and returned under the Office of the President of the Philippines.

On November 9, 1974, PD 576 abolished MAC and created the Philippine Council for Print Media and the Broadcast Media Council. This was seen as a step towards normalization because these were self-regulatory bodies that took the place of government agencies in overseeing the performance of the private media.

The martial law years saw a variety of methods by which the Marcos regime gagged the once free-wheeling Philippine press. First there was overt censorship or threat of legal sanctions in the form of presidential decrees. Among them were PD 33 (penalizing the printing, possession and circulation of printed materials which tended to undermine the government), PD 90 (penalizing rumor-mongering), PD 1737 (empowering the president to detain persons to prevent them from acting against national security or public order), PDs 1834 and 1845 (escalating the penalties for rebellion, sedition and other crimes related to national security, including "subversive journalism"), and PD 1877 (authorizing the incarceration for a period not exceeding one year of persons accused of national security crimes even without charges being filed against them).

Then there were the "guidelines" from the military and the government information agencies. President Marcos himself or his information minister, Gregorio Cendaña, used to call up the editors to tell them either to publish a story or play it down, or complain about even slightly critical stories. A National Press Club survey of nine desk editors in 1985 identified the Office of Media Affairs as chief censor.[32]

Then there was covert censorship, or "censorship by friendship." While Marcos started by saying that one reason why he declared martial law was to break up the mass media empires owned by the oligarchs who conspired against his government, he ended up by surrounding himself with a new breed of oligarchs with their own mass media empires (see Table 2). The biggest of these oligarchs was sugar baron Roberto Benedicto, who owned the *Daily Express* and its sister publications and collected radio and television stations. Benedicto took control of Radio Philippines Network, with six television and 15 radio stations; Banahaw Broadcasting Corporation with two television and seven radio stations, and finally Interisland Broadcasting Corporation with eight television and four radio stations to become the biggest mass media oligarch in Philippine history. He was also major stockholder of various telecommunications enterprises - Domestic Satellite Corporation (DOMSAT), Nivico Philippines, Inc. (television set manufacturer), Oceanic Winders Corp. and Eastern Telecommunications Philippines, Inc.

The other Marcos government weapon against recalcitrant Filipino journalists was libel suits. There were at least a dozen libel suits filed left and right by the government against newspapermen between 1980 and 1985 alone. The most celebrated of these probably were the two libel suits filed against Mauro Avena, Domini T. Suarez, and Mariano B. Quimson, Jr. of *Panorama*, and Lupino Lazaro, lawyer for the Galman family, because of an article titled, "Is the Agrava Board Afraid to Know the Truth?" One suit seeking P120 million in damages was filed by Marcos crony Eduardo Cojuangco and another seeking P100 million in damages was filed by General Fabian Ver, then Armed Forces Chief of Staff. Both men were mentioned unfavorably in the article. These two libel suits, eventually dismissed after the overthrow of Marcos, were the biggest libel suits in Philippine history.[33]

While bribery was practised before martial law, it became widespread and institutionalized during the martial law years as yet another Marcos technique of managing the mass media. The standing joke among journalists during this time was whether one was practising "envelopmental journalism" or not, in reference to payments which came in envelopes.[34]

But the most lethal weapon that the Marcos martial law regime unleashed on the Filipino journalists of this time was physical – threats, intimidations, closures, banning, deportation, detention and ultimately, if all else failed, death. Death was the ultimate form of censorship for many.

From 1976 to 1986, 25 journalists were killed in the Philippines, the highest mortality rate for journalists in the world, according to journalism historian Armando Malay. Fifteen of them were killed in 1985 alone.[35]

The Rise of the Alternative Press

In the beginning of martial law, these methods combined were able to stifle dissent in the mass media. Those who disagreed with the government were either in the stockades, in the hills or six feet underground.

Towards the end of the 1970s, however, a few brave souls began to test the waters, so to speak. When the government started to say that things were back to normal, they cautiously began to criticize.

The earliest of these few brave souls was Jose Burgos, Jr., who founded *We Forum* on May 1, 1977 as a weekly for the youth.[36] It began publishing news that could not be found in the muzzled crony press, as the newspapers owned by the Marcos cronies were then called. Some of the news stories were in the nature of exposes of conditions existing then that were a revelation to their readers, because the crony papers did not touch the subjects. One example is the story about the displacement of thousands of cultural minorities from their ancestral grounds when the Angat Dam was built in the province of Kalinga Apayao in the north.

Meanwhile, martial law was lifted in January 1980, after seven years and four months. But the lifting was only in theory. Later it was leaked out to the foreign press that on the eve of the lifting of martial law, President Marcos signed two "secret decrees" which among other things, increased the penalty for subversion to death. And the word subversion covered the use of "printing, broadcast, or television facilities, or any form of mass communication" for any activity that "tends to destabilize the government or undermine or destroy the faith and loyalty of the citizenry."

In the next few years, the *We Forum* became bolder and bolder and its circulation increased. It started coming out thrice-weekly and was planning on becoming a daily when it was raided by the military and closed down on December 7, 1982. Burgos and a number of his staff members, including columnist Soc Rodrigo (former senator) and Armando Malay (veteran newspaperman), were jailed.

The *We Forum* had overstepped its bounds. It had published a series of articles questioning the authenticity of the Marcos war medals.

When Jose Burgos, Jr. was released he published *Malaya* on January 17, 1983 as an English language weekly tabloid to take the place of *We Forum*.[37] Before *We Forum* was closed *Malaya* was its Tagalog sister paper.

At about this time, the *Philippine Collegian*, student paper of the University of the Philippines, had also been pursuing a militant brand of journalism, to the eternal shame of its counterparts in the professional media.

Table 2. Chain Ownership of Mass Media in 1973-1986

Owner and Business	Newspaper	Radio	Television
Roberto Benedicto Head, Phil. Sugar Commission, National Sugar Trading Commission, controlling interests in hotels, shipping, banking, Domestic Satellite Corp., Nivico, Oceanic Winders Corp., Eastern Telecommunications	Daily Express, Weekend, Pilipino Express, Evening Express, Express Week Magazine, Express Sports	Radio Philippines Network (14 stations): Baguio, Batac, Tuguegarao, Iriga, Binalbagan, Bo. Sumag, Dipolog, Zamboanga, Pagadian, Cagayan de Oro, Surigao, Tagum, Gen. Santos City, Mandaue	Radio Philippines Network (7 stations): Davao, Cagayan de Oro, Zamboanga del Norte, Bacolod, Cebu, Iriga, Metro Manila
Hans Menzi Holdings in citrus, rubber and coffee plantations, paper mill and trading company. Board Chairman, Holland Milk Products and Basic Food Corp., board member of four companies, including Phil. Airlines. Owns Menzi Foundation, which controls six companies and shares in at least 13 others with interests in paper production, hotels, food processing, agriculture, airlines	Bulletin Today, Tempo, Panorama, Who, Balita, Liwayway, Bannawag, Bisaya, Sine, Song Cavalcade	Banahaw Broadcastig Co. (5 stations): Quezon City, Naga, Dagupan, Legaspi, Iligan	Banahaw Broadcasting Co. (1973, 4 stations): Bacolod, Baguio, Cebu, Quezon City Intercontinental Broadcasting Network (1973, 8 stations): Manila, Baguio, Bacolod, Cebu, Tacloban, Cagayan de Oro, Davao City, Bislig
Benjamin Romualdez Brother of first lady, Imelda Marcos, governor of Leyte, assemblyman, ambassador to the U.S, major holdings in Philippine Engineering Co., PCI Bank, Pilipinas Models (assemblers of Datsun cars in Philippines) and Meralco	Times Journal, Manila Journal, People's Journal, People's Tonight, Taliba, Women's Journal, Parade, People, Seventeen, Observer		

Kerima Polotan-Tuvera
Biographer of Imelda Marcos, wife of Juan Tuvera, Executive Secretary of Preisdent Marcos, owns Oriental Media, Inc.

Evening Post, Metro Manila Times, Orient News, Focus Magazine and World News

Henry R. Canoy & Family

Radio Mindanao Network (1986, 24 stations): Baguio (2), Intramuros, Kalibo, Punta Tabuk (AM & FM), Pasig, Iloilo (2), Bacolod, Cetu (2), Calbayog, Dipolog, Pagadian, Butuan, Surigao (2), Cagayan de Oro (2), Davao, Koronadal, Anda, Iligan

Intercontinental Broadcasting Corp.

Intercontinental Bctg. Corp. (6 stations): Kalibo, San Jose, Roxas, Quezon City, Iloilo, Bukidnon

Menardo Jimenez, Felipe Gozun, Robert Stewart and Gualberto Duavit

GMA Radio/TV Arts (6 stations): Quezon City, Metro Manila, Cebu (2), (AM & FM), Cagayan, Iloilo

Intercontinental Bctg. Corp. (10 stations): Quezon City, Davao, Laoag, Cebu, Iloilo, Bacolod, Cagayan de Oro, Roxas, Baguio, Tacloban

GMA Radio/TV Arts (17 stations): Quezon City, Benguet, Ilocos Norte, Mt. Province, Zambales (2), Batangas, Marinduque, Legaspi, Albay, Catanduanes, Cebu, Cagayan de Oro, Bukidnon (2), Lanao del Norte, Iloilo

Abelardo Yabut & Family

Nation Broadcasting Corp. (23 stations): Bonuan, Baguio, Laoag, Tuguegarao, Iligan (2), Santiago (Isabela), San Pablo, Makati, Cebu (2), Tawi-tawi, Zamboanga, (2), Cagayan de Oro (2), Davao (2), Bislig, Gen. Santos, Cotabato, Butuan, Bacolod

The *We Forum* and *Philippine Collegian* were the forerunners of what was to be called the alternative press in the Philippines in the early 1980s. They were called such because they provided an alternative source of information to the crony press which served only pro-government stories.

More than anything else, it was the assassination of former senator Benigno Aquino on his return from three years of exile in the United States on August 21, 1983, that released the floodgates of press freedom in the Philippines.

When Senator Aquino was shot as he stepped down from his plane at the Manila International Airport that day, the first reaction of the crony press was silence. They did not know whether to carry the story or not and waited for instructions from above -- their publishers and beyond, meaning Malacañang.

The very first indication that something was amiss was a small item on television saying that Senator Aquino was shot at the airport, and no further elaborations. According to Arlene Babst, one of the critical columnists of *Bulletin Today*: "I called *Bulletin* after the killing on the twenty-first and asked if the story would be headline. And they said they didn't know yet how they were to play it. Imagine that!"[38]

Even before Aquino's arrival, the crony press had been told to run nothing on his arrival. So until the tragedy at the airport tarmac, people were generally kept in the dark about the Aquino arrival.

But when the tragedy happened, there was no stopping the story from spreading, although at first the crony newspapers and radio stations tried to ignore the event.

Times Journal ran the story of the funeral procession, participated in by some five million people and lasting 11 hours from early morning to late night, below the fold on the first page. Channel 7 gave ten seconds to the event but the other stations ignored it completely. Then, first by word of mouth, then by Radio Veritas, the Catholic radio station, and by other means, the word spread like wildfire.

Radio Veritas was the only station that gave the story the importance it deserved, giving full day coverage for days to the events from the shooting at the airport to the funeral wake and historic funeral procession.

At the vigil for the slain Aquino at Sto. Domingo Church in Quezon City, meanwhile, the thousands of mourners were buying at P5 or more a copy xerox copies of the front page of the *Japan Times* English edition, carrying the story that soldiers had killed Aquino. Then video cassettes carrying footages taken by foreign correspondents of the shooting at the airport were being sold and circulated. The public was getting information from abroad through the wonders of modern technology.

Among other things, it was xerox journalism and cassette journalism that made it impossible for the authoritarian regime of Marcos to suppress information on this tragic event of national importance.

Meantime, among the print media, *Malaya* and *Masa*, sister publications of the padlocked *We Forum* of Burgos, took up the cudgels for free expression. They went from weekly to twice weekly to daily in the weeks that followed the assassination and their circulations increased steadily. The people were starved for information and they gobbled up every copy of these papers that were sold in the streets. About a dozen tabloids also sprang up in the streets at this time, including the *Manila Paper* of former Assemblyman Reuben Canoy and the *Philippine Times* of veteran newsman Rommel Corro, who eventually landed in jail for nine months because of a story he ran claiming that General Fabian Ver was linked to the Aquino killing.

Eugenia D. Apostol, publisher of *Mr. and Ms.*, decided to put out special editions in the first week of September 1983 to cover the post-assassination events and the trial of the accused assassins. Circulation of the *Mr. and Ms* special edition jumped to 800,000 copies in the first eight post-assassination issues. Apostol also put out *The Weekly Inquirer* on February 4, 1985 to report on the Agrava Board hearings on the Aquino murder. The newsweekly gave way to the *Philippine Daily Inquirer* on December 9, 1985 after the Agrava Board handed down its decisions. The *Inquirer*, because of its weekly reports which were not presented by the crony publications, quickly sold in the newsstands. On its third month, said *Inquirer* board co-chairman Betty Go-Belmonte, the endeavor netted P5 million.[39]

Veritas newsmagazine was founded on November 27, 1983 by a group of Catholic Church and business leaders, led by Jaime Cardinal Sin, head of the Philippine Catholic Church, and Vicente Jayme, head of the Bishops-Businessmen Conference of the Philippines. The Catholic paper then joined the other opposition papers in the fray and together they became the alternative press that started giving the crony papers a run for their money.

At this point, the government was too stunned by the turn of events - the growing boldness of the mass media and the growing size of the crowds that were demonstrating in the streets in anger at the Aquino assassination. The circulation of the alternative papers continued to increase while the circulation of the crony papers plummeted.

The business leaders who founded *Veritas* called for a boycott movement against the crony papers, which lasted from September 1983 to the early part of 1984. When the boycott movement was launched the crony papers trembled and their circulations dropped drastically during those months.

The boycott of dailies served as a barometer of public anger at the inability and timidity of the three established newspapers (*Bulletin Today, Daily Express* and *Times Journal*) to print stories on the Aquino killing. The first boycott was organized by the Anti-Cronyism Movement (ACRONYM). The second boycott, which was called by now President Corazon Aquino, caused the circulation of the three papers to tumble down. Richard Ching, *Bulletin* vice-president for circulation, said that during the ten days of boycott in March, the paper's circulation plunged by 15 percent, from

245,000 to 215,000 copies, and advertising linage decreased by 20 percent. Some people believe that the *Bulletin* circulation dropped by more than 15 per cent, and that the *Express'* and *Journal's* circulations went down to 15,000 or 10,000.[40]

In self-defense the crony papers changed their editorial policies and began carrying stories on the Aquino assassination. Thus the jab at these newspapers' most vulnerable spot, the cash box, was most effective in prodding them to return to objective, truthful reporting and bringing back press freedom. The crony press had to print the truth in self-defense.

By the end of 1985, when the fall of the Marcos regime was drawing near, the alternative press had pushed the crony papers into a corner. *Malaya's* circulation had jumped up to 300,000 and 400,000 at one point to compete with the *Bulletin Today*. *Mr. and Ms.* had overtaken the *Bulletin Today* in terms of circulations of 600,000 to 800,000 per issue at certain points during that period.

Then on December 9, 1985, the *Philippine Inquirer* became a daily and a wonder of Philippine publishing.[41] At the start of 1986, because of its trio of the most widely read columnists at the time -- Louis Beltran, Max Soliven and Art Borjal - the *Inquirer* becaue the circulation leader with 350,000 copies daily.

The *Inquirer* was followed by the revival of the pre-martial law *Manila Times*, by Ramon Roces on February 5, 1986, just shortly before the snap presidential elections.

So when the Marcos regime was finally overthrown on February 26, 1986, the alternative press had effectively taken center stage and ousted the crony papers, except for *Bulletin Today*. And today (1987), the alternative press has become the establishment press.

3. Lessons from Martial Law

There are a few lessons from martial law history that bear repeating.

First, when news is censored in an authoritarian society, rumors and gossip will proliferate because people become starved for information.

Second, when the mass media are muzzled, there is no check to government abuse and graft and corruption becomes rampant.

Third, when the press is gagged, it deteriorates. Journalists lose their initiative in gathering and commenting on the news, they lose their self-respect, and in the long run the press loses credibility. And without credibility the press is lost.

Fourth, when a government tries to hide the truth, it may succeed at first. But in the long run, the truth will come out from other sources. When that happens, people will lose their trust in their government. And when the government loses credibility, everything is lost.

Fifth, with the rise of modern communications technology, like the xerox machine and video cassettes, it is no longer possible for any society, however authoritarian, to impose complete or near complete censorship.

Finally, people will always demand to know the truth, and they will eventually get it from whatever sources, by whatever means. And then the truth will make them free.

Notes

[1] Jose Luna Castro, *The Manila Times Journalism Manual* (Manila: The Manila Times Publishing Co., Inc., 1963), p. 2.

[2] Edwin Emery, *The Press and America* (Englewood Cliffs, New Jersey: Prentice Hall, Inc., 1962), p. 29.

[3] Castro, loc. cit.

[4] Ibid.

[5] Jesus Valenzuela, *History of Journalism in the Philippine Islands* (Manila: Published by Valenzuela, 1933), passim.

[6] Armando J. Malay, "The Philippine Press." In *Philippine Life*, one of a series of pamphlets issued by the Cultural Foundation of the Philippines.

[7] Valenzuela, loc. cit., p. 28.

[8] Carson Taylor, *History of the Philippine Press* (Manila, 1927), p. 6.

[9] Castro, op. cit., p. 6.

[10] John Lent, *Philippine Mass Communications, Before 1811 After 1966* (Manila: Philippine Press Institute), p. 53. All subsequent references to magazines in this chapter came from his work.

[11] In an address delivered at the National Press Club in 1958, as quoted by Castro, op. cit., p. 79.

[12] This brief history of Filipino movies was prepared by Nicanor G. Tiongson, movie historian and critic.

[13] Lent, op. cit., p. 79.

[14] This brief history of Philippine advertising was prepared by Ludy Elvinia and Ramon Osorio, advertising professors.

[15] Emilio Salazar, "A good look at the great game," *Marketing Horizons*, July 1964, p. 44.

[16] References here to the development of television in the Philippines came from Lent, op. cit.

[17] Eduardo Sanchez, "Print Media in the Philippines," unpublished paper, 1971.

[18] *Philippine Mass Media Directory 1971* (Manila: Philippine Press Institute).

[19] Sanchez, op. cit.

[20] Ibid.

[21] According to a survey by Geoffrey W.J. Conwell, as reported in the *Manila Times*, Sept. 22, 1970, p. 20.

[22] According to a nationwide communication study conducted by Robot-Gallup Research Group for Media Research Foundation of the Philippines, March-April, 1966.

[23] According to a 1965 survey made by Crispin C. Maslog, director, Silliman School of Journalism and Communications, Dumaguete City.

[24] According to Sen. Rodolfo Ganzon, in the explanatory note to a bill he proposed at the seventh special session of the Sixth Congress of the Philippines, to regulate radio and television ownership in the Philippines. The bill did not pass.

[25] Lent, op. cit., p. 16.

[26] Ibid.

[27] Reuben R. Canoy, "Politics is Everybody's Concern," a speech delivered in Silliman University, October 3, 1969.

[28] Ferdinand Marcos, *Today's Revolution: Democracy* (Manila: Published by NMPC, 1971), p. 128.

[29] The Martial Law presidential decrees and letters of instruction implementing them have been published in a series of volumes by the National Media Production Center.

[30] This part of this history is based on original research by the author — the sources were the issues of the newspapers themselves and the various decrees and letters of instruction by President Marcos.

[31] Ruben Alabastro, Agence France-Presse editor, in an interview in October, 1972.

[32] John A. Lent, "Government-Media Relationship in the Philippines: A Mid-1980s Assessment," unpublished paper, 1985.

[33] Doreen C. Fernandez, "Artists, Writers and Intellectuals and the Culture of Crisis," unpublished paper, 1985.

[34] "The Local Press: An Appraisal," a white paper on the Philippine Press prepared by the Philippine Council for Print Media, 1977.

[35] Crispin C. Maslog, "The Old Information Order: An Era of Repression," unpublished paper, 1986.

[36] Alan Pearce, "Lonely Voices in an Era of Darkness," *IPI Report*, March 1986.

[37] "Important Dates for Malaya," in *Malaya,* January 17, 1987.

[38] Lent, op. cit.

[39] As quoted from Domini T. Suarez, unpublished paper, 1986.

[40] Suarez, op. cit.

[41] Fe B. Zamora, "Inquirer: The First Few Days," in *Philippine Daily Inquirer,* December 9, 1986.

Part Two

Overview

This second section gives an overview of the field of communication in the Philippines. It tackles the topics that are broad and run through the gamut of communication. Chapters II and III introduce the communication student to communication terms and explain the role of communication in society. Chapters IV and V describe the central role played by communication in the February 1986 Philippine Revolution which toppled the Marcos dictatorship.

Then Chapter VI talks about the crucial role played by the mass media in the formation of values. Chapters VII and VIII bring the reader up to date on development communication and development journalism, concepts which were recently introduced into the communication field by Filipino communication scholars, particularly from the University of the Philippines Los Baños and the Philippine Press Institute.

Chapter II

Introduction to Communication

Crispin C. Maslog

Communication, like breathing, is so much a part of human life that we take it for granted. And this is where the problem begins. Communication, unlike breathing, cannot be taken for granted. People assume that they are automatically communicating when they speak or write, but that is not always the case.

Communication happens only when someone listens, and when both speaker and listener, or writer and reader, attach the same meanings to the words they use.

A textbook on communication ignores this basic principle of communication at its own risk. Hence, the need to define the basic communication terms that will be used in this book.

Communication Versus Communications

The most basic term we are dealing with in this book is communication, which may be looked at from two aspects -- as a process and as a result.

As a process, communication is the transmitting of information, ideas, values, beliefs and attitudes from one person to another. To speak, therefore, is to communicate.

It is not enough, however, that we speak to communicate. What we speak of must be understood by the other fellow. Here, we are interested in the result. Otherwise, there is no communication.

The word *communication* came from the old English *comun*, to commune, which in turn came from the Latin *communis*, common. To communicate, therefore, is to commune, to create something in common between the communicator and his audience. As soon as the audience grasps the message sent by the communicator a "commonness" is established between them. When we communicate in the true sense of the word, we create a special bond between us and the other fellow -- we are "tuned in" to each other. In the current Manila lingo, *vibes tayo*. Our vibrations are on the same frequency.

For more precise thinking, Western scholars distinguish between communication and communications. The singular form refers to the process while the plural refers to the technical means to carry out the process.[1] Communication, therefore, is broader in scope than communications. It refers to the conscious and unconscious social behavior that communicates, while communications refers to the secondary techniques, the mass media that help carry out communication.

Communication in its most basic sense is the cement that holds society together. Without it, society would fall apart. This basic social process includes all the ways by which man shares with fellow man what are in his mind and heart. These include gestures, overt behavior and language.

Language is actually nothing more than a code or a system of signals among people belonging to a particular group, society or country. The code, of course, is only as useful as the number of people who can decipher it. In this sense, gestures and overt behavior can be considered as language. In this sense also, some people talk about the language of love, flower language, or stamps language.

By language of love, they mean the various gestures by which lovers communicate to each other their special feelings -- the touch of the hand, the moonstruck eyes, the inviting smile. They say that lovers wink with their right eye to say, "I love you."

Flowers also are supposed to speak a language of their own, starting with three red roses which mean "I love you." Stamps also can be used to convey a message depending on how they are positioned on the envelops. An inverted stamp on the envelope is meant to tell the receiver of the letter that the sender is angry at him.

All of these examples are just a way of saying how ingenious man is in finding ways to communicate to his fellow humans. But a word of caution must be raised here: in using these special languages, be sure that the other person knows your code, or you might end up with a misunderstanding instead of a communion of ideas.

Sometimes, what we say is not as important as how we say it. "Good morning," and "Kumusta Ka" are two expressions we use so often when meeting friends that they have become ritualistic rather than meaningful phrases. They assume meaning only according to the tone of our voice or the smile on our faces when we say them.

"Good morning" can be said happily, sadly, indifferently, even angrily, and friends will know whether you really mean it according to your behavior at the moment.

Sometimes also, what we say is not as important as what we do not say. It is not only when people talk that they communicate. They also communicate when they do not talk. As a matter of fact, silence sometimes becomes more eloquent than words, especially during those moments when you are expected to say something. Remember that favorite saying, "Speech is silver, but silence is gold."

Talking about gestures, the wave of the hand says goodbye, just as the outstretched palm says give me.

The problem with gestures is that they are a product of their cultures -- the same gestures may mean different things from one society to another.

All these ways of communicating -- by gestures, overt behavior or unconscious behavior -- are informal language which is not always precise and efficient. Man had to invent formal, written language to help him carry out more effectively the act of communicating to others. Formal language is more widely understood, more systematic and more effective for the purpose of communication.

From the point of view of the communicator, communication may either be *verbal* or *non-verbal*. When a man wears a long, gloomy face, for example, he is telling other people how he feels without being conscious of it. This is non-verbal communication.

From the point of view of the receiver, however, all communication is verbal in the sense that all signals or stimuli must first be translated into words in the head before they can be comprehended.

Non-verbal communication is the province of psychologists and sociologists. At this point, we leave this type of communication to them. We turn our attention to verbal communication, which is more the province of mass communicators.

Person-to-Person and Mass Communication

Verbal communication may be categorized into two: *person-to-person communication* and *mass communication*. Note that we are using the singular form of the words here, which means that we are referring to the primary process.

Person-to-person communication is communication by one or a few persons to another or a few other persons in a face-to-face situation.

There is person-to-person communication when two lovers whisper under the moonlight, when a teacher lectures to a class of 20 students on the meaning of communication, or when a politician speaks over the microphone to a rally of 2,000 people in the town plaza. The meaning of person-to-person communication might even be stretched to include persons talking to each other over the telephone or using the walkie-talkie.

Mass communication, on the other hand, is the delivering of information, ideas, beliefs, values and attitudes to a large and diversified audience in different places at the same time through the use of a channel or medium.[2]

Of the two, person-to-person communication is easier to accomplish and more effective. It is easier because you are usually dealing only with one or a few persons at a time and you can see their faces as you talk to them.

First of all, you will know who compose your audience and, therefore, you can tailor your message to their level of intelligence, their interests and their command of the language. Second, you can see them and so when they look bored you can tell a joke to wake them up and adjust your message to the situation immediately. Hence, the message can be more effective.

The job of mass communication is more difficult. Most of the time, you do not even know who are listening to you (if you are using radio) or reading what you write (if you are using the newspaper). So you have to prepare your message for a general audience. You imagine an average person in your audience and address your message to him. This means that you have to make your message as simple as possible, if you want the majority to understand you.

For another thing, while you are delivering your message over the radio or through the newspaper, you do not know whether your audiences are interested or even understand what you say. You might get a reaction (feedback) from them (in the form of a telephone call or a letter, perhaps), but the feedback will be much delayed. You will have no chance to revise your message to suit the needs, interests and intelligence of your audience.

While mass communication is less effective than personal communication, however, it can reach more people, and if it is well delivered, it can affect more. Mass communication can be effective if handled by an expert. The effective mass communicator is one who can establish rapport with as many of the people in his audience as possible -- by speaking simply and in a personal tone, as if he were talking to them face-to-face.

Face-to-face communication was adequate in the good old days, when societies were small. In the villages of our grandfathers, it was so easy to pass the word around that Felipa eloped with Baldo, that Mang Teban was selling his old pair of shoes or that village elders had prohibited the pasturing of carabaos in the village plaza.

As the village grew into a city in a matter of decades, however, it was no longer possible to rely on face-to-face communication alone to disseminate information of interest to the general public.

Today if you have a car to sell, you have to advertise in the newspapers to get the best possible offer. If the city council has banned parking on the main streets, it has to announce this ordinance over the newspapers, radio stations and television stations so that all the people may know. If you suffer from the offensive smoke from the jeepneys, you can write a letter to the editor to win more people to your side and hopefully attract government attention to the problem.

As the towns became urbanized and industrialized, life became more complicated. As the population expanded, the job of communicating with others became more complex. A system of delivering information to many people at the same time became necessary, and so mass communication was born.

This does not mean, however, that there is no more use for person-to-person communication in modern society. It still has its place, especially in developing countries like the Philippines, and public relations people and government extension workers are finding it an effective way to reach the masses in the rural areas. Face-to-face communication can profitably be used hand-in-hand with mass communication even in modernized countries.

At this point, we note that we are leaving person-to-person communication behind to the province of the psychologists and sociologists to which it belongs. We turn our attention more closely to mass communication and its instruments, the mass media.

Mass Media

The mass media are the tools for mass communicating; they are the channels, therefore, media, through which information, ideas and attitudes are disseminated to the masses. These media are primarily the newspapers, magazines, pamphlets, books, radio, television, film and billboards.

These happen to be Western definitions of mass communication and mass media, where they originated in the first place. An important component of the Western definition of mass communication is that it must be accomplished through the mass media which are institutionalized. The mass media are organized instruments for communicating to the public, as exemplified by newspapers or radio stations.

By Western standards, therefore, a Mahatma Gandhi who moved thousands upon thousands of Indians with the spinning wheel and the spoken word was not a mass communicator. Not even Christ who touched the heart of humanity with his Sermon on the Mount.

But, on second thought, were Gandhi and Christ not among the world's greatest mass communicators?

Another point to note in the Western definition of mass communication and mass media is that the word mass has a simple connotation--it means the general public, whatever your socio-economic class. In some countries of South America, however, it has a derogatory meaning--it refers to the "masa," the great unwashed, the lowest class in society. In the Philippines this would be the common *tao* or the *bakya* crowd.

The reason they are referred to as mass media, of course, is because they are supposed to reach the majority of the people, whether upper, middle or lower class. But is that true in the case of books and television in the Philippines? In industrialized countries like the United States and Japan, for example, where 98 percent of the homes have TV sets, there is no question that TV is a mass medium. But in developing countries like the Philippines, where only an estimated 10 percent of the homes outside the Manila area have television, how can it be a mass medium?

Books, and even magazines and newspapers, are also in the doubtful category. Outside of the students who are forced to read books in the schools, and the professors who force them to read, who else reads books with any amount of regularity in the Philippines? As for newspapers, the readership of dailies in the Philippines is appalling, something like 1.8 copies per hundred Filipinos, compared to 43.9 per hundred among Japanese.

In short, we should use the term mass media with caution. They have a long way to go before they can become truly mass media in the Philippines and other developing countries of Asia.

While the mass media are being developed, there are other supplemental ways to reach the masses in the developing countries: person-to-person communication, which we have discussed earlier, and the traditional, or folk, media.

Traditional Media

The traditional media are those folk arts -- plays, puppet shows, musical dramas, poetry jousts, etcetera -- which were/are popular forms of entertainment among the rural people in our country and other parts of Asia.

The traditional medium that is highly developed in Indonesia is the *wayang*, a popular puppet show whose characters were well-known by rural Indonesians long before the advent of movies or radio or television. In recent years, the Indonesian government has used the *wayang* as a vehicle to propagate family planning messages and other government development programs.

In the Philippines, our traditional media which used to be popular in the rural areas years and years ago and which are being rediscovered include the *zarzuela, balak, balagtasan, bugtong* and *moro-moro*. The *zarzuela* is a musical drama which was the most popular form of entertainment among Filipinos in the early 1900s.

Research and rediscovery of folk media might yet become a distinctively Asian contribution to the scholarship on mass communication which developed first in the West.

Community Media

There is a new trend in the use of communication media for community development. This trend is towards demassification--from mass media to small media. While the mass media are more efficient in mass dissemination of information, they are not as effective in getting people involved in problems and issues of their communities.

The small media, sometimes referred to as group media, but more often as community media, provide better access and opportunities for people participation in community development.

According to Frances J. Berrigan, who made a study for UNESCO in 1979, community media are "media to which members of the community have access, for information, education, entertainment, when they want access. They are media in which the community participates, as planners, producers, performers. They are the means of expression of the community, rather than for the community."

One of the earliest examples of the use of a community medium for community development was the Fogo Island (Canada) film project in 1971. It started out as a fairly typical documentary on the poverty of the people of this isolated settlement in Newfoundland. But the views of the community were also recorded and played back to the community. The film began to be the medium of dialogue. Individuals gave views on what could be done to make the settlement viable again and lively discussion followed. Out of this film-based dialogue emerged concrete plans for action.

The Fogo Island process showed that the community was capable of finding solutions to its own problems and that media could help people to articulate. It was the beginning of a community media technology.

Community media include theater, audio cassettes, slide sets, flip charts, dance, video cassettes and even radio. The key concepts are the use of these in small groups with maximum audience participation.

In the Philippines, the following might be considered community media: community newspapers, community radio, blackboard newspapers, rural mimeo newspapers, audio cassettes and development theater.

The Process of Mass Communication

It might help us understand the process involved in mass communication if we diagram it in its most basic form:

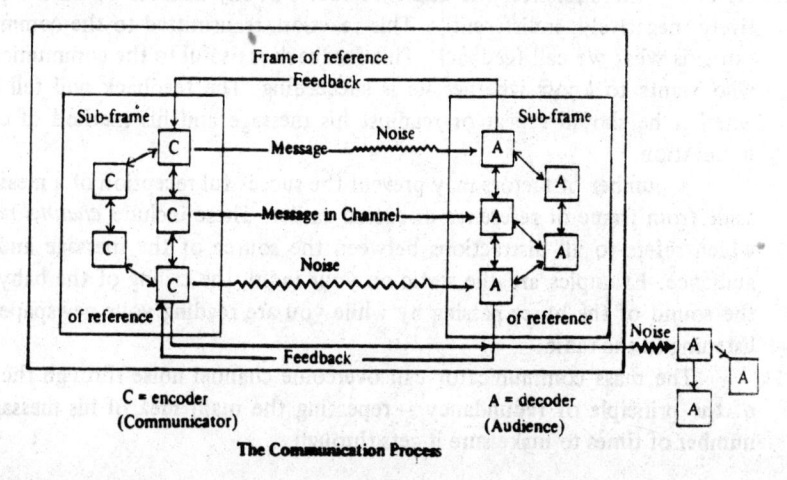

C = encoder
(Communicator)

A = decoder
(Audience)

The Communication Process

There are four aspects of the mass communication process: *communicator, message, channel* and *audience*. In the technical jargon of the communication researcher, the communicator is the encoder, the message becomes the symbols, the channel may be any of the mass media, and the audience is the decoder.

The process starts with the communicator who encodes, or puts his ideas into words. These words, the message, are transmitted through a channel, perhaps a newspaper, to the audience at the other end of the line. The audience (which may be one or more persons) decodes, or translates the message into ideas in his head, according to his own frame of reference.

The frame of reference is a psychological concept which refers to the point of view from which an individual looks at things. It is the window through which an individual looks at the world and what are in it. This frame of reference is determined by a person's experience, background, cultural values and beliefs, which necessarily color his perception of things.

Thus, for example, if the message a woman receives from her boyfriend is "You walk like an elephant," her reaction to the message would depend on her own cultural background. If the woman were a Filipino, she would probably slap her boyfriend, no questions asked. How dare you insult me! If she were a Laotian, however, she would probably kiss her boyfriend passionately. Because, according to Laotian culture, it is a supreme compliment to tell a woman that she walks like an elephant. To the Laotians, the elephant is a beautiful and noble beast of burden, and the elephant walk is a graceful walk.

This is an important principle for the mass communicator to remember, if he wants to be effective: Talk to the audience in terms of their own background and experience.

Going back to the communication process, once the message is received by the audience, the audience reacts in any number of ways -- positively, negatively, indifferently. This reaction, transmitted to the communicator, is what we call feedback. This feedback is useful to the communicator who wants to know whether he is succeeding. The feedback will tell him whether he should repeat or readjust his message and his method of communication.

A number of factors may prevent the successful reception of a message, aside from frame of reference discussed earlier. These include *channel noise*, which refers to all distractions between the source of the message and his audience. Examples are the static on your radio, the crying of the baby, or the sound of the buses passing by while you are reading your newspaper or listening to the radio.

The mass communicator can overcome channel noise through the use of the principle of redundancy -- repeating the main idea of his message a number of times to make sure it gets through.

Another factor that may interfere with the successful reception of the message is *semantic noise*. This occurs when a message is misunderstood even if it is received exactly as it was sent. This happens when the communicator uses words too difficult for his audience or words with double meanings. Or when he speaks of things never encountered before by his audience. Semantic noise can be reduced if the communicator takes care to define his terms, as we are doing in this chapter, and to adjust his language to the level of intelligence and background of his audience.

There are activities or organizations which may not be called mass media, but help in the process of mass communication. They are adjuncts of the mass media, and they include advertising agencies, public relations firms, government information offices, research organizations, news agencies and press syndicates. All of these, except press syndicates, are found in the Philippines, and will be discussed in detail in the chapters that follow.

Journalism

A term that is often confused nowadays with mass communication is journalism. Of the two, journalism is the older term and the older profession, but with a narrower scope.

Mass communication embraces all types of communication to the general public, and may be divided into two general classes: entertainment and educational. Journalism falls under the category of educational.

Traditionally, the journalist performs two functions: to report the news and comment on it. The report and the comment, however, must be timely. Thus, a book on the fall of Vietnam may not be considered journalism, even if it is a detailed commentary on the event, if it comes out a year after the fall. The newspaper reports on the downfall of former Philippiine President Ferdinand Marcos coming out the day after the fall is journalism. Journalism deals with immediacy, with events as they happen, with history as it unfolds.

Because of the nature of journalism, it has been called literature in a hurry. Just because it is written in a hurry, however, does not necessarily mean that journalistic writing is poor and careless. The work of the professional journalists can stand up in quality with creative writing and many of them became classics.

Journalism applies not only to the print media but to radio, television and film as well. But print media journalism is the oldest and most popular. When we talk about journalists we usually refer to the newspaper reporter.

With the development of radio, television and film (now often referred to as the electronic media), however, journalism embraced a wider field. So we speak now of the radio and TV journalists as well. The newscasters and commentators over the radio and television and the people involved in making public affairs documentaries and video news reports are as much journalists as the newspaper reporters and magazine article writers.

Journalism Versus Writing

In the Philippines, there is a term which is often confused with journalism--creative writing.

Journalism, however, as shown earlier, is only partly writing. Not all writing is journalism. Neither is all journalism writing.

To illustrate: writing poems is not journalism. On the other hand, reporting events by radio is journalism, although it is not writing. Writing fairy tales is not journalism. TV reporting is.

By writing, we Filipinos usually mean literary writing or creative writing. By creative writing, we mean writing of poems, short stories, essays, novels.

Journalism, on the other hand, means the reporting and interpreting of events -- whether by newspapers, magazine, radio, television, or film. A journalist may be a reporter, editor or columnist -- in print, over the air or on television.

A journalist writes an account of newsworthy events: one who writes for sheer entertainment, like a movie scriptwriter, for example, is not a journalist. We might say, then, that while creative writers write fiction, journalists write about facts. Both, in their own ways, arrive at the truth.

Press and Others

A term used often as a synonym for journalists is *press*. In the early days, before the electronic media came, "the press" referred to the newspaper and magazine journalists. Today, many print media men still claim that "the press" is an exclusive nomenclature for them, although radio, television and film journalists have as much right to the appellation as they.

It seems, however, that the trend among electronic media people nowadays is to identify themselves with their own medium, rather than as journalists or " the press," even when they are functioning as journalists and not as entertainers.

The mass media may be classified into print media (newspapers, magazines, other periodicals, pamphlets and books), electronic media (radio, television and film) and outdoor media (billboards, streamers, neon signs). Broadcast media is used to refer to radio and television only.

Periodicals are publications coming out at regular intervals and include newspapers, magazines and journals.

Newspapers are publications of general circulation that come out at least weekly in recognized newspaper format and containing stories of current and general interest. If they come out less often than once a week, they may not be considered as newspapers since they would no longer be timely. In newspaper parlance, news stories that are not timely are "history."

Magazines are publications that come out anywhere from once a week to once every three months (quarterly) in recognized magazine format containing articles that are both entertaining and educational and written in the more subjective feature style. Although many magazines in the Philippines tend to have contents of general interest, the trend in the United States and other industrialized countries is for magazine to become more specialized.

Examples of specialized U.S. magazines are *Sports Illustrated, Seventeen, Field and Stream, Farm Journal, Presbyterian Life, Popular Mechanics, Parents Magazine* and *TV Guide*. Examples of specialized magazines in the Philippines are *Sabungero* (Cockfighter), *Architectscope, Pambata, Parents Digest, Greenfields* and *Filipino Teacher*. There are also special magazines for the professions like medicine, medical technology and law, and for hobbyists, like stamp collectors, bird watchers and car racers. As a country becomes more industrialized it develops special audiences which need their own magazines to serve their interests.

No magazine comes out more often than once a week. Magazine journalists, therefore, have more time than the newspaper reporter or editor to research and write a particular story. They have a better opportunity to write in-depth articles about current events and trends.

Journals are the more scholarly type of publication that usually come out monthly, bi-monthly or quarterly. They contain articles based on scientific research or essays on more serious topics, and usually the style of writing is scholarly and full of technical jargon only the specialists understand. Examples those journals are *Journalism Quarterly, Journal of the Philippine Medical Association, Lancet, Science, Journal of Pediatrics, Journal of Public Health, Silliman Journal* and *Philippine Agriculturist*.

Opportunities for the Communication Graduate

What are the opportunities in the field for the communication graduate? Plenty and varied, whether in the Philippines or abroad.

For purposes of giving the prospective communication graduate a broad picture of the opportunities in the field of communication, we might divide it into: journalistic, non-journalistic, research, teaching, management and technical.

The most popular area to which the communication graduate is generally drawn is journalism because this is the most challenging and the forerunner of mass communication.

In this field the new graduates can work as reporters, proofreaders, copyreaders, photographers, feature writers, columnists, editorial writers and editors of newspapers, magazines and journals; as news gatherers, newscasters, scriptwriters, news editors, TV and video news writers and producers, camera men and commentators of radio, television and film; and as reporters and deskmen of news agencies.

All of these have to do with the exciting job of getting the news first and accurately, interpreting and commenting on it, and transmitting it to the public as fast as possible.

In the non-journalistic field, the communication graduate may work as copywriters, account executive, press release writers, and artists of advertising agencies; as public relations officers in public and private organizations; as advertising salesmen, continuity writers and continuity editors of radio and television commercials; as program directors, scriptwriters, directors, actors and producers for radio, movies, television and video features; and as writers and editors for industrial publications.

The non-journalistic field deals mainly with advertising and entertainment, whatever the mass medium used. It is a bourgeoning and lucrative field for many new graduates.

A relatively new field that is opening up for communication graduates is research. The new graduates can fit into a research job -- surveys, public opinion polls, market research, content analyses, case studies, historical research and others--even as soon as they finish college. It would help if they took up research and statistics courses.

Most of the communication research in the Philippines is done in the schools, like the Department of Development Communication, University of the Philippines, at Los Baños, Asian Institute of Journalism and the Institute of Mass Communication, University of the Philippines.

Market research is also done by advertising agencies for their business clients and by commercial market research organizations like Gallup Polls, Media Research Foundation, Far East Research, Inc. and Advertising and Marketing Associates, Inc.

Communication graduates can also land jobs in government information offices, like the Public Information Agency, Philippine News Agency and the information offices of the various ministries.

Also opening up for communication graduates is the area of communication planning and management. This is especially fitted for development communication graduates. With their communication as well as technical subject matter knowledge, devcom graduates are prepared to land jobs in media and information offices, development agencies using the media in their outreach programs, research utilization offices, and offices which require planning in the use of communication. They are also prepared for management positions related to communication.

Teaching in high school and college has always been a field open to communication graduates, but usually a master's degree is required before one can teach English or journalism in college.

There is an adjunct field that is open to communication graduates who have additional skills or training. This is the technical side of the profession or industry. All these huge mass communications outfits need engineers and technical men to run and maintain the machines and equipment --

printers, photoengravers, television camera operators, radio technicians and others.

In short, the world is wide open and the sky is the limit for the communication graduate with the proper training and the proper attitude in this age of the computer and the communications satellite.

NOTES

[1] William L. Rivers, Theodore Peterson and Jay W. Jensen, *The Mass Media and Modern Society*. (San Francisco: Rinehart Press, 1971), pp. 21-35.

[2] Edwin Emery, *Introduction to Mass Communication* (New York and Toronto: Dodd, Mead and Company, Inc. 1966), Chapter I.

Chapter III

Communication and Society

Crispin C. Maslog

Even the average person who has not studied sociology would know instinctively the importance of communication in society. Communication is the fabric that holds society together.

Society is people talking, working, living, dying together. Society is a consensus among people -- they agree on certain norms and rules of behavior that govern their living together. Without consensus there would be no society but anarchy.

To achieve consensus, people must be able to communicate to each other their wants and desires, their attitudes and ideas. This power to communicate is what makes man superior to animals.

The role of communication in society might be categorized into *political, economic* and *social*.

I. POLITICAL ROLE

Under political, communication has the role of providing information upon which political decisions of leaders and the general public are based.

In this age, when modern means of transportation and satellite communication have caused our world to shrink into a global village, the average educated man is better informed about what is happening in most parts of the world outside his country. Today, John Donne's phrase, "No man is an island," is more relevant than ever before.

1. Disseminating Information

People have come to accept what is happening in South Africa, the Middle East, the United States and China as part of their daily lives. They share the sufferings of the millions of Iranians and Iraqis being orphaned in a senseless war of attrition that has lasted almost a decade so far and they feel the terror of the victims of the Arab terrorists. They sympathize with the millions who were victims of the Mexican earthquake and the Ethiopian famine.

The Vietnam war was perhaps the most vivid example of a historical event that unfolded for two decades from the mid-fifties to mid-seventies right before the eyes of the world. It was the first televised war in history. And because of this, people knew all about the Vietnam tragedy, about the civil war that resulted in millions of casualties, about the American intervention that brought the napalm bombs. And because of what they knew, they demonstrated in the streets against this senseless war. Some went on hunger strike and others burned themselves in public in protest.

And yet, how many people knew first hand about this war? How many had been to Vietnam? How many had friends who had been there and came back to relate the gory details that they saw with their own eyes? Only a handful. Most, if not all, of what they knew about Vietnam were what they read in the newspapers, magazines and books, heard over the radio and saw on the TV and the movie screens. They had formed their opinions on the basis of what the media reported. In other words, people were ranting and raving about the Vietnam war all those years on the basis of second hand reports.

Just suppose, if only for a moment, that all those reports by the mass media were false. Suppose, if only for a moment, that there really was no Vietnam war at all, that it was all just a figment of the mass media men's imagination. Then people would have been ranting and raving and going on hunger strike and immolating themselves in vain!

Unfortunately, however, there really was a Vietnam war, as confirmed later by the thousands of refugees who passed by the Philippines on their way to the United States. But the point is that people are dependent upon the mass media for most, if not all, of the information about the outside world. And they have to trust that the mass media are reporting the truth -- they have no other choice. Without the mass media people would be helpless, lost, isolated.

People's dependence on the mass media for information applies not only to world affairs but even to domestic news as well. What people know about the Muslim rebellion, the Green Revolution, the trial of the people accused of assassinating former senator Benigno Aquino, the government plan to declare amnesty for the Communist rebels, the pregnancy of Janice de Belen, and other countless events, big and small, momentous and inane, all came from the mass media.

If one day all the Philippine mass media should shut down, our country would indeed become islands of ignorance.

Something like this happened when martial law was proclaimed in 1972. It was signed on September 21 but announced September 22, 1972. Before it was announced, there was a news blackout as the military carried out seizures and arrests and shut down the newspapers, radio stations, television stations, news agencies and other mass media.

For one whole day, the entire nation was in a mental strait-jacket -- except for a few communities like Dumaguete City which had its radio station picking up the news from Radio Australia that martial law had been proclaimed in the Philippines.

The Manila population, on the other hand, woke up in the morning of September 22 ready for another normal day of work. Manilans turned on their radio sets -- nothing but static. Many brought their radio sets to the repair shop, thinking they were out of order. They waited for their newspapers -- nothing came. For a few hours that morning, Manilans were befuddled. They did not know what the score was until later that day when some radio and television stations were allowed to operate and President Marcos announced that martial law had been proclaimed.

Libertarians put great store on the importance of the mass media in a democratic society. Since the basis for government in a democracy is the popular will, it is important that the people be informed if they are to participate wisely and actively in the affairs of government: this is the essence of political democracy that Thomas Jefferson postulated.

> The basis of our government being the opinion of the people, the very first object should be to keep that right; and were it left for me to decide whether we should have a government without newspapers, or newspapers without government, I should not hesitate for a moment to prefer the latter. But I should mean that every man should, receive those papers, and be capable of reading them.

That last sentence is important. It is essential that the people are able to read if they are to be effectively informed by the mass media. This might be called the "democratization function" of the mass media especially in developed countries like the United States.

2. Creating Public Opinion

Corollary to this information function of the mass media is the function of creating and reflecting public opinion. This holds true not only for democratic countries but also for authoritarian societies.

Governments can succeed only to the extent that they are supported by their people. The support of the people can be won either by persuasion or coercion, or both. But governments would rather rely on persuasion because a "people convinced against their will are of the same opinion still." Voluntary cooperation certainly is more desirable than cooperation at the point of a gun.

So in all societies, whether democratic or authoritarian, the mass media play very important parts in mobilizing public opinion in support of government programs. In democratic countries, the process is slightly more complicated. In the classic definition of a libertarian society, all shades of opinion are allowed in a free marketplace of thought -- right, wrong or left -- and the public was to be the judge of what is right. And what is right becomes public opinion. The government is not supposed to interfere in this free marketplace of thought because it is liable to disturb the balance of forces and, therefore, prevent the public from freely choosing what is right.

The role of the mass media in democratic societies, which are patterned after this classical model, is to bring in all kinds of information and all shades of opinion to the market so that the public may choose. Other groups -- political parties, economic blocs, civic clubs, labor unions, and others -- but never the government -- lobby for their interests in this marketplace of ideas by either going directly to the public in rallies, by door-to-door campaign, or through the mass media. Some use public relations firms to conduct their propaganda campaigns for them. But in the end the public is king: they make the final choice at the polls during elections, at the box office, or at the supermarket cash box.

3. Reflecting Public Opinion

Reflecting public opinion is the other side of the coin. After public opinion is created on a certain issue, or even before it is created, a government that is responsive to the people's needs would want to assess the public mood.

What the people think about the government -- its programs, policies, administration -- and other vital issues concerning them are effectively brought to the attention of the rulers through the mass media -- in editorials, columns, commentaries, letters to the editor, even in the patronage or non-patronage of certain newspapers, magazines or other media.

While the matter of gauging public opinion is more crucial in democratic countries, where the governors are elected and stay in office with the consent of the governed, it is also considered important by authoritarian governments.

4. Watchdog on Government

Related to the function of creating and reflecting public opinion is the watchdog function of the press, or mass media, in democratic societies, a function unheard of in authoritarian societies.

The watchdog function refers to the role of the press as a check on government. In the classical libertarian tradition, the press was looked upon as a "fourth estate" independent of the other centers of power (the monarchy, church and parliament) and existing as a power to challenge the power centers when they became abusive and corrupt. In modern democracies the press is a "fourth estate" following the three branches of government -- the executive, legislative and judicial.

The mass media are the conscience of government and the champions of the people. That is why the so-called adversary relationship between government and press exists in many democratic countries today, especially the United States. Under this setup, government and press are suspicious of each other.

The primary function of the mass media in these democratic societies is to make sure that the government is honest. If it does well and serves the people, it deserves praise. If it turns traitor to the public trust, it deserves to be criticized and exposed to the people. The mass media then lead the way in creating public opinion unfavorable to the government. It is important, therefore, that the mass media are truly independent, politically and financially, from the government.

More recently, however, this watchdog function of the press has come under attack, especially from governments in developing countries which have a tendency to be authoritarian. Many questions have been raised to question its wisdom: can societies which are still beset with many problems that threaten their very existence as a nation afford to engage in divisive debates with the mass media? Should the mass media not instead become a partner of government in unifying the nation and promoting economic and social development? Is freedom of the press a luxury that only the highly developed and stable societies can afford? Should individual freedoms not be sacrificed for the greater public good?

In authoritarian countries, like the Soviet Union and Communist China, the process of mobilizing public opinion is much simpler. In these countries, the mass media are simply instruments of the government and the Communist Party. So the media carry only one line -- the Party line. There are also no organized opinion groups to contest the official line. Individuals may have opinions of their own, but they keep their opinions private. There is no going against government policy, which is all you will find in the mass media. Because of government monopoly in the marketplace of ideas, it would seem that authoritarian governments would have an easier time mobilizing public opinion to their sides.

II. ECONOMIC ROLE

Mass communication in highly developed countries like the United States and Japan boosts the economy through the power of advertising.

In these countries the standard of living is high and the public has money to spend on consumer goods -- the things we consider luxury items in developing countries like cars, air conditioners, electric dryers, and sundry other things.

Manufacturers engage in mass production of these goods, whether essential, consumer or luxury goods, and then use the power of mass communication (advertising) to sell them to the public. Advertising makes people aware of their needs and then aware of products to satisfy their needs. Advertising moves the mass-produced goods from the factories to the supermarkets and eventually to the homes of the consumers.

Mass production and mass communication have thus led to mass consumption and today you will not find it unusual to see the same dishwasher manufactured in New York used in a New England home and in a southern California apartment. Or the same Ford Mustang made in Detroit driven in the flat highways of Minnesota and Texas and in the mountain roads of Colorado. Mass production and mass communication made all these possible.

Some social critics flay advertisers and the advertising industry for allegedly manipulating people into buying what they really do not need and encouraging wasteful spending. The advertising industry's answer is that advertisers only make people aware of their needs and products to satisfy these needs, but people ultimately decide whether to buy or not. And because people buy, money is poured into the economy, businessmen make profits, laborers earn more, industry expands, more people are employed, people's buying power increases, demand goes up and people buy more. The "vicious circle" that is healthy for the economy.

This role of advertising, however, does not hold true to the same extent in less developed countries. In the Philippines, for example, the market for consumer goods is more restricted and the power of advertising to move these goods, therefore, is restricted to that extent.

In developing countries, advertising can be harnessed to boost the national economy in a different sense. The advertising industry could, if it has not done so yet, help raise the standard of living and create a market by assisting in the development of correct economic attitudes and habits among the people.

Take, for example, the savings habit. The Philippines is reported to have one of the lowest savings rate per capita in the whole world. Filipinos do not put their money in banks. One reason might be poverty, but that is not the entire picture. There are people who have money but do not put it in banks.

Perhaps another factor is the *bahala na* attitude of many Filipinos -- never mind saving, God will take care of tomorrow. It is difficult to sell the idea of fixed deposits and insurance policies to a people who put their fate in the hands of a God who will provide for tomorrow.

Another likely factor is the "piggy bank mentality" of many Filipinos. There are many who do save money -- but not in banks. They hoard their coins in piggy banks, their cash in tin cans, bamboo tubes, earthen jars on wooden *bauls* somewhere in the house or buried under the house. It is not unusual to read in the papers about a household being robbed of P10,000, P20,000 or even P50,000 in cash and jewelry. Many Filipinos, alas, still hoard their money in the house and take their chances with robbers rather than entrust their savings to banks.

This is where advertising can come in -- a campaign to promote savings in banks, thereby harnessing national wealth for investments and economic development. This is already being done to some extent by the Philippine National Bank, with its "mag-impok movement" among school children. The idea behind this campaign is to develop the savings habit early.

Advertising can also be harnessed by the government for specific campaigns like food production. In 1974 the Philippine government went all out to get the farmers to produce enough rice for this rice-hungry nation. For the campaign, they hired the services of an advertising agency. The agency drew up the strategy, the slogans, and the approach for the campaign, which they named "Masagana 99." The idea was to make each hectare produce at least 99 cavans of palay, and from all indications the campaign was a success. The Philippines became self-sufficient in rice.

In general, therefore, the mass media can be utilized to educate the Filipino in economics.

III. SOCIAL ROLE

Mass communication in developed countries also helps strengthen the social fabric of the nation and influence its pattern. The mass media, in other words, contribute to the dissemination of information and popularization of practices that all add up to the cultural heritage of a nation.

1. Popular Culture

The various strands that are woven into this social fabric include customs, fads, fashions, folk songs, pop tunes, folk art, pop art, lingo, technology, norms, beliefs, personalities and even superstitions.

Take the Beatles who took the whole world by storm in the late 1960s. They started as an unknown singing group in Liverpool, England. Their singing voice was nothing outstanding, although they had something different, a style perhaps. But with the help of a press agent they parlayed their style into millions of dollars and a place in the hearts of millions of teenagers all over the world.

Their "invasion" of the United States in the mid-1960s was as carefully prepared and carried out as any military campaign. Weeks before they came feature stories and photographs were sent to the magazines and news stories were released to the newspapers and other media by their press agent. Recordings of their songs had already been put on sale. The groundwork was meticulously laid.

When the Beatles arrived in New York, the first stop in their cross-country singing tour, teenagers mobbed them at the airport (some claim that this, too, was arranged by their press agent). The American homage to the Beatles had begun.

Sometime during their act, teenagers started screaming and swooning. (Some claim, again, that this was arranged by their press agent.) Others followed. This screaming adoration for those long-haired apostles of the rock music was seen on television by millions of other teenagers in other cities of the United States.

So when the Beatles arrived at the next stop, the local teenagers did not need prompting anymore from any press agent. Mass hysteria had set in, influenced to a great extent by what they saw on television. By the time the Beatles reached California on the other side of the American continent, their conquest of America's teenagers was complete. The Los Angeles teenagers would not be outdone by the New York teenagers and so when the Beatles started their performance the teenagers started screaming. And they did not stop until the Beatles had stopped singing and departed from the stage.[2]

The Beatles are no longer there as a group -- they have broken up. But some people think they have left a legacy behind -- the Beatle music and the long-haired look, which have become part of the contemporary scene.

The story is the same for most of the early or current idols of the masses: Elvis Presley, Marilyn Monroe, Louis Armstrong, Frank Sinatra, Bob Hope, the Commodores, Burt Bacharach, John Wayne, Madonna, Michael Jackson, Sylvester Stallone, and among the Filipino idols: Nora Aunor, Dolphy, Vilma Santos, Fernando Poe, Jr., Pugo, Freddie Aguilar, Pilita Corrales, Sharon Cuneta.

These people live for the masses on the movie and television screens, and their images assume giant proportions because of the wide-screen color movies and because of the colorful publicity they get from the mass media, with the help of press agents.

Somehow some of them manage to project their own styles and their own distinct images, which become a model for their fans. Sometimes also these public idols through their programs or personalities are responsible for introducing new lingo like the Beatle look, the Monroe figure, cool, groovy, dig, *erap* (for pare), Bonjing, 007, *siga-siga, pogi, dehin goli, type kita, vibes tayo, kilig to the bones, kuno* and *naku ha*. Some of these phrases may eventually find their way into the language of the nation.

Some of these public idols introduce songs and dance crazes that become for a while part of the popular culture. Only those with integrity are likely to endure and become part of the culture. The rest are thrown into the dustbin of history. Examples of the more enduring musical contributions, perhaps, are the Beatles music, the Elvis rock and the Armstrong blues.

In the field of fashion, the mass media play an important part. Every year the high priests of fashion, led by Christian Dior, from their fashion olympuses in Paris, London or New York, make their latest pronouncements about the newest thing to wear for milady. And every year the mass media dutifully report these pronouncements to a female world waiting with bated breath to wear what Christian Dior thinks they should wear. It is fantastic to see how a few men can dictate to a world of women what they should wear year after year.

Remember how the mini skirt started in a small way in London way back in 1967? Within five years the mini skirt enveloped the whole world, caused a drop in textile sales, and became the symbol of the female liberation from social restrictions, thanks to the mass media.

Then came the maxi, a reaction to the mini, and then the midi, a compromise. If it is not the hemline it is the neckline that is going up or down. Marilyn Monroe, the GI pin-up girl of Vietnam, popularized the plunging neckline and the cleavage. Then came the see-throughs and the Cardigan top — nothing more than a loose shirt or jacket worn over hot pants or bikini wear.

What will the fashion designers think of next? Whatever it is, you can bet on one thing -- milady will surely know from the fashion magazine, the fashion pages of the newspapers, from television and movies.

What we have discussed here are only the most obvious examples of how the mass media can influence what a nation wears, sings, or dances. In many other ways also, they shape the nation's culture and pass this social heritage from one generation to the next.

2. Building a Nation

This task of building a common culture is an important role for mass communication, both in developed and developing countries. In developed countries the nation is already built and that social fabric is woven to add to an already existing culture. But in developing countries, like the Philippines, the building of a common culture is more like building a nation.

In an analysis of the problems plaguing Philippine society, one sociologist[3] has said the cause can be traced to our lack of unity.

We are a fragmented society, he said. We are split into the rich and the poor; the elite and the masses; the English-speaking and the dialect-speaking; the Catholics and the Muslims; the "stateside" and the native, the Ilocanos and the Bicolanos. We are divided into clans and barangays, with only a seeming sense of attachment to national values.

The sociologist continued:

> Because we have no strong sense of national unity or accomplishment, we expect little from the nation or government. For our security and welfare we turn to those close to us, our family, relatives, our friends, our personal connections... And so when the chips are down, and the choice is between the common good of the country and the particular advantage of my family and those close to me, I prefer my group's well-being (and my well-being) to the common good of the country... Thus, for all the trappings of a national government we are not far from the era of the barangay, and we conduct our affairs pretty much in the manner of Lapu-lapu and Humabon.[4]

There is much that is true in this analysis of the problems of Philippine society and much that also apply to other developing societies in Asia and the rest of the Third World. Our problem at this stage is a lack of a national conscience. We talk about lack of self-discipline: this is only part of the problem. We lack self-discipline because we have not learned to subordinate private interests to a higher good, whether it be God or a nation.

The mass media, together with the other social institutions like the home, church and school, can play a vital role in creating this sense of nationhood.

3. Entertaining a Nation

Another role of mass communication in society is to entertain. This applies to mass media in all societies, whether developed or developing, democratic or authoritarian.

A nation needs some respite from the daily grind of work and solving problems. For relaxation it looks to sports, travel, and entertainment from various sources, including the mass media.

Some of the mass media are especially geared to play the role of entertainer -- the movies, television and radio. While they also perform other functions, including informing the people, they are for the greater part entertainment media. In the Philippines, the movies are the most popular form of entertainment. Filipinos perhaps are among the most addicted movie fans in the whole world, judging by the number of movie houses in Manila and the smaller cities in proportion to population. There are about 1,200 movie houses today in this country of 56 million Filipinos. The Philippine movie industry is among the top three in Asia today in terms of number of movies produced.

Next to movies, television is the most popular form of entertainment in the urban areas, while radio leads the way in the rural areas, with the housewives patronizing the soap operas.

We should not forget, of course, the comics magazines and the comic strips. Comics magazines are the bestsellers among magazines in the country. They are read by everybody, especially the *bakya* crowd. The magazines in the vernacular also provide escapist fare in the rural areas with their sob stories about ill-starred lovers, abandoned housewives, cruel husbands and kind mistresses. The Filipino reader, it seems, escapes from his personal problems by crying over the problems of others, even if they are only fiction.

While entertainment is the essential function of movies, television, radio, comics magazines and the vernacular magazines, they can also be useful vehicles for educational materials. They not only amuse but provide palatable learning situations as well.

COMMUNICATION AND DEVELOPMENT

There is another role of communication which is especially relevant to developing countries: the development function. This role combines the political, economic and social functions.

In the Philippines and other less developed countries, we can look at mass communication, or the broader term communication, as an instrument for national development.

The role of communication in development seems obvious: when a road is built into a village, things change. First the physical changes: more houses and markets are built. More offices and more stores. More money comes in. More goods are sold and more stores are built. Then a factory is built to supply the needs of the local people.

When newspapers, magazines, books and films are brought in through those roads, more things change. People change in the way they think and look at things. Then radio and television come in over the airlines and bring with them new words and ideas. They bring in the speeches of government officials calling for national self-discipline or advising farmers how to produce more rice per hectare or how to kill mosquitoes.

Some people might use the road and go to the outside world to learn new ways of doing things which they bring back with them to the village. Films show local people how people elsewhere live in plush apartments and drive around in flashy cars. Some of these new ideas they adopt. Some they cannot adopt and these cause either frustration or a determination to work hard and acquire these things.

Slowly the old order is undermined, tradition breaks down, and change is underway, a change hastened by the advent of mass media.

1. Mass Media as "Mobility Multiplier"

Perhaps the first major study on the role of communication in development was made in six Middle East countries -- Iran, Egypt, Turkey, Syria, Lebanon, and Jordan -- by Columbia University in 1950-1951. The study and its results are described in the book, *The Passing of Traditional Society*, by Daniel Lerner.

In this book, Lerner proposed his theory of modernization, derived from history and supported with data gathered by Columbia University which he analyzed. Lerner compared from 54 to 73 countries, and found out that there was a pattern in their development. First urbanization, followed by development of literacy skills. Then media participation, followed by political participation. These four factors go together in the process of modernization, according to Lerner.

Lerner thus had in his hands a model of modernization. But, he complained, the historical model at this point was static. There were a few unanswered questions. How does a country move from one phase to the next? Why does an urban person regularly become a literate, a reader and a voter? Why do some people modernize faster than others? And others not at all? He searched for the dynamic component to explain these, to relate institutional changes with the changes in personal style. And he came up with empathy.

Lerner defined empathy as the "capacity to see oneself in the other fellow's situation, the skill in imagining oneself in another's shoes."

Lerner identified the more empathic individuals among the 1,357 Middle East respondents interviewed by Columbia University by the way they answered questions that called for imaginative answers. If you were head of the government, what would you do? If you were editor of a paper? Lerner found that the more empathic individuals (i.e., those who scored high in the questionnaire) had more mobile personalities. As people read newspapers, listen to the radio and go to the movies, they become more imaginative and develop a wider range of opinions. Lerner demonstrated that the mass media accelerates the development of empathy by developing psychic mobility. Lerner thus ties in empathy beautifully into his theory of the role of the mass media in the development of modern society.

The mass media, therefore, according to Lerner, serves as the "mobility multiplier."

Between the time the Lerner theory of modernization first appeared in the 1960s and today, however, a lot of water has flowed under the bridge, so to speak. The meaning of development itself has developed from purely economic growth to total human development.

And the concept of the role of communication in this process has changed from that of a reporter, mainly providing information upon which individuals in society may base their decisions, to persuasive communication, meaning the use of communication in a massive and systematic way to motivate people to action. And this has given rise to the new concept and new discipline of development communication, which will be discussed more fully in another chapter.

Notes

[1] Thomas Jefferson, as quoted in Edwin Emery, *The Press and America* (Englewood Cliffs, New Jersey: Prentice-Hall, Inc., 1962), pp. 166-167.

[2] These conclusions are based on the author's own observations and on newspaper reports from 1960 to 1967, when he was in the United States as a graduate student.

[3] Fr. Francisco Araneta, S.J., in an article, "The Fragmented Society," in the August 26, 1968 issue of *Graphic*.

[4] Ibid.

[5] Daniel Lerner, *The Passing of Traditional Society* (New York: The Free Press of Glencoe, 1964).

Chapter IV

The Role of Communication in a Crisis

Crispin C. Maslog

The Vietnam War, from the early 1950s to 1975, was said to be the first televised war in history. The senseless slaughter that was going on in the jungles of Vietnam, in a war of attrition between Americans and Vietnamese, was daily fare on American and European television for more than a decade.

On the other hand, the Philippine Revolution of 1986, from February 22 to 25, has been acclaimed as the first televised revolution in history. For four days in February, Americans, Europeans, Asians, people all over the world, were glued to their television sets, watching in awe and admiration, as millions of Filipinos fought a strange revolution -- not with guns and bullets, but with bare hands, rosaries, religious images, hymns, placards, prayers, songs, flowers and faith.

It was a stunning performance that ended the 20-year rule of one of the most corrupt dictators of modern times, and put the Filipino on a pedestal in the eyes of the world -- for how could one mount a successful revolution, indeed, without the shedding of blood?

But, that was what the Filipinos did, and the world watched it live, with bated breath, with wide-open eyes, thanks to the wonders of modern telecommunications and mass communication. About 1,000 foreign correspondents from all over the world were there to cover it for an unbelieving world. It was fortuitous, indeed, that so many journalists from foreign countries were here when it happened -- because they had been here weeks before February 22, to cover the snap election campaigns waged by an aging dictator and an inexperienced housewife vying for the presidency, and they were here to witness the incredible cheating during election day and during the counting of votes in the days that followed.

It was high drama that made good copy for the journalists -- the sight of thousands of nuns, seminarians, professionals and students protecting their ballots with their bodies, risking lives and limbs, a people determined to win back their lost freedoms. High drama piled upon high drama, as the tabulation of election returns went on and conflicting reports were given by the mass media.

Radio and television, particularly, led in the election coverage because of their immediacy. There were three sources of election results reported by different outlets -- the superquick count, called Media Poll Count, conducted by the Kapisanan ng mga Brodkaster sa Pilipinas (KBP) and aired over most radio stations and four television stations in Metro Manila (Channels 2, 4, 9 and 13); the super slow count, the so-called official count conducted by the Commission on Elections and covered by the same stations; and the quick count conducted by the National Movement for Free Elections (NAMFREL) and aired only by Radio Veritas.

The first two counts (the super quick and the super slow) showed then President Marcos leading, while the quick count (NAMFREL) showed Cory Aquino ahead. While some people loyal to Marcos believed the first two counts, most Filipinos stuck to the NAMFREL-Veritas count. Credibility, of course, had a lot to do with it. A survey in Metro Manila in 1985 showed that Radio Veritas and the alternative press had the highest credibility ratings among the mass media, way above the crony press which had negative ratings.[1] The same survey had also shown that the credibility of the government and its high officials was zero, and these two counts (the super quick and super slow) were government-sponsored.

Thus it was that the people were already tuned in to their radio sets, particularly Radio Veritas, when the high drama reached a crescendo on February 22, 1986.

Saturday, February 22

At 6:45 p.m. of that day the spark that ignited the revolution was announced at a dramatic press conference attended by local and foreign journalists at Camp Aguinaldo. The two principal *dramatis personae* in this high drama were there: Defense Minister Juan Ponce Enrile and Armed Forces Vice Chief of Staff General Fidel Ramos. One after the other they announced that they were resigning from their positions and withdrawing their support for the Marcos government. They said they could no longer, in conscience, support a government that did not have the mandate of the people.

That moment was electric. This author remembers it very well. We had just come home from work and we turned on the radio for the latest election results, as we had been doing for the past few days. Then this press conference. And when we suddenly realized that Enrile and Ramos had finally rebelled, the thought sent chills running up and down our spines. It was a moment Filipinos had long been waiting and praying for.

According to Minister Enrile, after confirming from various sources that then AFP Chief of Staff General Fabian Ver had ordered his arrest and that of the members of the Reform the Armed Forces Movement (RAM), he and his RAM officers decided to make a do-or-die stand at Camp Aguinaldo. Before going there, he made a succession of telephone calls.

He called up General Ramos to ask if he would join him, to which Ramos replied yes without hesitation. Minister Enrile continued:

"Then I called back my house and I talked to my wife and instructed her to contact Mrs. Eugenia Apostol of the *Philippine Daily Inquirer* to tell her what was happening and to please contact other members of the media about it. I also then after that, called another friend to contact and warn some acquaintances in the Opposition and requested them to lend us their political assistance...

"Finally, he (Ramos) arrived at about six o'clock. We went to the ceremonial hall (of Camp Aguinaldo), where the local and foreign news media gathered and that was the first time we announced what was going on. Luckily, Radio Veritas was there, and we were interviewed. Incidentally, I would like to tell you that when I talked to my wife, I told her to call Cardinal Sin. . . I appealed to our people over the airlanes to help us and also to our brother officers and military men. . . We announced over the radio, over the media at this point, that we will never surrender, that if they will assault us, we will have to go down together, they will have to kill all of us. . . After that press conference, we waited and then people were coming in to us here in the Ministry. . ."[2]

Then negotiations between Malacañang and Camp Aguinaldo ensued. While this was going on, the newsmen kept arriving. There must have been hundreds of them by this time, both local and foreign journalists. According to Enrile, "They asked if they could stay with us, and I said we would be happy if they did, but it would be inconvenient because we had no facilities. . ."

By this time, night of Saturday, February 22, appeals were starting to be made over Radio Veritas, anchored by June Keithley, for people to come to Camp Aguinaldo and Camp Crame to protect the two camps from the forces of General Ver. It was a strange twist to this revolution. The people were asked to protect their soldiers! The idea, of course, was to prevent the soldiers from killing each other, so there would be no bloodshed. At that point, no sane gambler would have bet his money that the revolution would succeed, much less be bloodless.

The first person to make the appeal was the Archbishop of Manila, Jaime Cardinal Sin, the third most important *dramatis persona* in this radio drama, for it was indeed a real life drama over the radio.

It was the Cardinal's authoritative voice over Radio Veritas that night that mobilized tens of thousands of Filipinos on to the streets in front of and around Camps Crame and Aguinaldo. The Cardinal summoned the faithful to nonviolent battle. Because of his role he was later aptly called the Cardinal of the Revolution.

"Leave your homes now," he pleaded, "I ask you to support them (Enrile and Ramos), "give them food if you like, they are our friends. Let us all go to Camp Aguinaldo."

It was the call that could save lives, according to one writer, bring "Cory's millions" out into the streets, including nuns who bodily stopped advancing tanks, and stupefy Pope John Paul II who did not want any of his Cardinals messing with politics. . ."[3]

In the Cardinal's own words: "When Betty (*Inquirer* co-chairman Betty Go Belmonte) was calling me about Enrile and Ramos, Ramos and Enrile also called me and they told me, 'Cardinal, help us, because in one hour we will be killed.'[4]

"The first thing I did was to call the contemplative sisters. We have three in Manila - the Poor Claire Sisters, the Pink Sisters in Hemady and the Carmelite Sisters. I said to them by phone:

"Come out from your cells. Go immediately to the chapel and before the exposed Blessed Sacrament with outstretched arms you have to pray, and prostrate before God on the floor. And you should start fasting tonight, and you should not eat solid food until the time when I will tell you, because we are in battle and you are the powerhouses. And the moment we do not win the battle, you will have to fast until the end of your life.

"That was what I told them--it was very strong.

"Then that was the time when I called the people: Get out now and go to Camp Aguinaldo."

"And the young people and the old went there and the sisters, and also this Ms. Monzon who died today (Ms. Francisca Sunico vda. de Monzon passed away on March 22 at the age of 88). She was 88. She jumped from her house in a wheelchair, and alone she went there with a crucifix. When she arrived there she met the tank, and she said, 'Stop! You can kill me because I am old, but do not kill the young people. Stop!'

"And the man operating the tank came down and embraced her...

"I did not leave the house because I was monitoring (the events). Every hour I say something (over the radio)... My security men told me not to go there because there were still Loyalists who might hit me. But the people heard my voice, that was enough..."

The fourth most important *dramatis persona* of this real-life drama was a veteran member of the Parliament of the Streets that blossomed since the death of Ninoy Aquino in 1983--none other than Ninoy's brother, Butz Aquino. He also played a crucial role in those critical first hours of the revolution. In his own words:

"I heard the replay (of the Ramos-Enrile press conference) on the radio.

"This was about eight o'clock in the evening. We were at a party, waiting for the other guests. While we were talking, the radio was going on, and of course this was the topic that night, since the news was that Opposition leaders were going to be picked up, martial law was going to be declared... there were so many rumors...

"We tried to get in touch with Cory (who was in Cebu at that time) and got as far as the radio room to transmit the message asking for any special instructions.

"By the time we started moving there were no instructions yet. Anyway we got to talk to Justice (Cecilia Muñoz) Palma, and I asked her, 'Do you believe in these two guys? ' And she said, 'I think so.'

"I told her, I'm going to Camp Aguinaldo and offer whatever support we can give."[5]

Butz went to Camp Aguinaldo in his old black Toyota Crown (where he was at first mistaken for a general) and looked for Enrile to offer his support.

The second Enrile-Ramos press conference that evening (still Saturday, February 22) was held around 10:30. After the press conference Butz Aquino, spying Radio Veritas' June Taña on the line to his station, plugged in and made his call for people to assemble at Cubao's Isetann for the march to the camps. Butz continues in his own words:

"From Camp Aguinaldo we proceeded to Isetann Cubao - about 10:45 p.m. There were only six of us there, looking at each other. How do we have a revolution with only six of us?

"By 11:00 o'clock there were about two to three dozen people. Then one of the ATOM (August Twenty-One Movement) guys came around and I told him to get our panel with our sound system. When he got back about 11:30, the panel couldn't go anymore because there were several thousands already."

Butz told the people they would march at midnight, and by that time there were already about 10,000 people, responding to his call over Radio Veritas earlier.

"And as we were marching," he continued, people were still converging, and by the time we got to Camp Aguinaldo we were at least 20,000... it was a beautiful sight."

By this time, almost everyone had his ears glued to the radio, in Metro Manila and throughout the archipelago. One writer recalls:

"Driving along Sucat, Parañaque at that time was eerie. The road seemed like one huge quadrasonic stereo, all glued to Radio Veritas. People turned off their aircon, pulled down their windows and looked at other motorists, seeming to seek confirmation for what they were hearing."[6]

Other people also heard the news, and each responded in his own way, as Cardinal Sin and Butz Aquino did. Three of these were soldiers.

First Lieutenant Tito Robles, Basa Air Force, had just come from Manila when he got the news from Radio Veritas. He immediately rushed to Camp Aguinaldo and joined the 600 or so rebel soldiers at the time guarding the Ministry of Defense building.

Capt. Jesus Durian, Special assistant to the Defense Minister, was at home with his family when friends called him up. "Listen to Veritas," they said. Capt. Durian right away told his wife, "I must go to Camp Aguinaldo, he needs me now." The wife said goodbye and prayed, afraid that she might be a widow soon.

Meanwhile, Col. Antonio Sotelo, commander of the all-important 15th Strike Wing of the Philippine Air Force, was sipping a bottle of beer at home when the news came over Radio Veritas. Col. Sotelo said:

"I listened in shock to their press conference when my phone suddenly rang. The caller was an aide of Minister Enrile, someone I know well. Our conversation was very brief. He said Minister Enrile is asking for my help. I said yes. The time was about 7:00 p.m...

"As I motored to Sangley at around 10:00 p.m., listening all the while to Radio Veritas, I started reviewing my life. I said to myself: I am fifty-two years old, with four grown-up children, two grandchildren; have savored the pleasures of the world; and so there was not much more to aim for... my mind was set to give up my life for my country..."[7]

Meanwhile, Marcos had two press conferences that night. He was on all the five Manila TV stations and most of the radio stations. The first press conference came about two hours after Enrile and Ramos announced their mutiny. Marcos claimed that his men had uncovered a coup d'etat plot by the men of Enrile and Ramos. He presented a nervous-looking military officer who was asked to read his confession of participation in the plot. In the second conference, Marcos presented another officer who was also supposedly part of the same plot.

Radio Veritas did not sleep Saturday night. From midnight up to the darkest hours of dawn, until Sunday morning came and again into the night, the brave and hardy souls manning the radio station, led by June Keithley, took turns at the microphone, to plead, cajole, entreat people to come out of the comfort of their homes to EDSA, to prevent the soldiers from fighting each other, ensure peace and prevent bloodshed. This was certainly Radio Veritas' finest hour. By this time the only station for the people was Radio Veritas, "on the dial 848, the number of truth," as the announcer kept repeating.

Sunday, February 23

By Sunday morning, the people were responding in tens of thousands. From all walks of life they came, from all directions, from mansions and from hovels, from Forbes Park and from Tondo, they poured like an unending stream into EDSA, the eight-to-twelve-lane highway running between Camps Aquinaldo and Crame north of Manila. It was an awesome sight, a sea of humanity answering the summons of this one radio station, playing like the Pied Piper of Hamlin.

Just before Sunday noon, Cory Aquino was heard for the first time since the start of the revolt, coming over Radio Veritas from Cebu. Her soft, clear voice was heard by the nation, a nation that had not slept the previous night. She rallied the country behind Enrile and Ramos and pleaded for calm and non-violence.

In the afternoon, the first serious threat to the two camps came in the form of about a dozen tanks and a Marine contingent under the command of Gen. Artemio Tadiar. The story of that dramatic confrontation at corner EDSA-Ortigas between the soldiers and the people with their anti-tank weapons, like rosaries and statues of the Virgin Mary, has been told in detail elsewhere. Butz Aquino was there. The nuns were there. The Filipino and foreign journalists were there, to record the intense drama that was going on. Looking back at the whole EDSA scene those days, people remember noticing the hundreds of foreign newsmen with their ubiquitous video cameras and audio cassette recorders, all over the place. It seemed that every hundredth person was a foreign correspondent, in his own vehicle, walking the streets, perched on top of cargo trucks used for barricades, astride the high cement fences of Camp Crame, their cameras clicking and whirring away. They were having a field day. Perhaps this was the first revolution that they had covered with such abandon and with such freedom, with little risk to their lives and limbs, as it turned out.

In the stand-off that Sunday afternoon, between the tanks and unarmed Filipinos, the people won. The tanks retreated to Fort Bonifacio. The first major victory of the revolution.

Meanwhile, the drama over Radio Veritas continued. Every few minutes throughout the night, Manila auxiliary bishop Ted Bacani was on the air with his appeal for more volunteers around the two military camps. This continued appeal was important because the crowds always thinned starting about midnight and early morning.

Then it happened. A military commando group, led by no less than Marcos crony Eduardo Cojuangco, attacked the unguarded P40 million microwave facilities of Radio Veritas in Malolos, Bulacan. The attackers were wearing yellow, the color of Cory Aquino's movement. Momentarily, Radio Veritas was off the air, and there was panic.

June Keithley, however, with the encouragement and help of Fr. James Reuter, was able to negotiate for the use of another radio station, DZRJ, 810 on the radio dial. The new station's 10 kilowatts was certainly less than the 50-kilowatt power of the destroyed Radio Veritas transmitter, but it served just as well, because by this time other radio stations, especially in the nearby provinces, were already hooked up to the "number of truth."

For security reasons, June Keithley did not reveal where she was, and she baptized her new station, as DZRB, or "Radio Bandido." It added an air of romance and mystery already building up around June Keithley and Radio Veritas during those fateful days in February. As June would recall later, she was really scared to death, announcing alone that whole day, with only two boys assisting her in the studio and two security men guarding outside. She could have been attacked by another Marcos loyalist commando team anytime, especially because her new station was located about a kilometer from Malacañang, right on top of the former Office of Media Affairs in the Jacinto building on Magsaysay Blvd. and Old Sta. Mesa. But at that time not more than a handful of friends knew where she was.

As it turned out, no attack came, and June Keithley's voice was heard throughout the country and through the night, calling for more volunteers, in her fluent English and broken Tagalog, for which she continually kept apologizing. Minister Enrile and General Ramos were alternately on the air appealing for more "People Power." They must have known that the huge crowds had thinned out alarmingly by this time.

June Keithley, in the meantime, kept apologizing for not having the "Mambo Magsaysay" record requested by many listeners. It was becoming popular after June played it at the old Veritas studio. The substitute "Onward, Christian Soldiers," however, turned out to be more inspiring.

Down at EDSA, in the meantime, the mood was desperate. One EDSA veteran recalled later a scene he saw: "Returning to the main gate, I saw a line of 8 or 9 persons on the west side of EDSA with bowed heads. They were facing Ortigas, positioning themselves as if they wanted to be alone. My curiosity so overwhelmed me that I decided to approach them. But before I could reach them, I saw all of them make the sign of the cross and each one kissed everyone else. I figured that this was one entire family, and when they joined the human barricade I said to myself, 'They are ready to die. . .'[8]

Monday, February 24

It was June Keithley on the air, at dawn of Monday, February 24, who kept people awake with reports of the second major attempt by the Loyalist forces to take over Camp Aguinaldo. June implored her listeners to turn up their radio sets, hoping that the soldiers who heard the National Anthem would be moved to retreat.

The battle royale was heard over the radio by someone who later that morning was going to play a major role in the series of events that marked the revolution, Col. Antonio Sotelo. In his own words:

"Sunday was a long day. I was walking on razor's edge. Exhausted, I slept at about 10 p.m. and woke up at 2 a.m. of Monday. Immediately, I started tuning in to Radio Veritas only to find out that it was already gone. But somehow I managed to recognize a familiar voice, that of June Keithley. She was giving a blow-by-blow account on what was going on and it was saddening. . .

"The radio in my car was on so I knew what was going on. It was pretty bad and deteriorating rapidly. Appeals by Eddie Ramos to Manong Andy to call off the attack. Appeals to Comparing Fabian. Tear gas was already being used to clear the people. Instructions on how to handle the tear gas. Wet towels. Wet blankets. Put on the lights. Ambulance. Medicine. . ."[9]

The government forces used tanks and lobbed tear gas at unarmed barricaders but the wind shifted and the teargas hurt the soldiers who promptly withdrew. In another confrontation with unarmed people, the soldiers again retreated. And June Keithley announced this triumphantly over Radio Veritas.

Later that morning, Colonel Sotelo landed his 15th Strike Wing, composed of six helicopter gunships, at Camp Crame. He had decided to go over to the rebel camp, and Marcos was deprived of his control over the air. According to General Ramos later, this was one of the major turning points in the four-day snap revolution.

By 7 a.m. loud cheering could be heard in the office of General Ramos at Camp Crame. Since Enrile joined Ramos in the office, it had become the command post of the revolution. MP Alberto Romulo was reported later to have come out of the office with the announcement that "Marcos had flown the coop" the night before. This was carried immediately by Radio Veritas, and a euphoric June Keithley kept repeating the announcement.

By 7:30 a.m. a news bulletin was flashed over Channel 7: "Enrile, Ramos in control. Watch out for further developments."

Then just as Enrile and Ramos were to have another press conference at Crame, Marcos came on the TV screen. He was surrounded by his family.

The First Lady Imelda and daughter Irene were seated a little to his right. Grandson Borgy was playing all over the place. Bongbong came in later, dressed in battle fatigues. Still insisting he was in control, Marcos announced that his inauguration as President would be held as planned the next day. Irene seemed to be forcing a smile. Imelda silently handed her husband the day's newspapers. Bongbong was running after Borgy.

Marcos declared a state of emergency even as he lambasted the mass media for their alleged irresponsibility in announcing that he had fled. As the First Family quietly left camera range, the press conference began. This was to be Marcos' last press conference over TV 4. But before it was over the televiewers were treated to a strange spectacle that will long be remembered.

During the conference, General Ver arrived in full battle gear and asked Marcos for clearance to launch an artillery and air attack on Crame. Ver was visibly agitated and argued with Marcos when he said no, use only "small arms fire." Ver wanted to use heavy artillery. Marcos was trying to appear cool and in control, while Ver was fidgety and shaken. All these live on television!

Then as Marcos was about to answer a reporter's question on how he was in control, the television screens blacked out. Rebel troops had wrested control of the government television station.

Meanwhile, no one among the high officials in Camp Crame was able to clarify where the false story that Marcos had fled came from, nor would anyone admit that it was intentional, a psychological warfare ploy. Whether deliberate disinformation or not, the story that Marcos had fled spread panic among government forces and started a series of defections to the rebel camp, even before Marcos could deny the story over television.

Meanwhile, also, Radio Veritas was getting weaker. It had to go off air for short periods of time because of technical problems. "Our station is dying, but the spirit lives on," June Keithley said.

When Col. Mariano Santiago and three truckloads of rebel soldiers, all in civilian clothes, arrived at TV 4, a loyalist unit was already inside. Santiago at first negotiated.

"We are brothers," said Santiago. "If we shoot each other, this would be our last meeting. We don't shoot fellow 'mistahs,' we shoot enemies."[10] ('Mistah' is the nickname for graduates of the Philippine Military Academy.)

The Loyalists didn't shoot at first. Then quickly some of the rebels climbed up the side of the television tower until they held a commanding perch about 150 feet above the street.

Santiago planned to knock Channel 4 off the air as quickly as possible. But Marcos was still able to get on the air to announce that he had not left the country, before his press conference was cut off.

It was a brief siege that left one civilian dead (chief engineer Fred Arias, who died of a heart attack) and a few soldiers injured. By 9:50 a.m. the rebels had knocked TV 4 off the air. This was another turning point in the snap revolution. This bastion of the Marcos propaganda machine, which once featured the by-now hated Marcos apologists Ronnie Nathanielsz and Rita Gaddi Baltazar was now liberated.

Radio Veritas announced the takeover of Channel 4 and its sister radio stations in the government-run complex and its staff moved to the liberated facilities. They told their listeners that their moving in to the swankier and more sophisticated complex was providential. Poetic justice after their P40-million equipment was destroyed by Marcos Loyalists.

At 1:30 p.m. the reformists, as the men of Enrile and Ramos were now called, started telecasting over TV 4. The first few hours were chaos. There was no air-conditioning, some of the equipment were not working, the volunteers did not know where things were.

The government-now-rebel station was renamed Voice of Free Philippines, then Radyo Pilipino and finally Radyo ng Bayan. Shortly after lunch, Radio Veritas anchorman Orly Punzalan and Maan Hontiveros, sans make-up, went on the air amid cheers from their studio audience. Recalled one writer:

"The telecast was spontaneous. Without any format, just about anyone came to sit in a hastily-made panel. They all telecast their unscripted euphoria, fears, opinions and apprehensions. All of them became instant anchorpersons, analysts and advisers to the mass movement outside as they aired appeals and announcements that deluged them from their television audience."[11]

There were attempts by the loyalists to retake Channel 4 but they were thwarted by people power. Human barricades spontaneously formed outside TV 4. Barricades were set up at the approaches and intersections of Bohol Avenue where Channel 4 was located. At a side gate a poster read: "Wanted Dead or Alive: Ronnie Nathanielsz."

Another writer recalls that first day: "No one and everyone was in charge. June Keithley in the studio later was called a General. Faces from the past reappeared on the screen -- Bong Lapira, Jose Mari Velez, Ninez Cacho

Olivares, Tina Monzon Palma. Maan Hontiveros would run in and out. Johnny Manahan and Maria Montelibano directed. Girlie Rodis took charge of the food brigade. Noel and Subas and Jim turned from performers to field communicators. Mel Cancio screened the barrage of people who wanted to air their piece. Freddie Webb called on his fellow athletes. Marilou Diaz Abaya, Ronnie Henares and Celeste Legaspi came in from the frontlines to join the others..."

That was how it was during the first day of liberated Channel 4. With Radio Veritas going, and finally gone, Channel 4 and Voice of the Philippines became the communication center for the revolution. They were rebaptized People's Station and Voice of Free Philippines, later Radyo ng Bayan.

For the people of Metro Manila, it was a culture shock to tune in to TV 4 and not find Ronnie and Rita. It was a strange sensation to see on the television screen for the first time in 14 years the reality of things outside. People Power made its debut on national television with the televising of the sea of humanity at EDSA and Cory Aquino's thanksgiving rally at Rizal Park. The crowd scenes and close-ups were enough to send chills up and down the spines of even the uncommitted televiewers watching from the comfort of their homes.

Said one housewife, "This is the very first time I've ever seen a rally or so many people in one place." Observed another viewer: "I've become so used to not believing television news. I can't believe this is happening. It's like culture shock because it's on Channel 4, too."[12]

Some unforgettable sights and sounds from this smiling people's revolution:

• Images of the Virgin Mary atop huge hauling trucks used to barricade streets, surrounded by people singing "Ave Maria," "Our Father," and other religious hymns.

• Nuns and students, middle class people and well-dressed elite, on their knees in the streets praying the rosary in front of the heavily-armed soldiers atop their tanks.

• An invalid in a wheelchair manning one of the barricades.

• A three-year-old child flashing the Laban "L" sign, perched on the shoulders of his father.

• Seminarians carrying huge crosses, their only weapons in this war.

• Contingents of poor people from the slums, children and adults, marching behind drum and bugle corps, waving banners with all kinds of slogans and all colors -- yellow, black, red, white and blue -- or singing the alternative national anthem, "Ang Bayan Ko."

But Marcos was not yet finished.

Around 7:00 p.m. that Monday, February 24, the other three television stations phone-patched Marcos from Malacañang. He fielded questions from a panel of four at the studio that included police reporter Ruther Batuigas and a Gen. Pacifico de Leon. When Batuigas asked him if he was imposing a curfew, he replied: "Well, now that you mentioned it, I hereby declare curfew all over the country from 6:00 p.m. to 6:00 a.m. effective tonight." The million people or so at EDSA that night laughed — practically laughed him out of Malacañang. There was no one to implement the curfew order. And if anyone did, there was no jail big enough for all the curfew violators. Marcos was kaput.

After the loyalist tanks and Marines were neutralized, the major battlefield in this revolution shifted to the mass media. After the reformists took over TV 4, the loyalists sent forces to secure the other television stations.

The battles for control of each of the television stations are interesting episodes in themselves, which some day can be told in all dramatic detail. In this paper there is only enough space to narrate the highlights.

Inday Badiday was on the air over Channel 7's DZBB at EDSA when loyalist soldiers entered the station and demanded that she sign off the air. She refused, saying only the station head could tell her to stop. After an hour of negotiations, her station manager finally told her to go off the air. While the loyalist soldiers controlled the station inside, they were surrounded by human barricades outside, obviously sympathetic to the reformists. The crowd outside was asking the loyalist soldiers to give up, but that night there was a stalemate. It was only the following day, at about 3 p.m. when the Marcos downfall was imminent, that the loyalist soldiers gave up and left Channel 7 premises by way of the back fence. But not before destroying the station's transmitter.

Tuesday, February 25

The battle for the television stations continued into the fourth day of the snap revolution. While TV 4 was firmly in rebel hands, the other stations early that morning were announcing that they were covering Marcos' inauguration at Malacañang.

Cory Aquino had her inauguration as president first at about 10 o'clock at Club Filipino, on Ortigas off EDSA, not too far from Camp Crame. This was taped and aired over TV 4 after its transmitter was fixed while Marcos was having his own inauguration at Malacañang. Channels 2, 9 and 13 in Broadcast City were getting ready to cover the Marcos inauguration, using the Channel 9 transceivers that were used to hook up the ceremonies in Malacañang.

As the three stations panned their cameras on the Malacañang crowd waving flags below the balcony, and as the emcee announced, "Ladies and gentlemen, the moment we have been waiting for...," the TV set suddenly blacked out. The rebels had neutralized the Channel 9 transmitter and Marcos was off the air for the last time.

The battle for Channel 4 was one of the more dramatic episodes in the snap revolution. It happened only 300 meters from President Cory Aquino's house on Times street in Quezon City. The crowds had surrounded Channel

4's transmitting station on Mother Ignacia Street, but loyalist Marines were perched atop Channel 4, trying to protect it. They exchanged high power rifle fire with the reformist rangers below. It was one of the more bloody incidents of the revolution. After more than an hour of gunfire exchange a helicopter gunship was called in by the reformists and the two Marine loyalists were finally shot down with machinegun fire.

With the capture of Channel 4, the battle for the airwaves was won by the reformists. This was the *coup de grace* to the embattled Marcos regime.

By 9:30 p.m., the news was confirmed on television -- Marcos had fled Malacañang and was on his way to Hawaii. The news struck many Filipinos deep inside and all the pent-up frustrations seemed to break loose in a flood of tears. As this author watched Channel 4, we saw that rare moment when three veteran broadcasters struggled with their emotions to no avail. Then Fr. Datu shouted a prayer of thanks to the heavens while Bong Lapira and June Keithley wept unashamedly. At that moment thousands all over the country were actually on their knees praying and crying with them. In Metro Manila millions were shouting and dancing in the streets as if celebrating Christmas Day, New Year's Eve and Easter Sunday morning combined.

ROLE OF THE PRINT MEDIA

While this account has been referring mainly to the electronic media when talking about the role of communication in the four-day revolution, the print media also did their share, particularly the alternative press led by *Malaya, Mr. and Ms., Veritas* newsmagazine, *Philippine Daily Inquirer* and *Manila Times.*

"We did our share in keeping people abreast of developments," *Malaya* publisher Jose Burgos Jr. said.

"Never in the history of the Philippine press have the newspapers played so gargantuan a task in keeping the people's hopes alive and urging them to do their share, by merely reporting truthfully — and, may I admit now, with some degree of sensationalism - the events shaping up during the four days before the Revolution was over. We tried to put a little order in the welter of confusion that gripped the nation. And we also helped quench the thirst for news brought about by those dramatic and tension-filled days."[13]

During that week *Malaya's* circulation jumped to as high as 500,000 copies a day. The demand was so great the paper was forced to spread the printing to cover four editions - provincial or bulldog, city, midday and evening editions.

The strongest selling point of *Malaya*, of course, was its reputation as a freedom fighter since the early days of martial law and the credibility it has attained since 1983, when it reported the truth about the Aquino assassination at great risk to its staff.

Malaya's main competitor for circulation during those days of the revolution and immediately after that was a newcomer to the field, the

Inquirer. The latter's circulation jumped to 350,000 during the week, as it reported the drama at EDSA to a nation hungry for news. People were now buying more than one newspaper, and if they bought two, it was most likely *Malaya* and *Inquirer*.

The *Inquirer*, a sister publication of *Mr. and Ms.*, whose publisher was Mrs. Eugenia Apostol, started out as a weekly during the Sandiganbayan hearings of the Ninoy Aquino assassination in September 1985. It became a daily three months later that year, in December, just as the snap presidential election campaign was starting.

The selling point of the *Inquirer* was its terrific trio of columnists, Art Borjal, Louie Beltran and Max Soliven, whose inside stories of the events during and after the revolution were avidly read by a public starved for information by the Marcos regime for 14 years.

The third competitor for circulation during those days of crisis was the *Manila Times*, the newest of the three leading papers. Published by Ramon Roces and edited by Vergel Santos, the *Times* started coming out on February 5, just two days before the snap election. And so it was able to cash in on the dramatic events that piled one on top of the other after election day and into the revolutionary week. Its appeal was to a middle class readership which relished the analysis pieces dished out by a veteran newsman who had just returned from Australia, Amando Doronila. Since then, of course, Doronila had left the *Times* to edit his own paper, the *Manila Chronicle*.

The crony press, during those exciting days of the revolution, was left behind in the circulation war because their credibility had been eroded by their spineless reporting during the Marcos years.

When the despot finally left, there was also drama in the newsrooms of Manila newspapers. A hard-boiled, veteran editor, Louie Beltran, later recalled events that evening as they affected him and his paper.[14]

"Some guys from foreign television interviewed me and I was explaining that elections were like a basketball game between the Celtics and the Lakers. Then they asked me how I felt. *Tinamaan talaga ako* (I was hit hard). Sometimes you never know the depths of your own feelings. I wanted to say something glib. Before I knew it I was crying. I've never felt so proud. Before they'd say, 54 million Filipinos and one son of a bitch. After the Revolution there was not a single Filipino you could be ashamed of. I remember many years ago when I saw Doronila off at the airport and he told me, the heroism of the Filipino died with Gregorio del Pilar. I'll never forget that.

"During the last hours, Fenix (*Inquirer* reporter) was outside the Malacañang gates. Sir, he called, the helicopters are taking off. People called, *baka raw hindi makuha ng Inquirer*. (Reporters) Formento and Logarta were in Camp Crame.

"When they came in I told them, gentlemen, I've never grabbed a story from my reporters, but tonight, you are going to sit down and I'll write the story. They saluted and said, 'Sir, you are entitled to it.' I've waited 14 years to write that headline story. But the people in production put a scandalously big byline. Oh, it was an incredible feeling! "

On the headline for that story in the *Inquirer* the following day, he added: "When Marcos fled I knew everybody will come out with 'Marcos flees' ; we had 'it's all over,' not just a sigh of relief or catharsis but to mark the end of the Marcos era."

MASS MEDIA IN THE PROVINCES

Meanwhile, from the provinces, the crucial role of mass communication in the February Revolution was further underscored.

I. RADIO DZLB IN LOS BAÑOS

by Felix Librero

Radio station DZLB, the rural educational radio station of University of the Philippines Los Baños, has always kept the public informed about current events and issues since it was started in 1964. Managed and operated by the Department of Development Communication, DZLB is used as a laboratory for broadcasting students, as a tool for research, as a channel for public service and extension and as a center for training in rural broadcasting.

Two important events covered by DZLB were the snap election of February 7 and the February Revolution.

Election Coverage

During the election, DZLB provided nonstop live coverage. DZLB staffers reported on voter turn-out, election frauds and the poll count. It aired observations about electoral behavior, interviews with various groups, officials and ordinary citizens. Whenever frauds were reported, DZLB announcers would call the attention of Comelec officials. Despite its limited equipment, DZLB reported electoral returns from nearby towns like Calamba, Bay, Sta. Rosa and San Pablo City where DZLB volunteers were posted. The broadcasts were well-received by the people of Laguna.

After the election, DZLB returned to its regular programming only to pre-empt all programs again during the three-day February Revolution.

Coverage of EDSA

Early in the morning of February 23, 1986, an emergency meeting was held at the residence of Vice Chancellor for Academic Affairs Edwin D. Magallona to formulate UPLB action plans. This writer was given the task of mobilizing DZLB to provide up-to-date reports on developments at EDSA and on efforts of UPLB to mobilize people to go to EDSA.

Starting at 7 a.m. of February 23 until the evening of February 25, DZLB was on the air continuously. DZLB announcers reported the developments in Los Baños and in Laguna, and in the entire country. To relay the latest information on the February Revolution, DZLB hooked up with Radio Veritas. When Radio Veritas went off the air, it hooked up with Radyo Bandido.

DZLB lined up panelists from the UPLB faculty, studentry, and community residents of Los Baños to provide listeners with views from a cross-section of the community. It also covered live the rallies organized by UPLB faculty and students on February 23 in support of EDSA barricades. The DZLB staff called for unity and fast action but at the same time counselled the people to remain calm.

DZLB certainly helped mobilize people to join the UPLB contingent to EDSA. Those who were unable to join the contingent remained tuned in to DZLB for news.

II. IN NUEVA ECIJA: RADIO AT FOREFRONT

by Rosita L. Rose

Radio was in the forefront in the Nueva Ecija election campaign. DWAY, a radio station in Cabanatuan City, aired some big rallies organized by the supporters of the Opposition. It thus provided its listeners the information needed to decide which side to take.

On February 7, election day, radio covered the events in the voting centers and in the poll count.

The print medium did not play an important role. The local newspapers, being weeklies, could not match the immediacy and timeliness of radio.

Not surprisingly, radio again took the front line during the four-day revolution, keeping the public informed of what was happing. Some radio stations hooked up with the Metro Manila stations. Some radiomen analyzed the situation and gave insights on the events.

Just as in the election, the presence of local papers was barely felt. At best, all they did was to recapitulate the events.

III. IN CEBU: MASS MEDIA WAS DIVIDED AND MANIPULATED

by Bien E. Fernandez, Jr.

Of the five daily newspapers in Cebu, only the *Freeman* and *Sun-Star* enjoy wide readership.

Visayan Herald can be considered an opposition newspaper following the path of *Pahayagang Malaya*. But it has low readership.

Sun-Star, with a circulation of 12,000 copies, is edited by Atty. Pachico Seares. It pirated from the *Freeman* Seares and many staff members. It is considered a crony newspaper, said to be financed by a Marcos crony, Anos Fonacier. Almost all of its columnists were Marcos apologists, among them, Godofredo Roperos, Johnny Brennan, Bong Layumas and Manuel Satorre, Jr. Only Wilfredo Veloso was oppositionist but only on the side of John "Sonny" Osmeña. News reporting for the front page was done by Leo Enriquez and Fred Espinosa, who specialized on Marcos news. If they had nothing good to report about Marcos, they usually wrote about killings mainly done by suspected NPAs. Eileen Mangubat and Thea Riñen reported news about the opposition, balancing off the pro-Marcos slant of the paper.

A quick look at headlines during February 1986 showed that *Sun-Star* carried pro-KBL stories at a ratio of 3-1. The paper conveyed to its readers that Marcos was winning. The February 9 headlines read: "3 Tallies place KBL on the lead." Later on, *Sun-Star* adroitly eluded being boycotted by Cory supporters through a shift in emphasis: news on robberies and killings instead of on politics. When the boycott took its toll, it turned "objective" on February 19 with the headline "Cory, Doy to file protest."

Still the *Sun-Star* tried to hold on to the slipping Marcos. But on February 25, before Marcos left the country, *Sun-Star* came out with the headline: "Cory, Doy take oath this AM."

The *Freeman* is the second largest newspaper with 9,000 copies circulated daily. It is owned by the Gullas family and therefore it tends to protect the interests of Gov. Eduardo Gullas. Since the governor is at odds with former Congressman Ramon Durano, the paper tries to play up news about the comical actuations of Durano, like his bolo and sandbags. Before the elections, it focused on the disunity of the opposition, particularly the Minnie-Sonny Osmeña family feud.

The majority of *Freeman's* columnists dished out opposition views. Ninez Cacho Olivares lead the pack that included Jose Logarta, Jr. and Ted Lugtu. Frank Malilong, Jr. and P. G. Aleonar are unreasonably pro-Marcos even until now. Lindy Maaba was quite confusing and editor Juanito Jabat struck at the Marcos excesses with his puns.

Soon after the elections, the *Freeman* went all-out opposition with pro-Cory news, perhaps to make fun of the Durano boast of a Marcos win in Cebu. On February 23, it headlined the Enrile-Ramos resignation with a follow-up of Gov. Gullas calling for calm. On February 26, the headline read: "Marcos is gone/Nation rejoices."

Broadcast Media

In broadcasting, DYRC-DYBU, DYLA, DYRF, DYMF and DYIM played major roles.

DYRF lead the anti's, being the home station of Mambabatas Pambansa Inday Nita Cortes Daluz. The station is run by the Divine Word order (SVD) of San Carlos University. Nanding Celeste's public affairs program TINUGDAN, is on the air every day, 7-9 AM, 12 noon-1 PM and 8-9:30 PM. It encourages public opinion on issues regarding the elections.

DYRF went on a 24-hour coverage of the election and poll count, fielding 15 reporters on motorcycles and 5 mobile units, and hooking up with Radio Veritas for the national poll results.

Worth noting is the bribery try on Nanding Celeste by a newspaperman to stop him from covering the NAMFREL count on February 8. The following day, he received death threats.

In its February revolution coverage, DYRF hooked up with Radio Veritas, had running commentaries on the events in Manila, and at the same time implored the people of Cebu to remain calm.

Station DYRC and its FM station DYBU were generally neutral, but at times leaned towards the opposition. DYRC's strong signal reached a lot of listeners who tuned in to its news and commentaries. Roy Ladiona anchored most of its public affairs programs. His DYBU counterpart was Rolly Chica.

A meritorious project launched by the two stations was the Radiothon which solicited contributions for those who barricaded EDSA. When they called for People Power in front of Camp Sergio Osmeña to prevent an attack by Gen. Renato Ecarma's loyalist forces, more than 6,000 people, together with their cars, trucks, and container vans, converged in front of the camp in less than 10 minutes.

DYMF, owned by an Ilonggo, Manuel Florete, was likewise neutral. Through an arrangement with RCPI, it got reports from many parts of the country.

DYLA, the radio station of the Associated Labor Union (ALU), has wide listenership but it was branded as pro-administration. Cerge Remonde was the moderating voice between DYLA's commentators and angry phone callers.

Very few really listened to DYIM, the government station, until Cory supporters took over the government radio and television stations in Manila.

The programs aired over the TV stations in Cebu were not much different from those of their mother stations in Manila because they are largely relay stations.

The most important contribution of Cebu mass media was its use as a forum for public discussion of national issues. Because people wrote to editors and phoned in to commentators, issues were discussed and crystalized. Readers and listeners became more interested and involved in the national life.

While the Cebu mass media served the selfish interests of their owners, they have also served the public interest by providing a forum for showing the truth in the interest of the nation.

CEBU MASS MEDIA - PART II

by Al Buenaventura

Manipulation of mass media in Cebu was a fact. It was not a monopoly of any political group. This was gleaned from interviews with lady journalists in Cebu.

Nini Cabaero of the *Freeman* said the offer was not outright bribery, but a show of gratitude by a political party for having covered its activities.

But Letty Suico of the *Visayan Herald* considered it an outright attempt to bribe her when cash was enclosed with press releases submitted to her by the Kilusang Bagong Lipunan (KBL). But she said,

> It did not alter nor affect the presentation of my news stories. I never interfered with desk work and I have no say what story should be published or printed. My task is only to deliver my stories to the desk.

Thea Rifien of *Sun-Star Daily* confirmed an attempt by the opposition to buy her off to slant her stories.

Both major political parties (KBL and UNIDO) made attempts, directly, or indirectly, to corrupt mass media. Some attempts may have succeeded, others have failed, but not a single mediaman would admit he was bought, for obvious reasons.

On the controversial nationwide Media Poll Count, how did the media react to the idea of pooled coverage? The members of the Cebu chapter of the Kapisanan ng mga Brodkaster sa Pilipinas failed to agree on the pooled coverage. Among others, each station had its own policy and idea of a poll count coverage. Some radio stations had their own network sources in Manila and they were asked to hook up with them for a wider coverage.

Sun-Star Daily columnist, Manuel Satorre, Jr., acted as Media Poll Count coordinator after he announced to the Cebu media in a press conference the mechanics of the operation. Nobody dared ask him where he got the funds. The only clue is that a Cebuano high-ranking official of the Ministry of Transportation and Telecommunications made the reservations for the luncheon press conference at the Lagkaw Restaurant. An investigation is underway to verify reports that the rumored P100,000 seed fund for the pooled coverage was part of a P2 million allotment handled by the Cebu office of the Finance Ministry Intelligence Bureau for media "lubrication." A government regional director is believed to have gotten hold of the seed money intended for the Media Poll Count.

What did the newspapers do during the election?

In an exposé in its April 5 issue, *Sun-Star Daily* news correspondent Eileen Mangubat reported that three *Sun-Star Daily* columnists were said to have secretly worked together to influence local newspapers to print stories favorable to KBL.

Satorre, one of those allegedly involved, denied it, questioning the authenticity of a report bearing his initials, saying it was an unsigned document. In his columns of April 5 and April 6, Wilfredo A. Veloso branded the expose as a smear campaign. Mangubat stated in her report that Godofredo Roperos, former regional director of the Office of Media Affairs in Region 7 and a *Sun-Star* columnist, could not be reached for comment. Roperos ignored the expose and did not bother to comment on it in his column.

Mangubat said she wrote the story because she considered it important, something the community ought to know. She was appalled about an orchestrated attempt by senior journalists to influence the media. She said she expected to be severely criticized by supporters of the mediamen. Their silence, she said, was more revealing:

> So when there was no comment at all on the radio, it occurred to me that the media community is like a cabal, the way at least the old hands maintain a cabal. There is brotherhood.

In November, months prior to election day, several Cebu broadcasters were invited to Malacañang for a briefing on the economic and political situation. DYLA News Director Sam Costanilla confirmed that some 60 of them were each given P5,000 by an aide of Antonio Barreiro, then commissioner of the National Telecommunications Commission.

'Envelopmental' Journalism

"Envelopmental Journalism" is an open secret. In more advanced countries, the practice is referred to as "amenities." To some radio commentators, it is a way of life. They do not deny being paid by politicians for their political broadcasts. Radio Commentators Vic Abangan of the KBL and Vic Canoy of the opposition admit this. Abangan said that it would be hypocrisy to deny it.

The KBP Community Advisory Board expressed alarm over the freewheeling character assassination and mudslinging by political commentators at the height of the campaign. The Board thus urged commentators to be responsible, and to strictly observe ethics and broadcast standards.

On election day, political groups tried to create a bandwagon effect by over-emphasizing some election returns. Remonde confirmed this. He said he was offered a sizeable amount in exchange for not sitting as anchorman during a specified period in the election. Remonde stressed that accepting the offer would mean no less than prostituting mass media at a crucial point in our history.

Print Media

During the February revolution, Cebu print media were largely dependent on radio broadcasts from Manila and abroad. Thea Riflen of *Sun-Star Daily* said she monitored overseas broadcasts which she rewrote for the paper and localized the events by adding the views of the military in the city. She added she would have wanted very much to be in Manila which was the forefront of an historic event - the toppling of a dictator with least use of force.

The broadcast media on their part showed initiative. Gary Bacolod, formerly of DYLA, fed monitored broadcast clips in a long distance call from Manila to DYLA in Cebu. DYRC and DYBU also monitored overseas broadcasts and aired parts of these. The government-owned radio station DYIM hooked up with MBS Channel 3 and DWIM while DYKC hooked up with KBS Channel 9.

The Cebu media expressed concern when three television stations and Radio Veritas in Metro Manila were attacked. Some mediamen understood the reasons behind such attacks. Nevertheless they considered the attacks as an assault on media institutions.

The Cebu broadcast journalists barely slept during those four days in February. Some of them were in mobile units in the field until the last minute defections of local military officials. Through the radio and television, local politicians were given a chance to be in touch with their constituents.

The February revolution had demonstrated once again, in no uncertain terms, the power which radio, as a channel of communication, wields, especially in helping mobilize people for a concerted action.

IV. IN DUMAGUETE: RADIO MOBILIZED PEOPLE

by Joy G. Perez

A few days before the February election, the *Vanguard*, one of the community newspapers in Dumaguete City, carried a headline that said Cory Aquino will win in Negros Oriental. The prediction came from a national survey, which the *Veritas* reported to have shown a landslide victory for Cory.

The four local radio stations - DYSR, DYWC, DYRM and DYEM-FM-- repeatedly appealed to its listeners to safeguard the ballots. But only DYSR and DYWC, both church-related, were very strong supporters of the National Movement for Free Elections (NAMFREL). DYSR is the broadcast arm of the National Council of Churches in the Philippines. DYWC is operated by the Catholic Diocese of Dumaguete. The other two stations are purely commercial stations.

The four radio stations decided to have a pooled coverage, but their poll count was so slow that people switched to Cebu radio stations.

While locally, the result was a Cory-Tolentino win, radio stations in Manila reported a Marcos-Tolentino win in Negros Oriental. It was a farce!

Days after, people listened to Cory's protest rallies which called for civil disobedience (what was known as Rally ng Bayan). Radio, TV and newspaper reports covered widely this protest.

From 3 p.m. through 6 p.m. on February 22, Cebu radio stations simultaneously covered the protest-rally of Cory and Doy. DYWC hooked-up with DYRF in Cebu.

At 6:30 p.m., Voice of America broke the news on Minister Enrile and General Ramos' break with Marcos.

Many could not believe at first. But Radio Veritas aired the Ramos-Enrile press conference.

Radio Veritas became the main source of news concerning developments on the February Revolution. When the Radio Veritas transmitter was destroyed on February 23, Dumagueteños switched to DYRC in Cebu City; every now and then, to DYMF.

At 6 a.m., on February 23, Silliman professor Rev. Lydia Niguidula and DYSR news reporter Glynda Descuatan rounded up the dormitory residents of Silliman University, telling them that they must do something. Over radio DYSR, an announcement was made. It requested faculty, students and any volunteers in the city to assemble at the Dumaguete Cathedral. Hundreds responded to the call.

At the PC/INP headquarters a religious service was said. Afterwards, the people remained outside the PC/INP headquarters to protect it from any attack. No one left the area until the PC/INP provincial commander, Lt. Col. Cesar Garcia, said: "We are with the people."

Copies of the *Philippine Daily Inquirer*, *The Manila Times* and *Malaya* that day (Feb. 23) were selling like hot cakes.

For the rest of the days, Sunday and Monday (Feb. 23 and 24), people huddled around their radio sets to listen to the latest news on the "revolution." Many had sleepless nights.

At past 9 p.m. of Feb. 24 (when it was officially announced that Marcos had left the country), people went out of their homes into the streets and rejoiced. Torches were lit and given to the people. The torches were the same ones used earlier in the street parade that climaxed the 6 p.m. Ecumenical Thanksgiving Mass held in front of the Dumaguete Cathedral.

V. IN BACOLOD: START THE REVOLUTION WITHOUT ME

by Ma. Cecilia L. Nava

The scenario for the mass media in Negros Occidental in the last election and four-day revolution might very well have been given the title of a 60s movie - *Start the Revolution Without Me*. Although it was obvious to everybody but the most rabid Marcos loyalist that Marcos was going to fall, many local media people continued (or at least gave that impression) in believing that Marcos would remain in power. Eli Tajanlangit, managing editor of the lone Bacolod daily, the *Visayan Daily Star*, recalled that when the February revolution started, three out of the seven pro-Marcos columnists in the paper called him up hurriedly to "kill" their columns for the next day. Their columns were singing praises to Marcos when the revolution started.

Pro-Marcos Media

The media, by and large, served the interests of the pro-Marcos establishment. Because of this, enlightened Negrenses considered Bombo Radyo in Iloilo more credible than Bacolod stations. Not surprisingly after the election, a major shake-up in Radyo Bombo resulted in the dismissal of two of its radio commentators, Fred Zapa and Ely de los Santos, for their marked pro-Marcos bias.

Anybody with knowledge of the history of Negros island will not find this surprising. Negros has always held a pro-establishment bias because of its ties with sugar. At one point in the past, the junta of Negrense leaders proposed a co-optation with American military forces at the height of the Filipino-American war just so the interests of the establishment could be protected. Economics has always played a major role in Negros politics and economics in Negros is invariably tied up with sugar. Not surprisingly, something as innocuous as "Snap Images," a photo and painting exhibit of Negrense artists, that was sponsored by Concerned Artists of the Philippines-Negros chapter, almost failed to open on election eve. Kagawad Atty. Romeo Geocadin, then in charge of the committee on culture and education, thought the pictures (which he had not previously viewed) might offend some members of the establishment because it mirrored Negros life too starkly.

The exhibit was also not deemed proper to be shown in the gallery of the Art Association of Bacolod City. As association president Dolly Gatuslao pointed out, the AAB building was on loan from the city government.

Utang na Loob

This strong sense of *utang na loob*, in the opinion of Edgar Billones, editor of a local fortnightly, *Forum*, was behind the delicate balancing act many media people had to play, while trying to remain credible. Some, like Bro. Mike Rapatan, FSC, principal and director of St. Joseph's High School, felt that the local mass media miscalculated and misjudged popular sentiments. In the process, he said, the media failed to reflect what was really happening in Negros. Billones said he felt that media reporting succeeded only too well in reflecting the dynamics of Negros politics and the hold of the patronage system.

Negros was the seat of no less than three Marcos cronies - Roberto Benedicto, Eduardo Cojuangco and Armand Gustilo. With the KBL conducting an organized and methodical campaign to woo media and voters (in Isabela, a small town with 18,000 voters, no less than P1.5 million was spent as "give-aways"), how could one possibly bite the hand that feeds? Although mediamen lambasted the Marcos administration abuses, they never went all the way.

Pressures on Media

The subtle pressures exerted on many a media man is perhaps best articulated by Millie Kilayko, former editor of the now defunct daily, *The Visayan Times*, and currently press information officer of new Negros governor, Daniel "Bitay" Lacson. Kilayko, as Namfrel co-chairman of politically-hot Cadiz City, wrote about her first-hand experience of election terrorism. She sent her article to a local daily. On the eve of its publication, she discovered the article was so watered down it failed to reveal what she really wanted to say. In disgust, she pulled out the article and mailed it that very day to *Business Day*.

No Opposition

Sandwiched between two strongly oppositionist provinces —Iloilo and Cebu -- Negros suffered the most under the Marcos administration due to the collapse of the sugar industry and the problems of military salvaging, malnutrition, hunger and child prostitution. Surprisingly, Negros delivered the elections to the KBL. A close look will explain why. Of the seven Batasan seats, only one was won by an oppositionist, Deputy Defense Minister Wilson Gamboa (he resigned in February 1987). Of the 18 mayoralty seats, none was won by the opposition. All barangay captains of the province are KBL party men. Small wonder that even when the stink in Malacañang was already beginning to spread in the province, Benedicto could still boast of delivering Negros to Marcos. History proved him right. How could he have lost when he had mass media in the hollow of his hand?

VI. IN LEYTE: RADIO RIDES AGAIN

By Lita Miguel

One thing was noticeable on that election day in San Jose, Tacloban City. As early as six in the morning, there were many people milling in front of the polling places. It was indeed a manifestation that people eagerly wanted to vote for Marcos' opponent. It did not matter anymore who the candidate was -- as long as the candidate would win and bring Marcos down.

People were silent, waiting for their turn to vote. Apparently, a good number of them had already sold their votes at the rate of ₱25 as an ordinary voter, or P50 for those close to the barangay chairman or the ward leaders.

From nearby houses, the three radio stations - DYPL, DYBR, and DYVL - kept the people of Tacloban abreast with the events in and outside Tacloban. DYPL and DYBR were markedly pro-Marcos. Announcer Lulu Palencia was all-out against Corazon Aquino and her tirades verged on personal insults. The main issues aired against Cory Aquino were: that she was inexperienced compared to Marcos; was ugly and unsophisticated compared to Imelda Marcos; and that she would deliver the Filipinos to the Communists if she won. DYVL aired the two sides of the issues.

After the elections only DYVL, a radio station in Surigao, could be heard in Tacloban. DYPL and DYBR were suddenly silent. People in Tacloban even thought that Lulu Palencia had probably joined the Marcos party when it left for Hawaii. Later, DYBR, keeping a low profile, switched to balanced reporting.

People flocked to DYVL to talk about their experiences during the elections. Foreseeing an Aquino victory, they became free, bold and vocal. They admitted having accepted money from the KBL, yet still voted for Mrs. Aquino. Frauds and terrorisms were reported.

The radio stations gave contrasting election results. DYPL and DYBR aired the Comelec results which gave Marcos an early lead and reported that Mrs. Aquino got zero in Southern Leyte, the homeplace of MP Nicanor Yñiguez. DYVL reported an Aquino win based on a NAMFREL tally. It was confusing. But in the end, Mrs. Aquino still won because people were more vigilant and watchful of the election results.

National dailies like *Malaya* and the *Inquirer* sold like hot cakes and kept Leyteños updated on events in Manila.

Fear gripped the city when DYVL reported that MV Legaspi, allegedly owned by the Romualdezes, was sighted in Babatngon, a coastal town some 20 kilometers from the city. The vessel was said to have been loaded with high-powered guns and money. The crew was reportedly paid P200,000 each. The bill of landing was addressed to Yao Ka Sin, a prominent Chinese businessman and supporter of the Romualdezes and the KBL.

Later during the week, money and guns were also discovered in the Governor's mansion.

VII. IN CAGAYAN DE ORO: LOCAL MEDIA IN A COCOON

by Ma. Theresa M. Rivera

Cagayan de Oro, a quiet city in the heart of Northern Mindanao, exists like a cocoon - all's well inside but everything seethes outside. A few meters outside the city, all kinds of problems exist -- militarization, evacuees, fighting between NPA and the Army and salvaging, among others.

Media Ownership

The mass media in Cagayan de Oro are owned largely by politicians. Two of the most influential politicians in the region - Oloy Roa, who owns PN Roa Broadcasting, and Reuben Canoy, who owns Radio Mindanao Network. Both politicians own printing presses and also publish local dailies. The television stations in the city, GMA (Channel 11) and RPN (Channel 3), although owned by other people, are to some extent controlled by these two politicians.

The pattern of media ownership partly explains the key role media played during the February election and revolution.

The people of Cagayan de Oro are neither heavy media users nor politically inclined. Even with the presence of celebrity politicians and with news of forthcoming elections, few were stirred by political events. The mass media also were not supportive of these events. They continued to feed their audiences with variety shows and soap operas. Very few broadcasters provided political analyses/commentaries of the situation. Media owners seemed careful not to prick the wrong balloon.

Campaign Period

During the campaign period, partisanship showed. Roa's radio station, DXOR, devoted its airtime to convincing people to vote Marcos-Tolentino. Cory's radio spots were unheard of until some Cory people demanded fairness. Only then did radio stations devote some time for the opposition's plugs. In the same manner, DXCC of Radio Mindanao Network propagated Canoy's candidacy. Only DXMO, owned by an opposition Cory sympathizer, became a lone voice battling for Cory.

At that time, even early during the pre-election time, most people in Cagayan were evidently pro-Cory although they did not show it openly. It was only a few weeks before and after the election that most people actively listened to the radio and watched television to find out how their candidates fared. DXMO attracted listeners from all classes. It was the only station that aired all opposition views. It even aired the rallies of Cory's Crusaders, Youth for Cory and Doy and Bayan. Thus, people learned of issues through DXMO.

Election Results

On election day, the pro-KBL stations openly displayed their sarcasm over the lead of the opposition, or when the opposition got a "0" mark. The stations in the city were not so much listened to because of their slowness in reporting results. People got accurate results over the Cebu stations and Voice of America. The distrust of people for local stations was easily seen during those times. And it was more justified when the people's revolution came. The radio stations then were at the height of passivity and lacked relevance and timeliness. Listeners were anxious to hear the latest news, but most of the stations continued airing soap operas and local commentaries, refusing to touch on the revolution. Hence, most people tuned in to Cebu, to DXMO, or to VOA and Radio Australia (ABS) to get first hand reports.

A "Media Monitor" group during the four-day revolution listened to all AM and FM stations in the city, in Cebu and abroad and saw the great disparity in reporting. This writer was in the group. Local media was airing its regular programs while history was happening. Because of this, most people switched to Cebu stations. The newspapers from Manila were grabbed by people as they arrived. It was only then that the mass media caught people's interest in the city. Without them, the whole of Cagayan de Oro would likely not have been aware of history being made.

VIII. IN COTABATO CITY: LOCAL MEDIA ACTIVE

by Patricio P. Diaz

Three local radio stations, DXMS, DXRO and DXCM, one locally published weekly, *The Mindanao Cross*, and a number of national dailies and magazines updated the people of Cotabato City and the surrounding provinces on issues and happenings during the snap presidential election and the February revolution.

Local Radio Stations

The local radio stations were the battleground of political propaganda. The Kilusang Bagong Lipunan bought, starting in the second week of January, more radio time than the opposition.

DXMS was the choice of the UNIDO but even here the KBL still had bought more time. In fact, on February 5, the KBL bought all radio time, from noon to midnight, in DXMS and DXRO, both of which have 10 kilowatt power. UNIDO had to content itself with DXCM, a station with low power, for its "miting de avance" broadcast.

While DXMS sold more radio time to the KBL, it was still identified as an opposition station. Yet, its newscasts did not show partiality to the opposition. And it did not have any news analysis or editorial. Perhaps the impression was created because DXMS is identified with the Catholic Church.

The two other stations were either pro-KBL or were just distancing themselves from the UNIDO. When the Cory-Doy team came to Cotabato on January 22, only DXMS sold radio time to them.

There is no doubt that the three radio stations in Cotabato City and DXND, the sister station of DXMS in Kidapawan, about 125 kilometers from the city, were most instrumental in bringing the election issues to the barrios. No newspaper could have done it.

Local Weekly

The Mindanao Cross, with its 5,000 circulation every Saturday, apparently had a strong impact on the city where it sells more than 3,000 copies. But it had lesser impact in the provinces of Maguindanao, Sultan Kudarat and Cotabato. It circulates only about 1,500 in these provinces. The paper is not an opposition paper. But the KBL called it as such and the UNIDO hailed it as an ally. The paper has the tradition of bringing out the truth about conditions and events as it sees them through its editorials and news analyses. Any objective analysis of the Marcos regime would inevitably have hurt Marcos.

National Dailies

The national dailies and weeklies, though limited in circulation, updated the people daily on what was happening in Manila and the other parts of the country.

The Mindanao Cross compiled materials for its news and editorial analyses from the national dailies. For the duration of the snap election campaign the paper carried "News Analysis" on page 1 (covering the latest development until the Friday deadline) and *"Comments on News"* on page 4.

Election Day

Election day and the week after was radio's show. All stations monitored election results round the clock. Here the party color of the stations showed.

Some stations also created confusion by broadcasting results from different sources. The results in the Manila dailies were more reliable even if they were 24 hours late.

The radio stations realized how much the people appreciated their special coverage. Matrons and refreshment parlor owners sent them soft drinks and food even at midnight.

Revolution

Radio Veritas, through DXMS, broke the news of the revolution to Cotabato City and surrounding provinces at 6:30 p.m. on February 22. DXMS resumed its 24-hour special coverage. In most homes, people listened to their radio sets throughout the night. Tension was as high as in Manila.

DXMS had an advantage over DXRO and DXCM. As a Catholic radio station, it maintains a link with Radio Veritas and DXND. The people followed closely the DXMS-DXND team broadcast.

DXMS supplemented its coverage with reports gathered through the PFCB-SSB system from station DZJO in Infanta. (Members of the Philippine Federation of Catholic Broadcasters are linked through a Single Side Band network.)

After Radio Veritas went off the air, DXMS and DXND covered the revolution primarily through the PFCB-SSB. Through the PLDT, DXMS called up either General Fidel V. Ramos, or Defense Minister Juan Ponce Enrile, so they could speak direct to the DXMS-DXND audience. Long distance calls were also made to Radio Veritas.

DXMS also got news through relays from PFCB sister stations. A friend of the station fed it with telexed and taped news, speeches, and press interviews of General Ramos and Minister Enrile.

Station Manager Jun Subido of DXMS, who is close to Brig. Gen. Cesar Tapia of Regional Unified Command 12, and Brig. Gen. Rodrigo Ordoyo of the 1st army brigade, had secret conferences with these generals to feel out their allegiance. On the second day of the revolution, when the three generals made known their support for Ramos and Enrile, DXMS-DXND broke the news to Central Mindanao.

Through DXMS-DXND, General Tapia assured the people of Central Mindanao that he would defy the orders of President Marcos to enforce martial law, starting with the curfew. He gave the same assurance to Archbishop Philip F. Smith, O.M.I., D.D., who was then leading the religious-civilian groups in planning emergency measures if martial law were reimposed.

When Radio Veritas went off the air, DXRO lost also a link since it had no links with its sister stations. On the third day of the revolution, it got permission to hook up with DXMS.

To the people of Cotabato City and Central Mindanao, especially the Cotabato provinces, the 10 DXMS broadcasters, who went on air in pairs, were also heroes. They were given food, drinks and commendations. Unsung, but as much heroes, were the technicians who stuck it out with the broadcasters.

Reflection

Through the snap election and the subsequent revolution, the Filipino people resurrected democracy and freedom.

In both events, the mass media that remained independent and did not accept bribes or did not allow themselves to be manipulated, demonstrated their indispensability to inform people, to link people, and to make them aware of the fact that the survival of their freedom and democracy lies in their hands.

IX. IN ZAMBOANGA CITY: LOCAL PRESS WERE CRONIES

By Fr. J.T. Bacatan

During the February snap election and revolution, this writer was in charge of our single sideband that, up to now, is linked with other stations of the Philippine Federation of Catholic Broadcasters.

In addition to our single sideband, we had a base transceiver and two mobile units. These pieces of equipment monitored the activities and the few irregularities at the polls at the east and west coasts of Zamboanga City. The only other time these units were used was during the "victory" celebration on February 25, originally meant to be a protest celebration if Ferdinand Marcos were proclaimed President-elect.

A first-hand account of how people perceived mass media in February was made by Fr. Raymond Miller, S.J., Principal of Basic Education at the Ateneo de Zamboanga.

Father Miller said that "for the past couple of years, it was easier to get anything published in *The Morning Times*, a leading local newspaper, or the *Zamboanga Express* than in the *Zamboanga Times*," the oldest paper in the city.

Just before the election, Father Miller reported encountering resistance from both *The Morning Times* and *Zamboanga Express*.

It was around that time when he started writing on the hard issues of justice and truth. When he started tackling the hard issues, one of his pieces was edited to his great dissatisfaction.

It was then that he discovered *Mindanao Special*, the only local paper that seemed to have remained free and non-partisan. *Business Star* seemed also free, but it did not come out regularly. He noted that *The Morning Times* and *Zamboanga Times* to this very day have maintained a crony orientation, pretty much the same way the *Daily Express* has been even after the revolution.

The Crony Radio

Father Miller said that radio was and is all but completely crony-owned and irresponsible, except DXYZ, DXTY and its sister station, DXTY-FM (there are 10 radio stations in Zamboanga). A government radio man gave him, upon his request, an insider's report on how media functioned. (To avoid reprisals on the man, his identity has been withheld.) This is the radio man's report:

From December 1 to February 4 - Most of the radio people in Zamboanga were directed to campaign for Marcos and were instructed not to say anything in favor of the opposition.

Most of the stations owned by the cronies of Marcos were given campaign materials to conduct house-to-house campaigns for Marcos.

All materials for broadcast emanated from Manila.

From January 1 to February 5 - All election materials were disseminated on and off the air by the broadcasters in the crony stations.

All music personality and public service programs were to air only the achievements of Marcos.

When Radio Veritas went off the air DXMS of Cotabato City became the main source of information for Zamboanga City.

SUMMARY AND CONCLUSIONS

A number of conclusions can be drawn after observing the performance of the mass media during this crisis in February 1986.

1. *World-wide Coverage.* Because of modern telecommunications and mass communication technology, and because of the critical events that converged at this point in Philippine history, the snap revolution and the events immediately preceding it were extensively covered by the world media. About a thousand journalists had descended upon the Philippines since December 1985 and so it was that when the revolution happened, it was recorded by the audio cassette and the camera, shown live on television screens and reported on the front pages throughout the world. This was probably one of the most widely covered and most vividly reported events in recent times and the first televised revolution in history.

In the global context, therefore, the mass media played the role of reporters. The Filipinos were the performers and the world was the audience in a real life drama carried live by the world's mass media.

2. *Role of Radio.* In the national context, radio played a primordial role in the crisis -- in reporting events as they happened, in airing public opinion, in serving as the communication link among the leaders of the revolution, between the rebel leaders and the people, and among the people themselves. Radio was the web that pulled people together, bound them in a communion of ideas and emotions that led to the explosion of people power at EDSA, elsewhere in Metro Manila and throughout the Philippines. The primacy of radio, of course, was mainly due to its very nature--its immediacy, accessibility, portability and reach. There was no question that during this week, radio reached the remotest corners of the nation. This was probably nowhere more vividly dramatized than in EDSA where about every tenth person was carrying a portable radio set surrounded by a group whose collective ear was tuned in to the set, intent on the unfolding events.

3. *Radio Veritas.* Among the radio stations, Radio Veritas was preeminent. This was mainly because of the Catholic radio station's credibility built over the years, probably starting with its reporting of the Aquino assassination in 1983. It was the only station that carried live and reported to a stunned nation the historic funeral procession for Ninoy participated in by about five million people and lasting 11 hours into the night of August 31, 1983.

Another reason for Radio Veritas' preeminence was its brave and balanced coverage of the snap elections at a time when the country needed to know the truth. It went on the air 24 hours a day in the four days following the election on February 7, and in the succeeding days broadcast from 5 a.m. to midnight until the revolution came. Then it again went on the air

The radio station stressed its policy of being a two-way vehicle for communication between the government and the people, and between the radio station and its audience. It gave people from both sides of a controversy a chance to phone in their views, raise questions, share perceptions and react to news and issues in a candid manner. As Radio Veritas phrased the station policy very clearly: "This is your station. Feel free to make use of it and share your ideas with others."

One writer paid tribute to Radio Veritas:

"Two other factors that were uniquely characteristic of the Catholic station's programming were the moments of prayer and reflection, and the wise choice of appropriate music relevant to this 'point in time' of our history as a people coming of age or reminiscent of a similar period in our past, as in the instant appeal of 'Mambo Magsaysay' or 'Stout-hearted Men' or 'I'll Live Again.'

"In the light of such selflessness in rendering public service at a time of national crisis, it is small wonder that the public response was spontaneous and equally generous. Volunteers flocked to the Radio Veritas studio to be part of 'the team' through the long, protracted vigil to share the truth. Families and individuals provided for the dawn-to-dawn work shifts, bringing meals, snacks, cheer-up notes to keep body alive and spirit hopeful."

For a time then, it seemed as if Radio Veritas was the only station on one side that reported the truth, and most of the other radio stations and all the television stations were on the other side. Truth was defined here as what NAMFREL reported was happening during elections and the counting of votes, and what most people saw with their own eyes and heard with their own ears at that time.

Then when the snap revolution came, Veritas became the veritable communication center for the revolution. In that sense, Veritas had taken sides, but then its side was the side of millions of Filipinos at EDSA and the great majority of the people in Metro Manila and the entire country.

After the snap revolution, a fund raising campaign was launched to raise at least P20 million to go towards a fund to purchase a new transmitter for the station. In the telethon organized over Channel 4 one day in March, P2.5 million was collected in cash and pledges from thousands of people in Metro Manila.

4. *Role of Television*. A major role, but still secondary to radio, was played by television, for a number of reasons. Aside from the fact that television still has limited reach, even in Metro Manila (it is not portable for one thing), it was blatantly partisan at worst or indifferent at best in the midst of the social upheaval going on at that time.

It was carrying the Marcos line during the campaign and the counting of votes, and therefore its credibility, which was zero to start with, was eroded even further. But when TV 4 was finally captured by the rebels, it became their communication center in Metro Manila and helped catalyze public opinion for President Cory Aquino faster. Television was so identified with Marcos that when all the TV stations were finally captured by the rebels, Marcos immediately came crashing down.

5. *People Power*. The new phenomenon called "people power" inspired the publication of books and the production of video tapes to record these events for posterity. The most prominent of these are "People Power: The Philippine Experience," a videotape by Communication Foundation for Asia; and *People Power: Eyewitness to History*, a pictorial history by Fr. James Reuter.

6. *Interpersonal communication*, while more difficult to document, obviously also played a most important role in the crisis. By word of mouth or by telephone, people in the Metro Manila area and throughout the country spead the word and extended the reach of the mass media.

In their own little groups or big institutions, people discussed, analyzed and reacted to what they saw and heard from the mass media, and planned their courses of action in response to what they saw and heard.

Even ham radio operators were in action. They were organized and covered the snap elections, monitored the counting of results and were there in the midst of the communication network when the crisis reached its final stages.

In UP Los Baños, Laguna, to use one example, people gathered spontaneously in the university quadrangle in the morning of the day following the Ramos-Enrile defection, paraded around the campus to show their solidarity with the rebel leaders, met with the top local military official to persuade him to join the revolution or at least stay neutral, and went to Metro Manila in car caravans to join the barricades at Camp Aguinaldo.

7. *Role of Print Media*. Finally, the print media also played a major role in the revolution, but still secondary to radio. It could never compete with radio for immediacy and reach. But it provided more details, more human interest stories about the revolution (and the revolution had a million heroes with their own interesting little stories to tell), more in-depth analysis, and certainly they provided a more permanent record of the times to which people can refer their grandchildren with pride in the years to come.

Many years from now, people will be showing the pages of *Malaya, Inquirer, Manila Times, Mr. and Ms., Veritas* newsmagazine and the other newspapers to their children and grandchildren, and perhaps with lumps in their throats and mists in their eyes, they will be saying: "My dear child, I was there at EDSA during that revolution of 1986. That certainly was the Filipino's finest hour. The world stood still during those four fateful days in February to salute us as we carried out our bloodless revolt, and I was never prouder to be a Filipino!"

Notes

[1] Des Retuerma, "Credibility of the Establishment Press and the Alternative Press: A Study in Receiver Judgment," a Master's Thesis, Department of Development Communication, UP Los Baños, Laguna, 1986.

[2] Johnny Villena, "Defense Minister Enrile Tells His Story," in *Sunday Inquirer Magazine,* March 9, 1986.

[3] Teodoro Benigno, "The Call That Saved Many Lives," in *The Manila Times,* March 13, 1986.

[4] Doreen G. Yu, "The Cardinal of the Revolution," in *Sunday Inquirer Magazine,* April 13, 1986.

[5] Doreen G. Yu, "What's Butz Aquino To Do," in *Sunday Inquirer Magazine,* June 1, 1986.

[6] Margie Ongkeko Cabrera, "Postscript to the Revolution: How Great Little Lives Went to War and Won Without Firing a Single Shot," in *Mr. & Ms.,* March 21-27, 1986.

[7] Antonio Sotelo, "Fighting Men in Their Flying Machines," in *Philippine Daily Inquirer,* March 12, 1986.

[8] Diosdado B. Peralta, "The Turning Point," in *Malaya,* May 27.

[9] Sotelo, op. cit., March 13, 1986.

[10] Joseph Albright, Associated Press, "Four Days in February: The Final Chapter," in *Malaya,* March 13, 1986.

[11] Gus Miclat, "One More Time," in *Sunday,* March 23, 1986.

[12] Candy Quimpo, "Channels to Freedom," in *Mr. & Ms.,* March 7-13, 1986.

[13] Jose G. Burgos, Jr., "The Philippine Press After the Revolution," in *Malaya,* May 13, 1986.

[14] Ceres P. Doyo, "How Do You Solve a Problem Like Louis Beltran?" in *Sunday Inquirer Magazine,* May 25, 1986.

[15] Esty Joco, in her column, "Woman in the City of Man," in *Malaya,* February 19, 1986.

Chapter V

A People Power-Media Coalition

Florangel Rosario-Braid

Something happened during the February 1986 revolution that may augur well for a new information order. The people power-media coalition in effect demonstrated the effective contribution of media to the downfall of the 20-year regime of Ferdinand Marcos. Of course, many would say that the third force is the invisible hand of God which directed both the power of the Filipino and the media (particularly radio and television) so that with the right timing and strategy both forces were able to bring the four-day drama to a nonviolent, successful end.

From the time the distress signal was sent from Camp Aguinaldo by Minister Enrile and General Ramos early evening of February 22, the media were prominently on the scene. Representatives of the press, who were contacted, quickly responded and hied to the camp where the two rebels were holed up. Thus, through the foreign press and Radio Veritas, the world had instantaneous access to the drama unfolding on EDSA.

Traditional communication theory looks at communication effects primarily in terms of their cumulative and reinforcement impact and less on what is described as the "hypodermic needle" effect - that is, their ability to have immediate and powerful impact. Only a few isolated cases such as the effect of "The Invasion of Mars" (a radio broadcast that simulated reality so well so that it drove thousands in an Eastern U.S. suburban town to evacuate their homes) and a few others have demonstrated that the mass media can indeed effect revolutionary change within a short span of time. The lack of theories which guide the behavior of media in revolutionary times can further be explained by the orientation of present social change theories. The latter have primarily evolved within fairly stable societies which did not recognize the importance of other means of control of violence such as peace movements, militarization and a coalition of populist forces with existing social institutions. Given the framework, one can understand why the Marcos government was unable to anticipate the scenario which unfolded on February 22.

Historical Precedents

The case of Iran was similar to the Philippines in the sense that the mass media were consciously integrated with the force of people power to topple the corrupt regime of the Shah. Xerox journalism and audio cassettes mobilized a heretofore inert citizenry. A religious revival from below fanned the collective spirit of the Islamic fundamentalists. In the same manner, xerox journalism which became more widespread after the Aquino assassination, audio and video cassettes, a vigorous alternative press and an upsurge in voluntarism (over 80 cause-oriented groups were born in late 1983) provided the alternative information in a society with a tightly controlled press and thus revitalized the democratic spirit which had been subjugated by years of repression. The effective use of communication symbols such as yellow confetti, the rally and the lobby, and the emergence of the Church as an active social force (through Basic Christian Communities, mass media and the pastoral letters) all contributed to the awakening of the citizenry. The analogy between Iran and the Philippines stops here. As we have witnessed during the four-day revolution, the media were very much in the forefront -- informing, inspiring, mobilizing and directing from start to finish. In Iran and El Salvador, the media were used by the instituted power groups -- the Khomeini rebels or the military as in the case of El Salvador. This was only possible after a complete takeover and after the collapse of previous regimes. In the Philippines, the first institution taken over by the rebels was Channel 4, a media organization. One can state with certainty that without radio and television at the height of the revolution, the Reformists and the people would not have stood a chance. In El Salvador, the military ordered a power blackout and subsequently a media blackout like it was in the beginning of martial law in the Philippines. It was then easy for the military in El Salvador to install its own candidates and to push out Duarte and his men after the latter had attempted a coup. Likewise, when Marcos declared Martial Law, he had full control because of the mass media. He was able to plan his strategy and consolidate power because the people were kept in the dark.

The Medium is the Message

An important lesson from these historical events is the critical importance of electronic communication during a national crisis. June Keithley became an instant heroine when she used radio to mobilize, to inform and to link people to centers of vigil. She and the other Radio

Veritas heroes allayed rising anxieties by providing reports on the state of the siege. When Radio Veritas was shut down, Keithley, armed with courage and determination moved to a clandestine location. She carried on with her marathon broadcasting from the DZRJ facilities in Sta. Mesa, only a stone's throw away from the Office of Media Affairs office and close to Malacañang.

The mass media showed the unique capability to dramatize, to focus, to reinforce and more importantly, to serve people in a process called bottom-up communication.

The early desperate cry over the radio from Minister Enrile during his interview with newsmen could not have had a more telling impact had it been sent through another medium. But radio has greater force as the listener has the added impact of embellishing the message in his imagination. The immediate response to the "SOS" and pleas for more vigilantes, barricades and food during the next few days was a tribute to the emergence of voluntarism and people force which was catalyzed by the broadcast media. Neighborhood associations, professional and alumni organizations and cause-oriented groups rallied around crisis points in response to media information and direction.

When Marcos "staged" a confession, accusing the two rebels of a plot to assassinate him and his family, it was Enrile's word that had a more sincere ring. In Malacañang, the camera focused on self-serving posturings in an attempt to obtain sympathy. The picture of the trembling aide reminded viewers of a similar staged kidnapping of the President's son-in-law several years ago. Likewise, the deposed president later cut a forlorn and dejected figure as he faced newsmen. One could hardly recognize the once invincible and arrogant Marcos who "did not intend to die." Instead, the camera, which panned around his family, showed a pathetic leader (no doubt a doting grandfather) who perhaps knew that this was the end although he did not wish to acknowledge it.

Perhaps one of the most memorable images on television was a scene that was aborted at its climax. Just as the former president was about to be sworn in, the Reformists cut off the power thus preventing the nation from witnessing another presidential oath-taking. Some wondered whether the Chief Justice had decided to abide by the people's wishes or whether Marcos himself had decided to call it off, or whether the Reformists had taken over the palace. But this and the take-over of Channel 4 indeed contributed to the continuing defection of high government and military officials and the rallying of people around the Aquino government.

Many viewers visibly wept with joy during the most informal presidential oath-taking in history. Television captured the essence of what this nation of 54 million people had long awaited -- the return of simplicity, honesty and integrity that the lady in yellow personified as she pledged in a crowded function room to serve the Filipino people.

Quick and Timely Action

A sense of timing and quick thinking vis-a-vis the use of the media by the Reformists helped win the revolution. One can perhaps attribute this to the media orientation of the military officials who immediately saw the need for a take-over of Channel 4. The success signalled more "victories" as other radio stations started to link up with the new government station so that the entire nation became participants of the "EDSA miracle." For a government which had successfully institutionalized dictatorship through media control, it is almost unbelievable to see that even its most sophisticated communication machinery was unable to save the Marcos regime. Its "hard sell' pitch and outright blatant distortion through the two arrogant anchorpersons during the pre- and post-election days helped in developing a greater awareness and a groundswell of antipathy towards television that made many turn to Radio Veritas. Thus, the latter became even more significant in effecting mobilization. The Marcos government had more than 36 hours to further secure Channel 4 after the rebels struck. It would have been the appropriate signal for a media blackout. But they hesitated. Perhaps historians would someday debate on whether the failure to act decisively was due to the lack of a central command on the part of government media or because God had a hand in the events that followed in that He provided the right mix -- people power, credibility and good judgment by the media in using the right messages at the right time.

Not Only the Medium but also the Message

Much has been said of the non-violent aspect of the revolution. If people acted the way they did -- meeting tanks and soldiers with flowers, food, and warm embraces -- it was because they had internalized the messages that were articulated often and again by Cardinal Sin, the bishops, the pastoral letters, Radio Veritas, and Cory Aquino -- non-violence even in civil disobedience. This consciousness was shared by a vast cross-section of the citizenry -- Catholics, Muslims, Protestants and all classes of society.

People's Media

A new information order described as "bottom-up"communication and characterized by high involvement of people in the communication process could presage the coming of a real participatory democracy. As an alternative development model, this power to inform loses its former character as a right only of the elite groups. It becomes a right of a wide spectrum of people to actually participate in the communication process and the right to be informed truthfully of events. To do this, media should be weaned away from the oligopoly which has controlled them for the past four decades. Any structural transformation of the media can only take place in a receptive social setting. The emergence of people power and the readiness and willingness of people to be involved in national life is the needed dynamic that could encourage the growth of this participatory model in communication.

Final Note

What is important to note is that media becomes an active force only when it joins in partnership with other social forces. In the final analysis, it was the people acting in solidarity who made decisions on how to cope with the problem -- mobilizing others to join human barricades, organizing food brigades, and inspiring one another. Media sustained the fervor and revolutionary spirit as they were omnipresent -- in homes where viewers acted in response to calls for assistance, in EDSA, Channel 4 and Santolan barricades where radio sets and occasional TV monitors kept people updated on the state of the siege. The steady flow of information therefore, prevented outbreaks of violence which normally happen when people do not know what is happening.

The initial television programming that greeted the people during the revolution and immediately after liberation was visibly reflective of a new type of people-orientation. There was casualness and spontaneity in the entire production process -- makeshift props, crude production techniques, media hosts sans makeup, an unstructured programming where people just walked in to share views and reflections and where anchorpersons served as facilitators and conduits of messages and opinions from the public. These processes should be built into the spirit of future TV programming. Those who have given up on the erstwhile idiot box may now want to partake of some of the refreshing changes -- intelligent panel discussions, a people's hour where groups may share concerns and views on what the government should be like. We also welcome the advent in a few days of a new daily -- *Ang Pilipino Ngayon*, which hopes to support and reinforce people power and the search for truth, justice and the common good.

The information and communication sector has a vital role to play in societal transformation. This is possible only if people accept that moral and value transformation must occur simultaneously along with the restructuring of the social, economic, political and cultural institutions.

Chapter VI

Mass Media and Values

Fr. Cornelio Lagerwey, M.S.C.

In formal education, the teacher is the central influence on the students in the classroom. In informal education the mass media - print, radio, and especially television — are the teachers of the biggest classroom ever, the world outside the school, including the home.

Values in the classroom are taught. Values presented in the media are caught.

In the classroom, teachers spend some of their daytime hours inculcating in children all the proper values, like frugality and honesty. At night, when the children sit in front of a TV set, programs and commercials convince them that their lives become miserable if they do not own a color TV set. Television makes people desire owning a watch, a toy, and other material things.

Mass media can negate the teachers' lessons to students about peace and justice, productivity and nation building, about clean and moral relationships between men and women. False or incomplete information in newspapers and magazines can lead to wrong impressions, if not wrong values. The violence and cruelty in the movies, the abuse of women in TV stories, make them more objects of sex than persons with dignity. These are only a few examples to illustrate the influence of the mass media on the public, especially the young people.

The mass media being the way they are should be not just a *problem* but a challenge for the schools and classroom teachers. This challenge enjoins schools and teachers to be creative and to find ways and means to counteract the harmful influences of media, and to recast their objections into a positive course of action.

How can this be done? There is the existing method related to television called TAT, which means *Television Awareness Training*. In a broader sense it is also called *Mass Media Education*. By mass media we include radio, television, newspapers, magazines, books, records, compact discs, audio tapes, video tapes and advertising. Mass media education can be made a part of the curriculum.

Such education means simply to teach children and adolescents how to use the mass media to enrich their whole personalities. It raises such questions as whether or not the media available to children are educationally good or bad. The field encompassed by mass media education is wide and comprehensive. It is linked to social education and artistic expression. It aims to provide the students with an adequate and varied knowledge of the theory of the mass media and instruct them in the use of these media for enriching their personal development. General curriculum models are available for this purpose.

During the past few decades the mass media have considerably changed the environment in which children and adolescents view life. Almost all families have a radio set and many have a TV set, and some have newspapers and magazines. Children become familiar with them from infancy. Through the media they receive information, acquire vicarious experiences, and develop attitudes and values that otherwise would not be within their reach. In this way, the media are performing the function of educators and teachers.

The influence of media on the youth is no longer a matter of conjecture. It has the potential for good as well as for bad. There is a need, therefore, to train teachers to understand deeply the role of media in the children's environment. Meeting this need could be a giant step towards forming the character and personality of students. Thus media can be turned into a positive instrument for developing values.

Another point which has a bearing on values and education is the franchise/license system in mass media. In the same way that the people united after the EDSA revolution they should unite and dare challenge the mass media to be more responsive to the yearning of the nation. Thus, a high government official saying that "A free press even if irresponsible is better than the deafening silence we have had before" is surprising. All may agree that the suppression of press freedom under the dictatorship was an evil thing. But the trauma of those years should not bring us to the other extreme—that press freedom is all right even if it is irresponsible. It would be like a license to kill the souls, minds and hearts of the most vulnerable, the young.

Here is where the role of good government comes in. The government should realize that the mass media industry is not the same as the garment industry or a shoe factory. Through the mass media, especially the broadcast media, the government permits media people to reach out to the hearts and minds of the people. This can never be equated with making shoes or garments. In media, the word profit should not enter. "Media" means service.

They are different. They should, therefore, have different roles. The government should not allow a broadcast license to be isssued to persons who do not care about their responsibility to the public so long as they get profit and political power.

Running a media enterprise is a public trust. A license has to be used for public service only.

Mass media, therefore, is a public trust for public service. This has been the orientation of the Communication Foundation for Asia (CFA) since the late 1960's. Through print, CFA supported agricultural development goals, population planning projects, social justice. It developed weekly and monthly publications like *Ang Tao* and *Action Now* before martial law. In recent years, it published the monthly *Gospel Komiks* and *Pambata Magazine* to aid the schools in character and moral formation. And soon a new magazine for teenagers will be tested. The name: *Barkada*.

All of these projects are intended to utilize positive mass media in accordance with the new morality. Development of the people, therefore, is CFA's basic commitment, whether through formal or nonformal education, wholesome entertainment, or people-oriented programs. This is the foundation of true, meaningful development communication. It recognizes the value of freedom and responsibility. True freedom always goes with a corresponding responsibility, purpose and direction.

Finally, a few observations:

True to the saying, "People get a government that they deserve," people get the kind of public institutions that they want and deserve. And people will get the kind of mass media and the kind of programs that they deserve.

The questions then are: Do people deserve a "freedom-for-all mass media, promoting values of rugged individualism, materialism and greed which inevitably lead to widespread graft and corruption in even the lowest level of public office? Do they deserve a powerful, influential media that systematically negates moral values which teachers diligently inculcate in the classroom? Or would teachers rather have a responsible mass media -- promoting, and actually leading by example, such values as social responsibility, public service as public trust, social justice, productivity, industry, and morality?

This leads to the next point. An enlightened mass media producing quality material would indeed enhance, reinforce, and hasten value education throughout the country. Thus, the teachers and media no longer need to be at cross-purposes, but true and real partners in value education.

The teachers have a special, critical role developing values in the students with regard to radio and television programs and printed materials. The schools and teachers can integrate mass media education in the curriculum and so influence the students on what newspapei, magazines and books to read. They can guide their choice of radio and TV programs to listen and watch.

In this area both the teachers and development communicators must forge a tight partnership. There are ways mass media practitioners can cater to the needs of value development. The mass media must explore different ways of supporting and complementing teachers' efforts.

Conversely, the teachers' wholehearted support is definitely required in development-oriented mass media projects.

Teachers may have to exert more effort in guiding students and pupils, by way of assignments or suggestions, towards wholesome and value-laden reading materials and broadcast programs. This would mean greater media consciousness for the teachers. Those in development communication are aware of this, and will help in any way to lighten this burden, e.g. by regular workshops and review sessions in the future.

Teachers must be aware that value education does not begin and end in the classroom, not even in the school. Value education, for better or for worse, is carried out in a more powerful way by mass media.

Chapter VII

Development Communication Today

Nora C. Quebral

Four months after the improbable, moving, wondrous happening at EDSA, media people still cannot quite believe that the press is free again. Exercising rusty vocal cords, they speak out once more with impunity. The good old freewheeling days of the 60s are back.

Free enterprise is the rule of the day in the print media. As of last count, 22 dailies* now compete for readership. Characteristically, all of them are bunched in Metro Manila. Waiting impatiently in the wings for another go at the newspaper and broadcast industries are the old media family oligarchs.

Political news again dominates the front pages of the more reputable papers, to the novel diminution of crime stories which, however, remain the *piêce de rêsistance* of the tabloids. Radio commentators once more blur the line between opinion and fact.

The then minister of information had vowed to defend press freedom at all costs. He may not agree with what the journalists say - and he is the first to feel their ire - but, like Jefferson before him, he will uphold their right to say it. An admirer of American liberalism, he is for public relations and a BBC-style Philippine broadcasting, but vetoes development journalism and "managed" culture.

Other government departments are rushing plans said to favor the countryside and its mainstay, agriculture, in order to lick mass poverty. This is not a new story. The feeling of *déjà vu* that not a few have remarked upon about government plans is noted here, too. But, as others have also said, the difference is in the doing. The enormous faith in President Corazon C. Aquino makes the statement easy to believe.

*As of March 1987

So where does all this leave development communication, assuming that there are some who care to know? Is it a creation of the Marcos era, as many think, and best consigned to the trashbin of history? Since the February revolution, the nation has been going through a massive catharsis, trying to rid itself of 14-year-old hangups as it rolls up its sleeves to deal with today and tomorrow. The urge to clean house and to take stock has infected everyone. In this spirit of beginning anew, an end-of-the-era appraisal of development communication makes sense before it is declared a loss or an asset.

BRIEF HISTORY

Most people reckon the start of development communication as a concept from a symposium on breakthroughs in agricultural development held in Los Baños in December 1971, nine months before martial law overran the country. Some are wont to point out that even before then, agencies like the National Media Production Center or the University of the Philippines College of Agriculture itself were already practising it, albeit not under that name. Be that as it may, development communication as a discipline of another stripe, distinct from public information, public relations, advertising, marketing and the other professional categories into which communication is usually subdivided, is taken to date back to that 1971 symposium.

Two features are said to mark it off from the other types of communication: its purpose to promote social equality and the unfolding of human potential and, by reason of the first, its bias for the poor who make up the most in any developing country. While basically growing out of current thought in development and in communication, the discipline drew as well from other bodies of ideas in the 60s:

- Agricultural communication as a subspecies of agricultural extension with its educational approach to improving the lives of farm families.
- Development journalism pioneered in the 60s by the Press Foundation of Asia and the Philippine Press Institute as another mode of defining and reporting news.
- Development support communication seen as a critical component of field projects of United Nations agencies.

In the next years after 1971, the concept was adopted by the information staff of some government and nongovernment development agencies. Three of them were the then Ministry of Agriculture, the Ministry of Public Information and the *Kapisanan ng Mga Brodkaster sa Pilipinas*. There were others that picked it up directly or indirectly. But these three agencies were among the first and they acknowledged Los Baños as the source. Notable as a parallel effort was the devcom program of the Social Communication Center, later to become the Communication Foundation for Asia.

Some degree of success in the country and outside proved to be a mixed blessing for the concept. Any innovation is bound to undergo change when applied in other environments. In the case of development communication, its adoption by government agencies bracketed it with government, there being more government agencies in development work - or what passes for it - in any developing country. Unfortunately, association with government gave devcom a propagandistic image - for three main reasons:

• It was unwittingly or deliberately misinterpreted to mean only the simplistic notion of "government telling people what it is doing for them."

• Government information officers made the label a convenient front to publicize their bosses and the latter's pet projects.

• It was used to legitimize certain communication projects meant to tighten government hold on the countryside.

Journalists schooled in the classical liberal tradition, sensitive to imagined threats to their independence and turned off by the terminology of the behavioral sciences, all too willingly accepted the image and took potshots at the offender. In recent years, it has gotten more flak, this time from the ostensible guardians of free flow of information, when it became involved - again, by association - in the international imbroglio over UNESCO's championing of the new world information and communication order.

Development communication has not been without gains in the Philippines, however, since it was conceived 15 years ago. Something of its unorthodoxy has diffused unnoticed so that a practising newspaperman's statement, for instance, that "...the rural press in particular must... be a communicator for change..."[1] hardly raises any comment. Perhaps its greatest influence has been on the schools. More universities are now offering whole curricula in development communication than in 1973. Only one school offered devcom then. In 1985, seven schools were offering devcom courses.

DEVELOPMENT COMMUNICATION TODAY

But what of outside the schools? What is the status of the development communication profession? What has been its impact on the rural areas? What is the present condition of the rural areas?

The Profession

The status of the profession is easiest answered. Judging from the appearance of professional organizations in agricultural or development communication, the calling has attracted a small following. Two such organizations are the Philippine Agricultural Journalists and the Communicators for Agricultural and Rural Development, both of which were organized after 1971.

Rural Communication

Poverty is the primal cause of underdevelopment. Any developing country must first and foremost wage war on poverty where it is rooted - in the rural areas. The poor are also found in cities, but they were once village poor. Poverty in the cities only reflects the poverty in the villages. The squatters, prostitutes, beggars and strays in Metro Manila are the effluent of the countryside. For this reason, development communication will be taken to be almost synonymous with rural communication. To check on the status of development communication, therefore, we have to look at what has been happening with rural organizations, with the rural press, with rural radio, and with extension workers.

Extension Workers

Extension workers and other knowledgeable persons are the chief source of information on livelihood, health, family planning, and other developmental topics in the villages. Radio comes second. Newspapers, magazines and television are hardly ever used for this purpose. But while extension workers head the list, they are not that available either. In 1971-72, only about one-fourth of the rice farmers were visited by extension workers. Of these, 40 percent were visited only once.[2] In 1981, about 50 percent of the farmers queried in a national survey did not contact, or were not contacted, by extension workers.[3]

Several factors may likely explain why contact was less. One of them is that there are not enough extension workers. The average ratio of extension workers to farmers in 1976 was 1:290 for the rice program, 1:204 for the corn program, and 1:500 for the vegetable program.[4] Even these ratios do not give the true picture because the workers are not equally dispersed across regions. In 1977, for example, Regions 11 and 12 in the south were said to have proportionately fewer extension workers than those in Regions 1 and 2 in the north.[5]

Two other factors work against more frequent visits by extension worker: The roads are bad in isolated communities and rural transport is poor.

Rural Radio

In reach, radio outstrips the extension worker. Because radio sets are relatively cheap, radio has been touted as the rural medium, and it has so performed in many ways. Of the 257 stations in 1980, 211, or about 80 percent, were in the provinces.[6] Today there are 308 radio stations, 261 of which are commercially run.[7] A little less than 50 percent, however, are massed in Luzon; 25 percent are in the Visayas; and 27 percent in Mindanao.[8]

In the provinces, radio ownership is about 60 percent.[9] But listening is found to be higher there because non-owners also listen to radio. Still, 40 percent do not own sets. It is a disturbing fact, since it applies to the poorest people, who are the focus of development. Also, the quality of the sets declines as the farm family's income goes down.[10] Cheap, or old sets, do not receive as clearly. They may be good enough for music listening but not for talk programs that need full attention.

Radio's wide coverage also often masks the barriers to transmission of signals, like mountains, weak transmitters, geographical location, and others. It is dismaying to note how they often crop up as problems when evaluating educational and pilot broadcasts beamed to the rural areas.

On the credit side, radio deserves mention for being ahead in consciously trying to promote rural development. After martial law was imposed, the broadcasters were among the first to respond to the call to assist in rural development, at the beginning by fiat through regulatory bodies, and later as a relatively independent group through the Kapisanan ng mga Brodkaster sa Pilipinas. KBP accepted early the development communication concept and applied it through its member stations. The KBP development communication committee report for 1985 mentions campaigns to promote nationalism and nutrition, and to combat drug abuse.[11] KBP member stations donate airtime for development communication programs as part of their public service.

Recognizing radio's built-in advantages, development agencies and educational institutions have used radio in projects on food production, family planning, forest conservation, values formation and other subjects salient to rural families. Perhaps radio's most solid success to date is the Masagana 99 program, for which it has been cited internationally.

The Rural Press

The term "rural," used in communication, is not as clear-cut as it sounds.

Radio stations in cities and towns in the provinces are labeled rural in spite of their urban location. The label is justifiable because radio reaches the villages.

The "rural" press is another story. Newspapers outside Metro Manila are produced in provincial cities and towns and circulate there as well. Journalism scholars, therefore, call them the provincial or the community press, not the rural press. This is not unusual in a country where a prevailing definition of "rural," as "any place that is not urban," betrays a deep urban bias.

The fact that community newspapers are published either in English or a combination of English and a local language or dialect, says much about their AB readership. True, the rural elite who read them have their part to play in development. But what is needed is a truly rural press that is read in the villages.

Experiments were made in the 70s to promote a rural press. Program Genesis was started in 1974 by the Ministry of Public Information to bring developmental information to the rural masses. A network of cooperative newspapers was first set up in 11 regions. An interpersonal and radio phase was later added to it.[12] What happened to one of the newspapers, *Iwag*, in Bacolod City, makes an interesting commentary on the viability of a rural press at this time.

Iwag started out on a high note by only publishing news on food production, land reform, family planning, and other subjects deemed important to rural families. Subscriptions to the paper for the village people were borne by the municipal governments, barangays, schools, civic clubs, businesses and other groups. The local police distributed the copies and collected the subscription pledges. The village folks liked and read the paper, although they could not afford its price of P0.50 a copy.

In the first year, the 10,000 copies run off weekly reached the farthest barangay in the region. The subscriptions came in regularly. By the second year, the policemen and community leaders were finding their end of the venture harder and harder to sustain. The city-based advertisers, on the other hand, were increasingly showing their displeasure with the editorial policy. By the third year, *Iwag* had become just like any other provincial paper in content and business procedures. The staff sincerely regretted the change, having seen the response to barrio-relevant information, but felt they had no other choice if the paper was to stay alive.

The Catholic clergy has run other newspaper experiments using small town resources.[13] The *Moalboal Times*, a "newspaper" written on 26 blackboards located in the poblacion and barangays of Moalboal in Cebu, was a brainchild of Fr. Francisco Silva. The "daily" was well read by the people it intended to reach.

Encouraged by Father Silva's experience, the National Office of Mass Media set up 26 more blackboard newspapers edited and managed by parish priests in the Visayas and Mindanao. The Rural Mimeo Papers is another project of the Jesuit-run National Office of Mass Media. It started with 26 mimeographed news sheets produced by parish priests in small towns, mainly in the Visayas and Mindanao.

Rural Organizations

Given the dismal media picture outside Manila and other cities, the government move in the early 70's to create rural organization as conduits of both services and information to the barangays appeared to make sense. The decade saw the start of a number of them - the barangay councils, *samahang nayons*, irrigators' associations, compact farms, social laboratory farmers' associations, to name a few.[14] Not all were government-sponsored. Some were organized by non-government agencies. Either way, the life of the associations rested on the continued support of the sponsoring agency.

Notwithstanding their potential as media of information and interaction among farm residents, rural organizations have so far not lived up to their promise. In 1981, most of them were still immature. They were unable to fend for themselves and were dependent on their mother agencies.[15] They still were preoccupied with laying down norms and operating procedures. Their slow growth - even regression - is attributed to agency rivalries, community factionalism, a paternalistic type of leadership, among others. In other words, rural organizations at this time do not make much more effective development communication channels in the countryside than the more impersonal media.

The Rural Poor

Development communication is not communication channels alone but is equally the purpose for which they are used. A profile of development communication would have to include the answer to at least one more question: What has been happening to development?

Not much, it seems, during the Marcos era. If anything, poverty has worsened. The backlog of wants which sprang from centuries of social injustice, was increased further by the Marcos brand of economic pillage. In the last 15 years, the Filipinos' average annual income ostensibly grew 10 times but it actually dropped by 7 percent.[16] This means that if the Filipinos' average income in 1971 was P3,736, it is now P30,748. But it is actually only worth P3,471 in real terms. Unemployment and underemployment are the highest ever with 15 to 20 out of 100 Filipinos without jobs and 35 with only part-time jobs.[17]

Small wonder that 70 percent of Filipinos are now said to be living below the poverty line, which is measured at P2,800 a month for each family.[18] Since 70 percent of all Filipinos live in the rural areas, it is not hard to figure out where the poverty predominates. The rural folks' average annual income of P21,409 is less than half of the city dwellers' annual income of P46,209.[19]

This poverty translates into moderate to severe malnutrition, bad housing, unsafe drinking water, and minimal health care and sanitation for most of those 70 percent who fall below the cut-off level. The children are among the hardest hit. Seventy percent - obviously an unlucky figure in the Philippines - are malnourished.[20] For every 10 babies born, three die and three become malnourished before they get to the age of five.[21] For every 1,000 births, 41 to 44 do not even complete their first year of life. (By international standards, an infant mortality rate of above 10 is considered high.) Western and central Mindanao, where 112 babies die out of 1,000 births, have the highest infant mortality rate.[22] It would seem that to be a poor child in the rural fastness of Mindanao is to be deprived, indeed. Perhaps only the children of Negros, at this time, can claim a worse plight.

The poor children, who survive their fifth year, are usually put to work early.[23] Because they are young, they work under harsh conditions, they are prone to illness and death and, for those earning a living in the cities, to social traumas as well.

PROBLEMS AND ISSUES

All in all, the problem of development is a mammoth one against which to pit the country's emasculated resources, including those of communication. Nevertheless, the Aquino government, from all accounts, is determined to utilize them to correct the ills of agriculture, to resuscitate a blighted countryside. So far, in the general rejoicing over a newly freed press, the government, either through the Philippine Information Agency, or the Office of the Press·Secretary has not said a word about how it might use communication resources to help bring about development.

Perhaps it is just as well. Perhaps that function should now be officially returned to the agencies that are directly responsible for agriculture, nutrition, social development, natural resources, education and culture, health, and all the other aspects that bear on improved rural and urban life. The Department of Local Government and Community Development should be somewhere at the top of the list because it must see that rural people learn to know the true meaning of self-governance. Someone in government must think about creating and nurturing avenues for dialogue among ordinary people, for non-formal education, for transmitting information to bypassed areas, and for other types of communication that are not attractive to private enterprise.

For while poverty is the immediate problem, it affects and is affected by social, political and also cultural and ethical considerations. Planning and doing which are required to propel meaningful development is not the province of only one department, but of other departments as well. They are increasingly the job of non-government organizations. They are equally the job of the people themselves.

The next question is: How prepared is everyone to do what has to be done? To answer this, the attitudes and competence of policy makers, communicators and users of information have to be examined along with the forces that have shaped them. Either through their presence or absence they have collectively been a block to development communication. Some of the more stubborn constraints are:

1. The lower value placed on what is rural or agricultural, whether it be communicators, media programs or people. This attitude reflects the low purchasing power of the rural sector for both economic and social goods. Rural folks themselves share this attitude. They aspire for their children to be out of agriculture and the barrio.

2. The knowledge system is heavily skewed to research; at the expense of extension and communication, or teaching, in general. Researchers get

more prestige and money than teachers, in either the classroom, or the farmer's field. Equipment and facilities for research are funded far ahead of those for teaching.

3. Fragmented and conflicting policies on how communication technology will be used for rural nonformal education. There have been enough successful pilot projects on use of community technology done here and abroad, to justify its use for countryside development. But findings were either unread or ignored.

4. The commercial beginnings of broadcast media in the Philippines which have identified them with non-educational content. This in turn has conditioned most media consumers to turn to radio and television mainly for entertainment.

5. The commercial sponsorship of most of our print and broadcast media which has made profit the ultimate standard. Parallel to this is the use solely of economic criteria in judging the success of communication projects for rural development.

6. The perception by administrators and communicators that communication stops at publicity and public relations. Many administrators want nothing more. They may even disapprove of subordinates who exceed that expectation - and communicators oblige for the most part.

7. The development communicators' view of their role as simply producers of communication materials. They are not expected to interact on site with farm people, or be involved in thinking on why, how, and when the materials are used, much less in program planning.

8. Insufficient education for communication and extension workers not only on communication skills, but also on the worth of their calling, on the new roles opened to them by changes in the country and in the world, and on the values that give the development of people prime importance.

9. The knee-jerk reaction of journalists when words like "policies" or "planning" are placed in conjunction with information because they think that press freedom is on the line. The truth is that in these last decades of the 20th century, information has become much more than news and the media are no longer the exclusive preserve of the press. Also, information is seen as a resource easily accessible to the rich and educated but denied to the poor. Hence policies that will correct the imbalance are needed.

PROSPECTS

None of the problems ticked off can be solved soon enough. Yet in the words of one department secretary, it must be rural development now or never. What are the prospects that development communication will be able to contribute in spite of its constraints? Obviously there must be political will that can be thrown into the breach with whatever extension and communication knowledge, facilities and people that are now at hand. With or without that will, non-government organizations can move ahead on their own, as many have done in the past with encouraging results. Their special virtue is that their people work right in the villages.

The problems mentioned imply these four steps that merit doing by development agencies, whether government or non-government:

1. Make policies that truly favor the poor in rural areas.
2. Place a good deal more communication facilities and resources in the countryside where most Filipinos live.
3. Train field workers and professional communicators in social responsibility, in communication skills, and in information appropriate for villagers.
4. Conscienticize not only rural people, but also communicators and policy makers.

To move rural development, four kinds of information are critical at this moment:

- Information to increase food and income, improve health, and upgrade education.
- Information to fight illiteracy which, belying official figures, is said to be at least 80 percent in the rural areas.[24]
- Information to diminish rural isolation, promote interaction among villagers, and to link them with decision centers.
- Information to help rural people form and maintain their own organizations and to help them achieve economic and political power.

A whole range of means, from word of mouth to satellites and computers, can be used for the information exchange needed. Except for the first, few of them are plentiful in the rural areas at present. Practicality dictates that we start with what there is. The challenge to communicators is, first, to be creative and, second, to bone up on knowledge and experience that already exists.

Given our new climate of hope, the common will to rise above the present has never been stronger. Rural development can be evolutionary or revolutionary. It can be done slowly by working through long-standing institutions. Or it can made quicker by breaking new ground, by trying alternatives, by replacing faulty structures with better ones. This is as truly said about communication as of other components of rural development.

In sum, development communication has been around for 15 years. Although laboring under many constraints, it has won some real gains. The opportunity for it to help rural development become a reality today has never been as marked or as badly needed. How much it can help depends on policy makers, communicators, and the rural people themselves. What would be ironic is if development communication, originally conceived to benefit the country's poor majority, is nullified by a wholesale reversion to the national communication system of the 60s, in effect making development communication a casualty of the People's Revolution.

Notes

[1] Pat H. Gonzales, as cited by R.A. Gabuya, "The Provincial Press During Martial Law," Journalism 205 report on developmental reporting in the provincial press, Institute of Mass Communication.

[2] Gelia T. Castillo, *Beyond Manila*, Ottawa: IDRC, 1977.

[3] Philippine Training Centers, "Primary Resource Employment Strategy to Intensify Development Effort," January 1983.

[4] Philippine Training Centers for Rural Development proposal, 1976.
4Philippine Training Centers for Rural Development proposal, 1976.

[5] PTC, loc. cit.

[6] Cesar M. Mercado, et. al., "Studies on Radio for Education and Extension," April 1980 (mimeographed).

[7] KBP Broadcast Media Yearbook, 1985.

[8] Bernardo M. Villegas, et. al., *The Philippines at the Crossroads: Some Visions for the Nation*, Manila: Center for Research and Communication, 1985.

[9] Ibid.

[10] Nora C. Quebral, *The CTRE Study: Piloting a Distance Learning System for Small Farmers*, Laguna: UP at Los Baños, 1982.

[11] KBP, loc. cit.

[12] Raul R. Ingles and Rebecca F. Maceda, *The Provincial Press in the Philippines*, Singapore: AMIC, 1981.

[13] Crispin C. Maslog, "Philippine Print Media: A Profile," (Mimeographed, n.d.).

[14] F.L. Dumagat, "Some reflections on the factors of effectiveness and viability of rural organizations," *Journal of Agricultural Economics and Development*, January, 1981.

[15] Ibid.

[16] *Philippine Daily Inquirer*, "Incomes grow 10-fold but drops 7% in value," June 5, 1986.

[17] *Manila Daily Bulletin*, "Aquino government needs massive aid, lots of luck," May 6, 1986.

[18] Ibid.

[19] *Philippine Daily Inquirer*, loc. cit.

[20] Elizabeth Lolarga, "Children are innocent victims," *Manila Bulletin*, May 14, 1986.

[21]*Philippine Daily Inquirer,* "High infant mortality, malnutrition among Marcos' legacy," April 6, 1986.

[22]Lolarga, loc. cit.

[23]Ibid.

[24]Evelyn Opilas, "Fighting poverty and mendicancy," *Philippine Daily Inquirer,* May 5, 1986.

Chapter VIII

Development Journalism: An Update

Juan F. Jamias

Developing countries are typically characterized by massive poverty, low productivity, scarcity of jobs and social inequality. Compounding these problems are their exploding populations, unfavorable balance of payments, and spiralling prices. In these countries, the people's priorities are how to gain a higher living standard and to improve the quality of life in general.

The first development decade of the sixties ended dismally, its aspirations for a better life for the newly-independent nations in Asia and elsewhere unrealized. In 1968, a Manila-based group of Asian journalists, which organized themselves into the Press Foundation of Asia, started an approach to communication for development. The press, the pioneers declared, would help its readers better understand national problems and their solutions. Their approach became known as development journalism.

Development journalism may be defined as the purposeful use of the print and electronic media to bring about desirable change both in groups (e.g. society) and individuals. *Desirable* means bringing about the greatest good for the greatest number in society, and for the individual, fulfilling his or her own potential.

A holistic or systems conceptualization of development journalism defines its role in a country's *social, economic, political and cultural development.* Development may be substituted for the word *change* in the definition stated in the previous paragraph.

Indeed development journalism has turned out to be a rich, multi-dimensional concept like a gem refracting various points of light.

In the first facet, there is a new job cut for today's journalists. As a specialized news reporting, development journalism focuses on a key problem of the Third World — poverty - and on issues concerning the poor. Ten Asian countries account for some 70 percent of the non-socialist Third World poor who since 1960 have been becoming even poorer. The World Bank in 1985 revealed that 2.3 billion persons, nearly half of the world's population, had an average income of $400 or less a year.

"Let us spell (the job) for you," began Alan Chalkley in his pioneering *A Manual of Development Journalism*. "Here in Asia are millions of people who are poor, because their countries are down in the 'vicious circle' of poverty.... This is the development problem — how to punch a hole in that circle somewhere. That is where you (development journalists) come in."

The second facet highlights a new newsbeat - development. Media critics have pointed out that the development story has frequently become a bad fourth after politics, crime and sex. Yet it spotlights the moving daily drama of people trying to make a better life, of society's efforts to enable individuals to achieve their full potential.

Amitabha Chowdhury, an Indian journalist, pointed out that development journalism is the coverage of "news beats that are relevant to social and economic changes."

The third facet of the new journalism is its in-depth reporting that leading development journalists use in depicting development. Chalkley spelled out this type of reporting as "a new way of expressing news and analysis which would reach down further into the readership, be brighter, be rigorously honest and accurate, be pictorial and human." He cited at least three axioms to make development journalism readable, interesting, colorful, informative, and have impact.

• Simplify, translate horrible technical jargon into language which is more like ordinary speech. Use plenty of colorful phrases, swing the copy along to keep the reader's interest up, but do not lose accuracy.

• Humanize the economic and social story. Remember that economics is not the prerogative of bankers and high treasury officials, or the people who draft those awful reports in the United Nations. Economics is trying to earn a living, by everyone, including housewives.

• Illustrate stories more, use pictures and charts. One diagram is worth a thousand words.

Chalkley emphasized that in addition to changing the manner of telling the development story, the subject matter covered had to change, too.

He said, "Spot news events are okay, of course - they inform, and to some people they mean events of great importance. But in a story there is also a process at work. And it is process that is the name of the game in development journalism."

The fourth facet ties the three facets described, namely, the new job for media reporters, the new newsbeat, and the new writing style. It sets the role of the new breed of reporters and broadcasters. As reported in the first Press Foundation of Asia training course for Asian economic writers held in 1968, "They [the participants] decided that they would no longer regard themselves as economic writers but as development journalists who should now consciously serve as a part of the efforts of their nations to develop their resources and not merely as recorders of economic events."

Development Journalism at UPLB

The emergence of development journalism has had a close connection to agricultural communication as this special area developed at the University of the Philippines Los Baños.

The UPLB's Department of Development Communication began as the Office of Extension and Publications in 1954 in the College of Agriculture. It was established to popularize and disseminate the results of research done at the College and other information on improved agriculture.

In line with its objective, the Office of Extension and Publications started a press service. It prepared news and feature articles and sent them to national and provincial newspapers and magazines. A radio farm news service was later added.

In the summer of 1959, the first communication course in the country was offered at Los Baños.

In 1962, the office became a full-fledged academic department. Like the other departments of the College of Agriculture, it had three basic functions - teaching, research and extension. The then Department of Agricultural Information and Communications at UPLB started studies leading to the Bachelor of Science in Agriculture, major in agricultural communications. Agricultural journalism formed one of the fields of specializations in this curriculum. Others were radio broadcasting and audio-visual communication.

Since then agricultural communication has expanded to such specializations as forestry, cooperatives, agrarian reform, nutrition, population programs, including family planning, and the environment.

To keep up with the expansion, the department was renamed Department of Development Communication on March 28, 1974. At about the same time, it started its four-year Bachelor of Science in Development Communication, the present course, with majors in development journalism, community broadcasting and educational communication. This course is the first communication study program with a technical component, in the Philippines. It requires 24 credit units in at least one technical field to be communicated. The student may take agriculture, including crop or livestock science, forestry, nutrition, environmental science, or any of the other science fields offered on the campus.

Communication scholar Wilbur Schramm himself has batted for communicators who have in-depth understanding of some technical subjects to be communicated. In 1974, he wrote in the first issue of *Media Asia*, "Most thoughtful critics of training for journalism and news broadcasting feel that in the years to come it will no longer be sufficient for a new entrant to the profession to be able to write about 'anything'; he must be able to write with depth and understanding about something. That is, he will need a specialty in which he is substantively trained and able to interpret professional findings for lay leaders..."

Development Journalism and the Working Press

In a sense developmental stories are nothing new. They were published long before the term "development journalism" was coined.

In September 1969, the Press Foundation of Asia started the Depthnews, a rough acronym for development economics and population news. Executives of the PFA and the Philippine Press Institute worked out the lively, popular writing style. They slashed the hoary technical terms and jargon and put color on the phrases and sentences in the new material. Depthnews stories were sent via air mail weekly from Manila to hundreds of newspaper editors in Asia. Depthnews stories were at first available in English. Versions in the Korean, Bahasa Indonesia and Indian languages, and in four major Philippine dialects were later added.

Developmental reporting has found its way into communication schools, in mass media, in government agencies, and in private research and development agencies.

This writer suggests that the term "development journalism" be set apart from the broader term "developmental writing." The former refers to specialized reporting in the mass media. The latter includes information disseminated by government departments and agencies, research and development agencies, banks, industrial corporations and other non-governmental organizations (NGOs).

Characteristics of Development Journalism

Development journalism may be characterized by its purposiveness, pragmatism, relevance, mass-orientation, and scientific outlook. These attributes are suggested by some writers.

1. Development journalism is purposive. It means the writer or broadcaster must consciously work towards an objective or objectives.

A development story or series of stories may aim to promote the adoption of a new rice variety, improved health practice, land reform, urban uplift, or family planning. The writer thus asks when writing a story, "What do we want to happen? In what way do we want the reader, or listener, or viewer to change after reading the story?"

Such objectives do not have to be stated for every story. But the development journalist must bear in mind what his story can contribute to development.

In contrast, general news reporting is non-purposive. In a mass communication model, two American communication scholars Bruce H. Westley and Malcolm S. MacLean, Jr., specified different functions for the advocacy and channel roles of the mass media. The former role is purposive, as in public relations. The latter role is non-purposive, as in newspaper reporting.

According to the Westley and MacLean model, the news reporter's task is merely to inform, to record the events or facts as they are, without any ax to grind. Development journalism goes beyond conventional news reporting. The development journalist does not merely report and interpret the facts. He also promotes them (that is, help bring about the change desired).

2. Development journalism is pragmatic. This means that journalism is to be judged by its results. It implies that the writer, editor or broadcaster must also be concerned with results.

While this position is controversial, it has not been wanting of supporters.

George Verghese in 1975 emphasized that the developing world's media must be both observer and participant in the development process. Putting belief to practice, Verghese launched the project Chatera in the *Hindustan Times* where he was editor. The project showed how a newspaper could be a catalyst to rural development through a fortnightly column depicting life in an Indian village. The project ran for nine years, from 1969 to 1977.

3. Development journalism is relevant. As Tarzie Vittachi had observed, "Asian editors are rapidly learning such hard facts of newspaper life. Many Asian newspapers - particularly 'language' papers - began as political pamphlets, dedicated to achieving political freedom, and to them views were much more relevant than news. But too many of them, long after political goal had been achieved, continued to be almost exclusively political."

This would not necessarily be wrong, Vittachi continued, but it is essential to realize that "political reporting is not merely a recording of the activities and soundings of political personalities and the movements of the partisan political balances of power. What is important (and interesting) to the reader is how politicians are using their power, how they affect the pockets and the general well-being of the people. Economics, population trends, the performance of health and welfare services, industrial and agricultural growth or stagnation, crime waves, money, education, military developments - all these ingredients of national life are intimately relevant as they affect the daily life of the people."

The PFA lists the topics that the new breed of journalists would cover. They include government plans and budgets, land reform, taxation, banking and finance, industry, agriculture, population, manpower, community development, public health, social welfare, environment, and science and technology.

On the whole, the development journalist's beat ideally covers these specialized reporting areas, namely, development in general; political development; science and technology; economics and business; labor; food and agriculture; human ecology and the environment; consumerism; health; education and culture.

4. Development journalism is mass oriented. Majority of the 24 daily newspapers published are in English and are elitist. The newspapers are circulated mainly in the cities. Very few newspapers reach the countryside. The same lopsided distribution holds for the Tagalog publications.

Komiks and radio have wider reach than newspapers and magazines. Television, a potent medium, is viewed mostly in the urban areas. Thus development journalism challenges media practitioners to reach the masses. Toward this end, innovations are needed.

5. Development journalism is scientific in outlook. Development journalism is mainly centered on people. Because it deals with development and human behavior, it underscores exposure to the social sciences like economics, rural sociology, demography and research methods.

Moreover, the social scientist's tools, such as sampling and surveys, are also expected to influence the gathering of reliable and accurate facts. Such sophisticated professional demands requires that the development journalist have grounding in the social sciences and in conducting simple research.

Chanchal Sarkar, then director of the Press Institute of India, described in 1969 the training needed for development writers. He said that they should be able to assimilate economics and sociology, psychology and administration, research methods and demography. The syllabus he cited consists of three parts:

● selected concepts in the social sciences;

● their relationships to specific issues with which journalists in Asia are, or ought to be concerned; and

● techniques of development writing and other forms of presentation.

REFERENCES

Ali, S.M. 1980. "Notes on the changing role of the press in Asia's economic development." *Media Asia* 7(3): 153-155.

Chalkley, Alan. 1972. *A manual for development journalism.* Manila: Philippine Press Institute.

_____. "Development journalism: a new dimension in the information process." *Media Asia* 7(4): 215-217.

Chowdhury, Amitabha. 1975. "A new newsbeat has arrived -- development." *Philippines Daily Express,* February 16-17.

Jamias, Juan F. 1987. "A specialized reporting area for humane development." *Philippines Communication Journal 1(2),* March 1987.

_____. 1977. "Beyond conventional reporting – development journalism." *The Journalist* 1(5): 15-21. (First delivered at SEARCA Professorial Chair Lecture, University of the Philippines Los Baños, College, Laguna, 1977.)

Lent, John. 1970. "Philippine media and nation-building: an overview." *Gazette* 15(1): 2.

Press Foundation of Asia. 1974. Syllabus of advanced course in development journalism. Manila: Development Journalism Guidebooks.

Manila Chronicle. 1987. "Poorest nations getting poorer – World Bank." (April 8, 1987).

Sarkal, Chanchal. 1976. "Development and the new journalism." In Sinha, P.R.R. (ed.). *Communication and rural change.* Singapore: Asian Mass Communication Research and Information Center, p. 73.

Schramm, Wilbur. 1974. "An open letter for Media Asia readers." *Media Asia* 1(1): 5-11.

Westley, Bruce H. and Malcolm S. MacLean Jr. 1957. "A conceptual model for communications research." *Journalism Quarterly* 34:31-38.

Verghese, B.G. 1976. "Project Chatera -- an experiment in development journalism." *Media Asia* 3(1): 5-11.

Vittachi, Tarzie. 1976. "Relevance is all." *Press Forum, pp. 6-7.*

Part Three

Print Media Today

This third part of the book tackles the oldest of the mass media—the print media. Chapter IX gives a profile of the daily newspapers and magazines of Metro Manila while Chapter X deals with the community press in the provinces. Then Chapter XI draws a portrait of the book publishing industry and Chapter XII describes komiks as the most widely read and most potent among the print media.

A more detailed introduction to the print media follows in the next few pages.

Print Media Today

Of the various media of mass communication, the print media are the oldest -- in the Philippines, Asia and the world. The origins of the newspaper in Asia dates back to 700 B.C. in China, when the *ti-pao* (government gazettes) were circulated in the Chinese imperial courts. The *ti-pao* antedates the first newspaper in Europe -- Julius Ceasar's *Acta Diurna,* which was posted in the Roman Forum about 600 B.C.

In the Philippines, the first of the print media was the book *Doctrina Christiana,* printed in 1593, followed by the newspaper *Successos Felices* in 1637 and *Del Superior Govierno* in 1811.

The term newspaper refers to publications which come out regularly (at least weekly) in recognized newspaper format, containing information of general interest and circulated to the general public. If the paper comes out less often than once a week, as in the case of fortnightlies and monthlies, they do not fulfill one important element − coming out at least weekly − of the accepted international definition of a newspaper. By international standards, therefore, they are not considered newspapers.

A good number of them come out more often than once a week -- many of them bi-weekly, some tri-weekly, a few four times a week, and a number daily. If the paper comes out from five to seven times a week, it is considered a daily. There are a few papers, especially those in big cities, which come out anywhere from two to ten times daily. These are the metropolitan dailies with multi-editions. *Bulletin Today* in Manila, for example, has two editions daily − a provincial and a city edition.

The modern newspaper, whether weekly or multi-daily, fulfills essential roles in society, whether the society is democratic or authoritarian. Its basic functions may be grouped into two: the information function and the opinion function.

The newspaper has often been referred to as a modern-day university because in its pages, as in the halls of academe, you find information of all sorts -- ranging from the trivial to the profound.

On any given day you will read in the newspapers the story of man in all its tragic and comic aspects -- murders, suicides, arson, thefts, robberies, drought, dope addiction, rebellions, coup attempts, wars, lost babies and newfound husbands. You will also find in the newspaper man's attempts for splendor and the sublime: peace talks, heroism in the midst of disaster, achievements in art, increased rice production, improving the quality of life, protecting the environment, self-sacrifice, love, service to fellowmen, sports heroics, martyrdom.

In the newspaper pages, you will find current events as well as timeless features, spot news as well as interpretative articles.

In the front page alone of one issue of a Manila daily, for example, one can read a variety of stories: Supreme Court drops petition to annul presidential polls; Manila Bank depositors calmed down; Estrada denies accusing Enrile of mishandling funds; fears of cement, milk shortage allayed; proclamation of five congressional winners voided; freed kidnap victim says he's okay; media banned from President Aquino's talk with soldiers; government criticized on slay of rebel priest; labor bloc to file charge before ILO on vigilantes; Miss Chile wins Miss Universe Crown; quake kills 1, hurts 2; land reform flaws noted; Kris Aquino nervous on camera.

The information function of a newspaper has traditionally been carried out on the front page, and the inside news pages of the paper. The stories are written in journalistic style -- objective, factual, inverted pyramid style, where the more important facts are put in the opening paragraphs and the less important in the later paragraphs.

There are two main reasons for this. First, the newspaper reader is a busy man and he wants to get at the information right away. Sometimes he is so busy he has time to read only the first few paragraphs. So if the most important facts are placed at the beginning of the story, he will be able to know the main ideas even if he does not finish the story. The second reason is for convenience in editing. When the editor, who is always racing against the deadline, runs out of newspaper space for the story, he simply deletes the last paragraph or paragraphs as needed, without danger of cutting the most important facts of the story.

The news reporters are not allowed to express their opinions in their stories.

The opinion function of the paper has been traditionally carried out in the editorial-opinion page, usually on page four. The paper is allowed to express its opinions on the issues of the day on this page -- and not on the news pages. The paper expresses its opinion in the editorials. Its columnists express their personal opinions in the columns. Its staff writers may express their opinions in their by-lined articles which can be subjective and analytical. Its readers express their opinions in letters to the editor and opinion articles. The editorial page therefore serves as the forum for the exchange and creation of public opinion on issues of the day.

There is a third, less important function of a newspaper, especially in democratic countries: to provide entertainment through feature articles and comic strips. However, the newspaper is considered less of an entertainment medium than the other media, like film and television, for example. It is mainly an information medium.

Newspapers used to be first with the news, but with the advent of radio and television, they are now only second or third. But although radio and television are now first with the news, newspapers are still read because they are able to give more details, and people can read and re-read them at leisure. They also provide a permanent record of the activities of the society of which they are a part. A good newspaper records history as it unfolds. Future historians will use today's newspapers a lot when they sit down tomorrow to write history.

Philippine print media might be categorized into two: the metropolitan press, printed and circulated mainly in the capital city of Manila, and the community press, based and disseminated largely in the provinces.

Sometimes newspapers in the provinces are referred to as the provincial press, or local press, but the term more commonly accepted and used by Filipino newspapermen is community press.

The term rural press is generally eschewed in the Philippines because strictly speaking there is no rural press here. There is a metropolitan press, composed of 24 dailies, 9 weekly newspapers, 4 magazine supplements and at least two dozen popular weekly magazines (as of 1987), at least two-thirds of whose circulation is in metropolitan Manila. The 24 daily newspapers have a circulation of approximately 2,000,000 for example, and only about 30 percent of this circulation goes to the province. Of the other publications, only the four magazines in the vernacular and komiks are circulated widely in the provinces.

Then there is the community press, 164 local newspapers circulated mainly in the small cities and big towns (as of 1987). Beyond these big towns, usually the provincial capitals, there are no print media in circulation regularly except the four fiction-oriented magazines and comic books in the dialects.

There were some attempts to extend the reach of the print media into the rural areas in the 1970s. One of them was Project Genesis, a cooperative newspaper project of the defunct Ministry of Public Information (MPI). The idea was for MPI to organize regional newspapers in the dialect, one for each of the 12 MPI regions in the country, which was eventually to be owned and managed by the people in each area. The concept was grand, but the project did not get off the ground.

Another attempt is the Rural Mimeo Papers project of the National Office of Mass Media, a Catholic organization run by the Jesuits and based in Manila. The project was started and managed by Catholic priests from their parishes in various small towns of the country.

The experiment is still going on. There are now 83 such rural mimeographed papers, printed in the dialect and circulated in the small towns, mostly in the Visayas and Mindanao. The average circulation of these mimeographed papers is about 1,000, although the biggest circulated 12,000 at one time.

The best known of these rural mimeo papers was *Ang Bandillo*, with a circulation of 12,000, which was managed by controversial Catholic Bishop Francisco Claver in Malaybalay, Bukidnon (northern Mindanao). It was eventually closed down by the Marcos government. Two other widely circulated papers in this group were *El Agong* (2,000 circulation) in Basilan (southern Mindanao) and *Bayan-Liham* (3,000) in Infanta, Quezon Province (southern Luzon).

The Rural Mimeo Papers project got its start with an initial support by Pathfinders, Inc., which gave the mimeographing machines, paper and ink for the first year's operation. Today most of these rural mimeo papers are just breaking even financially. They range in circulation from 100 to 4,000.

A third experiment aimed at reaching the rural Philippines is the blackboard newspapers project also managed by the Office of National Mass Media. This project was inspired by the *Moalboal Times* of Fr. Francisco Silva, a Catholic priest of Moalboal, a small town in Cebu in the Visayas in Central Philippines.

The *Moalboal Times*, started in 1968, was an unusual newspaper -- it was not printed on paper, but written on 25 blackbroads located in strategic places in the poblacion and barrios of Moalboal. The editor was the town priest, Fr. Silva, who used market vendors as reporters and schoolboys as "staff writers" -- the people who transcribed the news, features and editorials on the different boards. This blackboard newspaper was a daily, it was well read, and had high credibility among the people of this town.

Inspired by this experience, the National Office of the Mass Media launched in 1974 26 more blackboard newspapers in various small towns of the Visayas and Mindanao, all managed and edited by Catholic priests.

It is perhaps too early to tell if there are any success stories among these various experiments in rural journalism worth studying in detail. Because of this, when we talk of community journalism in the Philippines we turn to the area between metropolitan Manila and the small town of the Philippines -- the theater of operations of this country's community journalists. We discuss the Philippine community press in more detail in Chapter X.

Chapter IX

Manila's Metropolitan Press

Domini T. Suarez

The heady days of the bloodless February Revolution at EDSA presaged startling, albeit amusing, developments in the print media. With a new government at the controls, and with the words "press freedom" dangling from their lips, people made a dash for the publisher's chair. Today, there are 24 nationally-circulated daily newspapers - - 9 morning dailies, 3 afternoon dailies, 5 morning tabloids, 2 afternoon tabloids and 5 Chinese newspapers. Of the dailies four are in Pilipino. There are also nine newsweeklies, four magazine supplements, and a host of women's, entertainment, and specialized publications.

Some observers view this with alarm. They hold the pragmatic view that only the fittest among the papers will survive, and so those given the false hope of succeeding will only be wasting their investments.[1] Even so, Art Borjal, National Press Club (NPC) president, says the proliferation of publications, while symbolizing freedom of the press, forces all newspapers to compete with one another through quality writing.[2] Another advantage is that with more newspapers, more people are being reached.[3] But former NPC president Antonio Nieva disputes it, saying that more newspapers mean fewer readers for each newspaper.[4]

The overriding consideration in assessing what brought about the trend is the freedom with which people can now run after truth and write and publish it without fear of anyone or anything. The unhampered reporting of truth is, after all, essential in a democratic and free society.

How the press lives up to its many roles as purveyor of information, disseminator of truth, mirror of society, fiscalizer and carrier of ideas, dissent and criticism, will determine, to a great extent, its survival. Because, while media is alive, as Greg Brilliantes puts it, "what it needs is restraint."[5] Former *Pahayagang Malaya* publisher Jose Burgos, Jr. says, "In the long run, it is the reading public that will judge which paper will survive. The readers' expectations now are different from those of the Marcos years. Before, they were hungry for information. Now they are more selective. They get the news everywhere, so they want analysis, objectivity and sobriety. It will be a matter of coming up with the right mix."[6]

Indeed, in a year's time, two morning dailies (*The Philippine Tribune* and *Philippine Daily Express*) and a weekly (*Veritas*) folded up. But a new daily (*Standard*) and a weekly that turned daily (*Observer*) took their places.

The writer's atmosphere today ("lively, confusing and unrestrained")[7] may be better appreciated when juxtaposed against the unhappy, oppressive climate of the martial law regime. It was not so long ago that martial law's repressive claws continued to hang over the heads of those who dared to write or speak out against the dictatorship until February 1986.

THE PRINT MEDIA TODAY

The most obvious manifestation of press freedom today is the proliferation of newspapers and newsweeklies. Under the new regime, the publishers vow objectivity, and to give the public what it must know. As if to break away from the stigma of being crony publications, the *Bulletin Today, Daily Express* and *Times Journal* changed their names to *Manila Bulletin*, the *New Daily Express* and the *News Herald* (later the *Manila Journal*).

The *Observer*, a newsweekly whose first issue came out on June 23, 1986, says it for all the post-Marcos publications:

> (To) strive rigorously to be a medium of accurate and reliable information and a vehicle for thoughtful public discussion; to contribute something vital and fresh to national life. *Observer* intends to do its part by digging out the facts of issues and events, and by airing the various ideas and alternatives on which may be based the resolution of issues and problems.

The morning dailies and their owners/publishers/editors are: *Business Day* (Raul Locsin, publisher); *Manila Bulletin* (Napoleon G. Rama, publisher); *Manila Journal* (Philippine Journalists, Inc., publisher); *Ang Pahayagang Malaya* (Amado P. Macasaet, publisher); *Philippine Daily Inquirer* (Eugenia D. Apostol, chairperson of the board); the *Manila Times* (Ramon Roces, publisher); the *Manila Chronicle* (Eugenio Lopez, Jr. and Joaquin "Chino" Roces, publishers); the *Philippine Daily Star* (Betty Go Belmonte, chairperson of the board, Max Soliven, publisher) and the *Manila Standard* (Rodolfo Reyes, publisher). In early 1987, two papers folded up — *The Philippine*

Tribune (Roberto Cuenca, board chairman); and the PCGG-sequestered *New Daily Express* (Roberto Benedicto, publisher; D.H. Soriano, president). The afternoon dailies are the *Evening Post* (Kerima Polotan-Tuvera, publisher/editor-in-chief), *Ang Masa* and *MidDay*. MidDay was formerly published by Jose Burgos, Jr. who later sold it to the *Manila Standard* group. Rodolfo T. Reyes is now publisher of *MidDay*. Burgos resigned as publisher of *Malaya* and *Ang Masa* when President Aquino appointed him officer-in-charge of Ilocos Sur. E.S. San Diego is now publisher of *Ang Masa*.

The tabloids are *Tempo* (Napoleon G. Rama, publisher); *People's Bagong Taliba* (Philippine Journalists Inc., publisher); *People's Journal*, and *People's Tonight* (of both *People's Journal* and *People's Tonight* (Philippine Journalists Inc., publisher), *Balita* (Liwayway Publishing Company; Buenaventura M. Gonda, president); *Ang Pilipino Ngayon* (Betty Go Belmonte, chairperson of the board and Antonio Roces, publisher); and the *Observer* (Antonio A.S. Valdes, president). The *Observer* was formerly a weekly.

There are five Chinese morning dailies: the *Chinese Commercial News* (the Yuyitung brothers, Quentin and Rizal, publishers); *United Daily News* (Leoncio Go, publisher); *World News* (originally owned by Kerima Polotan-Tuvera, now published by Florencio Mallari); *The Chinatown News* (Ramon Sy, publisher); and *Universal Daily News* (Billy Chan, publisher).

The newsweeklies are: *Mr. and Ms.* (Eugenia D. Apostol, publisher). *Dispatch* (Antonio Nieva, publisher); *Midweek* (published by a group of intellectuals, writers and businessmen, edited by Greg Brilliantes); *We Forum* (Jose Burgos, Jr., publisher); *Philippines Free Press* (Teodoro Locin, Sr., publisher); *The Economic Monitor* (Wilfredo S. Baun, editor); *Filipino Times* (Elizalde D. Diaz, publisher); *The Guardian* (Marcelo B. Soriano, publisher); and *Philippine Times Recorder* (Rodolfo M. Acob, publisher); *New Day*, a weekend supplement of *Business Day*, ceased publication after coming out for several months. *Veritas* (Felix Bautista, editor), widely known as the mouthpiece of the Catholic Church in the Philippines, bowed out of existence in May 1987.

Magazines

The weekly supplements are *The Sunday Inquirer* (The Philippine Daily Inquirer); *Philippine Panorama* (Manila Bulletin); *Sunday* (Malaya) and *Sunday Times Magazines* (Manila Times). The popular entertainment magazines are *Mod Filipino, Liwayway, Song Cavalcade, Bannawag, Bisaya, Parade, Woman's Home Companion, Women's Journal* and *Woman Today*.

Comics

The combined circulation of all newspapers does not add up to one million copies. In contrast, the 50 or so komiks have a combined weekly circulation of more than two million copies and an estimated 16 million readers. Around as an institution since the 1920s, the komiks is the cheapest entertainment reading fare, and can be effectively used as "a carrier or communicator of values, popular consciousness, or legitimate literature, and reflector of the people's beliefs and aspirations."[8]

PROBLEMS OF THE INDUSTRY

The Economics of Publishing

In order for a paper to survive, it must have printing and typesetting equipment and building to house the editorial staff. Only one "crony" publication and *Ang Pilipino Ngayon* and *Daily Star* owned printing and editorial facilities in 1986. Owning facilities, of course, is no sure-fire formula for success. One must be ready to sink P200 million into the enterprise and not expect any returns during the first two years. The *Philippine Daily Inquirer* is an exception. Capitalizing on a public hungry for news, the *Inquirer* turned in profits in a very short time. Its circulation soared to a peak of 333,554 during the first month and netted ₱5 million in the third month.[9] Its circulation is now pegged at around 160,000. With everyone writing and publishing freely, the *Inquirer* will have to offer something different to go back to its premiere position.

Printing equipment is expensive. A web offset press costs around P100 million. A printing press' high price, however, has not deterred the ambitious publisher from publishing. A second option is to rent its facilities, and pay a commercial printer to put out the newspaper. The *Inquirer* was renting its editorial building until it bought its own building. At one point it used the printing plants of *Pilipino Star, Hiyas, Times Journal*, Cacho Hermanos, *Focus* and APO-Neda to print its increasingly thick issues. *Malaya* has been renting four different presses, two of them in Quezon City and the other two in Makati. The *Philippine Tribune*, which rented one of the *Focus* buildings for its editorial offices, also rented the *Express* printing plant to get its circulation of 40,000 copies rolling. The *Tribune* spent P4.8 million a month under this arrangement.[10]

Nieva's *Dispatch* is subsidized by his own small offset press which also runs commercial jobs, like printing textbooks and others.

The *Manila Chronicle* used to print with Graphic Arts Services, Inc., a big komiks publisher-printer. Now it is printed at APO-Neda. Typesetting is done at its production department at the Chronicle Building in Pasig.

The high paper cost is another deterrent to publishing — at least for the soft-hearted. Betty Go-Belmonte says that Paper Industries Corporation of the Philippines (PICOP) charges ₱14,500 for a metric ton of newsprint. That means ₱0.75 for a 32-page newspaper. To run 333,534 copies of a 32-page issue, *Inquirer* had to pay PICOP ₱600,000.

There are two sources of paper -- PICOP and Bataan Pulp and Paper Mill. PICOP agrees to deliver only after cash payment, and Bataan collects a day after delivery.

Imported paper is cheaper, about ₱8,500 a metric ton. But taxes and freight cost may push the cost to as much as what PICOP offers.

Would government's importing paper tax-free help lighten the publishers' load? Maybe it will. Something to watch out for, however, is how government will manipulate the press by setting up quotas for paper supplies, and allocating the bulk to its favored newspapers.

Agents and Dealers

The economics of publishing includes offering attractive packages to agents and dealers who are crucial in making a paper sell. They can be spoiled by the more established newspaper companies with contests or high street sales. Prizes may include trips to Hongkong, a brand new car and appliances.

Again, it is the small entrepreneur or the amateur who will suffer from the whims and caprices of dealers and agents.

Transportation

Part of the circulation strategy is getting enough allocation on the Philippine Air Lines flights to the key cities and provinces. New newspapers will have to bargain patiently for allocations. The *Manila Bulletin* has the highest allocation of 9,315 kilos every week.

Advertising

The economics of publishing is such that the bigger the circulation a paper has, the higher the printing costs are. That is why advertising is the crux of publishing. Circulation and advertising go hand in hand. A publication cannot attract advertising if its circulation is very low.

The paper's high production cost is offset by advertising income. The 60-40 advertising-editorial ratio assures a paper enough revenues to keep it going. But some newspapers have no qualms about having a ratio of 73 percent advertising to 27 percent editorial. Are those papers in the business solely for profit? There is a need to check on the unethical practice of giving a reader only 25 percent of the product he pays for.

An ominous sign for the newspaper publisher is the downward trend of print media in advertising lineage and credibility. In an address to the Philippine Association of Publishers Inc. in October 1985, Antonio R. de Joya, chairman of Advertising and Marketing Associates, Inc., said that the "problems of viability faced by the publishing industry has its roots in the total economic downtrend. This is something they have in common with the rest of the communication media, radio and television.

"However, the economic downtrend apparently has a more serious effect on the print industry than on the broadcast sector, as indicated by print's loss in market share in media advertising expenditures."

In 1980, for example, Joya said that print captured 45 percent of total media advertising expenditures. Four years later, print's share dropped to

29 percent. In contrast, television enjoyed 46 percent of total advertising spent in 1984, up from 32 percent in 1980.

Joya noted that print advertising grew by only 13.5 percent annually in the last two decades, whereas television advertising increased at an average rate of 30.8 percent, a tenfold growth in share from 1960 to 1980. Print is losing to TV at the rate of four percent annually despite its apparent advantages as an ad medium.[11]

Joya cited the major causes of the problems of the print industry — increases in prices of newsprint (at an annual average rate of 25 percent) and the high cost of money.

Print Credibility

A bleaker trend is that audience preference for entertainment and news has shifted from print to radio/TV. "The broadcast media have become more popular and acceptable to Metro Manila audiences, as shown by a Philippine Mass Communication Research Services (PMCRS) survey. TV is the medium most preferred by AB and C homes. Newspapers are the second choice of the AB group, and radio, of the C group."

From the advertisers' viewpoint, Joya said that television has become "the prime source of product advertising awareness for consumers in the ABC sectors in Metro Manila as well as in other areas. Newspapers rank lowest as advertising awareness source for all consumer sectors in Metro Manila and outside. Radio far exceeds print as the second main advertising awareness source for provincial consumers in all socio-economic sectors. In Metro Manila, the second place is a near tie between radio and magazines."

A Question of Ethics

As more newspapers organized their staffs, piracy became common. The flurry of piracy left a bad taste in the mouth, but then piracy may be viewed philosophically as a hazard of the trade. The good it does is that journalists' salaries are raised, because the new publications offer higher rates than the older ones in the business. The now defunct *Philippines Tribune* paid the highest salaries; in some cases, double those of other publications. In effect, the *Tribune* upgraded the newspaper writer's salary scales.

Newspaper employees used to be among the most underpaid. Because of their low salaries and their need to augment their income, they became vulnerable to bribes. Politicians, bureaucrats and society matrons paid their way easily into the newspapers, thus giving rise to the term "envelopmental journalism."

Today, however, newsmen are relatively better paid. But that doesn't mean that "envelopmental journalism" has disappeared. As they say, old habits die hard.

The *Philippine Tribune*, which opened in March 1986, upset the media industry pay scales by offering unprecedented high salaries to its reporters, editors and columnists. The starting salary of columnists and senior reporters was ₱10,000. The editor-in-chief reportedly received ₱25,000 a month plus allowances.

The other newspapers had to increase their rates. The starting rate now for a reporter with no experience is ₱1,500 plus transportation allowance of ₱500 a month. Senior reporters get as much as ₱4,000 - ₱5,000 a month and senior desk editors, ₱10,000 - ₱12,000.

Circulation

Circulation figures are like tires — inflatable and deflatable, depending on who is giving the figures. The exaggerated claims a newspaper company executive or employee gives is intended, of course, to sell space to as many advertisers as possible.

Inquirer columnist Hilarion Henares, Jr. put out his figures — in favor of his paper, of course. His claims are included in the following table. One word of caution: Do not always believe what you read.

Advertising Rates

The *Philippine Daily Inquirer* at first did not depend on advertising. Because people were hungry for news, they lapped up the *Inquirer* stories. Street sales hit the half-a-million copies mark. The paper became a success — with no thanks to advertising.

But with the proliferation of newspapers, the *Inquirer*, like all other newspapers, had to turn to advertising for survival. Shown in Table 4 are advertising rates and other basic information on some newspapers.

Sequestration

While opening the windows to the free flow of information, the new government, through the Presidential Commission on Good Government (PCGG), has imposed what journalists perceive as a real infringement on press freedom. Three newspapers have already been sequestered -- the *Manila Bulletin*, the *New Daily Express* and the *News Herald (Manila Journal)*.

The sequestration teams, headed by a fiscal agent, are empowered to look into the books of the company in question, to inventory the company's assets, to prevent removal or concealment of those assets, funds and records, and to determine the company's true owners. The objective is to determine if Marcos or his relatives, or both wholly or partly own the newspapers so that their shares of stock can be turned over to the government.

There are guidelines in determining those assets. As a sequestration team member puts it, "We are not guided as a team, except that we are given some guidelines. Now normally we just do it on our own. I mean what others do may differ from what the other teams are doing in form and style, depending on the situation. Me, I have only stock and transfer book on hand."[12]

D.H. Soriano, *Express* president, does not look at the sequestration team's decision to stop *Express* management from hiring and firing people with alacrity. The move, he says, is clearly "an infringement of our freedom. How competent are the sequestrators to tell us if writers are competent enough to be hired, or incompetent not to be hired?"[13]

The National Press Club, says Art Borjal, considers sequestration of media as "an indirect form of censorship. Firstly, sequestration is not properly defined theoretically. In actuality the way sequestration is implemented has affected the day-to-day operations of newspapers. The effect is that whatever ideology you want for the paper can be interfered with."[14]

On January 15, 1987, the Supreme Court upheld the PCGG decision to stop the *Express'* publication on or before January 31, 1987. In effect, the verdict denied the *Express* union's petition to temporarily stop the government from closing the paper for its blatant violation of the freedom of expression and of the press.

The verdict upheld the agreement between the PCGG and the representatives of former Ambassador Roberto Benedicto, a Marcos "crony," who owned more than 70 percent of the *Express*, to close down the paper because of mounting losses. The *Express* incurred a ₱30 million loss in 1985 and was losing ₱1.4 million a month. Only the collection of ₱15 million in receivables kept the company going. The receivables could be considered bad debts.

Where is Press Freedom Going?

Antonio Nieva, representing the Organizing Committee of the Union of Journalists of the Philippines, wrote a memorandum to his media colleagues decrying the "threats to our very professions and freedoms."

Here are excerpts from his letter:

"Journalists and all other Filipinos who care for the people's basic right to freedom of expression cannot afford to ignore what has been happening in the mass media the past few weeks.

"The sacking of commentators from the government's *Radyo ng Bayan*, the censorship of television news footages, the sequestrations and imminent closure of a newspaper belonging to the administration's political rivals, the presidential order expanding the office of the press secretary -- these may all be seen as absolutely unrelated developments.

"But they do define a pattern, an ugly one. And we, print and broadcast mediamen of the National Union of Journalists of the Philippines, call upon our colleagues in the profession as well as on the rest of the citizenry to express serious concern over the implications of these developments.

"We are not ready to condone media repression tendencies from any quarter, be they from the assistance of a popular President and directed against those forces identified with the thoroughly discredited Marcos loyalists.

"Neither are we about to go along with the Press Secretary's assertion that government has the right to judge which opinions it would allow to be aired over government stations -- after all, taxpayers are not asked their political beliefs whenever they are bled white to sustain the government's operations and commitments.

"When the people toppled the Marcos dictatorship, they had vowed never again to allow such a regime of terror to rule their lives. We may have to be reminded, however, that the rule of repression may not necessarily take place in full scale with a stroke of the pen. The curtailment of our basic rights can come to us very gradually, in small bits and pieces that can go unnoticed and can pass without resistance until they choke our very standards and our own judgments as to what constitutes curtailment of press freedom. Let us not allow this to happen."

Power Brokers in the Media

The media oligarchs of the martial law dispensation were Benjamin "Kokoy" Romualdez, Roberto S. Benedicto, Hans Menzi and Kerima Polotan-Tuvera. If Burgos had more money, he would have been considered oligarchic, since he had four publications under his name (*MidDay*, one of his papers, was recently sold off). By his own admission, his operations are hand-to-mouth ventures. Emilio Yap, with his varied interests, had taken Gen. Menzi's place, until the *Bulletin* was sequestered in 1987.

Media owners do not just own media outlets; they own, if not have, controlling interests in other enterprises either related or not related to media. Pre-martial law oligarch Eugenio Lopez, Jr., who escaped from military detention, left behind the Meralco, a public utility firm, the *Manila Chronicle* and ABS-CBN in the hands of Marcos' relatives. He has returned and was given by the new government authority over the properties that the Marcos relatives took away from his family. Emilio Yap, former board chairman of *Bulletin Today*, is in banking, shipping and automotives. Aside from putting out *Bulletin Today*, *Tempo*, *Panorama* and *Balita* and the Liwayway publications (*Liwayway*, *Bisaya* and *Bannawag*), the Menzi corporations also deal in agriculture and paper. Three branches of the Roces family, who were mass media oligarchs before martial law, are back in the newspaper business. Joaquin "Chino" Roces, along with Eugenio Lopez, Jr., is behind the *Manila Chronicle*; Antonio Roces together with Betty Go Belmonte, is a moving force behind the *Philippine Star;* and Ramon Roces puts out the *Manila Times*. The Gos, who publish *Fookien Times*, are also the publishers of *The Philippine Star* and *Ang Pilipino Ngayon*.

The danger in families running a chain of media outlets is that they may control and manage information, and ultimately, public opinion. If these families are more interested in profits than in pursuing the truth, then they weaken press credibility. That is what journalists' associations should be vigilant about. The new Constitution's disallowing media empires and encouraging a broad base ownership of media may prevent that danger.

Alejandro Roces, the *Manila Times* editor-in-chief, however, says the Roces families may be in media, but they belong to different organizations. In fact, the *Times* and *Chronicle* considered themselves stiff competitors.

That we have press freedom is "illusory," says Nieva. "This time, liberation means essentially the dispersal of the propaganda utilization of media to that of producing a particular interest, such as business or politics. So, press freedom is still illusory. The media again is being made to sell vested interest under the illusion of press freedom."[15]

Conclusions

If the Philippines is to be a democratic society and its press continue to enjoy freedom to serve the people:

1. mass media outlets must not be placed in the hands of single - family proprietors, but must be owned by as many persons as possible. The *Philippine Daily Inquirer* and the *Philippine Tribune* sold shares of stock to their employees. When employees feel they are part of the organization, they perform better and show real concern for the company's welfare.

2. the industry should monitor what's going on in government and see to it that the government does not impose controls on press freedom.

3. journalists should form newspapermen's guilds to standardize salaries and develop members' professional skills.

4. journalists should create a Code of Ethics to establish the print medium's credibility and uphold the media practitioners' dignity.

The smell of freedom and the roar of the presses are causes for celebration among today's writers, intellectuals and artists. The print medium, much like the government, faces a myriad of problems and challenges in institutionalizing credibility within the bounds of its perception of freedom, comitment and responsibility.

Table 1. 1986 Publications According to Types

Type of publication

68 Publications
24 Newspapers   15 English
                       4 Tagalog
                       5 Chinese
48 Magazines   18 general interest magazines
                       8 women's magazines
                       7 specialized magazines
                       11 vernacular magazines
                       3 children's magazines
                       1 Chinese general interest magazine

Notes

[1] Art Borjal, personal interview, June 19, 1986.

[2] Ibid.

[3] Ibid.

[4] Antonio Nieva, personal interview, June 2, 1986.

[5] Greg Brilliantes, personal interview, June 2, 1986.

[6] Jose Burgos, Jr., personal interview, June 5, 1986.

[7] Rosalinda Pineda Ofreneo, *The Manipulated Press: A History of Journalism Since 1945* (Manila: Cacho Hermanos, 1984), p. 135.

[8] Soledad Reyes, "The Philippine Komiks (Manila: Philippine Mass Media, CAA Publications), p. 169.

[9] Betty Go-Belmonte, personal interview, June 1986.

[10] Richard Ching, personal interview, June 19, 1986.

[11] Antonio R. de Joya, "Credibility and Viability of the Print Industry; the Advertising Perspective," paper delivered at the annual convention of the Publishers Association of the Philippines, October 26, 1985).

[12] Comment of Bobby Gozon, member of the Fiscal Team assigned to sequester the *New Daily Express*, before the National Press Club committee looking into the problem of media sequestration.

[13] D.H. Soriano, personal interview, June 19, 1986.

[14] Art Borjal, personal interview, op. cit.

[15] Antonio Nieva, op. cit.

Table 2 1985 Print Media Circulation in Philippines*

National Newspaper (20)	Number of publications		Combined total circulation/issue
National Newspaper (20)	AM	PM	
Broadsheet (9)			
English dailies	5	1	935,143
Chinese dailies	3	-	98,141
Tabloid (4)			
English dailies	1	-	150,000
Filipino dailies	1	-	186,000
Eng-Pil-Chi	1	1	645,362
Business newspaper (3)			
English (Mon-Fri)	2	-	156,011
English (weekly)	1	-	25,000
Weekly newspaper (3)	3	-	506,123
Special edition (1)	1	-	50,000
Local magazine (31)			
General interest	17	-	1,418,000
Women-oriented	5	-	393,700
Children-oriented	3	-	224,000
Sports-oriented	3	-	202,700
Newspaper supplement	2	-	538,400
Comics	36	-	3,433,700
Provincial newspaper	54	-	215,827
Local trade journal/ Yearbook/In-house	18	-	185,000
Foreign publication			
Newspapers	3	-	34,800
Magazines	9	-	160,100
Trade journal/Yearbook	32	-	224,480
In-flight magazine	9	-	1,359,000

*Not a complete list

Table 3. 1986 Circulation of Metro Manila Newspapers

Publication	Henares sources	"Independent sources"	"Biased" sources (Claims)
		(As of Oct. 19, 1986)	
Philippine Daily Inquirer			
Week days	260,687	255,755	
Sunday	261,660		
Manila Bulletin			
Week days	227,616	252,540	
Sunday	255,365		
Malaya			
Week days	173,896	93,800	
Sunday	148,204		
Manila Times			
Week days	153,574	59,000	100,000
Sunday	154,082		(Source: Alejandro Roces)
Daily Express*			
Week days	117,210	52,850	
Business Day *			
Week days	53,000		
People's Journal			
Week days	53,000		
Sunday	221,164		
Philippine Tribune*		36,800	
Philippine Daily Star		33,000	80,000
			(Tribune management)
Manila Chronicle		22,300	10,000
			(Source: Alejandro Roces)
			50,000
			(Chronicle senior editor)
			85,000
			(Chronicle Bus. Manager)
Manila Journal		17,450	
Evening Post		5,700	
Balita		186,200	
Tempo		151,875	
People's Journal		149,500	
People's Tonight		96,500	
Ang Pilipino Ngayon		73,000	

*Defunct

Table 4. 1985 Circulation and Advertising Rates of Manila Newspapers

MORNING BROADSHEETS

	Bulletin Today	Daily Express*	Times Journal	Malaya	Metro Manila Times*	Philippine Tribune* (1986)
1. Circulation[a]						
a. Monday-Saturday	314,831	181,498	174,814	44,000	117,000	36,800
b. Sunday	356,871	181,498	174,814	44,000	117,000	-
2. Language	English	English	English	English	English	English
3. % Readership rating[b] (past week)	36.3%	6.4%	4.3%	5.7%	-	-
4. Rate per col. cm. -						
a. Monday-Saturday	75.00	60.00	60.00	45.00	37.50	55.00
b. Sunday	90.00	65.00	63.00	-	-	65.00
5. Cost page (B/W)						
a. Monday-Saturday	36,450.00	29,160.00	29,160.00	21,870.00	18,225.00	-
b. Sunday	43,740.00	31,590.00	30,618.00	21,870.00	18,225.00	-

[a]Based on publishers' statements.
[b]PMCRS Metro Manila Print Survey, December, 1984.

*Defunct

Table 4a. 1985 Circulation and Advertising Rates of Manila Newspapers

	MORNING TABLOIDS			AFTERNOON DAILIES	
	People's Journal	Balita	Tempo	People's Tonight	Evening Post
1. Circulation					
a. Monday-Saturday	466,004	186,000	150,000	179,358 (Mon-Sun)	103,000
b. Sunday	466,004	186,000	150,000		
2. Language	Eng/Pil	Pilipino	Eng/Pil.	Eng/Pil.	Eng/Pil.
3. % Readership rating (past week)	31.8%	23.9%	19.9%	7.1%	0.9%
4. Rate per col. cm.					
a. Monday-Staurday	100.00	45.00	60.00	30.00	37.50
b. Sunday					
5. Cost of page (B/W)					
a. Monday-Saturday	23,100.00	10,552.50	11,520.00	6,930.00	18,225.00
b. Sunday	23,100.00	10,552.50	11,520.00		

[a] Based on publishers' statements except for *Balita*.

[b] PMCRS Metro Manila Print Survey, December 1984.

Table 4b. 1985 Circulation and Advertising Rates of Manila Newspapers

| | BUSINESS PAPERS ||| CHINESE PAPERS |||
	Business Day	Economic Monitor	Makati Business Daily	Chinatown News	World News	United Daily News
1. Circulation[a]	31,001	25,000	125,000	43,270	27,213	27,653
2. Edition frequency	Mon-Fri	Weekly	Mon-Fri	Mon-Sun	Mon-Sun	Mon-Sun
3. Language	English	English	English	Chin/Eng	Chi/Eng	Chin/Eng
4. % Readership rating[b]	1.6%	-	-	-	-	-
5. Rate per col. cm. -	70.00	40.00	40.00	18.50	20.00	23.00
6. Cost of page (B/W)	19,600.00	11,200.00	19,440.00	8,991.00	9,720.00	11,178.00

[a]Based on publishers' statements.
[b]PMCRS Metro Manila Print Survey, 1984. December,

Table 4c. 1985 Circulation and Advertising Rates of Manila Newspapers

	WEEKLY NEWSPAPERS		SPECIAL EDITION	
	Veritas	Glitter	Philippine Inquirer	Mr. & Ms.
1. Circulation[a]	51,300	30,000	120,000	304,823
2. Edition/Frequency	Weekly	Weekly	Weekly	Weekly
3. Language	Eng/Pil.	English	English	English
4. % Readership rating[b] (past week)	1.1%			
5. Rate per col. cm.	55.85	35.00	45.00	100.00
6. Cost of page (B/W)	12,500.00	8,085.00	9,765.00	9,300.00

[a]Based on publishers' statements.
[b]PMCRS Metro Manila Print Survey, December 1984.

Table 5. Newspaper Circulation Breakdown by Region as of 1985

		Bulletin Today (M-Sat.)	Bulletin Today (Sunday)	Daily Express* (M-Sat.)	Daily Express* (Sunday)	Times Journal	Balita	People's Journal	Malaya	Total
Metro Manila		210,200	253,653	108,231	117,375	93,479	128,927	364,397	26,101	1,302,363
	%	60.70	70.30	62.60	64.67	54.51	80.18	79.12	60.00	69.55
Ilocos Region		10,624	10,869	66,708	7,078	7,734	1,125	9,965	568	54,671
	%	3.40	3.01	3.88	3.90	4.51	0.70	2.14	1.30	2.92
Cagayan Valley		4,758	4,532	2,127	2,051	1,149	949	1,620	798	17,984
	%	1.50	1.25	1.23	1.13	0.67	0.59	0.34	1.80	0.96
Central Luzon		24,018	29,203	15,820	16,335	16,995	17,752	25,719	4,118	149,960
	%	7.60	8.15	9.15	9.0	9.91	11.04	5.21	6.30	8.01
Southern Luzon		12,721	17,953	5,723	5,681	8,849	7,879	24,280	2,745	85,831
	%	4.10	4.98	3.31	3.13	5.16	4.90	5.51	9.50	4.58
Bicol Region		7,548	6,370	3,544	3,394	1,492	2,155	3,851	1,585	29,939
	%	2.40	1.76	2.05	1.87	0.87	1.34	0.82	3.60	1.60
West Visayas		10,489	9,329	10,737	10,781	6,156	257	8,065	2,991	58,805
	%	3.30	2.59	6.21	5.94	3.59	0.16	1.73	6.90	3.14
East Visayas		12,593	10,540	10,304	9,311	15,503	595	12,025	893	71,764
	%	4.00	2.92	5.95	5.13	9.04	0.37	2.58	2.00	3.83
North Mindanao		9,292	6,581	3,873	3,521	4,527	402	6,275	949	35,420
	%	3.00	1.82	2.24	1.94	2.64	0.25	1.35	2.20	1.90
South Mindanao		12,713	11,789	5,809	5,953	15,588	756	10,240	2,807	65,655
	%	4.00	3.27	3.36	3.28	9.09	0.47	2.20	6.40	3.51
Total R.P.		314,956	360,819	172,876	181,480	171,472	160,797	466,437	43,555	1,872,392
	%	100.00	100.00	100.00	100.00	100.00	100.00	100.00	100.00	100.00
Foreign		13	16	17	18	17	.	.	. .	81
Grand Total		314,969	360,835	172,893	181,498	171,489	160,797	466,437	43,555	1,872,473
	%	100.00	100.00	100.00	100.00	100.00	100.00	100.00	100.00	100.00

Table 6. Readership Profile of Leading Newspapers/Tabloids as of 1985

	Manila (%)	Legaspi City (%)	Cebu City (%)	Cagayan de Oro (%)	Davao City (%)
Sex:					
Male	54	60.7	54.6	58	52.1
Female	46	39.3	45.4	42	47.9
Age Group:					
14-19	17.0	18.8	21.3	19	17.5
20-29	39.0	27.9	33.5	32	31.9
30-44	27.0	28.4	29.8	34	34.1
45-59	11.0	14.4	10.7	10	10.5
60-over	6.0	10.5	4.6	5	6.0
Student:					
No	82.0	75.5	74.8	73	79.6
Yes	18.0	24.5	25.2	27	20.4
Socio-Economic Class:					
(AB)	12.0				
(C)	50.0	59.8	62.4	60	56.3
(DE)	38.0	40.2	37.6	40	43.7
Educational Attainment:					
Elementary or less	7.0	7.4	2.0	3.0	4.7
Some high school	11.0	17.0	11.3	16.0	10.9
High school graduate	22.0	22.3	12.2	18.0	34.6
Some college	32.0	26.2	31.7	32.0	34.6
College graduate	27.0	25.3	40.0	32.0	31.7
Post graduate	-	1.7	2.8	-	0.3

Source: PMCRS Print Survey, December 1984

Chapter X

The Community Press

Crispin C. Maslog

Publishing newspapers in a country splintered into 7,107 islands poses unique problems - and challenges.

The men and women who publish, week after week, the 164 or so community newspapers scattered throughout the archipelago are doing critically important work. They seek to make our provinces and cities better places to live in; they help in national development. They inform the people in the rural areas, making them intelligent participants in government.

Of these newspapers, the PAPI Directory lists 12 dailies, most of them in Cebu City; 1 triweekly in Zamboanga City; 2 biweeklies; 117 weeklies; 2 fortnightlies and 6 monthlies (Twenty-four papers did not state their frequency).

This list however may be misleading. The PAPI Directory includes some papers that had folded up before 1979.

Profile

The typical community newspaper in the Philippines is a weekly, tabloid in size, measuring 6 columns by 16 inches, with an average circulation of 3,630. It is printed by letter press. The number of pages normally run from 4 to 8. It is usually published in a provincial capital and other cities with populations between 50,000 and 100,000.

The community paper is either in English entirely, or English and local language dialect combined. A study made by Raul R. Ingles and Rebecca F. Maceda for the Asian Mass Communication Research and Information Center (AMIC) in 1977 showed that 33 percent of these community papers are published in English entirely while 65 percent are published in English and a local language-dialect combined. The reason for the use of English is because their readers are still the middle class and elite.

In an earlier study by Crispin C. Maslog (1965) of the Silliman School of Communication, a little over 50 percent of the Philippine community papers then were published in English entirely.

English-local language dialect means, usually, three pages in English (in a four-page paper) and one page in Pilipino or any of the other local languages or dialects. Most of the papers in this category use English-Pilipino and English-Cebuano Visayan combinations. Cebuano Visayan is the most widely-spoken language in the country.

Circulation of the weeklies ranges from 500 to 10,000, and of the dailies, 3,000 to 12,000.

Majority of these papers are sold on the streets by newsboys. Only a small percentage is delivered or mailed.

The circulation of most weekly newspapers is not audited. However, they submit to the Bureau of Posts, twice a year, a sworn statement on their claimed circulation as required by Republic Act 2580.

Community papers are sold between P1.50 and P2.00 a copy. In 1969 the average price was only 10 centavos a copy. But those were the good old days.

Subscription rates vary. The average annual rate of a weekly like the *Mindanao Times* of Davao City is P78; that of a triweekly such as *Zamboanga Times* of Zamboanga City, P234; and that of a daily like the *Freeman* of Cebu City, a bargain at P126 a year (normally worth almost P700).

Advertising rates also vary from place to place. By and large, commercial ads solicited in the province or city costs P18-P25 a column inch. Some papers in Luzon charge between P45 and P62.50 a column centimeter (between P112.50 and P156.25 a column inch).

Front page and back page ads normally cost 50 percent more.

A commission of 15 percent is deducted by advertising agencies from the cost of national ads placed in community papers. For local ads, commissions are higher - 15 to 25 percent.

Rates for legal notices are uniform since they have a ceiling set by law (Republic Acts 4569 and 4885, amended by Presidential Decree 1079). The ceiling is P35 a column centimeter. In practice, some newspapers charge from P10 to 18 a column inch.

Contents

The Ingles-Maceda study for AMIC in 1977 showed that 50 percent of the editorial space of these papers is devoted to news, and 27 percent to columns. This indicates that Philippine provincial papers tended to carry too many columns.

The AMIC study also showed that the papers devoted 36 percent of their editorial space to local items which is to be expected of community papers. The 18 percent space devoted to national items, however, seems to be too much.

Another study by Crispin C. Maslog of ten selected community papers in 1975 showed that the papers devoted 57 percent of their space to advertising and 43 to editorial matter, indicating good income to support their operations.

It is unlikely, however, that this ratio would apply to the average community paper. More likely the ratio would be reversed.

In style and make-up, community papers try to follow the Manila papers, which in turn are patterned after those in the United States. The inverted pyramid style of newswriting, headlining and front page make-up show the American influence.

Only a few community newspapers use pictures. This is due to the high cost of photoengraving. Outside the big cities, Cebu and Davao, photoengraving facilities are generally not available.

Some papers however have switched to offset, either fully or partially. Offset printing allows the greater use of pictures at minimal cost. *Mindanao Times* of Davao City and *Sun-Star Daily* of Cebu City are printed entirely in offset.

Combined offset-letterpress printing is used by papers as a middle ground between making its pages more attractive by publishing photos and keeping costs down.

Papers using the combined processes print their front and back pages in offset. This allows the use of more pictures and spot colors. Inside pages are usually printed in letterpress.

Very often, the absence of pictures is due to failure of editors to realize the value and impact of pictures.

The AMIC survey in 1977 showed that of the 57 papers studied, 25 owned their presses. That's roughly 44 percent. That leaves more than half of the community newspapers relying on commercial printers.

This means that most of these community papers are at the mercy of printers who can jack up prices anytime, and who will not always meet deadlines. The reason for this situation is that it takes some capital to start a newspaper with its own plant. Many editors are small enterpreneurs.

Staff

The average staff size of these papers is small -- seven, with four full time and three part time.

A typical full time staff consists of an editor and a reporter, and one or two men to handle the circulation and collection of bills. Very often, the publisher serves also as editor, reporter, printer, business and advertising manager, bookkeeper — and sometimes, as messenger.

The 1977 AMIC survey showed that nine out of 10 community editors are men, Roman Catholic and are married. They tend to be older; 30 percent are 55 years old and above. The majority are between 35 and 54 years old. And they have been editors for 10 years.

Seven out of 10 editors are college graduates, but only 15 percent have a journalism degree. However, nine out of ten editors had previous journalistic experience before starting their papers.

The AMIC study indicates that editors of community papers are highly educated, and have therefore a broad background.

However, since most of these degrees were in fields other than journalism, this means that they wandered into journalism from other fields. And even so, they have only one foot in the journalism threshold, because they are in it only part-time. To illustrate, 60 percent of these editors work only part-time with the paper. They spend an average of five days a week, eight hours a day on their journalism job; the rest of the time, they are teachers, businessmen, dentists, lawyers, pastors, engineers, etc.

Some papers employ stringers or part-time reporters. They are paid on a space-rate basis. The stringers may also act as advertising or subscription solicitors.

Kept Press

Unfortunately, there are a number of newspapers that are published irregularly, depending on seasonal political support or some subsidies from selfish interests. They operate at low cost since they publish only a few hundred copies. They offer unfair competition to regular papers. They do not adhere to the ethical standards of the established papers - and give a black eye to the legitimate, hard-working community newspapermen.

Survival

What are the chances for survival and success of a community paper?

The chances for survival and a modest profit are good — if the paper provides service to the community, is operated efficiently, and has integrity.

As of today, community newspaper publishing is generally a hand-to-mouth operation. Seven out of 10 papers, according to both the 1965 Silliman University School of Communication survey and the 1977 AMIC survey, were either earning some profits or just making both ends meet.

Since 1984, the situation has worsened. Prices of paper and printing materials soared because of the series of devaluation of the peso.

To community newspaper publishers, it was like being caught between the proverbial "devil and the deep blue sea."

The sharp increases in production costs could not just be passed on to readers and advertisers. Readers were also financially pinched and would have likely resisted sharp price increases. Business was slow and advertisers were unwilling to pay for big increases in ad rates. In fact, many business firms have cut down on advertising.

To save on production costs, many newspapers reduced their circulation.

A community newspaper's performance will, in the long run, determine whether it will survive or not. The readers will ultimately decide the fate of a particular paper.

The community will expect some definite things from the paper and its staff. It will be expected to record, from week to week, the significant activities of the community. If the province needs a new bridge, a new industry, or a more honest government, the paper must fight for it.

The paper must also try to interpret the news for local readers, provide sober, well-informed discussions of issues affecting the community. It should also serve as a market place for those who want to buy or sell their products and services.

A newspaper is both a public service and business enterprise. It must make profits to be able to serve. In a democratic society, the most dangerous newspaper is one that cannot make both ends meet, because it loses its independence.

An editor of the Philippine News Agency summed this up: "A newspaper which becomes consistently identified with the private interest... loses readership and dies a natural death."

This is because while a newspaper is primarily a business as far as its owner is concerned, "it is a business vested with a public function identified with the public interest."

Editors, reporters and columnists, too, have a duty to observe.

There are many rewards in working with the community press. Most of the people who are engaged in it now seem satisfied with their work.

For example, to find out if they were satisfied with what they were doing, the community editors were asked in the 1965 Silliman survey if they would transfer to a Manila newspaper, given the chance. Three-fourths of them said no, and many were vehement in their opinion.

To some of them, Manila was synonymous with "corruption." The majority felt that they could not leave their papers because they owned it, or because they felt they could be more useful to their communities as small town newspapermen. Some of the more financially stable editors replied, proudly, "I make more from my own paper than any salaried newspaperman in Manila."

Then others found work in the local paper more challenging than "newspapering" in the big city. Many of them enjoy being their own boss. This sentiment was vividly expressed by one editor, who said, "I would rather be the head of a fly than the tail of a lion!"

The 1977 AMIC study also showed that 74 percent were not willing to work in Manila if given the chance. Of this number, however, only nine gave reasons signifying a real commitment to their job. Is this an indication of a dwindling sense of satisfaction on the part of these community newspaper editors?

The Philippine community press, like its counterpart the world over, has its share of black sheep. But it has also produced heroes like Antonio Abad Tormis of the *Republic News* of Cebu City, Ermin Garcia of the *Sunday Punch*, and recently, Jacobo Amatong of the *Mindanao Observer* Crusading editors, they were gunned down while fighting corruption in their cities.

You will see in the journalistic careers of Tormis, Garcia and Amatong the challenges and opportunities for service in community newspaper work.

Chapter XI

Book Publishing Industry

Pacifico N. Aprieto

Historians invariably trace the beginning of book publishing in the Philippines to two events: the printing of the first book, *Doctrina Christiana*, and the setting up of the first printing press in Manila.

EARLY HISTORY

Doctrina Christiana, a religious handbook in Spanish and Tagalog, antedated by nearly half a century the earliest book in America, the *Bay Psalm Book*. The *Doctrina* was printed in 1593 by a Christian convert, a Chinese named Juan de Vera, who used the ancient Chinese method of block printing (xylography).

Three copies of the *Doctrina* have thus far been discovered in existence abroad. The *Doctrina Christiana* in Spanish and Tagalog, which was donated by an American millionaire, is deposited at the Library of Congress in Washington, D.C. A *Doctrina* in Chinese was found in the Vatican Library in Rome. The third, *Tratado de la Doctrina de la Santa Iglesia y de Ciencias Naturales*, was discovered in 1952 in the Biblioteca Nacional of Madrid. Carlos Quirino, investigating these copies, established that the *Doctrina* in Spanish and Tagalog and the *Tratado* were the first books published in the Philippines. A facsimile edition of the Spanish-Tagalog *Doctrina* was issued by the National Historical Commission in 1973.

In block printing, the wooden block surface was rubbed over with a paste, probably made from boiled rice, to smooth it and prepare it for receiving the characters. The text was finely drawn on thin transparent paper which was then pressed to the block, face down, and rubbed off, leaving a reverse image. With a sharp tool, the engraver cut away all the non-image portion, leaving the characters in relief.

The image area was inked, then a thin sheet of paper was laid on the block. A dry brush was run gently over it to take on the impression. By this method, an experienced craftsman could produce 2,000 copies a day.

In 1602, Juan de Vera, under the Dominican priest Francisco Blancas' guidance, set up a printing press that used movable types in his residence in Binondo, a Chinese district in Manila. As in Europe, the introduction of movable types hastened the development of printing in the Philippines.

The first books that came off de Vera's press were the *Libro de las excelencias del Rosario de Nuestra Señora y sus misterios* written in Tagalog by Father Blancas; *Postrimerias, o Libro de los cuatro novisimos*, also by Father Blancas; *Ordinationes Generales; Memorial de la Vida Christiana*, written in Chinese by Father Domingo de Nieva; and *Simbolo de la Fe*, also in Chinese, by Father Tomas Mayor.

In 1613, de Vera's press was moved to the College of Santo Tomas in Intramuros and later to its present quarters on the University of Santo Tomas campus on España Street.

Among the first Filipinos to learn the printing trade from the Spanish missionaries was Tomas Pinpin, a native of Bataan and who is now known as the "Father of Philippine Printing." Between 1610 and 1639, while managing the Dominican press, Pinpin printed 14 books. His first printing job was *Librong Pag-aralan Nang Mga Tagalog Nang Uicang Castilla*. This bilingual book was 119 pages.

In 1613, Pinpin printed the first Tagalog dictionary, *Vocabulario Tagalog* by Father San Buenaventura.

The first lithographic printer in the Philippines was the Spaniard Salvador Chofre. Quick to recognize the commercial prospects of a modern printing press, he imported a lithographic machine from Germany and set up his own shop in 1880. The shop changed ownership several times until it was acquired by Jesus Cacho and became Cacho Hermanos, Inc. in 1927. Cacho Hermanos, Inc. is now owned by Alfredo Ramos.

Two Europeans combined their talent and money and established a printing shop in 1887. Eulalio Carmelo y Lakandula, an artist-engraver, and William Bauermann, a German lithographer started with a modest press, Carmelo and Bauermann, that soon became a leader in modern printing.

Among the first Filipinos to set up his own printing press was Juan Martinez. With a Minerva platen press, he started reprinting in 1905 literary works popular at that time, such as *Juan Tiñosa* and *Ibong Adarna*. In 1909-1917, he employed some 50 workers in his press and central bookstore in Intramuros, and had branches on the Escolta, Plaza Moraga and on Plaza Calderon de la Barca.

Imprenta-Libreria y Papeleria de Juan Martinez was one of the few successful Filipino establishments that published native literature. It had either published or reprinted over a hundred romances, novenas, vocabularies, alphabets, novels, almanacs and other publications. The owner's grandson, Roberto Martinez, Jr., now manages the National Printing on Quezon Boulevard which carries on the tradition started by Imprenta nearly three generations ago.

Many books published during the Spanish regime reflected the efforts of the Spanish missionaries to understand the Filipinos and to be understood by them. By 1800, 541 books had been published in the Philippines. They were mostly dictionaries, grammars, and religious instructions. The missionaries found Tagalog easy to learn and published most books in this language.

Authorship was wholly non-Filipino. Encarnacion Alzona described the period as the age of obscurantism. The Catholic Church censored and prevented the publication of Filipino writings. It limited publishing to books on the lives of saints, tales of miracles, novenas and devotions. The publication of *Florante at Laura* by Francisco Baltazar in 1833 was an exception. With allegorical characters and setting, the verse satirized and criticized the Spanish rule. It became a popular book. Jose Rizal carried with him a copy of the book in his trips abroad.

The American rule gave impetus to publishing by Filipino authors. Filipinos soon had their works published in English here and in the United States.

Among the early Filipino books published in the United States were the *Philippine Islands* (New York, 1899) by Ramon Reyes Lala; *Legislative History of America's Economic Policy Towards the Philippines* by Jose S. Reyes (New York, 1923); *The Philippine Republic* by Conrado Benitez (Boston, 1926); *Philippine Folk Dances and Games* by Francisco Reyes (New York, 1927); *America, the Philippines and the Orient* by Hilario C. Moncado (New York, 1932); *Evangelical Christianity in the Philippines* by Avelina Lorenzana and Camilo Osias (Dayton, Ohio, 1932); *Philippine Literature Series* by Ely Fansler and Isidro Panlasiqui (New York, 1923-1925); and *The Development and the Present Status of Education in the Philippines* by Vicente Catapang (Boston, 1926).

The Textbook Industry

During the early years of American rule, American textbooks were made the tools of instruction in Philippine schools. Later, some American publishers, notably Ginn and Company, encouraged Filipinos to write textbooks. Camilo Osias wrote the first readers in English for Filipino elementary students in 1918.

It was inevitable that Filipinos would feel the need to develop and publish their own textbooks. Serafin E. Macaraig was the first Filipino to set up an educational publishing firm in 1926 and to encourage Filipinos to write schoolbooks. Other pioneer book publishers were Delfin R. Manlapaz, whose first books in 1932 were his own laboratory manual in physics and handbooks in college mathematics, and Juan C. Laya, who published the prose and poetry series, *Diwang Kayumanggi.*

After World War II, more Filipinos went into textbook publishing. Notable among them is Dr. Ernesto Y. Sibal, who set up Alemar-Phoenix Publishing House in 1958. He constantly championed the Filipinization of textbooks. The others are Ceferino M. Picache, who organized Bookman Incorporated in 1947 and who became one of the biggest schoolbook publishers; Pablo L. Bustamante, who published his first reference books and teaching guides for the elementary and intermediate schools in 1948; Jose N. Francisco, who, with his wife, organized the Jonef Publications in 1948 "in the firm belief that the Filipinos, better than the foreigners; can write their own schoolbooks"; Olimpio L. Villacorta, who put up the Modern Book Company, initially a distributor of medical publications but which became a full-time publisher in 1947.

With the large market for textbooks, publishers soon saw the need to consolidate their gains against foreign publishers. In 1958, under the leadership of Alemar-Phoenix Publishing House, the Philippine Educational Publishers' Association (PEPA) was organized "to meet the challenges of educational book publishing in the Philippines and serve the national community with books written by Filipinos for Filipinos and of the Filipinos."

In 1954, copyrights were secured for 237 books, of which about half were textbooks. By 1984, only about 350 out of some 1,000 titles published were textbooks.

The Concern for Literature

Although less important commercially than textbooks, Filipino literary books in English have had a spectacular record.

Just 20 years after English was introduced in the Philippines, the first English novel, *A Child of Sorrow* by Zoilo M. Galang, was published in Manila in 1921. *Never Mind and Other Poems* by Procopio Solidum, and a collection of plays, *Types of Students and Unfortunates* by Jose Bernardo, made their appearance the following year.

In 1923, Galang came out with *Tales of the Philippines*, a collection of stories. The same year also saw the publication of Cayetano Arellano's biography by Jose Batungbakal.

Several anthologies came off the press in quick succession. *Filipino Poetry*, edited by Rodolfo Data, and an anthology of essays, *Thinking for Ourselves*, edited by Eliseo Quirino, came out in 1924. In 1927 the first anthology of stories in English, *Filipino Love Stories*, came out. It was edited by Paz M. Benitez. In 1930, the first anthology of plays in English, *Philippine Plays*, edited by Sol Gwekoh, was published.

In the United States, the first book by a Filipino, *Azucena*, a volume of Filipino poetry by M. de Garcia Concepcion, appeared in 1925. Scribners published Jose Garcia Villa's *Footnote to Youth* in 1933. Among the first novels that were published in the U.S. were *His Awakening: A Romance of Manila and Hollywood* by Ernest Lopez (1929); *The Lonesome Cabin* and *The Brown Maiden*, both by Felicidad V. Ocampo (1930-1931). Alfonso P. Santos published in the U.S. in 1936 two volumes of poetry, *A Garland of Sampaguita* and *Flowers of Melancholy*. A prose collection by Luis Agudo, *Filipinos Digging Their Graves*, was published in 1935.

Sixty-four Filipino novels in English had been published by 1966. Abdul Majid, a scholar from the University of Malaya, found this literary output remarkable. He observed that in none of the former British colonies in Asia, Africa and the West Indies was an English novel produced so shortly after the arrival of the English language. Even India, the first British colony to publish a novel, did so only after two centuries of British rule.

Majid further observed that the number of Filipino novels in English in 1966, was second to India's and was formidable when compared with that produced in other former British colonies which had a much longer experience with the English language. Singapore, acquired by the British in 1819, had less than ten. Malaysia which came under the British rule in 1786 had less than 20.

This remarkable growth of Filipino literature in English was attributed to the United States colonial policy that differed from Spain's.

The Spaniards came to the islands primarily to spread Christianity. The missionaries found it more convenient to learn the native language for their work. Spanish authorities also were not averse to keeping the natives ignorant so they would be easier to rule. The limited opportunities for education in Spanish hindered the spread of Spanish. At the end of Spanish rule only about 1.6 percent of the Filipinos had Spanish education.

The Americans used popular education, using English as the medium of instruction, as their primary instrument for governing the country. Long deprived of opportunities for education, and for learning the colonial ruler's language, the Filipinos took to the schools and the English language with a passion. Thus, more than three centuries of Spanish rule had passed before the first Filipino novel in Spanish, *Ninay* by Pedro Paterno, was written. But it took only 20 years for the Filipinos to develop sufficient confidence and skill in the English language to write the first novel in English.

The fact that among the first Filipino books in English was a novel can be attributed to the narrative tradition based on epics and folklores that flourished long before the Spaniards arrived. This tradition assured the continuing popularity of literary works. Rizal exposed the abuses of Spanish authorities and the ills of society through his socio-political novels. Earlier, Balagtas had used narrative poetry to achieve the same goal.

Scholarly Publishing

Grammar books, histories, and dictionaries of native languages produced during the early years of the Spanish regime are considered the first scholarly publications in the country "since they were printed in the interest of scholarship and for a limited audience." However, the first signs of serious scholarship did not appear until about the middle of the 19th century when writers like Francisco Baltazar rebelled against the clerical tradition. Before that period, the church influence was strong. Thinking was uniform and unorthodox ideas were condemned. Original scholarship was non-existent.

Philippine scholarship today follows more closely the European and American tradition of rigorous and objective research and deals with a vastly wider variety of specialized topics. Its major outlets are some 200 journals, mostly in English, put out by schools and research groups.

Scholarly books, on the other hand, are sparse. A survey of books published in 1900-1935, in the University of the Philippines library, showed barely a dozen titles that could be considered scholarly by present standards. Among these, arranged by dates, would be Albert Ernest Jencks, *The Bontoc Igorot* (1905); Frank Ringgold Blake, *The Tagalog Literature and Analogies in Other Languages* (1908); Constantino Lendoyro, *The Tagalog Literature* (1902); Fernando Salas, *El Habeas Corpus* (1913); Anonymous, *Construction of Coordinated Words in the Philippine Languages* (1916); Pedro Alejandro Paterno, *Historia Critica de Filipinas* (1920); Rufino Luna, *The Philippine Municipality at Work* (c. 1929); and Candido Bartolome, *Philippine Recreational Games* (c. 1936).

The picture today is different. Whereas only one book could be produced in a year before World War II, today about 15 scholarly titles are published annually. In 1974-1984, the Copyright Office registered 157 scholarly books.

Textbooks have become the mainstay of book publishing because they are more profitable to publishers. A dozen publishers control the textbook industry. Competition is stiff. Publishers vie for authors, manuscripts, and even for editors, promotion managers, sales staff, and printers. Most textbook publishers have their own printing plants, which usually are the best in the country, but they still send jobs to printers to meet the heavy demand for textbooks when school opens. Most of them have well-established distribution outlets. A few of them own bookstore chains in greater Manila.

The textbook industry's size, in terms of revenues, is hard to determine. Publishers are reluctant to give out sales figures. Persistent rumors which are hardly denied, of some publishers using "grease" money to hasten approval and payment of big orders, especially during the pre-martial law years, attest to the lucrativeness of selling textbooks.

Publishing literary works, as earlier mentioned, has flourished fairly well because of society's concern with literature and literature's universal interest. Inspite of frequent complaints from writers about the national neglect of literature, literary publishing has enjoyed a much greater variety of support than any other type of publishing. The government and private groups encourage literary writing by giving awards, sponsoring workshops, conferences, training and writing fellowships, and offering publishing opportunities here and abroad. This concern is also reflected in the works of scholars. There is more published writing on Philippine literature, especially in English, than say on textbooks or scholarly publishing.

Scholarly publishing has not enjoyed as much profitability as textbook publishing nor as much national concern as literary publishing. Uneconomical to publish, scholarly books are avoided by commercial publishers. The Filipino scholarly book has yet to capture the national attention and imagination. Thus scholarly publishing has largely been the function of higher education and research. The schools, however, have not been as efficient as they should be in publishing scholarly books. In some big universities, no central publications office takes charge of publishing scholarly works.

Three universities lead in scholarly publishing -- the University of the Philippines, Ateneo de Manila University, and De La Salle University, which have set up their own university presses or academic publishing programs.

The typical scholarly book is written by a scholar to communicate information and ideas in his field. It conveys new knowledge or new interpretation, usually the results of the author's research, for academicians, students and others interested in scholarly discoveries.

There are also scholarly books that appeal to a large audience. Whether their readership is limited to a small group, or to a wide audience, scholarly books share a common quality: they are the result of disciplined study.

The "esoteric" books make up the majority of scholarly books. Specialists most need them. Although their demand is low, their need is big. Their need is large in the sense that it is a qualitative, not quantitative, need; and that it is imperative.

THE TEXTBOOK PROJECT

A project that had a major impact on the publishing business is the government's large-scale production of textbooks. Funded from a World Bank education development loan, the project developed all basic textbooks for the public schools, and printed and distributed close to 80 million textbooks and teacher's manuals.

The textbook project (1976-1988), is the largest book publishing activity undertaken in the Philippines. It calls for developing 109 titles for the elementary and high schools and distributing them loan-free, one textbook for every two pupils, in some 40,000 schools.

Textbooks and accompanying teacher's manuals were developed by government curriculum centers. Editing and production were undertaken through the Textbook Board Secretariat. The printers and binders are chosen through international bidding, in accordance with World Bank procurement procedures.

Unprecedented in scale, complexity and organization, the Textbook Project came to mean different things to different groups. For the first time in years, textbooks were available in every school throughout the country. These books were produced under exacting educational and publishing standards. The project infused into the printing industry more than US$3 million every year in the last 10 years. The large demand for typesetting spurred typesetting companies to expand and improve their facilities. Art and design studios, as well as independent copy editors, designers, illustrators and photographers found their most challenging jobs in the project.

Paper merchants and manufacturers, commercial forwarders, ink manufacturers and other sectors of the graphic industries felt the impact of the Project.

International competition and the strict standards set for the project appeared to have increased local printers' productivity, upgraded quality and provided experience in large-scale printing and binding under tight schedules.

The traditional textbook publishers, however, appeared to have suffered from the project. The government ceased to buy privately-produced textbooks. However, under the project's second phase, which was programmed to produce 10 million textbooks every year from 1983 to 1988, the government announced its intention to reactivate the private educational publishers to help carry out the program. Thus an Instructional Materials Development Corporation (IMC) was set up under the aegis of the Department of Education, Culture and Sports.

Under IMC's charter, its main task is to carry on the Textbook Board Secretariat's function of keeping enough supply of textbooks through reprinting, revision, and development of new textbooks. IMC will also develop and distribute an array of instructional materials, print and non-print, to enhance teaching and learning in the classrooms beyond 1988.

IMC's emerging role is that of an educational broker, meeting requirements of schools through private publishers and printers.

PUBLISHING PROBLEMS

There are 30 full-time publishers in the country, which publish textbooks as their mainstay. Together they put out about a thousand titles every year at an average print run of 3,000 copies. As earlier mentioned, about 70 percent of their production are textbooks and general references; roughly 23 percent are monographs and miscellaneous publications such as indices, atlases and almanacs; around 4 percent are literary works; and the rest are university publications.

Sleek volumes referred to as "coffee table books" have made their appearance in recent years, catering mainly to rich collectors and tourists. They usually deal with a cultural facet, such as old streets, indigenous architecture, art or historical vignettes.

Of 30 publishers, only 15 can handle all aspects in book publishing, from purchasing or commissioning of manuscripts and editing them, and designing, printing and distributing the books. Almost all are family corporations. The large and successful publishers appear to depend much on their bookstores' earnings, like National, Alemar's and Goodwill Bookstores. In the Philippines these bookstores often operate like supermarkets carrying a variety of non-book merchandise, from greeting cards to school supplies.

Almost at the same time the government started the textbook project, the Book Development Association of the Philippines (BDAP) was organized by publishers, authors, printers, book designers, booksellers and allied professionals "to increase the number of books published and sold."

BDAP holds book fairs, participates in international book exhibits and conferences, cooperates with publishers especially in Southeast Asia, gives awards to outstanding books, and lobbies for such measures as liberalizing paper imports, lowering taxes on printing and publishing equipment, supplies and foreign books, and abolishing the export tax on books.

The BDAP sees the problems of book publishing as follows:

1. Distribution

The country's book market is far from developed. The smallness of the market accounts explains why publishers print only limited copies of books and hence, produce them at a high unit cost.

In addition, there is a gross imbalance between urban and rural areas on the availability of reading materials. Roughly 95 percent of all books, other than textbooks, are sold in Metro Manila and a few key cities only.

Many cities and large towns are without any real bookstore to speak of. Even those with bookstores are never exposed to substantial numbers of books. It is a known fact, for example, that not a few people from Mindanao come to Manila to buy books.

Distribution is expensive primarily because the country is made up of so many islands. Books in Cebu City, in Central Visayas, for instance, cost at least five percent higher than those in Manila, excluding postal charges. Besides being expensive, transportation and postal facilities are inadequate and often unreliable.

2. Book tax

The Philippines is a signatory to the UNESCO Florence Agreement which guarantees "free flow of information," i.e., books shall be duty free. The government does not impose any duty, but it collects advance sales tax or 12½ percent of the books' invoice value plus an additional 3 percent sales tax and 1 percent municipal tax imposed when books are sold.

This amounts to double taxation, and makes prices of imported books exorbitant.

Worse, due to high cost of importing books, booksellers and distributors are very selective in choosing titles and have thus limited the number of books available.

Some of the best books published in the world today are never seen in our country.

3. Printing cost

Virtually all the raw materials (paper, ink, film, etc.) for making books, not to mention printing equipment, are subject to an average 50 percent duties and taxes. This has caused locally printed books to become expensive despite their poor quality.

High cost is undoubtedly the foremost reason why the Philippines publishes the least number of books in Asia today.

The ratio of imported books to locally published titles is somewhere between 100 to 1.

The number of Filipino authors have diminished. Fewer companies are publishing their works due to high cost of printing and the constricting book market.

4. Poor reading habits

Worsening the undeveloped market the poor reading habits of the people.

The comics, television, and the radio have distracted people from reading.

Other contributing factors are:

a. Very few local publications, least of all, newspapers, publish book reviews and book news. While book reviews are part and parcel of most newspapers abroad, they are rarely found in local publications.

The Philippines never had a best-seller list, either of local or foreign books. A Filipino, therefore, walks into a bookstore completely unaware of the latest books, or of bestsellers. He is left to his own resources as to what books to buy. More often than not he judges a book by its cover.

If he ends up with a bad book, chances are it will take him a long time to buy another, if he ever buys again.

b. Filipinos profess to want to develop local publications. But it is a known fact that many schools do not even recommend local books, particularly in literature. The study of Philippine literature has not been encouraged enough.

This does not augur well for developing the book industry.

c. Comic books are sold by the millions every month. In fact, comic book publishers are given priority in procuring newsprint over other publishers. While comics is the cheapest form of reading material, it unfortunately, offers the lowest form of cultural and intellectual fare.

Efforts must be exerted to redirect the comic reading habit to book-reading. And always, the best place to start is at home and in the school.

d. In Western countries a library, or at least a book shelf, is part of the home. A Filipino home usually has a well-appointed den or lanai for entertaining, but hardly a bookcase.

This architectural characteristic indicates the Filipino's attitude toward books in general.

e. There is need for more libraries and reading centers in the rural areas and in most cities.

Only a government policy towards the nation's intellectual growth can make such public facilities available.

In housing government projects, hardly any attention is given to building libraries or reading centers.

The law requires a subdivision developer to provide a recreation area but not facilities for developing the mind. Thus the largest subdivisions, housing projects, and exclusive villages may boast of complex sports facilities, but hardly any of them have reading centers to speak of.

5. Over-protected industry

In the last several years, the government has protected some industries (e.g., paper and ink) to give them a chance to develop. But this has proved detrimental to publishing. It is common knowledge that local paper and ink are more expensive than imported ones.

It is high time the government takes a close look at the paper and ink industries. They have been overprotected for so long.

Protectionism obviously stunted the book industry's growth and consequently, the people's intellectual growth.

6. Not bankable

It is an axiom that publishing is a high-risk and yet a low-return business venture.

Coupled with an unattractive and unhealthy publishing environment, Filipino publishers have no choice but to switch to other investments, and thus become only part-time publishers.

Commensurately, book authors, editors, and designers are getting fewer. Most of them are in book publishing part-time only. Very few new talents are therefore developed.

To improve the situation, publishing must first be made financially attractive.

Again, while other businesses can avail of low-interest loans, publishers usually cannot avail of them. Publishing is regarded as a non-priority investment and books are not "bankable."

Saddled with the high interest on loans, publishers are further discouraged from publishing books which yield low returns. It normally takes at least two years to sell all the copies of most titles.

Providing low interest loans to publishers will redound to more books published at lower prices.

7. Government publishing

Textbook publishing by the government tended to retard further the book industry's growth. This is because the government would have a virtual monopoly of textbooks for the elementary and high school.

As in most countries, textbooks account for a big percentage of total book production. Since publishers have lost to the government a big part of their market, many of them had switched to other business, or had to scale down their publishing operations.

Nobody can dispute the government's aims and efforts in easing a serious educational problem by publishing textbooks. It should, however, allow the private publishers to play a major role in its program. Instead of competing with the private publishers, the government should make them its partner.

8. Red tape and venalities

Some undesirable practices in book purchases by the public schools have forced out some big publishers of textbooks. Their absence was filled in by fly-by-night publishers who lacked expertise and scruples.

Only in a healthy competitive environment can publishers help meet the increasing demands of our educational system.

9. Unprofessional practices

Unprofessional publishers demean the book industry with their disregard for generally-accepted trade practices.

This is partly because the copyright law is not strictly enforced, and the concept of intellectual property rights is not widely known.

Unprofessional publishers do not contribute to the industry's growth, save for one or two titles they add to the country's production. The problems they knowingly or unknowingly cause far outweigh their contribution.

Too often, authors who said they were not paid their royalties or were cheated, are those that had their works published by unprofessional publishers.

The BDAP aims to professionalize the book industry. But this can be accomplished only if there are laws conducive to healthy publishing.

10. Lack of book data

There is no mechanism for effectively monitoring and supplying vital information on books. The lack of statistical data and information on reading patterns makes it more difficult even for resourceful publishers to progress.

At present no office, private or government, can provide information on how many titles are locally published every year, much less a complete list of titles.

Many publishers do not bother to comply with the Decree on Legal and Cultural Deposit because they do not get penalized if they do not comply. A stiff penalty, for instance, must be imposed on publishers who fail to submit a copy of each of their books to the National Library.

The installation of the International Standard Book Number (ISBN) coding system provides a systematic monitoring system and accurate ordering guide for booksellers and librarians throughout the world. Its installation is a step towards professionalizing the book industry. All publishers should be required to join it.

11. Compulsory licensing

Presidential Decree 1203, of December 1977, authorizes the reprinting, under certain conditions, of any textbook or reference book, domestic or foreign, whose price may have become so exorbitant as to be detrimental to the national interest. The law prohibits the export of reprints and guarantees royalties to the copyright owners or original publishers every six months.

While the decree made textbooks and reference books more accessible to students, its disadvantages and ill-effects should not be overlooked.

For example, because they feared that their books may be "pirated," not a few foreign publishers have refused to show their new books in the Philippines, thus depriving the country of some of the latest books from abroad.

As a result of P.D. 1203, the country gained a bad reputation in international publishing circles. Filipino publishers have been called "pirates" at international conferences.

SUMMING UP

The problems BDAP describes give a good picture of Philippine book publishing. Some problems, however, were not mentioned by the association. For example, the most obvious reason for the poor sale of books is the low purchasing power of the Filipino family. The cheapest book in the market costs at least a half-day's work of most workers. For the majority of families, buying books has to be postponed in favor of food, shelter, and clothing.

As regards the doomsday prophets, evidence tend to show that despite the problems, book publishing has not only survived but even flourished. The number of book publishers and bookstores has increased, even if only slowly.

The Business of Publishing

It is a common mistake among laymen and even the more knowledgeable to equate printing with publishing. The first publishers were also the first printers. The history of printing is full of examples of one-man bookmakers who wrote, edited, designed, printed and sold their own books. The most visible publishing operation is printing which produced the finished book.

To a certain extent, many publishers still operate as the first Western publishers did: they print their own books and run their own bookstores. However, printing is only one aspect in book publishing.

Publishing may be defined as the intellectual and business procedure of selecting and transforming a manuscript into a book and promoting its use. Printing is the mechanical process of producing identical copies of the book.

Publishers must have the editorial, financial and managerial capability to originate manuscripts, transform them into finished book, and sell them to the public at a price that would give them a reasonable return on investment. The larger the publisher, the more specialized its departments. These functions usually are: editorial, design, production, accounting and management.

Small publishers may combine design with editing or production. Some publishers subcontract services from studios and free-lancers.

A publishing company may consist of a small office where the publisher/managers orchestrates the work of half a dozen assistants, or a large editorial, design, production, marketing, finance and management staff housed in a large building.

The editorial function, regarded as the heart of publishing, includes the acquisition, evaluation and editing of manuscripts.

While editing is intended to make the content readable, designing is aimed at making the book attractive.

The production department executes the design. It buys typesetting, paper, printing and binding according to the designer's specifications. It tries to maintain an orderly flow of work, according to schedule, set quality standards, and keep costs down.

The job of the marketing department is to get the books to the readers. It must know who are the readers and how they can be reached. Most books are marketed through wholesalers, bookstores, libraries and schools. Only a few books are sold by the publisher directly to the reader.

The accounting department helps allocate funds. It processess orders and controls credits. It analyzes and evaluates the costs of operation, keeps records, makes financial forecasts, prepares payrolls, and pays suppliers and printers.

The publisher is the over-all manager of the enterprise. He coordinates and makes decisions. When the publisher owns the company, as is frequently the case in the Philippines, his personal style, views and preferences are strongly reflected in the publishing philosophy, policy and direction. The university presses and government publishing agencies are exceptions to this rule. Agencies are guided mainly by public charters and university presses by institutional objectives.

In spite of the perennial complaints of publishers about bad times and the unfavorable conditions they operate in, book publishing remains a stable industry. It shows signs of continuing growth rather than of decay. More investors are venturing into publishing than are getting out.

Publishers constantly compete in recruiting talented fresh graduates of communication, journalism, literature, and the graphic arts. They pirate from each other experienced staff members. Piracy shows the paucity of expertise and of the need for specialized training. Top editors, designers, production specialists, and marketing managers are increasingly becoming mobile, freely moving from one publishing house to another.

Considering the on-going government programs to promote early interest in reading, there is every reason to feel sanguine about book publishing in the Philippines. Books will continue to be the most efficient, most convenient and the cheapest medium for instruction, communication and for conserving the national culture.

References

Aprieto, P.N. *Book Publishing and Philippine Scholarship*, Manila, Daily Star Publishing Company, 1981.
"The Philippine Textbook Project." Paris.
Prospects (UNESCO Quarterly Review of Education), 1983.
The Philippine Book Industry, Quezon City, Book Development Association of the Philippines, 1981.

Chapter XII

Komiks in the Philippines

Noel Bejo

Among the reading materials which have gained quite a numerous following in the Philippines are, aside from the daily papers, the *komiks* magazines or simply *komiks*. *Komiks*, an adaptation of the English term comic (or comics) as in comic strips and comic books, are phenomenally successful and widely popular in this country. Virtually every newspaper and magazine stand in the country is filled with *komiks* of all sizes and hues. And the "managers" of these outlets say that the *komiks* sell faster than any other periodical, local or foreign.[1]

Only some of the aspects of *komiks* are taken up here. The whole of the comic medium or comic art, which includes cartoons and comic strips,[2] is not taken up.

I. GENERAL HISTORY OF *KOMIKS* IN THE PHILIPPINES

It can be said, perhaps, that the introduction of the so-called "flying sheets" also marked the beginning of comics. But even earlier, comics, an American term used in the twentieth century to cover all forms of narrative sequence in pictures, usually with accompanying captions or dialogue enclosed in "balloons," can be traced back to the pictorial narrative of the Paleolithic era. That is, at least, what an author claims and this makes comics or pictorial narrative nearly as old as man.[3]

A. The Informal Beginning

The origin and development of *komiks* in the Philippines are no different from those in other countries, notably in the United States, where the comic books are not only considerably successful, but also a matter of controversy and debates.[4] There was first the appearance of cartoons, cartoon strips followed by continuous and serialized comic strips and, finally, the comic books or the komiks magazines.[5]

Dr. Jose Rizal is presumed to have been the first Filipino to draw cartoon strips that saw publication.[6] Other Filipinos during Rizal's time might have drawn cartoons for several comic periodicals published in Manila, among them *La Semana Elegante* (1884), *La Puya* (1885), *Manila Alegre* (1885) and *Manililla* (1887), and *Miau* and *Te Kon* in the nineties. It is then safer to say that Rizal was among the first Filipino cartoonists. Rizal transformed the fable, "The Monkey and the Tortoise," into a cartoon strip that was published in Truebner's Record (London) in July 1889.[7]

In the early 1900's, two politically-oriented magazines, the *Telembang* (corruption of *Kampana* for bell) and the *Lipang Kalabaw*, featured cartoons dealing mostly with the political figures of the era. (It has to be noted that editorial and political cartoons are still very much in vogue today.) These cartoons are considered the forerunners of present day *komiks*.

B. The Formal History[8]

It was Antonio S. Velasquez, regarded as "Father of Filipino Komiks," who in 1926 first saw the potentials and possibilities of the illustrated medium. He was with the Banaag Press until Ramon Roces, the publisher of *Liwayway* magazine,[9] bought the photo-engraving department. He retained all its resident artists and photo-engravers. Velasquez, in cooperation with Romualdo Ramos as scriptwriter, illustrated the cartoon character named Kenkoy. Kenkoy (nickname of Francisco; Iko or Kiko or Kikoy would have been too common) appeared for the first time in the January 11, 1929 *Liwayway* issue. What started as a single strip of black and white became within a year one whole page of comic strip in four colors. "Kenkoy," the funny and lovable guy, was clothed with the very human aspiration to succeed. He portrayed all the verities of life during the Commonwealth years, and became the very first cartoon strip to appear as a series in local *komiks*. "Kenkoy" was later translated into four other dialects: Ilocano in Northern Luzon, Hiligaynon and Bisaya in the South, and Bikolnon in the Bicol Region. The Ramos-Velasquez tandem produced yet another character named "Ponyang Halobaybay," a lady. The demise of Ramos left Velasquez to single-handedly continue "Kenkoy."

The Second World War saw *Liwayway* run by the Japanese. The Japanese Information Bureau utilized "Kenkoy" for its health drive throughout the country. In postwar 1945, Velasquez continued "Kenkoy" and "Ponyang Halobaybay" for *Liwayway*.

The arrival of the Americans with their comic books, which featured the creative combination of novel, painting and movie, hastened the development of the local *komiks* in a certain sense. The first Filipino *komiks* book named *Halakhak* (Laughter) came out to cheer the Filipinos up after the devastating war. *Halakhak* lasted for only ten issues.

C. Publishing Houses and Their Publications

On May 27, 1947, Don Ramon Roces, together with Tony Velasquez, organized Ace Publications, producing the progenitors of the present day *komiks*. Priced at 25 centavos, *Pilipino Komiks* hit the streets fortnightly starting June 14, 1947. From an initial 10,000 copies sold, circulation reached 120,000 copies in 1961. In 1949, *Tagalog Klasiks* came out. It was followed by *Hiwaga Komiks* in 1950, and the *Espesyal Komiks* in 1952. A pocket-sized *Kenkoy Komiks* joined the group also in 1952. The short-lived *Bisaya Komiks* also came out in the fifties.

The year 1950 saw also the publication of *Extra Komiks*, the fourth *komiks* magazine in the Philippines. Eriberto A. Tablan was its manager-editor and Ramon R. Marcelino was associate. It was published by Extra Komiks Publications. It was later sold to the Philippine Book Company, which also came out with a sister publication, *Romansa Komiks*.

The Graphic Arts Service, Inc., a sister company of Ace Publications under Damian Velasquez, was formed in 1959. What came out from this company was an impressive array of *komiks* magazines which are household names by now: *Kislap Komiks*, now a leading movie magazine, and *Pioneer Komiks* in 1959, *Aliwan Komiks*, *Pinoy Komiks* and *Pinoy Klasiks* in 1963, *Holiday Komiks*, and *Teens Weekly Komiks* in 1969. Later, *Lovelife Komiks*, *Precious Komiks* and *Silangan Komiks* were introduced in 1976. In 1982, Graphic Arts published *Damdamin Komiks*, *Nobela Klasiks* and *Kuwento Komiks*. It also published *Movie Flash* and *Sports Flash*. With its impressive showing, the company was asked in 1978 by Affiliated Publications, Inc. to manage and operate its company.

The Affiliated Publications was the first company to name *komiks* after movie stars. The military censors during the martial law period (1972-1980), however, frowned on personality cults, forcing the company to change its *komiks* titles. The Affiliated Publications included the *Superstar Komiks* (formerly called *The Nora Aunor Entertainment Magazine*), *Topstar Komiks* (formerly known as *The Pip Entertainment Magazine*), *Movie Idol Entertainment Magazine* which folded up, *Pilipino Reporter* which evolved from a tabloid-sized news magazine, *United Komiks* and *Universal Komiks*. *United* and *Universal*, together with *Kidlat Komiks* and *Continental Komiks* were published by Pablo S. Gomez Publishing House until Affiliated bought them in 1973, the time of an economic crunch.

The G. Miranda & Sons Publishing Corp. and its sister company, Mapalad Publications Corp., had the *Lagim Komiks* (later changed to

L'Amour), *Diamante Komiks, Sweetheart Komiks, Wakasan Komiks, Heart-Throbs Komiks* and *Sampaguita Komiks*.[10] *Wakasan Komiks* is still being published. The defunct Bulaklak Publications gave birth to *Manila Klasiks* and *Bulaklak Express*. A printing company, Soller Press, put up a publishing arm and came out with the *Wow Komiks* and *Romantic Klasiks*. The defunct Gold Star Publishing House had the *Dalisay Komiks, Kampeon Komiks, Teen World* and *18 Magazine* by RAR Publishing House. The company acquired the right to publish the *Bulaklak* from the Bulaklak Publications and renamed it *Bulaklak at Paru-paro*. RAR closed shop in 1983.

Ace Publications also folded up in the early sixties. In its place, the Pilipino Komiks, Inc. was set up in 1964 and the *Pilipino Komiks* was revived. *Pilipino's* sister publications, *Espesyal, Hiwaga, Tagalog* and *TSS* (formerly known as *Teenagers Songs and Shows* and renamed *Top Special Stories*), came out in succession. To avoid confusing the corporate name, Pilipino Komiks, Inc., and with the *Komiks* magazine name, the corporation was renamed Atlas Publishing Co., Inc. The name Atlas, a mythological hero, underscores the role of myth in the *Komiks* industry. The company later added *Darna Komiks* in 1969, *Kidlat Komiks* in 1974, *Extra Special Komiks* in 1976 and *King Komiks* in 1981.

In 1968, Marcelino resigned from Graphic Arts and organized the new Ace Publications. Ace put out *Bondying Komeex* and *Kiss Komeex* in the same year, *Bondying Komeex* later became *Bondying Movie Specials Weekly*. *Pogi Komiks*, which was bought as a magazine from the Pilipino Komiks, Inc., and *Hapi-Hapi Komiks*, which was later changed into *Happy Komiks*, were also added.

In 1971, Damian Velasquez organized Adventures Illustrated Magazines, Inc. It published *Adventure Komiks, Voodoo Komiks* and *Love Story Illustrated Weekly Magazine*. The first two folded up after several issues while the third one continues publication.

In 1978, Islas Filipinas Publishing Co., Inc. published *Pilipino Funny Komiks for Children*. In the same year, Rex Printing Co., Inc., the sister-firm of Rex Book Store chain, which publishes textbooks and other educational books, found a remedy to the slack after the "textbook season." The remedy was the forming of Rex Publications, Inc., a *komiks* outfit. The company immediately put out *Rex Komiks, Astro Komiks, Marvel Komiks* and *Gem Komiks; Tapusan Komiks* was added in 1979. Two years later, *Pag-ibig Komiks, Relax Komiks, Luv Komiks, Honey Komiks*, and *Darling Komiks* were also put out. The Rex group of *komiks* has become one of the largest groupings of *komiks* published in the Philippines.

D. The Present Scene and Future Prospects

The *komiks* industry is thriving. More *komiks* are being published. A new publishing outfit, the Artmark Publishing Corporation, made its debut in December 1985 with the publication of *Pilya Komiks* and *K'wela Komiks Magasin*. The old publishing companies are still adding more titles to their list. Atlas put out *Kasaysayan, Love-Drama* and *Bwisheart Komiks* magazines in 1984, and *Attack Power Komiks* in 1986. Rex has just added *Tisay Komiks* and *First Love Komiks*. Graphic Arts has just introduced *Commando Komiks* and *Shogun Komiks* in the same year.

Pocketkomiks are also increasing their share of the market. The Graphic Arts has *Speed Pocketkomiks*. Atlas boasts of *Bestseller Pocketkomiks, Starlord Pocketkomiks, Mighty Viking Pocketkomiks* and *Kasaysayan Pocketkomiks*. The Rex group of *komiks* has *Combat* and *Bulilit Pocketkomiks*. The Adventure Illustrated Magazine, Inc. has published *Pilipino Superheroes Pocketkomiks* and *Commando Pocketkomiks*. The Mass Media Promotion, Inc. produces the *Crimebuster Pocketkomiks* and *Western Pocketkomiks*.

The illustrated medium has also been rather misused. Some *komiks* are pornographic. They date back to the permissive sixties when pornographic *komiks* known as "bomba" *komiks* proliferated. Published by fly-by-night operators, *komiks* such as *Toro, Bikini* and *Sex-see*, served to satisfy the public's clamor for graphic sex in the *komiks*. A crackdown on mass media during the martial law years put a temporary end to their publication.[11] But these *komiks*, labeled "for adults only" are again being sold. They include *Playmate, Sakdal Sexy, Sakdal Bold, Sakdal Erotik, Macho* and *Tiktik* published by Sagalongos Publications[12]; and *For Gents Only* by R.G. Publication. Others like *For Adults Only* and *He & She* do not contain publication data.[13]

Perhaps the history of *komiks* in the Philippines can best be summarized by giving two lists of *komiks* magazines: composed of *komiks* of the sixties and the other of *komiks* of the present.[14]

II. THE CONTENT OF THE KOMIKS MAGAZINES

The *komiks* magazine explores immensely diverse topics and subjects in popular form. It is popular literature that makes use of the materials of serious literature. Proteus-like, this magazine type has demonstrated its uncanny ability to transform itself and manifest the complex mixture of folk and popular culture that shapes and structures it.[15] Let us now try to delineate the content of this magazine type.

A. The "Literary" Content: *Nobelas* and *Wakasan*

The "literary" content occupies the greatest number of pages. These *komiks* have an average of 34 pages per issue. There are two "literary" types. The first one is the so-called *wakasan* stories (short stories). *Wakasan* is usually restricted to a few pages of the entire *komiks* book. The second is the so-called *nobelas* (novels) or the serials.[16] The serials can last for months or even years. For example, the "Anak ni Zuma," a story culled from Aztec mythology, in *Aliwan Komiks*, is the longest running serial in *komiks* history. It is already in its ninth year of serialization.[17]

It has become an editorial policy that each *komiks* magazine should contain at least one established or potential supernovel to serve as its hallmark. Many times the magazine itself is also identified with its popular running serial.

There are *komiks* magazines which publish short stories only. Notable among these magazines are *Wakasan Komiks, Tapusan Komiks, Lovelife Komiks* and *Kuwento Komiks*. A *komiks* magazine may also run several serials at the same time. Except for those magazines publishing *wakasan* stories only, both *wakasan* and *nobelas* are the usual fare. For instance, a *komiks* magazine may have three serials and four or five *wakasan* stories. The number of *nobelas* and *wakasan* stories varies among the *komiks* magazines.

B. The Literary Content: Topics and Subjects

The "literary content" of *komiks* may be broadly classified. First, there is the fantasy story. The fantasy story usually calls for the presence and the use of magic and creatures from other worlds. Drawing heavily from mythology and fairy tales, the pages of fantasy teem with talking horses, roosters, birds and dolphins and an array of mythic creatures like satyrs, half-men and half-horses, half-spiders and so on. Usually, the hero is a victim of life's cruel jokes or society's scorn. He is given magical powers in the form of a magic stick or a golden gun or a magic piggy bank or some other object.[18]

The mystery genre as exemplified by the stories of *Hiwaga Komiks* comprises another group. In this bracket, the uncommon and the unreal abound.

The romance story, in which the opposition of good and evil is a basic feature, takes a large chunk of the *komiks* stories. The elements of love and drama can be put under this heading. A certain lightheartedness pervades the romance stories. In the end, however, these stories affirm life's goodness in the end. Even in the stories filled with the dark side of life the ending is that the dark forces will be annihilated eventually by the forces of light.[19]

The adventure stories can be considered another type. A willing disbelief is asked of the reader as he follows the exciting adventures of local Filipino sports heroes — world champions all — in basketball, boxing, chess and even bull-fighting.

An attempt at realism takes place in stories which include the biography of historical figures or the description of real life events. Contributions from the readers concerning their life experiences are also published. Many of these contributions take the theme of love and marriage and family-related realities.

It has to be observed, however, that a story cannot clearly be described as exclusively a fantasy or romance or adventure or mystery or realism. More often than not, a mixture of these types pervades the stories.

Hence, *Espesyal Komiks,* for example, has action-adventure-fantasy stories. The *Love Story Illustrated Magazine* has love-drama-action stories.[20] *Nobela Klasiks* and *Damdamin Komiks* specialize in love-drama content. It is also interesting to note that *komiks* titles can give an inkling of their content. *Tagalog Klasiks,* for example, features Tagalog translations of world classics.

Given those types of stories, it is not surprising to find an array of traditional and modern myths and legends (both indigenous and foreign), exploration of historical experiences, and accounts based on pseudo-scientific knowledge and mind-boggling excursions into the occult in these *komiks'* pages. Contemporary issues and events are also among the widely diverse *komiks* topics.[21]

The *nobelas* and the *wakasan* stories can also be classified as vernacular author, Mario S. Cabiling, puts it into the following: (1) *pag-ibig;* (2) *drama;* (3) *katatawanan;* (4) *aksiyon* o *pakikipagsapalaran;* (5) *katatakutan;* (6) *kabalaghan;* and (7) *sex.*[22] The last one, together with violence, has become quite common.

C. The Miscellaneous Content

Some *komiks* magazines publish household tips items on homecraft, health and cleanliness, and spiritual advice. Movie columns in the style of Hollywood's Hedda Hopper and Louella Parsons were first introduced by Atlas Publishing Co., Inc.[23] Later, the other magazines took up the idea and used it to boost their circulation. Atlas itself did away with this feature and introduced a raffle. Winners were awarded scholarships for vocational courses. Now and then, *komiks* magazines feature biographical sketches, accounts of delightful events, views on current issues, a pen pal section, crossword puzzles, and cartoons. They also publish educational materials. The *komiks* noteworthy in this regard is the *Pilipino Funny Komiks Magazine for Children.* It provides English vocabulary and general information. It has also reserved space for children's contributions of drawings and sketches. Advertisements are included now and then and many times they are presented in comics form.

III. THE USES OF THE KOMIKS MAGAZINE

It is generally thought that the lowly *komiks* belong to the low income Filipinos who do not have much buying power or influence in the running of society.[24] They barely have enough money to meet the basic needs of the whole family. Thus, they get leisure at the least expenses, and the *komiks* is one such leisure.[25]

The very first use of *komiks,* then, is entertainment. They provide visual entertainment. Their appeal lies in the simple, clear and funny drawings. Their language appeal lies in the authentic slice of life they reflect —

current issues, public affairs, social customs, fashion, sports events, personalities, behavior. Their overall impact lies in their human appeal.[26] The entertainment aspect appeals also to the Filipino's imagination, to his emotions and to his fondness for laughter.[27] Compared with other forms of entertainment, *komiks* is the least costly and the most available. A single copy is priced at P2.25 or less. It can be rented out at 50 centavos at rental stalls. Compared to *komiks* cover price, a movie costs P8.00 or more. Besides, *komiks* can be kept and reread at one's convenience. *Komiks* enable even the semiliterate to grasp the essence of the stories.[28]

Quite a number of *komiks* serials have been adapted for the movies, another entertainment medium. The film adaptation, according to Isagani Cruz, are "presold."[29] Unfortunately, such adaptations are not very successful. Cruz says that "*komiks* is a medium that has, in a hundred of films, proven to be unadaptable to the silver screen."[30] Just the same, such adaptations are intended to provide entertainment.

Secondly, the *komiks* magazines have become an effective source of information. Being informative, they have also an educational value. In fact, the government, especially during the martial law years, made use of *komiks* for disseminating information on government projects, social amelioration, tips on health care, family planning, child care and nutrition. The Ministry of Labor, Social Security System, Population Commission, Nutrition and the Ministry of Agrarian Reform were some of the government agencies which made extensive use of *komiks*.[31]

The use of *komiks* as "information disseminator" was evident during the 1986 presidential election. During the campaign, *komiks* magazines about Ferdinand Marcos and Cory Aquino did the talking. Their educational function was made use of by the Communication Foundation for Asia, when it published "The Decision, The Will of the People," under its "Civic Education Program" for the 1986 election in *komiks* form. *Komiks* have also been utilized for propaganda.[32]

In addition, *komiks* have become a medium for promoting the national language. The *komiks*, being written in Tagalog, give non-Tagalog readers free lessons in Tagalog.[33] In short, the *komiks* also have a linguistic value.[34]

IV. THE KOMIKS AND THEIR DISTRIBUTION

Komiks occupy a distinct place in most Filipino homes. They have reached people in the slums and the suburbs. Although they cater mainly to adults, they are at the same time attractive to the young.

Around 2.5 million *komiks* are said to be sold every week. Now, if a single copy of *komiks* is passed to four other readers, then roughly 12.5 million Filipinos read *komiks* every week.[35] The Audit Council for Media reported that for 1977-78, the audited circulation of the best selling *komiks* were as follows:

Komiks	Circulation
Pilipino komiks	144,616
Aliwan komiks	139,755
Tagalog Klasiks	134,275
Hiwaga Komiks	129,372
Espesyal Komiks	109,814
Superstar Komiks	108,260
Love Story Illustrated Weekly Magazine	106,273
Darna Komiks	103,076
Bondying Movie Special	97,061
Pinoy Komiks	71,952
Pinoy Klasiks	71,236
TSS Komiks	69,411
Pioneer Komiks	60,495
Holiday Komiks	55,274
Hapi-Hapi Komiks	51,051
Lovelife Komiks	48,144
Teens Weekly	44,246
Topstar Komiks	41,322
Kidlat Superkomix	39,564
Silangan Komiks	34,243
United Superstories	26,195
Universal Komiks	24,655
Pilipino Reporter	26,873
Precious Komiks	26,880[36]

Obviously, when the circulation of the unaudited *komiks* is added on, the over-all circulation is so large that it is something to reckon with.

Komiks are usually sold through newspaper and magazine stands. They are sold along with their publishers' other publications. For example, the Graphic Arts' *Movie Flash* and *Sports Flash* provide a pick-up point for *komiks* to all retailers. A delivery car brings the publications to a designated area and from there all outlet "managers" get their share.

V. THE KOMIKS AND THE CHURCH

The *komiks* has been utilized in Church work. The Communication Foundation for Asia publishes the *Gospel Komiks* monthly to bring the Gospel message to people. *Gospel Komiks* started in 1980 with 50,000 copies to provide points for discussion for lay leaders and community workers. In

1982, it was adapted for school use, and circulation rose to 80,000. *Gospel*'s circulation is now 300,000 copies, of which 50,000 copies are in Cebuano (Bisaya) and the rest in English and Pilipino. It is distributed mainly by Catholic schools and the parishes.

The Society of St. Paul also features *komiks* in *The Youngster*, a monthly magazine for the youth.[37]

One positive step undertaken by the Archdiocese of Manila is the inclusion of *komiks* in the Catholic Mass Media Awards.[38] This raises the status of *komiks* among mass media. The award is given to the "Best Comics Story."[39]

CONCLUSION

Among the print media, *komiks* is perhaps the only true mass medium in the Philippines -- with an estimated 12 5 million readers a week.

Like movies, however, it is mainly an entertainment medium that caters to the taste of the masses. There is a need to improve the quality of these *komiks* if they are to perform a useful role in Philippine society. Perhaps there is a need for more mass communication graduates to go into this field.

FOOTNOTES

[1] Gloria D. Feliciano and Crispulo J. Icban, Jr., *Philippine Mass Media in Perspective* (Quezon City: Capitol Publishing House, Inc., 1967), p. 32.

[2] It goes without saying that the comic medium is also much used in the Philippines. Cartoons and comic strips appear regularly in daily and weekly publications. Foremost among the cartoonists are Larry Alcala and Roni Santiago. See "Cartoonists are Born, Not Made," *Life Today* 42/3 (March 1986): 21-23.

[3] *The Encyclopedia Americana*, 1964, ed., s.v. "Comics," by Marya Mannes.

[4] The major personage in this respect is Dr. Frederick Wertham, a noted New York psychiatrist, with his work, *Seduction of the Innocent* published in 1954. See "Seduction of the Innocent: The Great Comic Book Scare," *Milestones in Mass Communication Research: Media Effects*, ed. Gordon T.R. Anderson and Ferne Y. Kawahara (New York, N.Y.: Longman Inc., 1983), pp. 233-266.

[5] For more information on the beginning of the comic medium under the pioneering works of James Swinnerton ("Little Bears"), Richard Felton Outcault ("Yellow Kid"), and Rudolph Dirks ("Katzenjammer Kids") and the subsequent development, see *The Encyclopedia Americana*. Some other authors trace a much earlier beginning of comics singling out William Hogarth (1697-1764), an English engraver, and Thomas Rowlandson (1757-1827), an English cartoonist, as the ones who took the initiative. See James Watson and Annie Hill, *A Dictionary of Communication and Media Studies* (London: Edward Arnold Ltd., 1984), p. 40; Cynthia Roxas and Joaquin Arevalo, Jr., *A History of Komiks of the Philippines and Other Countries*, ed. Ramon R. Marcelino (Quezon City: Islas Filipinas Publishing Co., Inc., 1985), 266-288; Ely Matawaran, "Cartoons Through the Years," *Life Today* 42/3 (March 1986):21-23; and Anderson, pp. 235-236. There is also an interesting work underscoring a thousand years of comic tradition in Japan. See Frederick Schodt, *Manga! Manga! The World of Japanese Comics* (Tokyo: Kondansha, 1983).

[6] Roxas, op. cit., p. 4.

[7] Fidel Villaroel, "Jose Rizal: First Filipino Cartoonist?" *Life Today* 42/3 (March 1986): 16. See also Feliciano, pp. 24-25.

[8] Villaroel, p. 17, writes that this more important cartoon work of Rizal "was drawn in 1885 when Rizal was in Paris, in the company of fellow physicians Trinidad and Felix Pardo de Tavera and of the two great Filipino painters Juan Luna and Felix Resurreccion Hidalgo. In a visit to the home of the Tavera brothers, their sister Paz presented to Rizal a personal album with some pages still blank, and she requested Rizal to do her the honor of drawing something. He obliged by drawing the story of the *Monkey and the Tortoise*, a Tagalog folktale he must have learned as a child in Calamba. The cartoon consists of 34 scenes - with narrative in Rizal's handwriting — telling the story of a monkey and a tortoise dividing a banana tree between themselves. The tortoise was the luckier with its part which produced bananas, but the astute monkey cheated the tortoise and ate all the bananas. In the end the tortoise avenged itself by cheating the monkey." For a reproduction of the cartoons, see Roxas, pp. 5-10.

[9] Unless stated otherwise, the main source for the rest of the history of *komiks* in the Philippines is the work of Roxas and Arevalo.

[10] It has to be noted that this vernacular weekly which has already become a household name is still existing. Published by Liwayway Publishing Inc., the same publisher of *Balita, Bannawag, Bisaya* and *PM News in Action*, *Liwayway* is considered as the only vernacular magazine that resembles serious literature. Aside from the *komiks* section (all of them are serialized novels and they occupy just a few pages), this 53-page magazine in the size of *Time* and *Newsweek* contains short stories and serialized novels, movie columns and human interest features written in Pilipino.

[11] The *Lagim Komiks* by GMS Publishing Corp. and *Sweetheart Komiks* by Mapalad Publications Corp. are still existing and can still be seen in newspaper and magazine stands. But they are now in pocket size only.

[12] Roxas, op cit., p. 50.

[13] An article in *The Bulletin Today* (29 January 1986), 1, entitled "2 Acquitted of Obscenity" cleared the publishers of *Tiktik Ngayon* of the charge of obscene publication.

[14] These reading materials contain almost all "short stories" and hardly a serial is included. Some of the stories included in the publication contain no pornographic pictures or language whatsoever. But a story of pornographic character is a usual fare to attract buyers and readers. The more daring publications feature more sensual coloration and pictures of foreign women in the nude or in state of undress to grace the pages.

[15] Here is a list of *komiks* magazines published in Greater Manila as of 30 June 1965, taken from Feliciano, pp. 305-325.

Alcala Fight Komix Magasin	Paraluman Komiks Magasin
Aliwan Komiks Magasin	Phantom Komiks Magasin
Barangay Komiks Magasin	Pilipino Komiks Magasin
Binggo Komiks Magasin	Pinoy Komiks Magasin
Dalisay Komiks Magasin	Pinoy Klasiks
Diamante Komiks Magasin	Pioneer Klasiks Magasin
Ditektib Komiks Magasin	Redondo Klasiks Magasin
Espesyal Komiks Magasin	Romansa Extra Komiks Magasin
Fantasia Komiks Magasin	Sampaguita Komiks Magasin
Fiesta Komiks Magasin	Sindak Komiks Magasin
Filipiniana Komiks Magasin	Sinderella Komiks Magasin
Filipino Movie Komiks Magasin	Superyor Komiks Magasin
Hiwaga Komiks Magasin	Suspense Komiks Magasin
Holiday Komiks Magasin	Tagalog Klasiks Komiks
Kislap Komiks Magasin	Teen-age Komiks Magasin
Karnabal Klasiks Komiks	Tru-Ghost Komiks Magasin
Horror Komiks Magasin	Tru-Life Komiks Magasin
Kulafu Komiks Magasin	Tru-Love Komiks Magasin
Lagim Komiks	United Komiks Magasin
Ligaya Komiks Magasin	Universal Komiks Magasin
Lola Basyang Komiks Magasin	Vida Komiks Magasin
Maharlika Komiks Magasin	Vista Komiks Magasin
Majestic Komiks Magasin	Wakasan Komiks Magasin
Makabayan Komiks Magasin	Waling-Waling Komiks Magasin
Pag-ibig Komiks Magasin	Walt Disney Espesyal Komiks

All of the magazines above are written in the vernacular (Pilipino) except for *Karnabal Komiks* which was in English and Tagalog, and all of them were published weekly except for the monthly *Barangay*.

[16] Soledad Reyes, "Romance and Realism in the Komiks," in *A History of Komiks of the Philippines and Other Countries*, p. 48.

[17] Karina Constantino-David, "The Changing Images of Heroes in Local Comic Books," *Philippine Journal of Communication Studies* (4 September 1974): 1.

[18] Roxas, op. cit., p. 39.

[19] Reyes, op. cit., p. 51.

[20] Ibid.

[21] Love is still a very appealing theme for the *komiks*. An author even says that many of these magazines are devoted to the proposition that love is still one of the most saleable items. Reyes, p. 48. See also Pio C. Estepa, "The Myth of Love According to the Filipino Komiks," *DIWA* (3 October 1978): 86-96.

[22] Reyes, p. 47.

[23] *May Sining, Tagumpay, at Salapi sa Pagsusulat ng Komiks* (Manila: Liwayway Publishing, Inc., 1972), p. 23. The classification can be translated as follows: love, drama, humor/comedy, action/adventure, horror, mystery and sex.

[24] Roxas, op. cit., pp. 31-32.

[25] Vicente S. Froilan, *Manual in Media Education* (Manila: Communication Foundation for Asia, 1985), p. 44.

[26] Roxas, op. cit., p. 3.

[27] Wilhelmina B. Amansec, "Comics: A Potential Diversion in the Classrooms," *Life Today* 42/3 (March 1968): 18.

[28] See Karolyn Molina, "Filipino Humor: For All Seasons and Reasons," *Life Today* 42/3 (March 1986): 18.

[29] Constantino-David, op. cit., p. 1.

[30] Isagani R. Cruz, *Movie Times* (Manila: National Bookstore, Inc., 1984), p. 77.

[31] Ibid., p. 82.

[32] "2M Comic Magazine Readers," *Philippines Today* 1 (January 7, 1978): 48.

[33] Schodt, **pp. 56ff.**

[34] The bulk of the *komiks* magazines published in the Philippines are in Tagalog or Pilipino.

[35] Amansec, op. cit., p. 19.

[36] Froilan, op. cit., p. 44.

[37] Compared with all the titles enumerated earlier, the audited number of publications is much lower. There is no doubt, however, which are the leaders and which are the most popular and easily sold *komiks* magazines. The information given by the Audit Council for Media confirms what the author heard from the "managers" of the newspaper and magazine stands.

[38] Actually, *The Youngster* is more of a religious magazine for the youth than anything else. Its use of *komiks* is minimal as it is limited to some three or four *wakasan* stories. It has more write-ups on Christian topics and other human interest themes.

[39] The Catholic Mass Media Awards are given annually by the Archdiocese of Manila in observance of World Social Communications Day and in response to Pope John Paul II's message to media practitioners during his visit to the Philippines in February 1981. Here is an excerpt of that message: "I would ask you always to be keenly aware of your responsibility. The image you film, the sounds you record, the programs you broadcast, cross every barrier of time and space... what people see and hear in your transmissions and commentaries heavily influences the way they think and act." First given in 1978, the awards are conferred to honor outstanding men and women, and their productions, in the field of advertising, television, press and film. They pay tribute "to their trade, to their industry, to their service to the people."

The awards are decided by a body of jurors chosen by the Archbishop of Manila, Jaime Cardinal Sin, for their competence, impartiality and integrity. The judges, aside from the great number from the practitioners in the field of mass communication, include academicians, priests, sisters and civic leaders. The selection of winners is based on broad norms: the entry must be a local production; produced and/or exhibited in the Archdiocese of Manila at any time during the year in consideration; presenting what is true, beautiful and good; and in a way that will promote the total human development of the receiver. And since the awards deal with mass media as a means for total human development, the awards body has stressed that the winning production need not be Catholic and the awardee need not be Christian. The decision of the body is based solely on the merits of the entries. See the introduction of the program of yearly awarding ceremonies.

Here is a list of the "Best Comics Story" award from the year of CMMA's inception until 1985: 1978 - "Mga Kuwentong Bayan" *(Silangan Komiks)* by Jose Lad Santos; 1979 - "Santiago" *(Silangan Komiks)* by Jose Lad Santos (for a continuing series by the same author), "Pepeng Kulisap" *(Holiday Komiks)* by Sergio Peñaflor (for short stories by occasional authors), "Paninindigan" *(Kayumanggi Komiks)* by Sergio Peñaflor (novel); 1980 - "Isang Impit na Hiyaw sa Sinapupunan" *(Rex Komiks)* by Flor A. Olazo; 1981 - "Isang Ama na Dadakilain" *(Love Time Komiks)* by Rene Villaroman; 1982 - "Kung Tawagin Siya'y Baliw" *(Holiday Komiks)* by Pablo Reyna Libiran; 1983 - "Si Mang Miguel, Nag-iisa" *(Kuwento Komiks)* by J. Pepito Marquez; 1984 - "Tatay ko si Mang Perfecto" *(Silangan Komiks)* by Andy C. Beltran; 1985 - "Ang Higit na Mapalad," *(Extra Special Komiks)* by Nina Enriquez (Ofelia Concepcion).

A LIST OF COMMONLY-SOLD KOMIKS
(As of February 1986)

NAME OF KOMIKS/ PUBLICATION	PUBLISHER	FREQUENCY OF PUBLICATION	SELLING PRICE
Pilipino Komiks Magasin	Atlas Publication Co., Inc.	Bi-weekly	P2.25
Hiwaga Komiks Magasin		Bi-weekly	P2.25
Extra Komiks Magasin			P2.25
Tagalog Klasiks		Weekly	P2.25
TSS Komiks Magasin		Weekly	P2.25
Espesyal Komiks Magasin			P2.25
Darna Komiks Magasin			P2.25
King Komiks Magasin			P2.25
Attack Komiks Magasin			P2.25
Bestseller Pocketkomiks			P1.50
Starlord			P1.50
Mighty Viking Pocketkomiks			P1.50
Kasaysayan Pocketkomiks			P1.50
Aliwan Komiks Magasin	Graphic Arts Service Inc.	Bi-weekly	P2.25
Lovelife Komiks Magasin			P2.25
Pioneer Komiks Magasin		Weekly	P2.25
Pinoy Komiks Magasin			P2.25
Weekly Komiks Magasin			P2.25
Silangan Komiks Magasin			P2.25
Holiday Komiks Magasin			P2.25
Kuwento Komiks Magasin			P2.25
Pinoy Klasiks			P2.25

Precious Klasiks Magasin			P2.25
Speed Pocketkomiks			P1.50
Universal Komiks Magasin	Affiliated Publications	Bi-weekly	P2.25
United Superstories		Weekly	P2.25
Pilipino Reporter Komiks			P2.25
Superstar Komiks Magasin			P2.25
Topstar Komiks Magasin			P2.25
Wakasan Komiks Magasin	Mapalad Publishing Corp.		P2.25
Love Story Illustrated Weekly Magazine	Adventures Illustrated Magazines, Inc.		P2.25
Rex Komiks Magasin	Rex Publications, Inc.		P2.25
Luv Komiks Magasin			P2.25
Astro Komiks Magasin			P2.25
Marvel Komiks Magasin			P2.25
Gem Komiks Magasin			P2.25
Tapusan Magasin			P2.25
Combat Pocket Komiks			P1.50
Bulilit Pocket Komiks			P1.50
Happy Illustrated Komiks	Ace Publications, Inc.	Bi-weekly	P2.25
Pogi Komiks Magasin		Weekly	P2.25
Movie Special Komiks Magasin			P2.25
Pilipino Funny Komiks Magasin	Islas Filipinas Pub.		P2.25
Crimebusters Pocketkomiks	Mass Media Promotion, Inc.		P1.50
Western Pocketkomiks			P1.50
Gospel Komiks	Communication Foundation for Asia	Monthly	P2.50

For the purpose of comparison, we include these **"for adults only"** komiks.

Playmate	Sagalongos Publications	Weekly	P3.00
Sakdal Sexy			P3.00
Sakdal Bold			P3.00
Sakdal Erotik			P3.00
Macho			P3.00
Tiktik			P3.00
For Gents Only	R.G. Publications		P3.00
For Adults Only	Not given		P3.00
He & She	Not given		P3.00

Part Four

Electronic Media Today

This section deals with the newer of the mass media — the electronic media. While Chapter XIII introduces the communication student to the fundamentals of radio broadcasting, Chapter XIV goes into an in-depth analysis of the problems and issues confronting the broadcast industry today, and Chapter XV proposes one possible alternative: a public broadcasting system. Then Chapter XVI introduces the communication student to the basics of Filipino film before Chapter XVII analyzes the problems and prospects of the movie industry.

Chapter XIII

Fundamentals of Radio Broadcasting

Ernesto I. Songco

Radio broadcasting in the Philippines has not yet attained an image of its own nor a personality that is distinctly Filipino. In many respects it has not succeeded in shedding off its "American" personality, which dates back to its introduction by Americans during the early thirties.

RADIO BROADCASTING SYSTEM

Radio broadcasting in the Philippines operates on a system of free enterprise. The broadcast industry is therefore primarily in the hands of the private sector. Ninety percent of radio stations are operated by private enterprises. They compete with each other for audience listenership and advertising money.

Since programs are financed by advertising, they are largely determined by advertisers. Before World War II programming was entertainment-oriented. After the war, many programs were content-oriented, emphasizing information and education. This new direction in programming was given impetus during the martial law period when the Kapisanan ng mga Brodkaster sa Pilipinas (KBP) and the Broadcast Media Council (BMC) supported and encouraged development broadcasting.

The problem of linking together 7,100 islands, which comprise the country, through broadcasting is compounded by the diversity of languages spoken. About 87 different languages and dialects are spoken. The most widely used languages are English, Tagalog, Cebuano, Ilocano and Panay-Hiligaynon.

The system of broadcasting in the Philippines follows a pattern of regulation rather than direct control or operation by the government. In fact, this is the significant difference between the Philippine system and the systems in Southeast Asia and other countries. In Indonesia, Malaysia, Singapore and Thailand, radio broadcasting is operated and controlled by the state. A limited "commercial" operation has been reportedly sanctioned recently in Malaysia.

Before September 1972, the Radio Control Office regulated the industry. It was first renamed the Telecommunications Control Bureau, then the National Telecommunications Commission under the Ministry of Communication and Transportation. When President Ferdinand E. Marcos adopted a policy that provides that media must be run by the private sector, the government created another regulatory body, the Broadcast Media Council.[1]

The BMC, among others, was:

to assist and support the government in developing the masses, through the massive dissemination of broadcast information and development broadcasting.

The National Telecommunications Commission (NTC) is empowered to enforce local and international radio laws and regulations. It also regulates the establishment, uses and operations of all radio stations and all forms of radio communication, construction, manufacture, possession, ownership, transfer, purchase and sale of radio transmitters in the Philippines. It supervises and exercises control over private and government-owned radio stations as regards assignment of frequencies and call letters. It also issues licenses to deserving operators who have passed a government examination for radio-telephone operators.

The commission sends out regularly investigators to find out whether radio stations have violated any regulations. Four centrally-located radio monitoring districts are assigned to inspect and monitor radio stations, and to detect unregistered radio transmitters.

The BMC later formed the Performance Audit Team. Starting in October 1976, the teams travelled around the country to discuss with station managers the various guidelines and resolutions passed by BMC and KBP. Problems discovered in these visits are relayed to the central office in Metro Manila.

The most common violations committed by provincial stations are:
● Not preparing operation logs.
● Commercial materials longer than contracted length.
● Not meeting requirements for a station library.
● Not airing two 15-minute daily newscasts.

The team, after consulting the central office, warns and reprimands the violators.

The teams also extend much needed broadcasting advice and expertise to the provincial radio stations.

RADIO BROADCASTING OPERATIONS

Radio stations are operated by individuals, offices, or corporations. All operators must be Filipino citizens or corporations, cooperatives or associations wholly owned and managed by Filipino citizens.[3]

Before September 1972, Congress issued the permit to operate. When Congress was abolished, the Department of Public Information took over the function. Later, the BMC was empowered to grant permits. Now the NTC has such power.

The broadcast media operators are categorized into the commercial sector, the non-commercial sector, and the government sector.

The *commercial sector*--This group is composed of private corporations or associations, private schools or civic institutions or independent business entrepreneurs. Stations run by them are business- and profit-oriented.

The *non-commercial sector*--This group is made up of civic or religious organizations with specific target audiences for their programs.

The *government sector*--Under this group, the radio stations are operated either by a government department, agency, organization or by a state/public university, or academic institution. They are to provide public service, information, cultural and educational programs designed to motivate and reinforce development activities. They also disseminate information on government activities.

Organizational Set-up

The BMC, new defunct, had a prescribed organizational scheme for a single station.[4]

In this plan, the station manager, aside from overseeing the entire operation of the station, carries out all policies, goals and guidelines set up by the station's operators.

Working under the station manager are the program director, the sales director, the chief engineer, and the administrative officer.

The program director supervises the program content, format and production. Being in charge of production, he supervises the producer, announcers, the newswriters, scriptwriters, the talent and traffic man.

The sales director coordinates and supervises the salesmen.

Heading the technical department is the chief engineer who supervises the technicians in the transmitter and in the studio.

The administrative officer is responsible for the administrative, accounting, and library departments of the station. He also supervises utility and auxiliary services in the station.

Under these department heads are their respective staff personnel.

Operating Costs

Much of what the radio station can do to serve the public depends on its financial capability.

The Pre-Investment Study on Communication Technology for Education (1967-77) conducted by the Educational Development Projects Implementing Task Force (EDPITAF) showed that the average annual operating cost of a typical radio station in 1975 was P300,000.00.[5] The cost could easily have doubled in ten years, to P600,000 in 1985.

Salaries of employees and talents make up 50 percent of the annual operating costs. Studio maintenance and repair, rentals of studio space and facilities, and depreciation account for 33 percent of the annual expenses. And the remaining 9 percent is credited for expense account like advertising, taxes, license fees, office supplies and equipment, plus Social Security and Medicare premiums.

Because the financial capability of the station is barely enough to keep it afloat, it cannot afford to produce programs beneficial to the community.

This does not mean the industry is not serving the public interest and welfare. Many radio stations are financially solvent and can adequately venture into development broadcasting if they want to.

Revenue

Essential to radio advertising are airtime rates and the maximum commercial load. Basic airtime rates are updated from time to time. The maximum commercial load for every clock-hour for radio was set at 13 minutes. But commercial loading is actually 15 minutes in Metro Manila and 17 minutes outside it.[6]

While the economic picture of the broadcast industry seems to be hopeful, all is not well in the provinces where some radio stations are not earning enough.

A study made by Sycip, Gorres and Velayo for the then Department of Public Information claims that a primary problem, in most instances, is not due to market conditions but to the poor performance of individual stations. Because of their performance, they have difficulty getting advertising. The SGV study also took into consideration the fact that some radio stations are operating in poor areas.

Manpower in the Broadcast Industry

At the very core of the radio operations are individuals on whose performance the survival and growth of the broadcast industry depend.

That performance, even from the very beginning of radio broadcasting, has never been adequate. As keenly observed by veteran broadcaster Francisco "Koko" Trinidad: "... The training of most of the people engaged in the various phases of broadcasting has remained incomplete. It follows that the end results of their efforts will be wanting in something. That something will be quality."[7]

Radio broadcasting had expanded quite fast that small scale training of personnel could not cope with the rapid change.

FUNDAMENTALS OF RADIO BROADCASTING

But to the credit of the Filipino imagination, patience, and industry, radio made some modest contributions, in spite of the broadcasters' inadequate training.

This lack of competence among broadcasters is reflected in a manpower profile made by the Broadcast Media Council.[8]

Here are some significant findings of the study:

Educational Attainment

• Of the 895 employees studied, 47 percent are vocational graduates, 27 percent are college graduates, 2 percent are high school graduates and 2 percent are postgraduate students.

• Of the 187 station managers studied, 50 percent are college graduates, 31 percent are college students, 12 percent are postgraduate students, and 3 percent are postgraduate degree holders. Only 2 percent are high school students and another 2 percent are high school graduates.

• Of the 414 announcers, 43 percent are college students and 37 percent are college graduates. Only 10 percent are vocational graduates and only 4 percent are high school graduates. Six percent are postgraduate students.

• Of the 94 scriptwriters studied, 44 percent are college students, 31 percent are college graduates, and 13 percent are vocational graduates. Only 6 percent are high school graduates. Three percent are postgraduate students and another 3 percent are postgraduate degree holders.

Training

• About 10 percent of the broadcast media employees had attended media-related training courses aside from formal schooling, and 40 percent had not.

• Thirty percent of the 374 station managers did not have any media-related training, and only 21 percent had. Only 23 percent of the 414 announcers had media-related training.

• Twenty-six percent of the 94 scriptwriters have had special training related to media, as against 24 percent who had none.

• Regarding participation in media seminars, conferences, symposia and workshops, 10 percent of the 895 had attended broadcast media seminars. Among the 187 station managers studied, about 37 percent had attended them.

• Of the 414 announcers, 44 percent had attended media-related seminars and 10 percent had not. Only 19 percent of the 94 scriptwriters have attended such seminars; 30 percent have not.

Work Experience

• Twenty-seven percent of the 895 employees had worked with a broadcast entity before joining their present radio station, and two percent had not.

- Among 187 station managers, 35 percent had previously worked with a broadcast entity; 15 percent had not.
- Of 414 announcers queried, 32 percent had worked with a broadcast entity, and 18 percent had not.
- Of the 94 scriptwriters, 37 percent have been scriptwriters for 2 to 5 years, and 21 percent have been writing scripts for 6 to 10 years. Twenty percent have been scriptwriters for a year or less. A small number of scriptwriters (13 percent) have had 11 to 15 years of experience, and 7 percent had 16 years or more of writing experience.

Programming in Radio Broadcasting

At the heart of radio broadcasting is programming.

Programming depends partly on the competence of station personnel, especially those in production, and on station policies.

To better understand radio programming, the various types of programs are classified here into (formal and non-formal) educational, informational, and entertainment.

Educational (Formal) -- These are radio programs integrated within the regular school, from the primary grades through the university.

Educational (Non-formal) -- This category includes programs designed for training and learning experiences pertaining to technical/vocational work, and to good citizenship.

Informational -- These are programs intended to develop and encourage public awareness and to disseminate information related to development. These programs include a variety of formats like: news, public affairs, news analysis, interviews, speeches, lectures, documentary, panel discussions, plugs, spot announcements, etc.

Entertainment -- These are programs designed to entertain the listeners. They include: variety shows, drama, situation comedies, contests and specials.

In 1976, the Broadcast Media Council studied the programming patterns of the radio stations in the country. The following were its findings:[9]

- The bulk of broadcast hours are allocated to entertainment programs: 22,558 hours a week are devoted to entertainment (79.22 percent).
- More broadcast hours are devoted to informational programs than educational programs. For informational programs radio stations give 5,662 hours a week, or 19.88 percent.

The broadcast media programming profile for radio is quite clear: 3/4 entertainment and only 1/4 education and information.

If radio broadcasting is to play its role in development, something must be done to correct the imbalance in the programming services of our radio stations. A new dimension of its mission must be properly recognized and adopted. Then broadcasting can become more relevant and meaningful beyond its present role to entertain.

MAJOR INDUSTRY PROBLEMS AND THEIR SOLUTIONS

The industry has always been beset with many problems. They have cropped up because of rapid changes in technology and in economic, political, and social conditions.

The biggest problem of all in the past was organization. The industry lacked organization, or was over-organized.

When a body is properly organized, its goals and objectives are identified, and its activities are properly coordinated and competently managed, such a body can adequately stand up to whatever problems that may confront it.

Such bodies were organized during the martial law years and these were the Kapisanan ng mga Brodkaster sa Pilipinas and the Broadcast Media Council.[10]

The BMC and the KBP formulated this "megapolicy":

> It is the primary responsibility of the broadcast industry to actively participate in the development of the country and its people. In the discharge of this responsibility, it becomes incumbent on the industry to provide for the continued well-being of the constituent broadcast companies and of its personnel.[11]

This policy gave the broadcast industry a sense of direction, and at the same time strengthened its relationship with the different publics it has to serve.

Manpower

Because the industry lacked competent manpower, KBP and BMC started training radio personnel in 1975. BMC's manpower development program was done through workshops and seminars, and was intended to upgrade competence in broadcast operations, management, and writing.[12]

From 1975 to 1977, BMC trained 213 managers, 385 announcers, 56 chief technicians, 113 sales managers and representatives, 44 newswriters, and 34 drama writers.[13]

In addition, 74 participants, composed of radio-TV program managers, directors, performers-talents, scriptwriters and newswriters attended the seminar-workshop in program code.

In 1975, 100 presidents and general managers of all broadcast companies attended the Top-Level Management Conference to formulate policy recommendations to provide the direction of the broadcast industry for 1976.

Another dimension was added in 1976: training by correspondence. Under the Distance Study System for Announcers, 861 announcers enrolled for courses on communication, social effects of radio, history of Philippine radio, development communication, and oral skills. The Distance Study System for Technicians started in July 1977 with 1,350 technicians enrolled.

As of August 1977 about 320 registered for the Distance Study System for Managers.

In its program of manpower training and development, BMC and KBP had recognized a partner, the academe.

Today, there are 50 schools offering degree programs in communication or special courses in communication.

On June 18-19, 1977 the KBP-BMC sponsored a seminar-workshop for the faculty and/or chairmen of mass communication schools in Metro Manila. Their purpose was to begin a dialogue between the broadcast industry and educators. Twenty-five academic representatives attended.

A result of this workshop was a consensus on standardizing basic course offerings in radio. Such changes were expected to enable communication students to adjust easily during their internship in radio stations.

The internship of broadcast students has not been without problems. But to minimize them, the KBP and the communication schools of Metro Manila formulated guidelines. Some of these are:[14]

• The internship program will be designed to provide the students adequate exposure to broadcast operations and to provide them with opportunities to train in as many areas, such as writing, programming, research, performance, production and merchandising.

• KBP shall see to it that interns of comparable knowledge and skills levels are sent to the same station at the same period.

• The stations are free to impose their own rules of conduct and discipline. "Friends" of the interns may be refused admission by the stations. Interns are also responsible for damage they may cause to equipment or other station property.

To ease the congestion due to the burgeoning number of interns each term, the KBP is seriously considering setting up a small radio station for internship. But this is still under study.

Another area of cooperation between the KBP and the communication schools is the *KBP-PACE Outstanding Student Thesis Award*. This KBP project was conceived not only to encourage but also to recognize research made by communication students. Results of such research studies are expected to ultimately benefit the broadcast media in the country.[15]

Cash prizes and trophies are given the first three winning theses.

Programming

One of the major concerns of KBP and BMC is to improve the programming of radio stations. They believe that broadcasting is more than entertainment. It can provide support to the government's efforts for human and community development.

Because of this, the now defunct BMC required radio station operators to "list down at least 10 needs and interests of the community to be served" and "to propose programming format" to meet these needs when they apply for renewal of their permit.[16]

FUNDAMENTALS OF RADIO BROADCASTING 207

On its part, the broadcast industry has taken significant steps to improve programming. One such step was the adoption of a Program Code, a set of guidelines on program standards. The guidelines were prepared by KBP's programming and production committee in the latter part of 1975. In March 1976, program managers, production talents, radio directors and scriptwriters met to examine and discuss the prepared program standards. They recommended revisions and additional provisions which were incorporated by BMC into the Program Code in November 1976.

As a matter of policy, the BMC did not directly interfere in a station's programming. However, BMC had warned and reprimanded, and sometimes imposed fines on violators of the Program Code. For instance, in September 1977, some announcers were suspended for violating a BMC order that prohibited them from airing Jai Alai results and materials related to illegal gambling.

A source of annoyance to listeners are the commercial loads and program interruptions. Recognizing this, the BMC in 1974 limited commercial loads and program interruptions.

Whereas BMC came up with guidelines for program interruption for television, it has not done so for radio. However, BMC had given radio stations some degree of freedom to regulate program interruptions internally, among themselves.

Program content was another concern of the KBP-BMC.

Radio is expected to inform its listeners of current events. Towards this end, the BMC required all radio stations to schedule two 15-minute newscasts daily, one in the morning and another in the evening. In 1979, BMC increased its requirement from 30 minutes to 45 minutes daily. However, several radio stations asked for more flexibility in programming the newscasts. Thus the BMC allowed a 15-minute newscast to be aired between 6:00 AM and 8:00 AM, and a 30-minute newscast to be scheduled between 8:00 AM to 10:00 PM.

To further help broadcasters handle issues of great importance to the people and community, BMC issued guidelines for public affairs programs. These guidelines are useful in dealing with controversial issues.

The BMC also formulated guidelines for children's programs. These deal primarily with the treatment of violence, sex, and other human attributes in programs for children.

Music is one of the big program services that radio stations give to their listeners. Because of this, BMC suggested to programmers that they should emphasize the selection of good music, and fight commercial interests trying to influence the music programs. In addition, BMC encouraged the development of Filipino music by requiring every radio station to play at least three original Filipino compositions in every clock-hour.

Radio dramas, which enjoy big listenership particularly in the rural areas, were used to help transfer technology to the rural areas, and to disseminate vital development information to provincial radio listeners.[17]

And, of course, one big factor in the improvement of programming on radio was the setting of professional standards and the accrediting of broadcasters. BMC banned all unaccredited announcers from going on the air. A fine of P500 was the penalty each time a radio station allowed unaccredited announcers on air.

With all these steps taken, there was every reason to hope for a much better radio programming.

OPPORTUNITIES IN RADIO BROADCASTING

Radio broadcasting today offers more opportunities to graduates of mass communications than a decade ago.

As mentioned earlier, the emerging consciousness in the industry that broadcasting can be used to promote and encourage development, opens new employment opportunities for competent writers, producers, and talents who could produce development-oriented programs.

News and public affairs departments of radio stations need more competent personnel than they now have.

More and more radio stations are offering a multitude of services, many of them in small packages like traffic reports, sports and weather reports, information on agriculture, religion, education and public affairs; commentary, analysis, and homemaking hints. Again, preparation and production of these types of magazine programs need competent writers and producers.

The business side of broadcasting, which has considerably improved in the past few years, offers better opportunities for employment than before. Traffic work, which is quite complicated but challenging, needs more hardworking people who are also alert and patient.

While there are more job opportunities in the industry today, new graduates of mass communications should also be open to a wide gamut of opportunities that are available. They should not limit their job preferences to announcing and disc-jockeying. Radio work is not only that. There are other jobs that are equally important in radio. They may not be as glamorous as announcing, but nonetheless, they are as important and necessary to the over-all operation of a radio station.

To summarize, there are as many job opportunities in the industry as one is willing to see and discover. A mass communications graduate can prepare himself for any of them and give his best to it.

THE FUTURE OF RADIO BROADCASTING

Looking at the future of radio broadcasting necessitates making judgment on the relevance of radio programming. Is it relevant to the needs of the people and community?

According to a study made by Dr. Gloria D. Feliciano and Ms. Melina S. Pugne of the University of the Philippines Institute of Mass Communications,

.... radio and TV programs today are relevant, although to a limited extent, to the needs of the Filipino. BMC/KBP have laid the groundwork, with some good results. However, much more needs to be done to make our radio and television programs more relevant to the needs of the Filipino in the 1980's.[18]

In the future, the relevance of radio can be increased if BMC and KBP adopt and carry out the following recommendations made by the study:[19]

- To emphasize the present-day BMC/KBP efforts in communicating the economic needs through science-oriented broadcasts, e.g., agriculture, forestry, fishery, wherever possible.
- That BMC/KBP join hands with research-oriented communication schools in systematically monitoring radio-TV programs so that findings can be used by station managers and program directors.

Of course these are not all the essential factors necessary to insure more relevant and meaningful programs on radio, but these are basic ones. If these recommendations are carried out, they will make a great difference in the relevance of radio programs.

There is no denying the fact that the broadcast industry has achieved so much in the past decade because it is organized as one body. This solidarity has given the industry a good image, and most importantly, the bargaining edge in its dealings with advertisers and advertising agencies, especially on issues that threaten the survival of many small radio stations.

The future of radio broadcasting in the Philippines is bright because of the oneness that binds the broadcasters together for the common good.

What is the future of broadcasting in the Philippines as a business? There is a steady growth in the total gross billings of radio stations in the country since 1974.[20]

The increase in billings in 1978 has resulted in the re-classification of many radio markets into the higher categories. The number of areas whose billings have exceeded P1.2 million (key market) have increased from 8 to 18 in 1979.

The pursuit for excellence in public service programming means good business. It builds listeners' loyalty and inspires advertisers' confidence. Any radio station that has both can face the future with greater certainty.

NOTES

[1]Created on November 9, 1974, under Presidential Decreee No. 576.

[2]Chito Ramolete, "Here Come the PATS," *The Broadcaster*, February 1977, p. 9.

[3] Article XVI Section II, Subsection 1, the 1987 Philippine Constitution.

[4] In 1975 the Broadcast Media Council formulated an organizational set-up for radio stations.

[5] EDPITAF arrived at this figure by taking the 1974 BMC data on operating costs, and adding to it 20% average annual increase in cost prices. The cost today is probably double this figure, or P600,000.

[6] PSRC, May 1982.

[7] Franciso "Koko" Trinidad, "Broadcasting," *Philippine Mass Media in Perspective*, Capitol Publishing House, Inc., November 1967, p. 69.

[8] Derived from a BMC broadcast staff study in 1975 covering 233 radio stations in the country. Approximately 60% of the stations responded, and the total number of broadcast personnel is 895.

[9] BMC solicited fact sheets and program descriptions/schedule from 226 radio stations. The fact sheets and program schedules cover a period of one week.

[10] The Kapisanan ng mga Brodkaster sa Pilipinas is an organization of all broadcasters in the country, while the Broadcast Media Council was the regulatory body for the broadcast industry created by a Presidential Decree during the Marcos regime.

[11] A Paper on Radio, prepared by BMC/KBP, p. 3 (unpublished, mimeographed, and not dated).

[12] Ibid, p. 4.

[13] Ibid, pp. 6-8.

[14] The 1979 KBP Annual Report to the Industry, pp. 24-25.

[15] Mimeographed guidelines given to panel of judges for the KBP-PACE Outstanding Student Thesis Award.

[16] Item "f", Programming and Community Needs, BMC Resolution No. B79-12.

[17] Report of the Broadcast Media Council, 1979, p. 14.

[18] Excerpts from "Radio-TV Programming Today: How Relevant to the Needs of the Filipino?" In Proceedings, Second National Broadcasters' Convention, Baguio City, Nov. 10-13, 1979.

[19] Ibid.

[20] Report of the Broadcast Media Council, 1979, p. 15.

Chapter XIV

Broadcast Media at the Crossroads

Raul T. Pañares

Towards the late 1960s, after almost 40 years of radio and 15 years of television, problems of growth beset the broadcast industry. These problems were competition, lack of planning, inability of the industry to stimulate local mass production and sales, and dependence on U.S. – produced programs and sets.

The TV stations were so busy fighting each other for ratings and revenue that no one had time to consider and plan rational growth. Partly because the Radio Control Board lacked clout, no rules were laid out especially for television, nor did any plan exist on assigning channels. There was no comprehensive national policy on how to organize the networks and extend them in a systematic way throughout the islands.

Broadcasting before September 1972 was as free of government control as a runaway juvenile. Freedom of expression was virtually unrestricted. No politician or public figure could hope to be spared from the "bomba," the term for vitriolic and abusive comments.

In greater Manila alone there were 55 radio stations in 1970. Out of 350 in the whole country, 120 stations were in Luzon, 90 stations in the Visayas, and 85 stations in Mindanao. Such a number indeed had to be organized and controlled, to be "marshalled" both for political and economic expedience.

The "marshalling" came with Martial Law in 1972.

The drastic closure by the government of many broadcasting stations, too many to be named here, were justified through numerous and vague reasons. One reason was that there were too many broadcasting stations. Another reason was that radio and newspapers were infiltrated by communist propagandists. They were, therefore, guilty of "subversive" communication that damaged the social fiber and weakened resistance to communism.

It made sense for a Department of Public Information to be set up after Martial Law was declared. One of its primary concerns was to regulate radio and TV so that these shall "broadcast accurate, objective, straight news reports of the government, to meet the dangers and threats that occasioned the proclamation of Martial Law." Furthermore, editorials, "opinion, commentary, comments or asides" were forbidden on the air.

In May 1973, the Media Advisory Council was formed to encourage responsible opinion writing of social and economic conditions, ban monopoly ownership, allocate radio and TV frequencies through a zonification system and under accepted international rules, and put up more radio and TV stations in the provinces.

The broadcaster's responsibility under the new order was to educate the masses by presenting cultural and genuinely artistic, or literary materials, and to promote Filipino moral and social values, especially among children. Program standards called for, among others, wholesome entertainment, respect for marriage, home, and family; and factual, fair, and unbiased news reporting.[1]

From all aspects, it looked like the "restructuring" and "rationalization" of the broadcast media was ushering in the "golden age" of broadcasting.

Or so it seemed.

In the process in which the martial law government gave Philippine broadcasting the directions, challenges and strife came forth fast.

After factional strife rendered the Media Advisory Council inefficient, President Marcos decentralized mass media in October 1974. Separate councils for print and broadcasting were created. The broadcasting industry came under the Broadcast Media Council (BMC) headed by Teodoro Valencia.

While Marcos broke up old broadcasting networks owned by oligarchies, he allowed the rise of a new oligarchy and allowed monopolies, especially for friends or relatives. For example, of the 209 stations listed in 1975, 117 were owned by only 10 companies. Marcos controlled Kanlaon Broadcasting System (through Roberto Benedicto) that managed three out of five television networks together with their radio stations. The three TV networks were Banahaw Broadcasting Corporation, Radio Philippines Network and Interisland Broadcasting Corporation. Under the Office of the President, the National Media Production Center operated the powerful 500 kilowatt Voice of the Philippines network. In 1975, the number of the radio stations were: 122 in the greater Manila area, 50 in Luzon, 19 in the Visayas, and 18 in Mindanao. Of the 27 active shortwave stations, 22 were owned by religious broadcasters. Far East Broadcasting Corporation owned 15 stations; Southeast Asian Radio Voice, now defunct, then had 5 stations; and Radio Veritas, 2 stations.

Broadcast media were most vulnerable to government dictation and control because the granting of the Certificate of Public Convenience (CPC) was made the "Sword of Damocles" over them. The mere threat of the non-issuance of the certificate was enough to cow any station owner or manager into submission and cooperation. That threat was in fact used to coerce the Board of Directors of the Kapisanan ng mga Brodkaster sa Pilipinas (KBP) into conducting the widely criticized KBP Election Coverage in February 1986.

This lack of CPCs created uncertainty about the companies' continued existence. In turn, it resulted in bankers rating broadcast companies high-risk business. Managers could not get loans to upgrade their steadily depreciating equipment. Only the profitable stations got to import spare parts and state-of-the-art technology.

That there was tremendous amount of government participation in the media is an accepted fact.

Indeed, regular programs were often interrupted to make way for a presidential speech or function. It gave Marcos infinite and quick access to audiences through a nationwide hook-up.

The martial law regime introduced the weekly forum on grassroots issues. Simulcast on radio and TV, at an early morning hour everyday, the forum took up development topics, mostly on agriculture. It had the overall effect of making people feel that, somehow, the government was doing something beneficial to everyone.

But broadcasting was still hindered by the same old problems. Then as now, more than 50 percent of TV schedules were taken up by foreign shows. The local programs showed the "bakya syndrome," a mind-set that favored stories about illegitimate children, forsaken wives, abused women, moribund fathers, poor girl/rich boy, poor boy/rich girl stories where the leading lady alternates between singing and weeping, or was forever caught between nagging and conspiring against a husband or lover suspected of two-timing her.

An observer, David Rosenberg, has noted that the communication media in the Philippines has had a dualistic development; radio catered mostly to lower classes and newspapers were for the elite who could understand and speak English.[2]

EDUCATIONAL BROADCASTING

An exploding body of knowledge available in the world and a shortage of teachers for the transfer of this knowledge to the next generation led many media visionaries to believe in the tremendous potential of broadcasting to educate masses of people. The development of satellite communications at that time enhanced this vision.

Educational broadcasting started as early as 1950. It was a joint project of the government's Philippine Broadcasting Service (PBS) and the Bureau of Public Schools, and was boosted by the Australian government's donation of 500 radio receivers for use in the schools. By 1967-68, 19 elementary and high school programs were broadcast over 18 private and commercial stations into 39,000 classrooms. There were 19,168 radio receivers available for the project then and 90 percent of these were purchased by the schools themselves. In addition, many government agencies, including the Radio-TV section of the Malacañang Press Office, were involved in educational broadcast projects. Adult education classes and farm broadcasts were aired in "Paaralan sa Himpapawid" (Radio Farm School), which graduated by 1986 2,000 farmers in radio correspondence courses on poultry raising, vegetable gardening, and miracle rice cultivation.

Television also turned into an educational, and "educated" medium -- at least for some time. The early 1960s witnessed Channel 9's "Education on TV" where a physics course was televised. It was sponsored by various groups, among them, the Metropolitan Educational Television Association (META). In 1964, the Center for Educational Television at Ateneo de Manila University initiated a closed-circuit TV pilot project with six receiving schools. In three months, 30 public and private schools of META were served by this project through a microwave link to a commercial channel.[3]

It was the rave of the times in education circles and 1968-72 was the peak of educational television (ETV).

From 1972 to 1974, ETV shifted to out-of-school youths, or informal education. Apparently, the government decided that ETV on the national level was its responsibility since majority of the schools serviced were public, anyway.

Only a token interest in using media for education remained in the 1980s, seen partly in the resumption of a Filipino version of the famous Sesame Street. Sesame Street was staple fare for the "martial law babies" who never seemed to grow tired of its reruns. Its counterpart here, "Batibot," came into being under a children's television workshop project. Lyca Benitez-Brown, the group head, ran it under the Ministry of Human Settlement's University of Life. The program is directed towards pre-schoolers in depressed urban areas. Rural children have yet to be served, however. Lack of funds again threatens the viability of "Batibot," a project intended to educate millions of pre-school children.

PRESENT SITUATION AND KBP's ROLE

One of the most enduring achievements of the martial law government is the organization of the Kapisanan ng mga Brodkaster sa Pilipinas (KBP), a self-regulatory body of the broadcast industry. KBP has 12 standing committees that perform functions aimed at professionalizing broadcast personnel. The committees are Standard Authority, Internal Relations, External

Relations, Government Relations, Trade Relations, Research, Personnel Standards and Manpower, Accreditation, Technical Standards, Program Standards, Public Relations and Promotions, and Ways and Means. An enforcement body, the Standards Authority, was also created to enforce association rules.

Formed in 1973 by 37 broadcast representatives, the KBP has formulated the rules and guidelines of the Radio and Television code, the Radio Code, and the Television Code through the Standards Authority to serve broadcasters in their program presentations. These codes and standards were never before addressed by government.

In the first National Broadcasters' Conference on October 21, 1974, general managers, station managers, journalists and broadcasters met to set up the rules and regulations for the broadcast media and to organize the provincial chapters. For this conference, President Marcos issued Presidential Decree 576 that created the Broadcast Media Council (BMC) to promulgate the self-regulatory policies. Thus, the KBP-BMC tie-up created a new image of the industry because it pursued vigorously and concretely supported developmental programming, announcers' accreditation and manpower training.

In its 13 years of existence, KBP has created many significant changes in the personnel standards and organization in the broadcast industry.

Nevertheless, much still remains to be done.

INDUSTRY PROFILE

Station Distribution

There are 308 radio stations now operating (in 1986) in the country, 236 AM and 72 FM. Eighty-five percent of these stations are classified as commercial, 7 percent (20 stations) as either educational or religious stations, and 8 percent (25 stations) as government-owned. Luzon accounts for the greatest number of stations (108), followed by Mindanao (79 stations), and Visayas (74 stations). Metro Manila currently has 47 radio stations -- 28 on the AM band and 19 on the FM band.

There are also 45 television stations, 24 of them capable of originating programs and 21 stations that only relay programs.

These radio and television stations are owned and operated by 93 broadcast companies. They range in size from single station ownership to networks. The largest network is Radio Mindanao Network which owns 24 stations.

In the urban areas, about three out of five (2.1 million) households are TV set owners. In the rural areas, only one out of five households (1.3 million) owns a set. In regional distribution, Metro Manila leads the list with 78 percent ownership, followed by Luzon with 34 percent and

Visayas and Mindanao with 26 percent. In terms of socio-economic class, the AB homes have at least one set, the C homes have 77 percent ownership while the D homes have 21 percent ownership.

Radio Audience Profiles

At least four out of five Filipinos (84 percent), aged 15 and above, listen to radio for about three hours a day, five to six days a week. This would mean that about 24 million Filipinos comprise the adult radio audience. Note that radio listening is higher in the rural areas, especially in northern and central Luzon, the Visayas and Mindanao, than in Metro Manila, southern Luzon and the Bicol region.

While the frequency of radio listening is about the same in all regions, Mindanao registers a frequency lower than the rest of the country. Another interesting fact is that contrary to popular belief, an urban radio listener spends more hours listening to the radio than his rural counterpart. This can probably be explained by the fact that urban listeners are radio set owners while in the rural areas, the radio audience include a substantial number of non-radio owners. The percentage is pegged at 15-20 percent. Listening levels among radio homes in the Visayas range from at least 18 percent in Iloilo to 30 percent in Bacolod during weekdays. In Mindanao, average listening levels range from 24 percent in Davao and Surigao to 31 percent in Ozamis during weekdays. In comparison, only about 12-21 percent of homes with radio in selected Luzon cities have their sets on at any time of the day during weekdays.

A brief broadcast industry profile shows what else could be done and why.

Radio listening is more a daytime activity than an evening past-time. Listeners listen at least two hours in the daytime and only an hour and a half in the evening. The possible explanation for this could be the shift from radio to television at night in the urban areas and the fact that many rural folks go to bed earlier than urban dwellers.

Studies show that the audience of pop music stations (AM-FM0) belong to class AB and C, are males and are 15-29 years old. Drama station listeners are characteristically DE, females below 15 and above 45 years old. Music personality stations have the same audience as drama stations in terms of socio-economic class (DE) and sex (females). As to age, however, the listeners of music stations are in the 20-44 age bracket.

TV Audience Profile

In areas where there are radio and television stations, television viewing is higher than radio listening. Sixty-six percent, or two out of three viewers, aged 15 and above, watch TV at an average of 4.3 days a week or 13.6 hours a week, or 3.2 hours a day. Radio, as was earlier noted, is listened to at an average of only two hours a day.

Metro Manila leads the country in television viewing, followed by northern and central Luzon, Visayas, southern Luzon and Bicol and lastly Mindanao.

Set Ownership

According to the 1985 figures of Philippine Survey Research Center (PSRC), 7.5 million households out of 9.7 million or 77 percent have at least one radio set while 3.5 million households (37 percent) have a television set. Radio is more egalitarian than television with ownership at a high 100 percent of AB homes and 49 percent of E homes. The reasons for this are rather obvious. Obviously, too, television still remains a relatively elite medium as ownership is limited at 100 percent in AB homes, to lows of 32 percent in D homes and 6 percent in E homes. Radio ownership has gone up by 40 percent, from 5.6 million households in 1984. In television, the increase is small -- 3 percent over that of 1984 when set ownership was pegged at 3.4 million households.

Gross Billing

In 1984, broadcast media registered gross billings worth ₱817 million, broken down as share and percentage of total billings:

AM   ₱173 million (21.18 percent)
FM   ₱102 million (12.48 percent)
TV   ₱542 million (66.34 percent)

The projected annual growth rate of the broadcast media's share of the advertising market is 7.95 percent. The bulk of these revenues will be derived from the top ten advertisers in the industry.

The host of problems, criticisms, and challenges to the industry today, is a virtual Pandora's box of complaints and "unsolicited advice" that makes the broadcaster, however successful and profitable, defensive.

Indeed, it has. Many Filipinos saw the "defense" of Channel 4 during the snap revolt, the bombing of the Radio Veritas transmitter, the battle for Channel 7 and Broadcast City, and finally the sequestration of Channels 9, 2 and 13. More recently, a group of soldiers held Channel 7 for several days as part of a coup attempt.

The following is a tabular summary of some issues and problems in the broadcast industry and some proposed solutions or remedies for them.

Area of Concern	Issue/Problem	Suggested Solutions
I. Program Staff 1. Owner-managers 2. Producer 3. Directors	Profit orientation: allow themselves to be dictated to by advertisers regarding scheduling of ads and content of programs to air.	Higher degree of "professionalism"
	a. Underpaid staff do not give their best.	Higher pay and incentives for professional growth
	b. Lack of updating and professional growth.	"Be in touch" with social and political realities of audiences
	c. Unaware of great social responsibility as communicators	Learn from the "old timers" and "fresh newcomers" alike
4. Scriptwriter	Writing stories only in popular taste or those catering to the lowest common denominator, i.e., the "bakya," "baduy" crowd.	
5. Talents	Tardiness at work	Educate talents in higher forms of entertainment
	Coming unprepared and unrehearsed	
	Careless with personal health (i.e., drug dependence, alcoholism, etc.)	
II. Audience: listening and viewing public	Uncritical/passive acceptance of low quality shows	Encourage public criticism through systematic feedback, i.e. ombudsman, etc.

	Preference for entertainment rather than informational educational programs	"Educate" public by exposing them to high-quality programs
III. Government	Political patronage	Government should not be involved in day-to-day operations of private media
	Government stations competing with private stations	
		Should be concerned only with "matters of grave and present dangers to the state"
		Supplement/support broadcasting system through subsidies and grants
		Recognize "job well done" or achievements of broadcasters
	Monopolies through multiple or cross ownership	Media monopolies should be abolished to maintain healthy competition among large units of the mass media
IV. Programming	Bulk of entertainment programs on TV	Improve quality of entertainment shows
	Public access to all points of view	Introduce more information shows both on TV and radio that encourage the public to explain their points of view (i.e. radio forum)
	Heavy drama orientation on radio	
	Foreign/imported shows dominate TV	Encourage local TV program production
	Too little relevant programming for children	Sponsor more educational programs for children and students

	Other Filipino cultural groups with their tastes and interests are not served	Cultural shows/programs depicting other Filipino cultural groups and their problems should be aired
	Public service programs	Segmented audiences with specific interests and motives must be addressed to with relevant programs
	Existing programs appeal to a very wide audience, using the lowest common denominator, with many programs becoming irrelevant to social issues and realities	For teachers, laborers, students, market vendors, drivers, government employees, housewives, parents, etc. in both rural and urban areas
	Scarce exposure of public to government affairs in general and provincial/rural affairs in particular	Put up regular slots for government ministries/agencies and for provincial/local governments to explain their programs and policies, using a "callback" forum/format
V. Distribution	Many depressed areas of the country are not reached by either radio or television. On the other hand, most urban areas have a glut of broadcast stations leading to cutthroat competition	Disperse transmission and relay facilities of broadcasting stations
VI. Research	Stale, stagnated knowledge on part of program staff about values and behavior of Filipino society	Update them on positive Filipino values and behavior that are productive and supportive of independence, equality, and social justice

Lag in current research data (both quantitative and qualitative) for use in programming, marketing, and management decisions	Allocate resources for quick and reliable data-base studies through a pooling of funds among members of the broadcast industry
	or
	Require market and media research organizations to come up with more uniform, standardized formats for monitoring changes in research data to avoid conflicting or widely disparate research data on similar population bases

QUESTIONING BASIC ASSUMPTIONS

The Pandora's box of problems and challenges in the Philippine broadcasting industry is not unique. In fact, similar broadcasting systems all over the world exhibit the same problems.

But the perspective from which such problems emanated needs to be recognized, distinguished and appraised.

Like all social systems and institutions, the broadcast media in this country operate from some basic premises about its nature, and roles in society, and what it hopes to become. A quick and cursory look into these assumptions could very well enlighten us on why some problems continue to exist.

Broadcasting in the Philippines has hewn most closely to the "market model... Its older and colorful cousin, the print medium, had earlier quite naturally adopted the "market model," owing to the country's colonial ties with the greatest market economy, the United States. In the "market model," advertising is the main financial lifeline of most mass media.

The history of newspapers has illustrated that "power had suddenly been vested in a new economic force: the advertiser."[4]

As they helped the newspapers become stable business ventures, advertisers did influence drastic changes in the nature of editorial content.

For many Third World countries, the technology of commercial broadcasting through which the expression of opinion is channeled does not come without a price. That price is a system of values that accompany the technology. The "professional" broadcaster or journalist, whether pursuing the traditional *public service* stance of BBC or the dramatic *public interest* posture of the American broadcaster, props up the status quo and favors proficiency over ideology.

This leads us then back to where we were. Do our basic premises still hold? For whom are we "professional communicators" and for what? Whither goest thou, broadcaster and journalist?

In an industry where humility is an exception rather than the general rule, a reexamination of conscience is in order. We recognize that what determines freedom is responsibility -- the responsibility to provide people with *access* to information, *access* to choice, *access* to education, *access* to collective opinion, *access* to collective power, both economic and political.

What concepts must be redefined? What hold-over, traditional, or conventional ideas must take on new and progressive dimensions?

The answers can only be found, perhaps, in the following days, the succeeding months, or the coming years. There are already suggestions.

Among these creative suggestions in the international scene:

1. In October 1980, the MacBride Commission studied the Unesco concept of a new international information order. The report[5] advanced the concept that if democracy must be sustained by communication systems, the crucial link between communication and power, and between communication and freedom must be recognized. Hence, it is necessary to move from the traditional philosophy of communication into what is now termed as "democratization of communication."

In this light, news, the Commission wrote, must be redefined: the proper role of the journalist is activist, not disinterested bystander. The mass media have the power to help strengthen peace, international security, and cooperation and to lessen international tensions. The press has a duty "to mobilize public opinion in favor of disarmament and of ending the arms race."

Furthermore, the MacBride Commission cited that the dangers of the existing world order was precisely the concentration on the *immediate and the dramatic*. What was overlooked and ignored were the great political, economic, and social issues.

2. A study conducted by Weaver, Buddenbaum, and Fair[6] showed that in the less developed countries, higher levels of economic productivity did not generally increase media development and decrease government control of the press, as was true in the more developed countries. What increased media development, and lessened government control, was education, measured in terms of school enrolment per capita. Increased urbanism is also associated with more accountability of government and less government control of the media.

These are hard facts to prove that mass media's primary role in "developing" countries is to inform and to educate, over and above entertaining and selling.

The February revolution was the first stage of the Filipino Satyagraha, a non-violent resistance to a repressive rule.

The broadcast media now stands at the crossroads: to reform itself and serve the Filipino people or to remain a profit-oriented industry and serve only the interests of its owners?

Table 1. Radio Ownership

	Total No. of Households	Number	Percent
Total Philippines	8,607	5,615	65.2
Urban Philippines	3,219	2,388	74.2
Rural Philippines	5,388	3,227	59.9
Ilocos Region	651	446	68.4
Cagayan Region	404	243	60.0
Central Luzon	838	600	71.6
Southern Luzon	1,107	753	68.0
Bicol Region	603	344	57.0
Western Visayas	787	490	62.2
Central Visayas	698	444	63.6
Eastern Visayas	511	270	52.9
Western Mindanao	439	230	52.5
Northern Mindanao	479	309	64.5
Southern Mindanao	591	400	67.6
Central Mindanao	72	49	68.7
National Capital Region	1,104	861	78.0

Source: National Census and Statistics Office, 1980

Table 2. Incidence and Frequency of Radio Listening

	Urban (%)	Rural (%)	Total (%)
Incidence of Radio Listening (Based on total interview)	82	85	84
Frequency of Radio Listening (Based on total who listen to radio)			
No. of days in a week			
Daily/almost daily	78	76	77
Two to three times a week	13	13	13
Once a week	9	11	7
Less often than once a week			3
			100
Total Ave. No. of Days			5.7
Average number of hours listening in a day			
Total day	3.6	3.2	3.3
Daytime	2.3	2.0	2.1
Evening	1.3	1.2	1.2

Source: Philippine Survey Research Center, 1983

Table 3. Number of Station(s) Usually Listened to Each Day

	Total Philippines Percent
One	42
Two	34
Three or more	24
Total	100
Ave. no. of stations listened to each day	1.9

Base - total who listen to radio

Source: Philippine Survey Research Center, 1983

Table 4. Audience Share by Type of Stations, Metro Manila*

	Year		
	1975 (%)	1980 (%)	1983 (%)
Drama/personality	37	25	17 (-)
Music personality	26	11	8 (-)
Pop music	24	17	9 (-)
FM band	7	42	61 (+)
Others	6	5	5 (+)
Total	100	100	100

(-) = increase
(+) = decrease

*The above data were taken from the PSRC Coincidental Radio Survey (CRS) for said years.

Source: Philippine Survey Research Center, 1983

Table 5. Profile of the radio audience by type of station

	TOTAL (%)	Pop-Music Stations (AM-FM) (%)	Music Personality Stations (%)	Drama Stations (%)
Sex				
Male	39	43	35	35
Female	61	57	65	65
TOTAL	100	100	100	100
Age				
Below 15	19	17	20	22
15 - 19	24	30	19	18
20 - 29	31	34	29	26
30 - 44	14	12	19	18
45 & up	12	7	13	16
TOTAL	100	100	100	100
Position in the Household				
Household head	8	7	8	10
Housewife	16	11	19	22
Other males	31	36	27	25
Other females	45	46	46	43
TOTAL	100	100	100	100
Socio-eco. class				
AB	4	5	4	2
C	35	43	33	23
DE	61	52	63	75
TOTAL	100	100	100	100

/ / = highest figures along horizontal line

Source: Philippine Survey Research Center

Table 6. TV Ownership Level

	Total No. of Households (000)	Households with TV 000 %		Ownership Distribution (%)
Total Philippines	9,316.2	3,352.4	36	100
Locale				
Urban	3,531.5	2,084.1	59	62
Rural	5,784.7	1,268.3	22	38
Region (Broad)				
Metro Manila	1,213.3	958.1	78	29
Luzon	3,884.6	1,313.0	34	39
Visayas	2,127.4	549.7	26	16
Mindanao	2,072.9	531.6	26	16
Socio-Economic Class				
AB	331.0	329.5	100	9
C	2,038.0	1,577.7	77	47
DE	6,947.2	1,445.2	21	44

Source: Philippine Survey Research Center, 1983

Table 7. Incidence of TV Viewing

Locale	Total Philippines (%)
Urban	82
Rural	58
Region	
Metro Manila	94
Northern/Central Luzon	70
Southern Luzon/Bicol	56
Visayas	65
Mindanao	54
Socio-Economic Class	
AB	87
C	86
DE	61

Base - total population aged 15 and up

Source: Philippine Survey Research Center, 1983.

Notes

[1] Media Advisory Council, Philippines, 1973.

[2] David Rosenburg, *The Development of Modern Mass Communication in the Philippines.* Ann Arbor, Michigan: University of Michigan Press, 1972.

[3] John Lent, *Philippine Mass Communication: Before 1811 and After 1966.* Manila: Philippine Press Institute, 1971.

[4] Herbert J. Altschull, *Agents of Power: The Role of the New Media in Human Affairs.* Annenberg/Longman Communication Books. George Gerbuer and Marsha Siefert, editions. New York: Longman, Inc., 1984.

[5] Unesco, *Many Voices, One World: Towards a New, More Just and More Efficient World Information and Communication Order,* 1981.

[6] In Press Freedom, Media and Development, 1950-1979: A Study of 134 Nations, *Journal of Communication*, Spring, 1985.

Chapter XV

Towards a Public Broadcasting System for the Philippines

Elizabeth L. Diaz

INTRODUCTION

The February 1986 revolution brought into focus the need for immediate changes in Philippine mass communications. The Marcos regime's control of the mass media had led to their loss of credibility. The revolution gave the country an opportunity to rectify the damage caused by the previous regime.

Reforms have to be immediately made in ownership and cross-ownership to prevent media monopolies as in the past, when media were in the hands of a few chosen associates. There is a need to phase out or minimize government ownership and control of media. In the previous regime, the mass media were used for propaganda. Providing representation from all sectors of society in the making of laws and regulations and the granting of licenses is another area that requires changes.

The February revolution, for the first time, created among many people awareness of media's overwhelming power, particularly of radio and television. Most media practitioners and educators knew media's great influence and power but had dared not question repression of the media.

The Aquino administration's abolition of the Ministry of Information is a move towards the right direction. It allows communication educators and practitioners to develop mass media along the lines of service and responsibility without much government intervention.

A starting point in making changes is to examine models and find out what features can be adopted.

ALTERNATIVE BROADCASTING SYSTEMS

Many media researchers and writers have pointed to the British Broadcasting Corporation (BBC) as one of the best broadcasting systems in the world. It is a suitable alternative to either a government-licensed free enterprise system (like that of the U.S.) or a government-owned and operated system employed by the majority of Asian countries. The Philippine broadcasting system is patterned after that of the United States. But even the Americans have realized the drawbacks of their system and came up with an alternative, non-commercial broadcasting system, officially called the Public Broadcasting System.

What would an alternative broadcasting system offer?

First, it will provide programming usually not available on commercial stations. This would include special interests like music, dance, fine arts, inportant foreign language films, superior dramatic programs and public affairs discussions. Through the public stations, the needs of ethnic minorities, children and other special interest groups in society, can be better met. Third, the system will allow localized programming, which would reflect and project local communities. Fourth, it will allow public participation in station and system policy.[1] And fifth, because the system is not profit-oriented, it can concentrate on making quality programs.

BRITISH VS. AMERICAN BROADCASTING

The British and the American broadcasting systems, both public and commercial, have peculiar advantages and disadvantages. England's BBC offers economy in programming in the sense that a single program is carried by stations throughout the nation. It has no competitor in hiring a talent. Thus, the artist's fees and program costs are kept low. The combination of a monopoly and centralized programming also contributes to national unity.

Government ownership and control allow the use of broadcasting as an instrument of culture and mass education to an extent not possible under a commercial system. Programs are chosen for their cultural and educational values, not for their popular appeal. There is no competition for listener attention, and no pressure from advertisers.

A disadvantage obviously is the absence of choice. The controlling agency decides what is to be broadcast with little or no regard for the preferences or interests of the public. The absence of competition stifles the initiative to experiment with new programs and forms. However, when commercial TV was introduced in England, BBC was forced to offer substantial entertainment programs in order to retain its viewers. Finally, a government-owned system can easily be made into an instrument of political propaganda. This is inherent in the system. The BBC charter requires stations to broadcast "any announcement" requested by "any department of the government." Even in democratic countries, there is always the likelihood that government-owned stations become instruments for either direct or indirect propaganda to support the controlling party.

The American broadcasting system is both commerical and non-commercial. There is no central planning and control of programs except to an extent, by the big TV networks. Non-commercial stations are owned and run by educational institutions, community or state organizations and by religious groups. Commercial and non-commercial stations compete for audiences but not for advertising revenues.

A disadvantage is that the wide ownership makes systematic planning impossible. Another drawback is wastefulness. There are far more stations than are needed to meet the needs of audiences, more than can be supported adequately by advertising. The competition for outstanding entertainers pushes program costs up.

The advantages include the following: it provides forums for controversial issues of public concern; the programs are free from direct government control; broadcasters are free to criticize as well as commend; there is a wide dissemination of information on issues of importance and free discussion of vital public issues; and audiences have a wider choice of programs. While the public can select or reject programs, it has no control over the range of choices offered it. Radio and television cater to the mass audience and largely ignore the interests of minorities. But their mass appeal is paradoxically the strength of the American system which match the country's political ideology – democracy.

Rationale for BBC

The reason for the BBC system lies in its belief that broadcasting should be subjected to a large measure of state control. Broadcasting holds social and political possibilities that ought not to be allowed to become an unrestricted commercial monopoly.[2]

Rationale for the American System

Freedom of speech is the primary basis of the American broadcasting system.

But because of too many abuses, Congress passed the Radio Act of 1927 which established the Federal Communications Commission to regulate the broadcasting industry.

The FFC set guidelines that stressed the importance of providing programs to meet varied interests and needs and of allowing people access to the broadcast media to express their opinions on important public issues.[3]

Historical Background of BBC

The BBC started out in 1922 as the British Broadcasting Company, a private company owned by radio manufacturers and makers of radio equipment. It was financed by license fees on receivers. The Postmaster General issued BBC's license to operate and exercised regulatory powers. Programming was centralized and broadcasting was a monopoly.[4]

In 1926, the government bought the company and renamed it the British Broadcasting Corporation. Under a Royal Charter, "BBC was to serve as a trustee for the national interest in broadcasting." The charter meant to avoid future political interference on BBC.

The BBC was a monopoly until 1954 when it became a "duapoly" which was financed by license fees on radio receivers and run by an independent public corporation. The BBC was responsible to the British government. Its director was appointed by the ministry in power for fixed terms. The policies were determined by the corporation's board of governors. Changes in the BBC operations were adopted from recommendations of special studies by committees, but the basic nature of BBC operations has remained the same.

Present Organization of BBC

The structure of the BBC has largely remained the same. It is a non-profit corporation with a board of governors serving a fixed five-year term. The Board's policies are carried out by an executive staff headed by a director-general, the chief executive officer. A general advisory council advises the corporation "on all matters which may be of concern to the corporation, or to bodies or persons interested in the broadcasting services of the corporation." Regional advisory councils and 20 local radio councils and specialist advisory bodies on agriculture, education, etc. were formed to insure that BBC would be in close contact with its audiences.

BBC Financing

BBC continues to finance its domestic operations from annual license fees on radio and TV sets. Income from the license fees are divided proportionately between radio and television. Government subsidy goes mainly to the external (foreign) services. Publications are a source of supplementary income. They include program guides (*Radio Times* and *Listener*), which also feature reviews, articles about music, art, films and the theater; manuals for BBC's educational/instructional programs; publications on BBC documentaries, children's programs, and on BBC itself.

BBC Programming

During the early years, BBC provided a national service, broadcasting from the London studios, and a regional service, coming from local studios. Emphasis was on "serious," "educational," and "cultural" programs, which also took popular tastes into consideration. The BBC's guiding principle was to offer programs to raise the intellectual and aesthetic tastes, and to give programs which are better than what public thinks it likes at the moment.[5]

In the last war, BBC radio had only one network, the Home Service. It was regarded throughout the world as the most dependable source of news about the war.

The BBC now offers four types of program service: the *Home Service*, which is designed for the broad middle section of the community. It carries news, reports of parliamentary proceedings, analysis of world affairs, instructional broadcasts; musical programs of great works, dramatic shows (including stage plays), serials and radio adaptations of popular novels. The second service is the *Light Program*. It caters to a large audience primarily interested in entertainment and relaxation. Pop music, comedy, light drama, and frequent news briefs and weather reports are its main fare. The *Third Service* also provides a wide range of high quality music, concerts and operas; "study session" in foreign languanges, history and art on weekday nights and a "sports service" on Saturday afternoon. A *Fourth Service*, which provides pop music programs, was added later.

BBC TV started operations in 1936, offering regular daily programming to a limited audience. Public clamor for a second service resulted in the creation of the Independent Television Authority (ITA), in 1954, ending BBC's broadcasting monopoly. ITA became the Independent Broadcasting Authority (IBA) in 1973. The IBA, although a government corporation, runs commercially. It leases stations to private companies which build and maintain their own studios, provide programs, and sell time to advertisers. IBA's programming consists of network, as well as local broadcasts. Despite its being commercial, the IBA takes measures to insure that advertisers would have no influence or control on programming.

BBC TV's programming aims to cover the full range of public tastes and interests to expand the viewer's awareness of the world in which he lives, and to set and maintain high professional standards. When it expanded its domestic services, BBC also expanded its foreign broadcasting services to include news reports and foreign language broadcasts.

BBC's Problems

Different groups have lately stepped up pressure on the BBC to accept advertising either as supplementary or alternative income. Many complain the license fee is regressive and burdens the poor and the old age pensioners. It is compulsory and paid as a single annual payment.

But BBC sympathizers contend that advertising would dilute program standards. Alastair Milne, BBC Director-General, stated that BBC believes competition for advertising income would reduce the range and quality of their programs. The license fee, according to Michael Tracey, head of the broadcasting Research Unit of the British Film Institute, is a form of financing best suited to the structure and philosophy of BBC - making programs free from commercial and political pressures, the two great threats to broadcasting independence. Only by maintaining a strong and independent BBC can one fend off those pressures.

The central problem now is whether the license fee is a viable and proper way of paying for the nation's major broadcasting organization. Should BBC look to other forms of finance such as subscription, sponsorship and government grants?

Future of BBC

Seventy-eight percent of the public seem more resentful to a reduction in the range of programs available on radio and TV than to continuing the license fee. Some have suggested modifying the way license fees are collected to make it easier on the public, like offering instalment payments, among others.

The Peacock Commission, however, recommends the continuation of BBC financing from license fees and for BBC and ITV to sell the 1 - 6 am time slot, during which they are not on air.[6]

The most promising source of supplementary funds remains the BBC's own commercial operations. Developing new markets from cable TV, satellite, or video can mean additional income.[7]

History of U.S. Public Broadcasting

In the early days of radio, many believed that stations should provide education and culture in their programs. If the commercial system cannot do it, then a "second broadcasting service" must be created to provide solely informational and educational programs. This is how public broadcasting came about.

Public broadcasting had its beginnings in educational broadcasting. Congress reserved channels for non-commercial use through FCC in 1945 as a result of the prodding by various educational groups since the early 1920s. FCC reserved 20 channels on the FM band as "educational channels" to be used only by non-commercial educational stations. In 1950, several groups of educators formed the Joint Committee (later Council) for Educational Television (JCET), and asked for reservations for educational TV. The National Association of Broadcasters (NAB), composed of commercial broadcasters, did not like the idea of educational TV reservations because it would mean fewer channels for them to operate for profit. The JCET argued that increased student enrolments, the growth in knowledge to be learned, and the shortage of teachers caused by the war, necessitated the use of television as a supplemental educational medium. In 1952, the FCC reserved 242 channels for the exclusive use of educational TV stations, which rapidly developed and expanded.

Financial assistance came from outside agencies, state and local grants, public subscriptions, local businesses and even commercial broadcasters who donated money or equipment. Foundations, like the Ford Foundation, provided financial support, especially for the National Educational Television and Radio Center (NETRC/NET) which produce educational and cultural programs on film or videotape.

Public Broadcasting Act

In 1969, Congress passed the Public Broadcasting Act. It was a result of the recommendations of the Carnegie Commission for Educational Television CCET.

By 1967, the U.S. had a "second television service" to provide educational, informative and cultural programs.

Programming

Educational programs offered during school consisted of locally produced programs intended for elementary and high schools. The materials are worked out by station producers and committees of teachers from the local school system. Instructors or "experts" appearing before the cameras come mostly from the local school authorities and station representatives.

Most programs use the "lecture and demonstration" format-with "master teachers" who appear, prepare, and present their own materials for subjects ranging from physical science to dinner education.

Other programs include those for out-of-school listening. They offer instruction and inspiration for the general audience and serve the cultural needs of the community. Non-classroom offerings consist of "how-to-do-it" type of roundtable or panel discussions and talks on a wide variety of subjects.

The National Educational TV (NET)

The NETRC, later the NET, was created in 1952. It distributed program materials using the mail, known as the "bicycle network." Most of its programs came from member stations which produced them under grants. Additional programs were purchased from the BBC and a few more were produced by private contractors. In 1964, Ford Foundation increased its subsidy. The subsidy enabled NET to have nearly all new programs produced by independent, professional program packagers.

Organization of Public Broadcasting (CPB)

A Corporation for Public Broadcasting was established as a non-profit corporation.[8] It has a 15-man board that the President appoints, with Senate approval. Not more than eight directors should belong to the same political party. The directors should be eminent in the fields of education, cultural, civic affairs, or the arts and radio and television and should represent a cross-section of various regions of the country. Their term was fixed for six years. The President appoints the chairman. The directors elect one or more vice-chairmen.

In 1969, CPB formed the Public Broadcasting Service (PES) to develop an interconnecting system among the stations. However, the Nixon Administration wanted a 'localized' system of ETV instead of a centralized network programming. President Nixon feared that PBS might control the entire public broadcasting system.

The Carnegie Commission had envisioned it to be a decentralized system where resources of public broadcasting would be drawn. Instead PBS emerged as a competitor to commercial broadcasters.

Public broadcasting modified its structure to blunt the criticism about "centralization." PBS circulated a list of programs to the stations. It asked these stations what they were willing to partly shoulder through the Station Program Cooperative. One dismal result was their choosing quantity over quality.

Financing

1975 was a promising year for public broadcasting. The Public Broadcasting Financing Act provided for a five-year funding scheme for the system. But Congress struck off the five-year appropriation. Instead, it decided on a two- to three-year funding which does not allow for medium-range planning. President Nixon's justification for this cutback was that CPB was exerting too much control over local stations, and that centralization threatened "to erode substantially public broadcasting's impressive potential for promoting innovative and diverse cultural and educational programming."

Congress encouraged raising funds from other sources. It authorized the matching of one federal dollar for every $2.50 raised from other sources.

Aside from Congressional appropriations, public broadcasting receives funding from other federal agencies and departments, state and local governments (including state colleges or universities), foundation grants (a major component), viewer/listener subscriptions/membership, donations from wealthy individuals, gifts from business firms (both cash and equipment grants), sale of program guides, annual fund drives, business underwriting of programs, and production contracts and rental of facilities.

In 1979, the Carnegie Commission II reported on the flaws of public broadcasting's financial, organizational and creative structure. One of the flaws was CPB's involvement in the programming process that subordinated its first function of insulating the system from political intervention.

The commission proposed that CPB be replaced by a Public Telecommunications Trust which will primarily hold the funds in trust and to insulate the system from political pressures. A separate Program Services Endowment was set up to prepare the national programs to be distributed by PBS.

Ownership Structure

By ownership, three types of public stations emerged. The first type is composed of stations licensed to a single private institution like a college or university, for training and servicing the community. The second type are those stations run by government agencies like a state university or public school system or a municipal board of education-state-operated stations. The third type are stations put up by cultural associations or institutions. These stations enjoy support from foundations, business and listeners and are usually more outstanding and significant on the national scene than the other types. Diversity of funding sources results in freedom in setting programming policies. The community stations' program mix include a broad cultural-arts-entertainment-educational fare aimed at a general audience.

PROBLEMS AND ISSUES IN PUBLIC BROADCASTING

In 1980, the federal subsidy for CPB was cut by 25 percent. This led to more funding difficulties.

Much of the time of public broadcasters are spent in searching for funds to the neglect of other important matters.

The Carnegie Commission recognized the danger of accepting federal funds. It tried to provide safeguards against political interference by specifying a non-political CPB membership and permanent funding. However, the stations in the beginning got funds from any source and then tailored their programs to the amount they had and to expectations of donors. When the donors were business companies, the stations made programs that reflected the corporations desire to project a favorable image among certain viewers. When donors were individuals they designed programs to please their donors' tastes and interests.

Another issue is the confusion over what public broadcasting is, its mission and purpose. Some say that public broadcasting should provide "alternative broadcasting" to fill the gaps in the commercial schedules with cultural and educational programs. Others feel that it should look at society and provide programs to meet societal needs. Still others expect it to provide instructional programs at all levels, and encourage children's and specialty programming.

Increasing competition from new technologies is expected to chip off the audience share of all types of programs. New distribution systems will likely raise costs for specialty programs, forcing public TV to offer fewer programs of this type.

Another problem is limited budgets which lowers program quality. The public stations find it difficult to hire competent and experienced program personnel because they cannot match the salary rates offered by commercial stations.

According to Wilbur Schramm, ETV has been "a shoestring operation, long on imagination but short on cash, high on ideals but low on salaries, strong on program standards but weak in money for talent and equipment."

Still many believers in public broadcasting foresee its becoming the "public telecommunication center" which will produce, acquire, receive, duplicate, and distribute all types of non-commercial, educational, cultural and informational materials.

PROPOSAL FOR A PHILIPPINE PUBLIC BROADCASTING CORPORATION (PPBC)

Based on the two broadcasting systems, a similar alternative to the commercial broadcasting system could be adopted in the Philippines.

The Post-Revolution era, characterized by the restoration of press freedom, provides the proper climate for innovation. There is now the opportunity to develop mass media into responsive channels for public needs and interests.

Rationale

What is a public broadcasting system?

A public broadcasting system provides programming usually not available on commercial stations. It can cater to minorities and special interest groups. It allows localized programming and greater community participation. Being non-profit, it can focus on making programs since it does not have to cater to the needs of advertisers.

Both radio and TV have enormous potential to aid economic, social and educational development programs. An appropriate, efficient, and effective system should produce programs which could help change the traditional attitude of the rural people and to enable them to acquire skills needed for their development.

Public broadcasting should provide diverse programs to help promote the growth and unity of the nation. They should be in either the local language or dialect. Their personnel should come from the locality, must know the local cultures of their community and speak the native language or dialect fluently.

Organizational Structure (PPBC)

The PPBC, like the BBC and CPB/PBS, shall be an autonomous, non-profit public corporation licensed by the government. Its board of directors shall be appointed by the President or the National Telecommunications Commission (NTC). Either the President or the NTC shall designate a chairman who will be recommended by civic organizations, groups and prominent citizens. The directors shall elect a vice-chairman. Patterned after the BBC set-up, the board shall formulate the basic policies of the corporation. Other committees will be created to help run the corporation. As in BBC, the PPBC shall have a general advisory council and 13 regional councils.

Financing

Funding should be permanent to prevent political intervention. Subsidy should come from the national government, its different departments and agencies, foundations, philanthropic institutions, individuals and business corporations. Sale of publications will also be another source of funds. No donor shall dominate the funding to prevent any undue influence on programming. Regional stations will be autonomous and will be owned by local citizens.

Programming

A separate committee should be in charge of either programming or production, or both. All public stations should provide local, regional, national, and even international programs. The products should be a balance and program of information, education, culture and entertainment for both mass and minority audiences.

Programming will be a mix of 60 percent national productions and 40 percent regional or local programs.

ETV would serve as a catalytic agent for overall educational reform - upgrading the quality of instruction, reforming curriculum, reaching larger numbers of students, equalizing opportunity, and reducing unit costs of instruction. In general, ETV can contribute teaching, as shown by the experience of many countries.

The thrust of public broadcasting should be to encourage independent producers to create high quality and distinctively Filipino programs to counteract the pervasive influence of foreign programs.

Canadian Broadcasting Corporation reports that foreign programs can seriously modify cultural perceptions and values and can diminish their sense of national identity.[9] The Philippines is not exempt from this type of modifications.

Public broadcasting's major characteristics which are laudable and applicable to national goals are:

- *Independence* of programs from funders;
- *Non-commercial* - Because it is not motivated by profit, it is mainly concerned with giving the best high quality programs to meet the the needs of specific audiences;
- *Public Service* - It is not a propaganda instrument; it is there to shape or change attitudes and opinions, inspire action and contribute to national unity and development;
- *Decentralized* - local stations could decide what is best for their communities; and
- *Broad spectrum of programming* - It serves all segments of the public.

The public broadcasting system, if adopted, can definitely help the government's democratization efforts in bringing about political, social and economic stability in the country.

Notes

[1] Eastman, Susan Tyler, Sydney Head and Louis Klein, *Broadcast Programming*, Wadsworth Publishing Co., California: 1981, p. 253.

[2] Emery, Walter B., *National and International Systems of Broadcasting: Their History, Operation and Control*. East Lansing: Michigan State University Press, 1969, p. 84.

[3] Agee, Warren, Edwin Emery and Philip Agee, *Introduction to Mass Communication*. Harper and Row Publishing, Inc., New York: 1981, p. 247.

[4] Ibid, p. 85.

[5] Ibid, p. 86.

[6] Milne, Alexander, "Future Broadcasting Policy in Britain – Fraught with Ambiguity," *Combroad*, London: BBC House, March, 1986, p. 22.

[7] *Philippine Daily Inquirer*, July 6, 1986.

[8] Summers and Summers, "Public Broadcasting," in *Broadcasting and the Public*, Wadsworth Publishing Company, Inc., 1978, p. 291.

[9] Milne, op. cit.

Chapter **XVI**

Fundamentals of Film

Amiel Leonardia

A look at the titles of Filipino films made today shows similarity in themes and reveals the current fad of movie audiences. From their titles, Filipino movies seem to have barely moved since 1964 when John Lent wrote:

> The other criticisms have become standard in the last 15 years: movies are not artistic, the same trite themes are used, continuity doesn't exist, people portrayed aren't real, and stars have no talent and are chosen on good looks, personality, and acting ability--in that order. Also, directors don't know how to direct because they are chosen according to what had made a hit in the past. If a movie with a child star succeeds, then all producers beat the bushes for child star scripts.[1]

Critics and observers of the movie scene in the Philippines tend to agree with Lent's observation. But Filipino film producers are not alone in riding on money-makers. American and European producers exhibit a similar propensity for profit at the expense of originality. American, European and Filipino imitations of James Bond movies are too numerous to mention.

T.D. Agcaoili, a film critic and director, noted in 1967 that film making requires some scholarship. But many film directors hardly reached college. He said:

Their lack of formal education should not be counted against them, for there are artists--writers, painters, poets, and composers--who have not acquired any college education at all, but whose creative works reveal great talent and artists make up for their lack of formal education with self-study, inquiry, and self dedication.

The average Filipino movie director today is concerned only with making money--an attitude that he shares with the average movie producers whose concern with making money is even greater.[2]

Such types of directors were still very much in the scene in the late seventies. A young man might be asked to direct a film because his uncle happens to be the producer, not for his practical and theoretical preparation. The problems in the industry in 1978 can be typified by complaints. Audiences complain about poor stories and sloppy productions; producers complain about *bakya* audiences. Directors complain against producers who do not respect their artistic vision; producers complain against directors who do not meet deadlines. Producers complain against actors and actresses who work on more than one movie at a time; actors and actresses complain about producers who are slow in paying them. Producers complain against the lack of government support; the government complains against the lack of commitment of the movie industry to the developmental thrusts of the nation. In spite of these problems, however, the Filipino film has survived and has even grown.

THE BEGINNINGS

Looking back, the early Filipino film audiences probably saw films of "a laborer felling a wall, workers leaving a factory, a baby eating breakfast in the garden."[3] Not until 1908 did Filipinos see a complete feature film.

"Dalagang Bukid," the first film produced by a Filipino, Jose Nepomuceno was made with the use of few pieces of equipment in 1919. Its star, Atang de la Rama, and another actress, Mary Walter, recall vividly that there was "only one camera, one reflector and lights which were so hot they almost cooked the stars."

Mary Walter recalls that only the director had the script and had to coach his actors on what to do.[4]

Nepomuceno is usually credited with having trained many of the early film actors, directors, cameramen, and other technicians. Others who followed Nepomuceno were Gerry de Leon and Lamberto Avellana who marked the introduction of creative cinema. Avellana started directing films in 1938, when he was only 23, a fresh college graduate from the Ateneo. His first film was "Sakay," which according to film critic, T.D. Agcaoili, employed organically in film some of the elements of modern stagecraft and dramaturgy that had been lacking in Philippine movies.[5]

Avellana has since produced "Anak Dalita," "Badjao," and other films. He has also been named national artist for film. Gerry de Leon is remembered for his movies based on Rizal's works such as "Sisa" and "El Filibusterismo."

In a country which delights in entertainment, the motion picture soon overshadowed the zarzuela, the popular theater form of the 1930s. By 1939, the Philippine movie industry was fifth in the world in number of talkies produced. The Big Four--LVN, Sampaguita, Lebran, and Premiere-- promoted the progress of the Filipino film by standardizing contracts and salary scales and exercising control and training of their movie stars.

In World War II, the Japanese, finding Filipino films too American oriented, revived the zarzuela.

After the world war, the production of films resumed. Lent observes:

> The first company to resume operations was Sampaguita, which formally opened June 1945. Its operations, however, were at first limited strictly to booking prewar pictures. LVN released the first popular picture in 1945--'Orasang Ginto.' It also was the first studio to team up with a foreign company to make movies. In 1952, it worked with an Indonesian firm. LVN made a total of 175 films from 1945 to 1954, 12 in full color. Sampaguita, in the same period, made 110 black-and-white movies.

The pace at which independent movie companies were formed paralleled the energy and vigor of the country's reconstruction after the war. Many of them were respectable, but some of them were merely out to make a quick profit, without regard for the aesthetic values or for the sensibilities of the audience.

Today, the Filipino movie industry has grown into a multi-million peso industry.

THE AUDIENCE

The most important element in the film industry is the audience, the reason for its being. The audience creates tastes, makes or unmakes stars, makes millionaires of producers or actors. The Filipino audience has often been criticized, maligned and called *bakya* for its undemanding tastes and indiscriminate preferences. Many movie producers excuse themselves from producing worthwhile and well-made movies by citing the tastes of the *bakya* crowd. Yet film director Lino Brocka, said:

> Too often has the *bakya* crowd been blamed for the sad state of Filipino movies. But what can one expect of an audience that has been fed nothing but secret-agent, karate, fantasy and

slapstick movies since time immemorial? A child raised on rock-n-roll would find classical music strange, discordant, unpleasant; an audience raised in an atmosphere of motion-picture commercialism and escapism would regard a good film totally alien. The film audience deprived of good, intelligent fare by irresponsible and unscrupulous film-makers cannot be expected to accept things overnight, no matter what artistic merits a production may have.[6]

A study conducted in 1970 by some students in mass communications at the University of Santo Tomas, noted that moviegoers consider the story element the strongest reason for seeing a movie. Forty-one percent of those queried said they went to see a movie because of the story, 36 percent because of the acting, and 18 percent because of the production aspect. The students further discovered that:

... Men see local movies more frequently than women.
Moviegoers, who are 40 years and above, watch films more frequently than the younger ones.
The more educated the persons are, the less frequently they watch local movies.
Local movie audiences watch movies most often on Sundays, followed by Saturdays, Mondays and Tuesdays.
Men prefer comedy and action pictures to other types of films, while women prefer comedy and drama.

Another study conducted in 1975 by the Philippine Survey and Research Center, Inc. showed that in deciding what movies to see audiences consider the cast (76 percent for local movies; 71 percent for foreign movies), the plot (52 percent for local movies; 53 percent for foreign movies), and the type (20 percent for local movies; 26 percent for foreign movies). Audiences also consider the following:

Director	33 percent
Award winner	29 percent
Language/dialect	36 percent
Producer	21 percent
Trailer	18 percent
Best seller	16 percent
Moviehouse showing	15 percent

Ben Lara, a *Bulletin Today* reporter, noted that while the tastes of a Filipino moviegoer may vary from one season to another, some of his biases die hard, including his preference for American films.

He pointed out that a recent Vilma Santos movie grossed ₱5 million in its entire run, but "Godfather," starring Marlon Brando, earned ₱6 million in its first few days run in six theaters.[7]

However, since 1973, the audience has widened. More and more college students watch Filipino films. Seminars on film and filmmaking held in many places in Manila show the increase of interest in film. Brocka suggests that in order to develop and enlarge the audience for Filipino films,

> The film-maker's task is to develop their tastes further in a conscious and patient fashion, in order to slowly wean them away from the false artistic and social values fostered by kiss-kiss, bang-bang, zoom-zoom, boo-hoo, song-and-dance flicks. One could work at first with the same commercial medium, but do it a little better, with more restraint, intelligence, characterization and motivation, so as not to insult the educated or alienate the *bakya* crowd.[8]

THE PRODUCERS

The Filipino producer has the ultimate responsibility for what the audience views on the screen. Although the director is artistically the production head, the director's creativity can either be inhibited or encouraged by the producer who holds the purse-strings. He can force the director to make a movie, which would be just a copy of other movies, or he can allow the director great freedom to be faithful to his creative vision.

The producer certainly has every right to expect to recover his investment or even to make a nice profit. What most directors ask, however, is that the producers should have an idea of cinema, that they should not be so willing to sacrifice quality for expediency. Because producers with a sense of commitment and devotion are very few, many young directors tend to work with producers with whom they have rapport. Behn Cervantes, film and stage director, makes the following observation on the producer:

> To these people, profit is foremost and quality is a word to bandy about to give themselves prestige. If the local films are to improve, the first people that have to be educated are the producers themselves because they decide what movies will be made, what stories to film, which directors to hire, which performers to be employed.[9]

Many producers do realize the importance of making significant films. Perhaps the most important development concerning the producers is their organizing the Philippine Motion Picture Producers Association (PMPPA).

In 1975, the PMPPA commissioned a study on the Filipino film which was edited by Wilfredo Nolledo. As a big business, Nolledo says:

> From its slender beginnings in 1917 the Filipino film, with no financial assistance whatsoever, has grown rapidly into a Big Business with a yearly intake of ₱100 million. Approximately 1,058,900 Filipinos go to the movies daily, accounting for ₱227 million in annual box office returns.[10]

Producers are also influenced by the quick return of, apart from big profits from their original investment. Nolledo says:

> The film industry probably represents the shortest cut possible between an investor's original capital and big profits. Unlike other stocks in trade with a long-term dividend yield, movie investment can be recouped, not infrequently, with substantial gains after a very short time span. The investment, thus, is not frozen.[11]

The holding of the annual Manila Film Festival initiated by the city of Manila to encourage Filipino film producers to produce quality movies has had very encouraging results. The ₱854,000 gross in 1966 had more than tripled to ₱2.5 million in 1973.

More Filipino films are being shown in first-run theaters. This favorable turn of events is attributable to, among others, the following factors:

- Between 1970 and 1971, the Manila Theatre Association entered an agreement with the Philippine Motion Picture Producers Association (PMPPA), to allocate 49 days a year in each theater to films produced by the PMPPA members;

- Filipino films exhibited in movie theaters, that show mostly foreign films, frequently outgrossed imported films;

- Fewer quality foreign films are being imported for exhibition.

Rodolfo L. Velasco, PMPPA executive secretary, expressed optimism that within the 1975-85 decade the film industry hoped to establish an ongoing demand from the outside market. He said that some of their films have already reached foreign audiences. However, some annoying problems remain. The Filipino film has not yet captured the market share it deserves. A look at the movie advertisements immediately indicates that foreign films still hold a large portion of the local market.

THE DIRECTORS

If the movie industry is to move forward, movie directors should also develop a sense of what is possible. Film critic Bienvenido Lumbera, commenting on the direction which a Filipino filmmaker should keep in mind, says:

> For the director who recognizes the boundaries set by an underdeveloped economy on his art, it is essential to cultivate less the technical, formalist side of filmmaking and concentrate instead on the human resources that are abundantly available to him.[12]

Some directors have directed films that are noteworthy for their consistency and seriousness of their vision. To name a few, they are Brocka, who has directed several award winning movies ("Tinimbang Ka Ngunit Kulang" and "Maynila: Sa Mga Kuko ng Liwanag"); Ishmael Bernal ("Pagdating sa Dulo," "Mister Mo, Lover Boy Ko"); Behn Cervantes who directed the much acclaimed "Sakada"; Celso Ad. Castillo ("Burlesk Queen"); Elwood Perez ("Beerhouse"); Mario O' Hara ("Tatlong Taon Walang Diyos"); Orlando Nadres, a scriptwriter and director; Lupita A. Concio ("Minsa'y Isang Gamo-Gamu"); and Mike de Leon whose work shows a mastery of the technical aspects of filmmaking.

Among the older directors are Eddie Romero ("Ganito Kami Noon, Papaano Kayo Ngayon"), Gerry de Leon and Lamberto Avellana.

Many of them were either nominated or awarded the Urian award, or the Famas for best directing. Romero has won an Urian award which is given by the film critics group, the Manunuri ng Pelikulang Pilipino. Lupita Concio won a FAMAS award for her direction of the moving and intensely patriotic "Minsa'y Isang Gamo-Gamu."

The new breed of directors has given the industry a look of respectability. Prospective moviegoers these days check out who is directing the film before they go to the theater. Many realize these directors turn out quality films.

Serious movie directors now receive better salaries. Brocka told a television audience in "Nothing But the Truth" that the movie director these days is well paid. In 1975, for instance, Nestor Torre, a movie critic and film director, reported that some directors in the past used to get as little as ₱5,000 for directing a quickie. In 1975, the top directors could command ₱40,000 or even ₱50,000 per film.[13]

The serious director has gained some respectability and can be considered seriously an artist due to producers giving him more responsibility, and rewarding him for artistically satisfying films that are also box-office hits.

THE ACTORS

Of all the persons involved in film production, the actor is probably the best known. This is only natural since the actor's work is the most visible in the film.

Some movie stars are bankable and hot in the box-office. Because they have an audience-drawing power, they also command astronomical salaries. In 1975, the asking price of Nora Aunor, Dolphy, Joseph Estrada, and Fernando Poe Jr. was under half a million pesos. In 1987, Seiko films signed up Dolphy for two films at P1.8 million a picture — the highest fee so far.[14] These movie stars virtually ensure the producer of making a profit at the box-office. Seiko producer Robbie Tan said he considers the Dolphy project not a gamble at all because it is "easy to recoup the fee" he paid for Dolphy.[15]

The "superstars" seem to thrive on their screaming, almost hysterical fans. They also consciously cultivate the loyalty of their fans by sometimes opening their houses to any fan who would like to spend the day with her favorite movie star. Movie fans are also more organized. Nora Aunor perhaps has the best fan club organization. The intense loyalty and adulation of the movie fan is aided and abetted by magazines, comics, radio programs, and even television programs which devote time to discussing the movie star's latest movie or love affair.

While some actors and actresses merit the respect and loyalty of moviegoers, many are simply amateurish and do not deserve to be viewed by a paying audience. Laurice Guillen, a movie actress and film director, explains it this way:

> First, why do aspiring actors go to the movies? There are, I think, three possible reasons. First, to make money (since the movies can be seen as a lucrative job). Second, to acquire glamor and popularity (the medium has a way of magnifying one's image). And third, to pursue therapeutic outlets for neurotic tendencies and hangups.[16]

Sadly, among the reasons given by Ms. Guillen, the need to act, the impulse to create, are absent. Yet, the audience deserves movie stars, who at least have a sense of acting for film. During the heyday of the Big Four, Sampaguita Pictures provided its stars some training before they were presented to the audience. According to the late Dr. Jose Perez of Sampaguita,

> This "build-up" program was incorporated in the contract and every signee (sic) had to undergo this phase in the course of his stay with the studio. Minors were made to further their schooling, with the company shouldering all the expenses. The contract stars were also made to enrol in special courses like

speech, dance, voice or music lessons if they had the inclination. Also a must in the contract was a requirement for the actor or actress to submit himself or herself to a dramatic and speech course.[17]

The decline of the studios in the late sixties and the emergence of independent companies have led to actors and actresses having to get whatever training they need themselves.

Nora Aunor's development from a singer to an award-winning actress gives the hope that others like her might be waiting somewhere in the wings.

THE SCRIPTWRITERS

Producers lately have recognized that the movie must begin with a script. Cesar Amigo, a scriptwriter and director, complains about certain practices in shooting. "In fact, we start shooting without getting to see the actual script. A director shoots in an island without even knowing what to do."[18] Clodualdo del Mundo Jr., scriptwriter of the acclaimed "Maynila: Sa Kuko ng Liwanag," states the importance of the scriptwriter to the production:

> He holds the sacred word for the film's visual and aural aspects. He is the producer's passport to the Board of Censors. He is the source of livelihood—for what will the director shoot without a script? What will the cameraman record if there are no sequences in the script? The scriptwriter is responsible for a lot of things. And if he is an intelligent writer, he has to know the visual requirements, write dialogue, establish the time and place and mood.

Nevertheless, the scriptwriter is still ultimately responsible to the producer. The writer must first submit his synopsis to the producer. If the producer is interested in the script, the writer may expand to a treatment. He may write a full shooting script once the producer gives his approval.

What kind of stories interest producers? A study submitted to the PMPPA gives an idea on what producers define as a good script:

Producer 1 "One which relays the message in black and white; moves the life of a character; understands the technical aspects of moviemaking; would sell the story to the public."

Producer 2: "Story with good qualities, the theme, message or moral lesson taken from it; not confusing, especially to the viewing public, the role of each character involved."

Producer 3: "Historical and with quality."
Producer 4: "One that has good down-to-earth and punchy dialogues, needless to say, and story must be 'in'."
Producer 5: "One with good story and message and at the same time marketable."
Producer 6: "A script that is original and does not drag."
Producer 7: "The theme should be impressive. The cast should suit the characters they portray. The theme and flow of the story should be centralized in one direction."
Producer 8: "A good script has a moral lesson."
Producer 9: "One with action, love, beautiful sceneries and solid story."
Producer 10: "The story must be meaty. The packaging must be good, i.e., stars included. Novelty counts a lot."[19]

Producers often mangle scripts or make unauthorized changes compelling scriptwriters to organize into the Philippine Scriptwriters, Incorporated to safeguard their interest. The PSI has set a ₱7,500 minimum price for a script. Some scriptwriters receive much more than the minimum price simply because of their reputation. This has already been upgraded, but scriptwriters are still fighting for the ₱25,000 minimum for each script.[20] Some still settle for ₱10,000 a script. The reputable ones get much more. Lualhati Bautista gets an average of ₱50,000 a script.[21] Ricky Lee, probably the highest paid screenwriter, gets ₱30,000 to ₱90,000 a script.[22]

PROBLEMS OF THE FILIPINO MOVIE INDUSTRY

Producers still complain about the movie industry's being one of the most heavily taxed industries in the country. High taxes pose extreme difficulty to many producers in turning out quality films.

Another problem which has not been resolved is the lack of professionalism among young actors and actresses. It is not uncommon for movie stars to be late for shooting schedules. Some are late because they have committed themselves to too many movies.

But the fact that Filipinos love movies and that the enthusiasm for moviemaking is undiminished seems to augur well for the film industry.

Because many people are genuinely concerned with the shape and direction of the Filipino film, the film industry, despite its problems, will grow even bigger. More importantly, it will reflect more and more the society in which it exists.

Notes

[1] John Lent, *Philippine Mass Communications* (Manila: A Philippine Press Institute Publication, 1964), p. 115.

[2] T.D. Agcaoili, "Movies," *Philippine Mass Media in Perspective*, eds. Gloria D. Feliciano and Crispulo Icban, Jr., (Quezon City: Capitol Publishing House, Inc., 1967), p. 146.

[3] Arthur Knight, *The Liveliest Art* (New York and Toronto: A Mentor Book, 1957), p. 19.

[4] Silent Stars Reminisce, *Philippine Daily Express*, May 13, 1977, p. 29.

[5] Justino M. Dormiendo, "Avellana Talks on Movies," *The Times Journal*, September 22, 1975, p. 8.

[6] Lino Brocka, "Philippine Movies: Some Problems and Prospects," *The Manila Review*, October 1974, pp. 59-60.

[7] Ben Lara, "RP moviegoers prefer US films," *Bulletin Today*, August 16, 1973, pp. 1, 15.

[8] Lino Brocka, "Philippine Movies: Some Problems and Prospects," *The Manila Review*, October 1974, pp. 59-60.

[9] Behn Cervantes, "Ganyan Lang Talaga Yan: or the harsh realities of Philippine Cinema," *The Sillimanian*, November 1977, p. 7.

[10] Wilfredo Nolledo, ed., "The Philippine Movie Industry: A Study on the Viability of Movie Production," (Manila: Philippine Motion Pictures Producers Association, 1975), p. 2.

[11] Ibid, p. 11.

[12] Bienvenido Lumbera, "An Approach to the Filipino Film: Guideposts for critics and directors," *Philippines Sunday Express*, November 2, 1975.

[13] Nestor Torre, Jr., "The Rise of the Filipino Film Director," *Philippines Daily Express*, July 18, 1975, p. 32.

[14] Crispina Martinez-Belen, "Celebrity World," a column in the *Manila Bulletin*, April 5, 1987, p. 47.

[15] Ibid.

[16] Justino M. Dormiendo, "The Stuff of which Actors Are Made," *The Times Journal*, October 9, 1975, p. 5.

[17] Crispina Martinez-Belen, "Stars Aren't Born; Studios Make Them," *Bulletin Today*, August 25, 1973, p. 5.

[18]Justice M. Dormiendo, "No Script, No Movie," *The Times Journal*, October 10, 1975, p. 5.

[19]Rey E. de la Cruz, "Factors Contributing to the Producer's Choice of Scripts: A Case Study," Thesis, Institute of Mass Communications, University of the Philippines, March 1976, p. 17.

[20]Constantino C. Tejero, "Screen writers of the Philippines: Felt Life and Disenchanted Moments," *Sunday Inquirer Magazine*, January 11, 1987, p. 20.

[21]Ibid., p. 17.

[22]Ibid., p. 19.

Chapter XVII

Film Making: Problems and Prospects

Nicanor G. Tiongson

Amused by the Filipino's obsession with movies, a critic once jokingly remarked that in the Philippines more people go to moviehouses than to churches. The comment was meant to be hyperbolic, but it probably comes close to the truth. According to one film scholar, about 1,200 moviehouses were operating all over the country in 1983, and an estimated 1,626,000 Filipinos viewed films every day of the year except Good Friday when all moviehouses are closed. The *cine* is indeed one of the most important institutions in contemporary Philippine society.

The power of cinema cannot be underestimated. Cinema catapulted a Nora Aunor to fame and fortune, and a Rogelio de la Rosa and Joseph Estrada to political prominence. It helped to get Ferdinand Marcos elected to the presidency (through movies like "Iginuhit ng Tadhana" and "Pinagbuklod ng Langit"). Later, it served as well to strengthen and perpetuate Marcos' dictatorial rule and the interests of the establishment that supported the dictator (mainly through the various censors' bodies controlled by the government).

On the other hand, cinema has fought the Establishment by exposing American domination ("Minsa'y Isang Gamugamu"), military abuses ("Boy Kondenado"), the problems of workers ("Bayan Ko: Kapit sa Patalim"), the journalists and the religious ("Sister Stella L."), the peasant ("Sakada"), and the urban poor ("Maynila, Sa mga Kuko ng Liwanag" and "The Boatman").

Clearly, the immense popularity of cinema has made it a power and disseminator of values and ideas. If only for this, cinema should not be ignored. It should be harnessed as an important agent for social change. Such an endeavor, however, will have to be premised on an understanding of the history, profile, and problems of the Filipino film industry.

PROFILE: 1982-1985

Since the film industry is now in transition, its present profile will have to be drawn from industry data from 1981 to 1985.

The Film

The *Filipino Film Review* reports that in 1981, 187 feature films were shown in the country, 183 of which were new, and 4 re-releases. In 1982, 172 feature films were shown, of which 150 were new and 22 re-releases. In 1983, 162 feature films were released, of which 141 were new, and 21 re-releases. In the first six months of 1984, 70 feature films were produced. Of these, 63 were new, 6 were re-releases and 1 was a co-production. Based on the 1981-83 figures, the average number of feature films shown yearly was 174.

Jackelyn A. Campos reports in the *Filipino Film Review* that of the types of films shown in 1978-1982, action films accounted for 47 percent, drama, 32.8 percent, and comedy, 20.2 percent. Of the action films, 83 percent are fiction, the rest are based on true characters and events.

The same pattern seems apparent in films in the first six months of 1984. *Filipino Film Review* reported that 70 feature films were shown. Of these, 63 were new − 31 action-dramas, 16 dramas, 8 comedies, 5 sex films, and 3 youth-oriented movies.

Typical of the action film is "Sumuko ka. . . Ronquillo" (1983). It traces the real-life story of Ronquillo (played by Rudy Fernandez) who suffers injustice at the hands of the law and who decides to fight the authorities. The most important ingredient of this type of film is the fight sequences which have to be scattered liberally throughout the film.

The melodrama or drama par excellence is "Mga Batang Yagit" (1984), a film based on Jose Miranda Cruz' popular TV soap opera of the same title. The film follows the lives of four children who are oppressed by hateful grandmothers, mothers, hostesses, call boys, but who manage to put one over their oppressors and even to have fun (e.g., singing while pushing a cartful of garbage). The film is replete with a lot of screaming confrontations and a hundred and one tearful breakdowns and reconciliations.

The comedy is typified by "Naku, Ha" (1984), which casts the comic trio, Tito, Vic and Joey, as overstaying students. Slapstick humor and witty lines, with a few songs and dances thrown in, are the life of most comedies.

The sex film is typified by "Scorpio Nights" (1985), which tells the story of a security guard and his young housewife. The latter has an affair with the young boy who lives on the floor above. When the husband discovers the two in bed, he shoots them and shoots himself. The movie, though technically well-crafted, presents us with a series of prolonged love-making scenes which seem intended merely to titillate the audience sexually.

FILM MAKING: PROBLEMS AND PROSPECTS

The youth film is exemplified by "Bagets" (1984), which presents five boys, played by Aga Mulach, J. C. Bonnin, Raymond Lauchengco, Herbert Bautista and William Martinez, as they go through their conflicts with stupid teachers, sex-starved women, and immature parents. Pretty faces and trendy costumes, the latest dance steps and songs, and lots of juvenile humor spell success for a movie for youth about youth.

The Producers

In 1983, 75 film companies produced 162 feature movies. Only 29 producers were members of the Philippine Motion Pictures Producers Association (PMPPA), which includes the big established film companies, like FPJ Productions (Fernando Poe, Jr.), Seven Stars (Jesse Ejercito), Wonder Films (Alex and Cheng Muhlach), Tagalog Ilang-Ilang (Esperidion Laxa), RVQ Productions (Rodolfo Quizon or Dolphy), Sampaguita Pictures (Marichu Vera Perez-Maceda), MVP (Marichu Vera Perez-Maceda), and JE Productions (Joseph Estrada). Twenty producers belonged to the Integrated Movie Producers, Importers and Distributors Association of the Philippines (IMPIDAP), which includes Regal Films (Remy and Lily Monteverde). Twenty-six outfits were independent producers.

In 1983, the top ten producing companies were: Regal - 11 films; Viva - 9; GP - 5; Cine Suerte - 5; Baby Pascual and Associates - 5; Seiko - 5; Bukang Liwayway - 4; JPM - 4; GPS - 4; and RVQ - 4.

Producers have to spend for (1) actors and actresses whose fees can eat up as much as 40 percent of total production costs; (2) production staff, which account for about 30 percent of costs distributed down the line (producer, director, writer, assistant director, production manager, cameramen, production designer, make-up artist, legman, stillman, film editor, music director, sound effects man, sound mixer, propsman, setman, two utility men, post-production coordinator, field cashier, looper, public relations officer, and lay-out artist); (3) raw materials, including color and black-and-white film rolls, sound recording rolls, and magnetic tapes, all of which take up about 10 percent of costs, and (4) promotions, in the print and broadcast media, which can take up, as in the case of Regal, almost 20 percent of costs.

The Theaters and Audience

The 1,200 theaters all over the country range from first to third-run theaters in the urban and rural areas. Based on industry estimates, there are about 591,864,000 moviegoers in a year.

Lucila Hosillos identifies the audiences of Filipino movies:

> Movies are patronized by the urban and town dwellers, workers, peasants and other low income groups who constitute

about 70 to 75 percent of the population and who live on subsistence wages and subhuman conditions. The habitues, however, who contribute the bigger income to the movie industry are of the upper and middle classes for whom movies are prime entertainment. A smaller percentage of the middle and upper classes are movie buffs, *aficionados,* dilettantes, censors, the cultural elite that prides itself in being the *avant garde* of film art, and the personnel and investors of the movie industry. . . . By sheer bulk and number, the low-income sector should be able to support the movie industry. It does not have, however, the financial means. In fact, low-income urban habitues frequent the neighborhood movie houses which show double programs and charge cheaper than first-class single-run cinemas downtown.

Knowing who make up the movie audiences, it is clear that the bigger percentage come from the low income groups. They have not even gone to high school, have not been exposed to artistic films, and have been raised to appreciate the simplistic characterization they encounter in popular magazines, radio serials, television dramas, and genre movies.

But in the minority are audiences who have gone to college, who have been exposed to the arts in and outside the country, and who demand a measure of technical expertise and artistry for any film. Some of them have banded together into groups, which try to upgrade the quality of Filipino films by giving out annual awards. In 1986, these awards groups included: the FAMAS, an industry award; the Urian Awards, which is given by the Manunuri ng Pelikulang Pilipino, the country's only group of film critics who judge films on pure artistic merit; the Catholic Mass Media Awards, which encourages technical and artistic excellence and emphasizes human values in films; the Film Academy Awards, where the guilds (directors, assistant directors, actors, production designers, cinematographers, editors, screenwriters) choose the best of the works of their members for the year; and the Star Awards, given by a newly-formed body of movie writers.

Government Film Agencies

When Ferdinand Marcos fled the country in February 1986, he left behind him several film bodies which he created. The best-known of these agencies is the Movie and Television Review and Classification Board (MTRCB) which was created by P. D. 1986 and which was activated in October 1985. MTRCB was to take over the functions of the Board of Review for Motion Pictures and Television (BRMPT). BRMPT then was headed by Maria Kalaw-Katigbak, whom the movie people wanted to oust for her outmoded criteria and repressive administration.BRMPT was created by Marcos just a few years back to replace the Board of Censors for Motion Pictures (BCMP), which became unpopular for its alleged corruption, ignorance of film, and repressiveness.

The MTRCB is headed by a chairman and a vice-chairman, and is composed of 30 members. Manuel Morato is the current censors chief. The board members seem to be people with little expertise in film.

Videogram Regulatory Board was created by P.D. 1987 "to regulate the industry and curb video piracy." It is composed of a chairman, a vice chairman and 18 members. But only seven persons were appointed to the board. Curiously, VRB's function was published only in March 1986, and therefore VRB could not be made fully operational. Some suspect that this was deliberately done to give certain video shop operators more time to pirate more materials.

The third government body is the Film Development Foundation of the Philippines. It was created by Executive Order 1091 and registered in October 1985 to replace the Experimental Cinema of the Philippines (ECP). ECP was criticized for becoming the producer and purveyor of sex films, although its original concept was commendable. Created by Executive Order 770 on January 29, 1982, it was governed by Director-General Imee Marcos-Manotoc, and a three-man board of trustees. Through the ECP, which was exempt from taxes and from any kind of censorship, President Marcos wanted to neutralize the repressiveness of Katigbak's BRMPT, and give his administration a wash of liberality.

In this liberal view, the ECP intended: (1) to foster film appreciation, particularly among the youth; (2) to expand the audience for films other than the average commercial fare via regular screenings and regional outreach programs featuring exhibitions and appreciation courses; (3) to develop parallel cinema by encouraging film to be produced outside the mainstream of commercial cinema; (4) to assist local talent to continually acquire film-making expertise; and (5) to promote other incentives (apart from financial) to develop filmmaking in the Philippines.

To achieve its aims, the ECP administered five divisions. The Film Fund provided production and financial assistance to producers. With a P50 million fund in the Development Bank of the Philippines, the Film Fund board gave as much as ₱250,000 in aid to film projects. The film projects, however, had to pass the criteria set by the artistic evaluation and marketing evaluation committees. The artistic evaluation committee required that projects should be an "artistic examination of the human condition," that they should have "social and cultural significance," and that they should "declare new directions in form and technique." The marketing evaluation committee looked into the commercial viability of a film. By June 1982, the Film Fund had given financial aid to 14 films. Majority of them did not seem to fulfill any of the requirements of the artistic evaluation committee. According to the Task Force on Film, the Film Fund was so incompetently managed that its receivables reached ₱11 million by 1986.

The Film Archives took care of the research, cataloguing and documentation, as well as the storing and conservation of film. Its collection-acquisition and archival departments collected and filed all films locally produced by Filipinos, all films produced by foreigners in the Philippines, all films produced abroad by foreigners and which had Filipino themes or Filipinos in the cast, and foreign classics readily available from archives and libraries. Its multimedia resource center took charge of continuing education (workshops and seminars) and exhibitions. In spite of the lack of funds, the Archives has completed a creditable amount of research on Filipino films, past and present.

Created by Executive Order No. 811 on June 12, 1982, the Film Ratings Board (FRB) was charged with the task of upgrading the quality of Filipino films through a film-rating and classification system. All locally produced films were evaluated according to these criteria: (1) technical qualities — 40 percent for good sound, color and cinematography; (2) artistic qualities — 40 percent for a clear, concise and well-structured screenplay that has credible characters and good narrative, dialogue, and conflict; for competent and creative direction, which harnesses all elements of cinema to present the film's message; for editing which creates continuity and rhythm appropriate to the film; and (3) scope and purpose — 20 percent for the film's message or insights which "make us a little more conscious. . . a little more caring about the world around us." Based on these criteria, FRB rates films A, B, or C. Films rated A get a 50 percent tax rebate of their amusement tax, films rated B get 25 percent rebate and films rated C get nothing.

Of the agencies under the ECP, the FRB, through its published evaluations and its film journal, *The Filipino Film Review*, contributed much to the industry by showing that enlightened classification of films is possible. In later years, however, FRB ratings were questioned. Too many films were getting Bs. The Task Force on film explained that in these years, the FRB was ordered to lower its standards "to collect more revenues for the cash-strapped ECP."

The Alternative Cinema took care of the exhibition of and education on alternative cinema fare, of managing the Manila Film Center, and producing ECP projects. Alternative Cinema had three sections under it. Film Programming took care of screening and producing art films (in 1982 alone, it screened about 158 films in various retrospectives). Film Education, on the other hand, upgraded the skills of film artists through various workshops (in 1982, on screenwriting, acting for the camera, writing for entertainment, and film direction) and encouraged film appreciation among laymen through its ECP Cine Club. Film Production held several scriptwriting contests and produced worthy projects like "Oro, Plata, Mata," "Himala," and "Moral." Like the FRB, the Alternative Cinema succeeded to a certain extent. But the films produced by its Film Production, which were later mangled by the BRMPT, showed the government's double standard and BRMPT's predominance over the ECP. Furthermore, the Alternative Cinema openly betrayed its noble aims and lost the little gains and credibility it had when it started showing pornographic movies, some of them co-produced by the ECP, at the Film Center to raise funds for the ECP.

FILM MAKING: PROBLEMS AND PROSPECTS

The Manila International Film Festival (MIFF) sought to "encourage understanding between nations, to foster the art of cinematography, to promote meetings in Asia among cinema professionals in the world and to stimulate film development." The MIFF '82 had five events, all held from January 18 to 29, 1982: the Film Competition which selected the best and second best films and the best actor and actress from about 20 international films; the Film Market which sought to sell Asian films to the West; the Film Retrospective, which presented some of the best films of Asia in the past and in the present; the Critics' Choice, which presented some of the best Filipino films ever made; and the Film Symposium, where international film artists and technicians shared their expertise with Filipino and international audiences. MIFF '83 followed a similar format.

The MIFF succeeded in calling international attention to the Filipino film, in particular, to the Philippines, in general. But this achievement was offset by many negative effects. The Philippine economy could hardly afford the millions of dollars that Mrs. Imelda Marcos non-productively lavished on these festivals which paid for the tickets, the hotel bills and the entertainment of international guests. The sale of Philippine films through the Festival's film market was minimal. Thus, the festivals were used more to project the benevolent image of the dictatorship at its height of oppressiveness, than to develop the industry.

As a whole, the ECP started out as a worthy project with very creditable aims. But as with most of Marcos' projects, it fell short of its noble goals. Although ECP served as a foil for the BRMPT's repressiveness, and it gave the regime the wash of liberality it desperately needed, Marcos did not think of ECP as a priority. So it was short of funds. The ECP thus compromised its own ideals by funding films with no artisitic merit but which looked commercially viable, giving minimal funds for the non-profit making archives, lowering the FRB standards, showing porno movies in the Manila Film Center -- just to raise money for its operations and apparently for other non-ECP operations. The Task Force reports that Mrs. Imee Marcos-Manotoc used the ECP funds for other purposes -- the last of which was to raise P10 million for the 1986 presidential elections.

PROBLEMS

Time and again, critics and film buffs have decried the low quality of Filipino films. Why are the stories of most films incoherent or badly-structured and often fatuous? Why are the characters and the acting so stereotyped? Why is sound and sound mixing so incompetently done? Why do they use canned music and derivative songs? Why is production design so anachronistic, illogical, and tasteless? Why is editing so badly-paced and the cinematography so declarative, tired and unimaginative? Is there a director on top of it all? Why are so many Filipino films so bad?

One can go on with a litany of complaints *ad nauseam*, but nothing can be done to improve the Filipino film if solutions are not provided for the industry's basic and perennial problems.

Popular Taste

After comparing the films that made good at the box-office and those that the FRB awarded with A or B ratings, Jackelyn Campos of *Filipino Film Review* concludes that: "Statistics strongly indicate that less artistic films are more attractive at the tills and that the majority of the local film audience shy away from artistic or highly artistic films." Shaped by decades of inane movies, the "bakya" crowd who comprise the majority of Filipino film audiences has been conditioned to like the following:

1. Genre movies or formula films. These movies provide escape from humdrum existence. They include action movies featuring supermen who can go through 15 fight sequences unscathed; musical comedies; comedies, and sex flicks.
2. The conventions of traditional cinema, which decreed that a director should merely narrate, not interpret, a story: that he be a raconteur, not an artist. Such conventions also dictate that a script should emphasize plot rather than character, and that the plot should be made up of colorful and convoluted events but narrated chronologically (flashbacks confuse such an audience). Dialogue should expose and narrate rather than show character. Acting and characterization must be black-and-white so that the good may be separated from the bad, and that actors and actresses play the roles they have been identified with (Dolphy must either be John or Facifica Falayfay; Nora must always be "api"; Ronnie Poe must always be a peace-loving man and turn violent only to avenge injustice; Rudy Fernandez must always play real-life criminal characters; and Vilma Santos is best cast as a mistress, never as a nun). Actors and actresses must be beautiful, i.e. mestizo and mestiza. In addition, the cinematography should be "declarative" in lighting and camera angles; and editing should be slow enough to accommodate a mind unused to complexity. To complete the list of conventions, a movie should have a message, an "aral" that in reality endorses and legitimizes the establishment (e.g., the poor must be content to be poor because luck will eventually take pity on them, that the rich are really kind and have immense problems of their own, that foreigners have always been good to us).

The Dominance of Foreign Films

The cultural multinationals like Warner Brothers, Twentieth Century Fox, Paramount, United Artists, MGM, Universal and Columbia dominate the local film industry. American films occupy half of the screentime of theaters in 100 countries and rake in the Philippines 4 billion of the 12 billion admissions all over the world. American filmmakers are well-capitalized and can do films which may not be all that significant but which showcase technological superiority of costumes, sets, props, sound and cinematography. Obviously, local films are no match for American movies. For how can a Filipino producer ever think of competing with Francis Ford Coppola's $30 million budget for *Apocalypse*, which is bigger than the budget of the whole Filipino film industry for two years?

And as if this were not bad enough, the government has never thought of other ways to protect the local industry from this unfair competition. The government instead allows foreign films to freely enter the country, and flood the market. Consider these data presented by Gualberto Lumauig in his Parliamentary Bill on the Philippine Motion Picture Industry:

> In 1973, the total Filipino film output was 146, whereas imported films totalled 412. In 1974, local films totalled 120, imported films, 519; in 1975, Filipino films totalled 145, foreign films, 390; in 1976, local films totalled 174, and foreign films, 301. Last year (1977), Filipino films totalled 141 whereas foreign films totalled 294. It is very clear, therefore, that the movie industry in the Philippines is under domination of imported films with the business being cornered at an average of 60 percent of the whole market.

In the past BRMPT favored foreign films in the matter of censorship. According to a *Malaya* columnist, the BRMPT used the Code and Rating Administration (CARA) of the Motion Pictures Association of America in evaluating American films to be exhibited locally. Because the CARA tended to be more liberal, especially in depicting sexual scenes, than the local censors' rules, American films had fewer cuts, and naturally, a larger audience than Filipino films.

Because the enemy is too big to "beat," local producers have decided to "join them," by slavishly imitating successful foreign films. Hoping to ride on the popularity of the original films, Filipino producers have come up with embarrassing copies like: "Disgrasyada," which copies "Turning Point," "Si Malakas, Si Maganda, Si Mahinhin," which combined "A Different Story" and "Love Story," "Ninong," which derives from "Godfather," "Ikaw at ang Gabi," which is "Torn Between Two Lovers," and the films of Tony Ferrer which were patterned after James Bond movies. For many a Filipino producer, imitation is a way of survival.

Excessive Taxation

Movie industry people contend that the cinema is one of the most heavily taxed businesses in the country, contributing almost P400 million in taxes a year to the government. And it seems true. Forty percent of a movie's gross receipts go to the following taxes: percentage tax, fixed tax, specific tax, flood control tax, amusement tax, ad valorem tax and withholding tax.

Brocka observes: "A film with a P1 million budget has to earn three times this budget in Metro Manila alone to recover that principal investment and pay the rest in taxes."

Since the burden is so heavy, film producers have to ensure huge earnings by getting superstars like Dolphy, Fernando Poe, Jr. or Nora Aunor to appear in their movies. Superstars charge much bigger rates (Dolphy in 1983 used to charge P2 million). Almost half of the production cost is lavished on just one or two actors, to the prejudice of the production staff that creates the content and artistry of a movie. The result is to be expected -- a movie that has very little sense or logic, but which brings in a lot of profit.

Furthermore, producers have to make sure that the playdates of their movies are ensured and favorable. Big film companies have created their own theater circuits which give preference to their own films (small producers have called this foul because it is tantamount to cornering the market). Most producers, however, have to reserve the dates much ahead of time and are often at the mercy of bookers. Once a playdate is fixed, the producer then rushes to finish the film. Sometimes, he forces a scriptwriter to finish a script in less than a week, a director to finish shooting a film in two weeks, and post production to finish in a week. More often than not, the result of such haste is cinematic waste.

The Film Producers

Given the adverse conditions earlier mentioned, local film producers understandably have no other consideration but profit.

Because they consider profit foremost, the producers have created and encouraged the star system, which, in turn, is among the causes of unprofessionalism. Pampered by the producers, superstars feel no compunctions about being absent from a shooting session, even if their absence means added expense in time, effort, food and transportation, and even if it deprives the extras and other "little people" of their salary for the day.

Producers want to stick to tried-and-true formula movies: the action film, the melodrama, the musical, the comedy and the sex flick.

But they also perennially search for new formulas. The *bomba* started out as an experiment which ended in success ("Uhaw," 1970). The same is true of the youth movie whose breakthrough was "Bagets" (1984). This "adventurousness" pushed some producers to finance projects like "Sister

Stella L." Unfortunately, Lily Monteverde's reading of the market (she thought such a film would ride on the post-assassination protest movement) proved wrong.

To ensure the film will make profit, producers meddle in the script writing. They stay away from "uncommercial" stories. They want to ride on the popularity of komiks materials that are already familiar to the "bakya" crowd. They snub socio-political themes, because these are "controversial." They have scripts tailored for certain actors, no matter how lacking in talent these actors are. They want at least five production numbers even if these cannot be justified in the scripts, to satisfy the fans. They order directors to put in such and such an actor or actress, and shoot the film so that it can be sold. They pay off movie writers to "review" their new films or create controversies about their stars so that they, and their latest movie, will be talked about. They tell a production designer not to demand expensive sets and costumes, even if these are really needed in a period movie. They tell cinematographers to scrimp on film, not to use too many complicated lighting equipment and techniques, and not to have too many set-ups that cost time and money. They tell any old dubber to finish off half of a movie that superstars can no longer dub because they are busy making three films at the same time. In general, they opt for action films because these are less of a gamble (these have a moderate cast and budget and these earn even in the smallest barrios).

Today, local producers also have to compete with foreign film companies who have started to make films in the country because of cheap labor and free use of scenic places. Eager to "sell" the country, Johnny Litton, MIFF Director-General, told the foreign filmmakers: "The Far East has a reservoir of talents and labor is cheap. It has many exotic locales conducive for film settings. Modern facilities are available."

Finally, local producers have to contend with yet another threat to their investment and profit -- video piracy. Of some 3,000 video outlets in the country, only 1,483 of them are registered with the VRB. The worst hit by video piracy are American films, which probably accounts for the drop in admissions to films like "Superman III," "Flashdance" and "48 Hours," as an industry man opined. But bomba movies have also been pirated quite freely by video shops.

Censorship

The hottest issue in the movie industry during the Marcos regime was censorship, especially under Katigbak's BRMPT. The BRMPT censored films, according to definite guidelines, which among others, prohibited too much sex, too much violence, and most of all, subversion in films. Since most of the censors do not have any film expertise, they cut films on the basis of scenes and not in relation to the totality of a given film. For example, in "Kisapmata," the scene showing Vic Silayan's fly as he approaches Charo

Santos to abuse her was cut because it was obscene. What the censors did not realize was that the camera angle was Charo's point of view, and the shots on the fly emphasized Charo's fear and revulsion at abuse from her father's hands.

Moreover, the BRMPT seemed to interpret the guidelines subjectively, according to their own (some would say "outmoded") standards of morality. "Moral" was cut up because it had too many "putang inas." "School Girls" was censored because it had pre-marital sex.

"Too much violence" is interpreted just as subjectively and according to individual scenes. The BRMPT censored the confrontation between the warring frats in "Batch '81," because it showed decent young men cutting off each other's heads. In censoring this portion, the BRMPT did not realize that it was cushioning the full impact of the film's message, i.e. that the frat mentality -- which is the fascist mind -- makes people so blind to other human realities and values that it can turn even decent young men into blood-thirsty barbarians.

"Subversion," however, is what the BRMPT was most afraid of. In their view, subversion is the depiction of a girl being raped by a man in uniform in "Boy Kondenado." (This is supposed to be far from the truth.) Subversion is a wife in "Moral" narrating how her NPA husband was "salvaged" by the military. Subversion is "Bayan Ko" being sung in a rally in "Kapit sa Patalim." Subversion is the depiction of poverty and oppression in films like "City After Dark," "Insiang," "Jaguar" and "Sakada."

All in all, the censors lopped off whatever offended the values and the image of the Marcos Establishment. But they saw nothing immoral in Sharon Cuneta movies, like "Dear Heart" and "P.S. I Love You," which flaunted fabulous houses, clothes, and cars, as though these were the ideal in life, in a country where the majority are living in poverty and subhuman conditions.

If the censors had their way, they would have wanted the film directors and producers to depict only "the true, the good and the beautiful" as the former First Lady would advise them to do. This, however, was what film artists could not stomach. As Lino Brocka put it:

> For one thing, the government will remind film artists that they must participate in the task of nation-building. And nation-building means trying to give a "beautiful" picture of the country, trying not to disturb people, trying not to make them angry by depicting the truth to them.

If there's anything good that came out of censorship in the Marcos era, it was the fact that arbitrary censorship exasperated producers, artists and technicians alike that it drove many of them to join forces and unite for the first time against a common enemy. The Free-the-Artists-Movement claimed that unity began the politicization of movie people.

Popular Taste

The patronage of local films by local audiences is probably the most important consideration among producers, film artists and technicians. If the industry is to improve, the logic goes, the taste of local audiences will have to be developed and improved.

Ironically, the solution lies in the film artists and technicians themselves. They will have to create films that will expose audiences to better stories, better direction, better acting, better cinematography, production design, editing and sound. For if audiences developed poor taste through constant exposure to simplistic genre films, then they can also develop better taste through constant exposure to films of higher quality. Education, they say, is simply exposure. And so it is with the film industry.

Crucial then in changing the popular taste is the continuing education of film artists and technicians. They must be the object of a massive program by the government, the private sector and the film industry. They must be exposed to good foreign and local films, sent to training workshops (such as the actors' workshop) and seminars (such as the directors' lecture series), and to other meetings where cinematic works are discussed and evaluated.

In addition, the exposure of moviegoers to intelligent but popular analyses of films in movie fan and other popular magazines could help deepen their appreciation for better films.

Finally, upgrading and popularizing standards used by award-giving bodies could elevate awards nights to recognition nights in the best sense of the word. Publishing the winners and why they won will allow for a free and (hopefully) intelligent discussion of issues, and put award-giving bodies above suspicion.

PROSPECTS AND RECOMMENDATIONS

Given the state of the local film industry, here are some suggested solutions to these problems.

The Dominance of Foreign Films

No doubt foreign films will have to be controlled to allow local films to develop. National survival takes precedence over all other considerations, including the moviegoers' freedom of choice.

One recommendation is to resurrect the Lumauig Bill of 1978, which was junked by the Batasang Pambansa because Filipino distributors of American films lobbied against it. This bill will gradually reduce the quota of foreign films, from a ceiling of 300 feature films in the first year to 150 films in the fourth year. Not more than $3.6 million foreign film earnings should be remitted to the U.S. in the first year and $1.8 million in the fourth year. The amount includes rights, prints and advertising accessories.

Furthermore, foreign filmmakers should be taxed based on their film budget for coming here so that they would not liberally take advantage of our cheap labor and free exotic locales. The tax shall go to the Film Fund.

Excessive Taxation

The government may have to restudy the taxes on the local film industry so the flood control tax and other taxes, which have no logical connection to film, can be eliminated. To make up for the lost tax income, the government should raise taxes on foreign films.

The Local Film Producers. If the tax burden were lightened, the local film producers will have little reason to think of profit alone. The government can then remind them, without infringing on their freedom, of their social responsibility as film producers.

To keep competition healthy, the government should institute measures to prevent any one producer or group of producers from cornering any aspect of the film industry, e.g., producers cannot be bookers and movie producers as well.

To encourage producers to make quality films, the classification board should continue giving tax rebates but explain in the print media why such classifications were given.

Finally, to remedy the present situation where a producer can control, and mangle, script, direction and general production to make more money, film artists and technicians should unionize so that their demands may be heard and granted.

Censorship

To prevent the recurrence of BRMPT's repressiveness and arbitrariness, the following changes could be made.

First, censorship must be replaced with classification. The Classification Board should merely rate films for the guidance of the community: as G (General Patronage); or O (Parental Guidance Recommended); or P (Restricted for persons 18 years and above). It should not cut, or ban films. Producers should instead be given the option to reedit their films to obtain a more general classification. Ideally, the board should, like the FACB now, explain its ratings in the print media.

Second, the persons appointed to the Classification Board should: (1) know film; (2) be reputed for their honesty and integrity; (3) have no commercial connections with the industry; and (4) have the time to view films. Obviously, political appointments and proxies will not do.

Third, to ensure that no one body will have such tremendous powers of censorship as the BRMPT, alternative cinema, especially video filmmaking, should be encouraged. Considering that the documentary movies of Asia Visions recorded and made public the abuses of the dictatorship, which the crony media glossed over, such type of filmmaking should be kept alive.

Finally, a mechanism for communication between the Classification Board and the industry should be set up. Film artists and technicians should have an alliance through which they can discuss issues affecting the industry and through which they can have their opinions heard. In case government agencies become as intransigent as the former BRMPT, such an alliance can function as a pressure group as well.

The Film Commission

Clearly, from the discussion of problems and recommendations, the government must study and act decisively to solve these problems. For this purpose, a Film Commission should be appointed.

The Film Commission should be premised on: (1) the freedom of expression in film; (2) the creation of a Filipino cinema that shall be artistic and commercially viable; and (3) the right of film producers, artists and technicians to be consulted in matters affecting the industry. Based on these premises, the Commission should then formulate government policies for the film industry and coordinate the activities of film-related government agencies.

Viewed from a wide perspective, the problems of the film industry are that of many Filipino industries as well. The film industry is only a part of the bigger reality.

If the Aquino regime will reexamine the many adverse realities in Philippine society of which the industry is part, then the film industry can look forward to a battle won.

SELECTED BIBLIOGRAPHY

Articles

Brocka, Lino. "State of the Filipino Industry," in Nicanor G. Tiongson (ed.), *The Politics of Culture: The Philippine Experience*, pp.48-51.

Campos, Jackelyn A. "Quality And The Local Film Industry." *Filipino Film Review*, Vol. 1, No. 4 (October–December 1983), pp.16-17.

Carunungan, Celso Al. "Early Years of Philippine Movies." in Rafael Ma. Guerrero (ed.), *Readings in Philippine Cinema*.

Lumbera, Bienvenido. "Kasaysayan at Tunguhin ng Pelikulang Pilipino (The History and Prospects of the Filipino Film)." in Nicanor G. Tiongson (ed.), *The Urian Anthology 1970-79*, pp. 22-47.

Martin, Perfecto T. "The 'Silent Pictures' Era in the Philippines." in Rafael Ma. Guerrero (ed.), *Readings in Philippine Cinema*, pp. 18-27.

Pilar, Santiago A. "The Early Movies." in Rafael Ma. Guerrero (ed.), *Readings in Philippine Cinema*, pp. 8-19.

Reyes, Jun Cruz. "Nang Mauso ang Pangit." in Nicanor G. Tiongson (ed.), *The Urian Anthology 1970-79*, pp. 62-71.

Santiago, Digna. "Why An Action Film." *Filipino Film Review*, Vol. 1, No. 7 (July-September 1984), pp. 18-19.

Torre, Nestor U. "Acting Stereotypes And The Vital Spaces In Between." *Filipino Film Review*, Vol. 1, No. 2 (April 1983), pp. 11-12.

_____ "A Sad Scenario." *Filipino Film Review*, Vol. 1, No. 7 (July-September 1984), p. 13.

Books

de Vega, Guillermo C. *Film and Freedom/Movies Censorship in the Philippines*. Manila. 1975.

Guerrero, Rafael Ma. (ed.). *Readings in Philippine Cinema*. Manila: Experimental Cinema of the Philippines, 1983.

Salumbides, Vicente. *Motion Pictures in the Philippines*. Vicente Salumbides, 1952.

Tiongson, Nicanor G. (ed.). *The Politics of Culture: The Philippine Experience*. Quezon City: Philippine Educational Theater Association, 1984.

Tiongson, Nicanor G. (ed.). *The Urian Anthology 1970-79*. Quezon City: Manuel L. Morato, 1983.

Documents

Experimental Cinema of the Philippines, Brochure, 1982.
Parliamentary Bill No. 85, Introduced by the Hon. Gualberto B. Lumauig. "An Act To Promote and Develop the Philippine Motion Picture Industry by Creating The Commission on Motion Pictures and for other purposes." Mimeographed copy.
"Rules and Regulations of the Movies and Television Reviews and Classification Board." *Philippine Daily Express* (December 28, 1985), p. 7.

Journals

Filipino Film Review, Vol. 1, No. 1 (January 1983). Manila: Experimental Cinema of the Philippines, 1983.
Filipino Film Review, Vol. 1, No. 2 (April 1983). Manila: Experimental Cinema of the Philippine, 1983.
Filipino Film Review, Vol. 1, No. 3. (July-September 1983). Manila: Experimental Cinema of the Philippines, 1983.
Filipino Film Review, Vol. 1, No. 4 (October-December 1983). Manila: Experimental Cinema of the Philippines, 1983.
Filipino Film Review, Vol. 1, No.5 (January-March 1984). Manila: Experimental Cinema of the Philippines, 1984.
Filipino Film Review, Vol. 1, No. 6 (April-June 1984). Manila: Experimental Cinema of the Philippines, 1984.
Filipino Film Review, Vol. 1, No. 7 (July-September 1984). Experimental Cinema of the Philippines, 1984.
Filipino Film Review, Vol. 1, No. 8 (October-December 1984). Experimental Cinema of the Philippines, 1984.
Filipino Film Review, Vol. 11, No. 2 (April-June 1985). Manila: Experimental Cinema of the Philippines, 1985.

Part Five

Small Media

A new trend in the field of communication is towards demassification — from mass media to small media. While the mass media may reach more people, they tend to be ineffective in moving people. Development communicators are using the mass media for promoting awareness, but they use the small media to follow up if they want to change attitudes and behavior. Hence, the growing importance of the small media, sometimes referred to as community media, group media or alternative media.

Chapter XVIII discusses the role of folk media in national development, while Chapter XIX describes the most common folk or traditional media in the Philippines. Then Chapter XX analyzes the concept and role of group media.

Chapter XVIII

Folk Media and Development

Victor T. Valbuena

It is becoming apparent that the mass media in their present form cannot adequately perform the roles expected of them by the development paradigms of the 1960s. The mass media do not reach enough of the Third World population to disseminate relevant information needed for social change.

Media experts have finally discovered in this decade what the peasants have known for centuries — the valuable contributions that traditional or folk media are capable of making. The use of folk media to support and promote national development programs in Third World countries seems to be "upstaging the paradigms of the 1960s that emphasized bigness in mass media development, non-participatory, uni-directional information imbalance, and that played up development in terms of economics at the expense of people's values, beliefs, attitudes and societal needs."[1]

As Coseteng puts it: "What the mass media in their high stage of development have failed to realize is that existing side by side with them on an actual village level that is quite different from the global village infrastructure... is another form of media, one which even antedates them — the traditional media of communication... Nevertheless, traditional media still survive and are used as meaningful channels of communication in traditional or developing societies. Their unobtrusive nature is, perhaps, the reason they have been ignored for most of the time by the mass media-oriented communication experts and development planners. Indeed, they are still viable forms of human communication."[2]

Fortunately, many development planners and decision-makers in the Third World now appreciate the value of using traditional or folk media as an alternative communication strategy in development programs. This may have been the result of their growing concern with cultural imperialism and the ineffectiveness of the mass media in reaching those who need change most. They are now taking a hard, second-look at folk media as alternative channels for development-oriented messages and as a means of generating local participation in planning and decision-making for social action programs.[3]

As Wang and Dissanayake put it, the emerging new paradigm for development also advocates using, among others, indigenous media and channels for development because they are locally oriented, easily accessible and relatively inexpensive.[4]

THE FOLK MEDIA

What are folk media? They include the customs, traditions, beliefs and practices embodied in folklore. As channels of communication, they could be defined as "those verbal, action, aural, and visual forms which are known or familiar to the folk, are accepted by them, and are addressed to or performed by, for them, for the purpose of entertaining, informing, enlightening, instructing, and educating."[5]

As folk creations or expressions, the folk media have identifiable forms, how they are organized and how they are presented. But more important, these forms contain messages which are generally understood by the audience because their meaning is derived from common folk life and experience.[6]

The folk media can include familiar religious rituals like the pasyon, cenaculo, moriones, putungan, panunuluyan, and santacruzan; indigenous spectacles like the ati-atihan and the sinulog; and literary, poetic and dramatic entertainment like the awit at corrido, the epic, the balitao, the duplo or karagatan, the balagtasan, the comedia or moro-moro, the zarzuela, other forms of folk drama, and speechways like proverbs and riddles.

Folk media can and tend to combine several formal elements into one medium. Thus a folk medium could contain both a religious and a social message, as in the pabasa or pasyon. It could also be in narrative poetry, presented in theatrical manner, as in the comedia and the balagtasan or the balitao.[7]

Coseteng stresses that folk media, like all forms of communication or expression, are dynamic. They are subject to change and adaptation. They take in new ideas, forms, methods, and techniques, dropping those which are no longer meaningful or functional to society. A new concept like family planning can be absorbed unconsciously into the group's values and become part of behavior. Coseteng adds that dynamism of folk media could be harnessed for social change and development.[8]

Between 1972 and 1979 at least seven existing forms of theater arts in the Philippines were demonstrated as viable channels for development communication: drama, the zarzuela, the cancionan, the balagtasan, the balitao, the bantayonon, and the puppet theater.

Drama. Performances of one-act plays, usually of the soap opera type, are standard offerings in many Philippine town fiestas. Plays with moral lessons are favorites of Filipino audiences, especially in the rural areas. Drama has a more serious function than mere entertainment in the Philippines. Watching a drama presentation is an opportunity for gaining insights into life, for learning lessons about man's relationships, and their implications for personal as well as communal welfare. Thus, standard plots of many Philippine dramas revolve around a wayward youth who returns to his family; a philandering husband who returns to his wife and family; a rich landlord and the poor, exploited tenant. There is conflict between the young and the old, between new, emerging values and age-old, traditional behavior patterns.

A performance provides an opportunity for the audience to hear the message of the playwright, who assumes the important social role of critic and teacher.[9]

Zarzuela. The zarzuela is a musical play similar to light opera. The Filipino zarzuela has its roots in the Spanish zarzuelas — simple, comic operas dealing with the manners, customs, and foibles of different segments of Spanish society. The zarzuela is always accompanied by dances and songs, making the play a type of musical.

The main appeal of the zarzuela lies in the satire and the biting social criticism underlying the sharp, witty, humorous, and often earthy language of the dialogue. "The musical score and the lyrics give flavor to the zarzuela, so much so, that the songwriter or composer is as important as the playwright, if he is not himself both; and a script is often built around a musical score."[10]

The home-spun wisdom, common problems, catchy tunes, lively dances, and attractive sets immediately involve the audience in the zarzuela. There is instant rapport, something not as possible with more sophisticated dramas and audiences.

The zarzuela has built-in originality and versatility. It is a flexible and dynamic dramatic form with local situations and issues, ordinary characters, familiar problems, and native songs and dances. The acceptability and versatility of the zarzuela as propaganda in drama form were apparent during the Revolution against Spain in 1896, against the United States in 1898, and in the struggle against the American occupation at the turn of the century.[11] The zarzuela is easily updated and the form can just as easily clothe the theme.

Although retaining the basic elements of the Spanish model, the Filipino zarzuela has developed into a full-blown, three-act melodrama. It may border on sentimentality, but it is complex in theme, plot, and characterization.

The play centers mainly on the family, and the conflict is usually due to family and social relationships, romantic love, or economic difficulties. The values, morals, and social traditions of the middle class prevail in spite of all the action. The Filipino zarzuela has a variety of topics: dowry, capital and labor, cockfighting, the trade monopoly of the Chinese, the corruption of native politicians, and native customs.[12] Its themes include: relationships between husband and wife and between in-laws; the love between young master and servant girl; between rich boy and poor girl, and vice versa; and the conflict between young and old. All these are favorite topics of the zarzuela.

Cancionan. Very popular in the Ilocos region, the cancionan is a form of argumentation in song and verse. It is a usual feature in town fiestas, a contest that pits male against female in argument on any topic. In many instances, it appears as a double bill or an intermission number in zarzuela presentations. The cancionan uses wit, humor, irony, and satire as natural components preventing it from becoming a dull musical contest. It has remained a popular medium because it lends itself to any topic and provokes the audience to take sides.

Balagtasan. This is a poetic debate between two protagonists using rhythmic colorful language, with humor, satire, and irony. It is a popular form in the Tagalog Region. The balagtasan can provoke arguments and generate thinking from the audience. The emotion that the balagtasan arouses is very much a part of the reaction of the audience.

Balagtasan can lend itself to any topic, issue, idea or sentiment, provided an opposing view (or several opposing views) exists, as it invariably does. Romantic, domestic, religious, ethical, political, or economic matters can be taken up in a balagtasan. Subjects range from ordinary, everyday problems to leftist sentiments and most controversial topics. In fact, the strength of the balagtasan is in argument and thought, giving it a directness which the zarzuela or the conventional drama could not approach.

Although the balagtasan is essentially a debate, it is invested with a sense of drama because of the fast and sharp exchange in the arguments between the protagonists which gives it an impression of a dialogue, perhaps planned, but certainly well-structured, compact, and rich. It is the kind of dialogue which demands the full concentration of the audience, broken only when the audience responds by applauding a protagonist who has won a point during the course of the argument or who has parried a counter-argument with a quick turn of wit and speech.[13]

Balitao. The balitao is a courtship-debate in song and dance, almost always extemporaneously performed by a man and a woman. The man presses his suit, and the woman, out of modesty, declines his advances and offers resistance to his sweet songs by singing and dancing her objections. In times past, at the end of a hard day's work in the fields especially during the planting or harvest season, the young men and women would gather and perform the balitao to entertain themselves. They would either divide into

FOLK MEDIA AND DEVELOPMENT

two groups, male and female, and sing the debate in chorus; or select a boy and a girl who would play the balitao to the cheers and clapping of hands and laughter of the audience whenever one contestant had made a verbal thrust or a sharp retort.

According to Coseteng and Nemenzo, although the subject matter of the balitao is mainly about love and courtship, it may have variations which are interspersed with other topics.[14] The elaborations and digressions of the debate involve the ability, intelligence, and wit of the performers, and how well and fast they can construct short verses for repartee. Tradition, history, religion, customs, and sociocultural values can all be used in advancing an argument, pressing a point, or in challenging or warding off an opponent's argument. At the end, resolution may come when the girl accepts the suitor's proposal, but with the promises she has exacted. Because of the girl's ability and wit, she may succeed at other times in warding off the suitor and win the argument. The audience and the occasion may decide the subject matter of a balitao.

Fortunately, the balitao has retained its abundance of wit, quick repartee, and humor reflecting traditional beliefs and practices. It also contains the omnipresent moral lessons. Allusions, suggestions, comparisons and other figures of speech are used often in appeals to both the emotion and the intellect. Strong sexual connotations bordering on the lewd and obscene are sometimes present, depending on the audience.[15]

Bantayonon. Another poetic debate form found in the Christian areas of Mindanao, the bantayonon usually focuses on love, courtship and marriage. Today, however, public affairs and other popular current issues are integrated into the bantayonon.

Puppet Theater. Puppetry is a prevalent art form in Asia. At one time there was a type of shadow puppet play in the Philippines called carillos, akin to the Indonesian wayang. Over the years, however, the tradition of the carillos was lost. In its place came the more colorful and popular hand or rod puppets now used in the development communication activities of at least four nationwide institutions in the country.

Forms of Theater Arts Used. Organizations seem to prefer the use of drama and musical plays in their communication campaigns. For example, the Commission on Population and the University of the Philippines are noted for their pioneering efforts in using the Ilocano cancionan, the Tagalog balagtasan and the Visayan balitao to support popular education and promote family planning. The Mindanao State University Sining Kambayoka use the Maranao bayok in its theatrical productions. The then Ministry of Public Information encouraged the use of the bantayonon as part of its theater activities in Mindanao. The National Media Production Center (now merged with the Philippine Information Agency) and Catholic Relief Services are proponents of puppet theater in development.

Much more can be done to promote greater use and to popularize these media forms. For example, they could be integrated with the more technologically-oriented media of radio and television to expand their audience. But utilization has been limited in this aspect of theater arts.

Very few institutions have made either quantitative or qualitative measures of the impact of theater arts as development communication. Available findings, nevertheless, support the assumption that theater presentations have an impact, not only in terms of drawing crowds but more important, on educational attitudes and on target audiences.

The lack of impact measurement is due to the inadequate recording and documentation by development agencies of data on the presentation of theater arts materials. There is a need for orienting the development agencies, both government and private, on the importance of maintaining an accurate record of significant events. The value of this material in planning and enriching the communication programs of other agencies is obvious.

Nineteen of 24 organizations surveyed by the author have used theater arts to promote their particular programs.[16] These include four colleges, three foundations, one educational theater group, one private family planning agency, one religious agency, one government commission and one government media office. In addition, seven government ministries have used theatrical fare at one time or another to carry their messages to target audiences: the Ministries (now Departments) of Agrarian Reform, Education and Culture, Human Settlements, Labor, Natural Resources, Public Information (now abolished) and Tourism. They do not implement theater activities directly, but through affiliated or contracted agencies, a number of which belong to the groups of other respondents in this survey.

For example, the Ministry of Agrarian Reform contracted with the University of the East, a private university in Manila, for the presentation of "Ang Bagong Filipina," a contemporary zarzuela on land reform by Ruben Vega, a local writer. The Ministry of Education and Culture linked up with the Dangerous Drugs Board and the schools through the Ministry's Youth Civic Action Program (YCAP) Coordinating Center to promote its campaign against drug abuse. The Ministry of Labor, from time to time, used the resources of La Tondeña Incorporada Workers Theater group to present plays on family planning. The Ministry of Natural Resources contracted with the Mindanao State University (MSU), Sining Kambayoka to present "Ambon, Ulan, Baha," a contemporary zarzuela on the ills of forest denudation. The Ministry of Public Information launched its "Movement for Cultural Revival," and, through its regional offices and other affiliate groups, presented plays with development themes.

Of the other organizations, the Commission on Population, the Population Center Foundation, the Family Planning Organization of the Philippines, the University of the Philippines Institute of Mass Communication, and the Capiz Institute of Technology have utilized theater arts to promote family planning; as have the National Nutrition Council and Catholic Relief Services on nutrition education.

The Zarzuela Foundation of the Philippines and the Philippine Educational Theater Association (PETA) use theater for carrying out their objectives. The Zarzuela Foundation presented a series of contemporary musical dramas on family planning, nutrition and land reform. PETA has also presented a family planning drama and has been used by NMPC and the Population Center Foundation/Development Theater Program to conduct theater workshops which call for the integration of development-oriented messages in their script writing classes.

The NMPC, through a number of its offices, used theater activities to support the government's population, nutrition and agrarian reform programs. The Communication Foundation for Asia had cooperated with the NMPC in conducting workshops on the use of theater arts for development. Mindanao State University implements development theater activities through its Sining Kambayoka theater group.

Rationale for the Use of Theater Arts

Organizations that have tried theater arts for communication purposes agree that they are effective in disseminating concepts and information geared towards development, particularly because they have wide popular appeal and encourage mass participation. The general opinion is that the use of theater for disseminating information, particularly at the grassroots level, is very effective.

For agencies like the Commission on Population, theater and drama are perceived to have certain advantages over more modern media. For them, theater is relevant and timely and audiences identify more closely with it than they do with film.

Attempts have been made as early as the late 1960s to integrate the folk media with the modern mass media, like radio. For example, since 1969 in the Ilocos region in northern Philippines, it has been common to use the *bucanegan*, a folk media form of argumentation and debate in verse, for discussing the pros and cons of family planning and other development programs.[17]

Other examples of media integration are the experimental radio broadcasts of *kabalaka* mobile theater presentations in Capiz, occasional telecasts of zarzuelas on family planning and nutrition, and regular telecasts of puppet shows on national values, dental health, nutrition and family welfare.

More notable are commercial films patterned after comic or dramatic zarzuelas with or without the songs, their storylines carrying development-oriented messages like those of environmental management, land reform, nutrition and family planning. Some of these commercial films have been partly financed by government agencies like the Commission on Population and the National Media Production Center. Examples are "Bato-Bato sa Langit," a comedy on family planning, and "Gisingin mo ang Umaga," a film on urban migration and country-side development. After having gone the round of the commercial movie distribution circuit for about one year, these films are reduced to 16-mm and shown around the country-sides through the mobile audio-visual units either of the Commission or of the Media Center. They are usually shown in community assemblies and are followed up with discussions and open forums, right after the film presentations or during home visits conducted by family planning or community development workers.

CONCLUSION

Experience in the Philippines has demonstrated that the folk media could be used as viable channels for communicating messages of development and social change. In spite of the great influence and impact of modern mass media, the folk media could be harnessed, revitalized, updated, even integrated with modern media, to serve the cause of social development.

Notes

[1] John A. Lent, "Grassroots Renaissance: Folk Media in the Third World," in *Media Asia*, Vol. 9, No. 1 (1982), AMIC, Singapore, p. 9.

[2] Alicia M.L. Coseteng, "Traditional Media in Developing Societies," in *Building Bridges Across Cultures: Perspective on Intercultural Communication – Theory and Practices*, Nobleza C. Asuncion Laude and Emy M. Pascasio (eds.), Solidaridad Publishing House, Manila, 1981, pp. 92-99.

[3] Debra van Hoosen, "The Barefoot Actors: Folk Drama and Development Communication in Asia," in *Continuity and Change in Communication Systems*, Georgette Wang and Wimal Dissanayake (eds.), Ablex Publishing Corporation, New Jersey, 1984, p. 128.

[4] Georgette Wang and Wimal Dissanayake, "The Study of Indigenous Communication Systems in Development: Phasing Out or Phasing In? " In *Media Asia*, Vol. 9, No. 1 (1982). AMIC, Singapore, pp. 3-8.

[5] Alicia M.L. Coseteng and Gemma A. Nemenzo, "Folk Media in the Philippines," in *Philippine Folk Media in Development Communication*, Victor Valbuena (ed.), AMIC, Singapore, 1974, p. 20.

[6] Ibid.

[7] Ibid.

[8] Ibid.

[9] Amelia L. Bonifacio, "The Social Role of Theater in Asia." In *Literature and Society: Crosscultural Perspectives* (The proceedings of the Eleventh American Studies Seminar, October 1976, Los Baños).

[10] Alicia M.L. Coseteng and Gemma A. Nemenzo, "Folk Media in the Philippines: Their Extension and Integration with the Mass Media for Family Planning." University of the Philippines Institute of Mass Communication, Quezon City, 1975.

[11] Amelia L. Bonifacio, *The 'Seditious' Tagalog Playwrights: Early American Occupation*. Zarzuela Foundation of the Philippines, Manila, 1972.

[12] Jean Edades, "The Zarzuela and Propaganda," *Sunday Times Magazine,* Manila, May 20, 1956, pp. 30-31.

[13] Coseteng, op. cit.

[14] Ibid.

[15] Maria Colina Gutierrez, "The Cebuano Balitao and How It Mirrors Culture and Folklife." University of San Carlos, Cebu City, 1961.

[16] Victor T. Valbuena, "Philippine Theater Arts as Development Communication: Perspectives and Prospects." Ph.D. Dissertation. Centro Escolar University, Manila, 1980.

[17] Jet C. Riparip, "Bucanegan: A Vehicle for DevCom," a seminar paper, University of the Philippines Institute of Mass Communication, 1982.

Chapter XIX

Traditional Media

Josefina S. Patron

The Philippines, like most Asian countries, is rich in folk, indigenous, literary and dramatic forms, which are referred to as traditional media. The more common of these traditional, or folk media, are the following:

1. Bugtong (Riddle)

The riddle is usually a test of wit which requires that the audience see the meeting between the object literally described and the object referred to. It has generally been described as an exercise of intellectual skill and quickness of wit. It becomes a test of memory especially with those riddles whose answers have to be learned by heart to be known.

The Tagalog riddle or *bugtong* is in very simple form, usually couplets — one line balanced against the other. The first line gives a general impression of subject, usually stated metaphorically. The second line presents a clue that only seems to complicate the problem created in the first. The clues, however, are not necessarily always added details. Sometimes they may be puns, metaphors, onometopoeic words that suggest the answer.

The imagery of the riddle is always homely, generally drawn from the immediate environment of the folk. Common objects are exaggerated when described, but there is no attempt to glamorize the common place. The tendency, as a matter of fact, is to pull down to earth (through the answer) what the imagination has raised to the level of fantasy.

An example of a Filipino *bugtong: Kong umupo ay mataas, kong tumayo ay mababa. Sagot: Aso.* (If it sits, it is tall; if it stands it is short. Answer: Dog).

2. Salawikain (Proverb)

Unlike the riddle, which reflects life without comment, the proverb makes a statement about what it describes. Proverbs are practical guides to living life. They provide man with lessons that allow him to cope with the problems of living.

Since the interest of the proverb-maker is in the idea behind the images used, the same proverb may be applied to entirely different situations which are limited only by the ingenuity of the individual. One proverb alone may be used to advise a person to learn patience, to chide another for wastefulness or to encourage a man's humility.

Like the riddles, proverbs generally consist of two rhyming lines. The first line usually refers to a situation and the second makes an observation about it. Another common characteristic of the proverb and the riddle is realism of imagery. Both derive their images from the daily life and environment of the folk. However, while the riddle tends to fantasize the subject, the proverb hardly ever does.

The *salawikain* employs irony, which may be created by using contrasts. The use of irony and homeliness of imagery combine to give the *salawikain* an earthy humor that tempers the censorious tone.

Example of a Filipino proverb: *Ang lumakad ng marahan, matinik man ay mababaw lamang.* (He who walks slow may step on a thorn; but the wound will not be deep).

3. Tanagas (or short poems)

These are pieces that contain more than two lines. The majority are quatrains that are made up of either seven or eight-syllable lines. The *tanaga* is "full of metaphors" only in the sense its single metaphor establishes an analogy between human experience and an aspect of man's environment. This metaphor is known as *talinhaga* which is associated with mystery, obscurity and parabolic speech.

While the *tanaga* and the *salawikain* both seek out the relevance to man of objects and activities around him, they are however, vastly different. The *tanaga*, considered a short poem, takes on an emotional and intellectual expressiveness not found in proverbs. But the *tanaga* appears as an extension of the *salawikain* in many cases. The four lines divide themselves into couplets, which could pass for two proverbs.

4. Folk Epics

The folk epic is a long oral narrative based on tradition, beliefs, customs, ideals and social values. It tells of an adventure of supernatural beings regarded as culture heroes. It may be recited or chanted or sung.

Some ethnic groups have preserved some epics, sometimes called *ethno epics*. It is interesting to note that of the ethnic groups, which were heavily evangelized, only two were able to preserve their epics, although they contain traces of Christian concepts. The Ilocanos have the *Lam-ang* and the Bicolanos have the *Bandiong*. Attempts to reshape the folk epics to suit the goals of Christianization were therefore very evident.

The ethnic groups that resisted Christianity — the Ifugaos of Northern Luzon, the Bagobos, Maguindanaos and the Tausogs of Mindanao — were able to preserve their folk epics. The Ifugao epic, *Hudhud*, glorifies Ifugao history and is usually sung during wedding feasts and other festive occasions. Another Ifugao epic, *Alim*, deals with the gods and spirits, and is quite similar to India's *Ramayana*. The Muslims called their epics the *darangans*. The *Bantugan*, *Indarapatra* and *Sulayman and Bidsari* are the most popular.

Except *Bandiong* and *Lam-ang*, which have been preserved mainly through their Spanish translations, the epics have been handed down orally from generation to generation. Old men recite them from memory. These epics tell of love, war, divinations, magic and charms — usually revolving around the life of the hero. Many episodes also attempt to explain the origin of things and other natural phenomena. For instance, the heroes could be the first men to practice agriculture, weaving and fishing.

5. Duplo and Karagatan

The *duplo* and *karagatan* had their roots in the pre-Spanish period in connection with mourning rituals and later with harvest celebrations.

Originally, the *duplo* was introduced to relieve the monotony and sadness of the prayers for the dead. It consisted largely of puns, jokes and riddles in the vernacular. These verses became so emphasized that the prayer itself became minor and was relegated to the end of the ceremony. This prayer in verse was called by the Tagalog people the *dalit*.

Later the *duplo* became an elaborate dramatic debate in verse. Riddles, banter, repartees and puns, poems, proverbs and conundrums are commonly used in *duplo*. Many people use the terms, *duplo* and *karagatan*, to refer to the poetic debates held on an elevated platform.

The *duplo*, for the most part, deals with contemporary personalities and social questions of the day. Generally, some of the players accuse others of fancied crimes and the accused defend themselves. The dialogue becomes very animated with quotations from the awits and corridos (native metrical romances) thrown into the debate. Rules of logic are hardly observed. When one debater gives an incorrect answer to a riddle, he is usually forced to give a *dalit*.

The *duplo* uses no formal stage. It usually takes place in the yard of the house of the dead person. A temporary shelter may be built in front of the house. Two rows of benches or chairs are arranged on a platform where the main characters of the play, the *villacos* and the *villacas* are seated. On a chair in the center of the group reigns the king or the star *duplero*. He is supposed to be the most respected man in the group and also the wittiest. The characters are identified by numbers. A typical *duplo* might begin with the "king" declaring that while he was away, his pet parrot got lost. Then he would ask if anyone knew who took it. A *villaco* would stand and ungallantly accuse a *villaca*. The *villaca* would cry out her denials, or a *villaco* might offer to defend her. A debate would then ensue. Eventually, the "king" would rise and decide the question.

The *karagatan* is less formal than the *duplo*. Whereas the *dupleros* are generally well-trained players, the *karagatan* players are merely guests who are called upon to extemporize verses.

The *karagatan* is essentially a play of words. It has no plot. Generally, it has a love team. The characters merely parade on the stage, speaking their versified lines.

Among the Visayans, the *karagatan* is by no means considered a parlor game. It is designed to idle the hours away during a wake and to comfort the bereaved ones. The losers in the game can reclaim the object of the battle only after reciting a *loa* or a declamation.

6. Pananapatan or Panunuluyan

This is a religious drama form that evolved and flourished during the Spanish era. It is a re-enactment of the hardships which Joseph and Mary underwent during their long journey into Bethlehem before the birth of Jesus. The *panunuluyan* is usually performed on Christmas eve, before the midnight mass. An elaborate affair, the *panunuluyan* is generally organized by a town school or the local parish. Joseph is played by a typical swain and Mary by a pretty girl of the community. Their looks, however, are not the only assets to be considered. They are also selected for their ability to sing. The play, in the form of a procession, shows Joseph and Mary going from one house to another, entreating for lodging. Each innkeeper denies them, using poetic language.

The procession winds up in church where the drama ends and the Christmas midnight mass begins.

7. Tibag

The *tibag* is presented during the Maytime festival in towns or barrios having devotions to the Holy Cross. The word *tibag* comes from the act of excavating the three mounds during the search for the cross. This is performed in commemoration of an event that brought St. Helena to the discovery of the true cross. The cross is "buried" somewhere in the barrio, usually in the church patio, in front of or near a chapel. A girl dressed as St. Helena, together with St. Constantine the Great, and some soldiers start looking for the cross at about three o'clock in the afternoon, on the day before the fiesta. The dialogue of the participants are all in verse form. When the cross is found, a procession starts and winds up in the chapel.

8. The Pasyon and the Cenaculo

The *pasyon* (or Passion of Christ) came around the 17th century among the various Christianized groups in the Philippines. The first Tagalog *pasyon* was produced in 1704.

As a literary form the *pasyon* is a narrative poem that tells about the life and passion of Christ. The other subsequent *pasyons*, however, start with the creation of the world to the death and resurrection of Jesus Christ. The *pasyon* was a very popular Lenten activity which was undertaken in order to "purify one's soul." It consisted mainly of chanting in vernacular Biblical passages. The chanters, who knelt devoutly for long hours, usually had memorized the entire book from the temptation of Adam and Eve, to the birth, sufferings and death of Christ. No interruption is to be allowed in the chant. Hence, stand-ins are ready to relieve the readers who want to eat or sleep. Often, however, challengers from another community sometimes interrupt the chanters by asking questions and riddles to test the reciters' knowledge of the Sacred Book.

The *pasyon's* interest lies less in the narrative as in the *aral* (lesson) that can be drawn from various episodes in the life of Christ.

The *pasyon* is also characterized by the prayer, which is to intensify the piety and religious fervor that would be induced in the reader after considering the lessons in the life of Christ. These prayers are also interruptions to the narrative just like the *aral*.

The *cenaculo* (passion play) is a theatrical presentation of the passion and death of Jesus Christ and may be said to be the *pasyon* on stage. Its name probably is derived from the word "cenacle," the place where the apostles gathered after the Resurrection. Often, the *cenaculo* is preceded by the enactment of the Creation, and other events in the Bible. The *cenaculo* is episodic, running for about nine nights to complete.

It used to be that every night of Lent, a *cenaculo* is presented by amateurs and professionals alike. A stage is set up on any vacant lot, with a curtain at the back. The dialogue is stylized. The actors usually chant the words, but at certain parts, they revert to the conversational tone.

The *cenaculo* may be presented in two ways:
- *Hablada* - the lines are spoken deliberately slow, rhythmically, emphasizing the rhyming in each stanza and conveying the dignity of the theme and the presentation;
- *Cantada* - lines are chanted also slowly. When the characters are important, such as Christ or Mary, the passages are sung. The other characters may speak their lines, even improvise them.

The actors are dressed in period costumes of the Biblical characters, with the men's faces covered with beards. In casting, those who portray Mary and Jesus Christ must have untainted reputations. Christ always wears a "halo" while Mary looks sorrowful from beginning to end. The Jewish and Roman soldiers are played as fierce, boastful, goose-stepping warriors, furnishing a welcome contrast to the sometimes monotonous meekness of the other characters.

In these presentations, a chorus remains on the stage throughout to sing the descriptive passages. The director himself stays with them and, besides singing a part, keeps a close eye on his actors. If anyone appears uncertain the director does not hesitate to call and tell the actor just where to go and what to do. Indeed he often loses his temper and when he does the play becomes even more exciting to the audience. Production details are ignored in singing the *cenaculo*. It does not matter, for instance, if Mary wears modern high-heeled shoes or if the major women characters wear today's clothes.

Each main character has his own leitmotif - - soft, sweet, strains of music for Jesus and His disciples, and martial, clanging marches for the Romans. The orchestra remains silent whenever a character chants his lines.

9. The Panawagan

The *panawagan* has the same theme as the *cenaculo*. It is usually held at around nine o'clock in the evening of Holy Saturday in a yard, fenced into an oval where the players perform. The audience sit or stand outside the oval while somebody at one end reads the *pasyon*. The performance is in pantomine although music is occasionally used to keep it from becoming monotonous. The presentation is usually crude. Mary wears a stiff, starched white cotton veil, trimmed with equally stiff cotton lace. Christ is wrapped in a mat during the Resurrection and is placed on a table in the center. At some climactic point, Christ unwraps himself, stands on the table and assumes the position of the Risen Lord.

10. Awit and Corrido

The English equivalent of the *awit* is the metrical romance. It is written in four 12-syllable lines. It usually deals with love between a Moro princess and Christian warrior, or a Christian princess and a Moro prince. The *corrido*, on the other hand, deals mainly with the lives of saints and biblical characters and comes in four 8-syllable lines. Both the *awit* and the *corrido* appear to be escapist, fantastic adventures or miraculous happenings set in the distant past.

Because the *awit* and the *corrido* evolved and developed side by side with the *pasyon*, in the 18th century, their anonymous writers incorporated into them the narrative strains of the *pasyon*.

The *awit* and the *corrido* became the center of family and neighborhood recreation on Sundays, holidays and hours of leisure.

The *awits* and the *corridos* immediately became popular principally because they provided temporary release from harsh realities. They provided "safest" entertainment during the Spanish period when political and literary censorship was strict.

11. The Carillo (Shadow Play)

The *carillo* is a play of cardboard figures projected on a white screen. Brought to the Philippines by a Spaniard, the *carillo*, like its counterpart in China and Japan, consists of manipulating figures by skillful hands. Oftentimes, these movements and gestures were without rhyme and reason, a sort of pantomimic cadenza. Action was usually accompanied by dialogue furnished by the manipulator or prompter. Generally the action dwelt on historical romances.

The theme of the *carillo* was most often drawn from legendary stories, largely from Europe. Often presented on moonlight nights after a harvest, the *carillo* offered a very simple but interesting entertainment with interludes of native songs.

The *carillo* through the years, underwent some changes. To evoke laughter, it began exploiting the adventures of Don Juan, the libertine of Seville who in a frenzy of passion slew the father of the lady whom he sought to seduce. At times the *carillo* told of the stories of Don Juan Tenorio, La Tia Norica, the Seven Infants of Lara, the Sadores of King Momo, and the Adarna Bird. All these stories were drawn from the same sources of the *awit* and the *corrido*.

During the early days of the American occupation, the *carillo* again underwent changes. Instead of cardboard figures, live actors performed on the stage behind a screen in the open air.

Because the *carillo* does not need many performers, it can easily be shown easily anywhere. It was not surprising, therefore, that carillo shows made use later of the Tagalog *comedias*.

12. The Bayok (Muslim Play)

The Muslim Filipinos have unfortunately no extant native plays. The Muslim Filipinos, however, perform today the *bayok* or the *embayoka*, resembling the modern *duplo*. It is a debate in verse between a man and a woman.

The formal *bayok* is usually followed by a handkerchief game called *sayatan*. The *sayatan* culminates with a young woman placing a handkerchief on the shoulder of one of the young men. In the Muslim tradition, the couple will be the first in the community to get married.

13. The Moro-Moro (or the Comedia)

The *moro-moro* is a theatrical presentation intended to convert. Knowing the powerful influence that plays had on the community, many author-priests used plays to convert natives to Christianity. The Spanish priest in every town decided the kind of plays to be staged. Thus inevitably the predominant theme of every drama was the triumph of Christianity over paganism or Islam. Family problems and love tangles were added to lend the plays color. But in the end, Christians always vanquished non-Christians by converting and baptizing them.

As a dramatic form, the *moro-moro* is supposed to have been inspired by a group of children playing "moros" (the name used for Muslim Filipinos) and Christians at war with one another. The usual plot of the *moro-moro* revolves around a Christian princess held captive by the Muslims. The king organizes a rescue party and pursues the enemy. They fight in the forest and in the plains. They are attacked by lions, tigers, giants, and other monsters and are bewitched by fairies and ogres. The rescue party undergoes many vicissitudes in addition to having a fight with the "Moros" who in the end are vanquished by some miracle or divine intervention. The Muslims are not only defeated. They are also converted. There is also a happy ending.

In these plays the *moros* are not the Muslims of Mindanao and Sulu alone; they represent Muslims, in general.

An indispensable feature of the "moro-moro" is the *torneo* (tournament). The *torneo* is preceded by a *paseo* or parade dress or a series of formations. The tempo of the musical background changes from the *marcha* to the *paso doble*.

The *escaramosa*, an interesting *moro-moro* feature, is probably derived from the word *scaramouche*. In the *escaramosa*, actors display their skill with twirling weapons as they sway. The movement is similar to that of folk dancing. In pairs, the combatants dance on the center of the stage. They bow to the royal personages on the stage and dance to the tune of the *fandango* and *balitaw* or other folk dances with similar tempo.

Stylistic stage movements are conventional in the *moro-moro*, making it attractive and fascinating.

The play, because of its brilliant pageantry, elegant poetic language, pompous gestures and exaggerated acting, appealed immediately to the masses. The country folk loved the *moro-moro* with its general appeal to the eye and ear, its clash of cymbals, stirring martial music as well as its sentimental songs like the *kundiman*. Moreover, the verses are sometimes geniune poetry and some of the loveliest native songs in the Philippines today originated from the *moro-moro* or the *comedia*. Many a rustic lover in the romantic Spanish days serenaded his lady with lyrics that had been sung first in *moro-moro*.

The *moro-moro* was often held in public plazas, in church patios or even on an improvised stage in an open field. It usually highlighted fiestas and other celebrations.

Conclusion

These traditional media are fast disappearing from our cultural heritage. There is, therefore, an urgent need to preserve them, and perhaps more important, to use them in communicating to the masses in places where the more modern mass media do not reach.

Notes

This chapter first came out as part of an article, "Mass Media--Philippine Style," in *Silliman Journal*, Vol. XXI, No. 1, First Quarter, 1974, pp. 29-59. The author acknowledges the contribution of Dr. Bienvenido Lumbera, Ateneo University professor, and Dr. Nicanor G. Tiongson, University of the Philippines professor, for the use of their personal materials on Philippine literature and drama.

Chapter XX

Group Media

Ibarra M. Gonzales

INTRODUCTION

The concept of group media continues its struggle for a name. The term has been long associated with audio-visuals, multi-media, little or mini media, folk media, traditional or local media, peoples' media, alternative media, or low-cost media. The concept also goes by another name, community media, but it smells just as sweet.

Some terms take on one perspective or emphasize one aspect of the concept more than the others. The terms are never exclusive of each other. Meanings overlap, categories are not distinct or clear.

The essential elements revolve around three concepts: (a) group, (b) media, and (c) methodology. Questions on group size, qualifications of participants, choice of medium or message depend on the group media practitioners. Group media methodology is essentially borrowed from the Freirean method of consciousness raising.[1]

In this chapter, we will be using the term group media.[2]

The initial task of group media is to establish a group, reorient, or enhance existing groups with the methods and processes of group media. The groups could be community groups or a network of groups, self-help groups, cause-oriented groups, media groups, production groups, study groups, etc. It is possible that group media is only one of the many "techniques" employed in group and community building. In other words, group media do not exist in a vacuum nor is there a "pure" group media.

The processes of group media hold certain value assumptions. Some of these value assumptions are maximum participation, dialogue and relevance. When the process is cut short, due for example, to time constraints, these value assumptions are undermined. Group media then, can just be another manipulative tool for oppression. The relationship between group and media is easily managed. However, the problems arise in accepting and being faithful to the value assumptions underlying its use, particularly for human development.

Here is an example of a group media session using photographs. A group of about 9 to 12 members and a facilitator (also called group leader or animator) gather around a set of pictures spread on the floor. The pictures, cut out of magazines, depicted the life situation of the participants. The facilitator gives the instructions: "Here are 50 or more pictures. Select one and only one picture that for you responds to our question 'How can we improve our living conditions today?' Study the pictures well, the lines, shapes, forms, the symbols, the meanings evoked by them. We will move clockwise in silence around the pictures. As we move, select mentally your picture. When you have selected your picture, sit down and wait till all of us have selected our pictures. When everyone is seated, we shall pick up the pictures you selected. Do not worry if somebody else has your picture. You can borrow it later. When everybody has a picture, put away the rest not selected. Then we can begin our sharing. Tell the group why you selected that picture."

The sharing begins. The facilitator can deepen the sharing by asking more provocative questions. Towards the end of the session, action plans can be discussed. Other media forms can be used to initiate and provoke dialogue.[3]

HISTORY

The practice of group media can be traced to four historical conditions: (a) economic, (b) political, (c) mass media system, and (d) failure of the last two "development decades." Precipitated by these four conditions, the group media phenomenon spread like fire, especially in the poor countries of Asia, Africa and Latin America.

Economic Condition

Because of limited economic resources, group media became an alternative to broadcast mass media. The latter needed a heavy layout of technology, skills, and maintenance, resources affordable only to developed countries. In contrast, group media needed minimum technology, skills and maintenance.

The main concern among these poor countries is national development and how communication can hasten the process. Prior models (e.g., radio schools, educational TV) of the early sixties suffered three major setbacks:

1) High technological cost which largely depended on foreign capital. When foreign aid stops, the project folds up.
2) Management, orientation and control of communication projects were easily coopted by the ruling political power, paying lip service to development.

3) Communication systems required skills and highly trained personnel to operate. The systems reach only a limited number of people or the wrong set of audience.

Group media offer alternative models which can overcome these shortcomings. It is in this context that "low-cost media," "micro media" and "alternative media" surfaced. Group media can make use of the most inexpensive medium like pictures cut out of magazines or newspapers. Possibly its most sophisticated medium is the Betamax tape.

Because group media involve "small" operations, activities can be easily monitored, directed (or re-directed) and managed by development agencies and voluntary groups.

Likewise, only minimal skills are required to run group media technologies. The communication environment in poor countries usually range from electrified to non-electrified areas and from literate to illiterate audiences. Group media provide wider access and more meaningful participation.

Political Conditions

More than the socio-economic conditions which set the stage for the emergence of group media, the political environment of most Third World countries serves as catalyst for group media development. Most developing countries have quasi-dictatorial or dictatorial forms of government. Communication systems are heavily censored. Peoples' access to the mass media is limited and controlled. Freedom of expression and speech are highly restricted. One possible outlet of communication is group media.

Group media thrives if not prospers in such conditions. Medium and content are made very relevant to the concerns and conditions of the audience. These conditions are similar to those that produced the "morality plays" of the middle ages. It is in this context that group media have been equated with "folk media," "traditional or local media," or "peoples' media."

Mass Media System

In developing countries broadcasting has been attacked as a tool of western cultural imperialism. It is cheaper to buy canned foreign programs (for TV and movies in particular) than to produce one's own. Broadcasting has been associated with entertainment and advertising, more than with education and development. Re-orienting the broadcasting system with development objectives has been tried with little success.

An alternative system is in group media. Radio lessons broadcast to small isolated study groups have been found successful.[4] Production cost can be reduced with the participation of small local groups. At the same time, the broadcast medium is being re-oriented toward development communication. This kind of modification can be done in print media. This is how the "rural mimeo press" and the community newspapers started.

Failure of Past Development Decades

Probably the most important condition that promoted the growth of group media was the failure of the two development decades in the 60s and the 70s. When the question "How to develop?" failed to produce results, it was changed to "Why is there underdevelopment?" Answer: The educational methodologies went unquestioned as well as the technologies and techniques of "How to develop."

The educational methodologies with their cultural superstructure have been imposed, maintained and controlled by developed countries. This produced "colonial mentality," a result of the cultural and media imperialism of the developed West. To change this attitude, a new consciousness has to be created, a new educational process has to be formulated.

Group media utilized the methodologies for consciousness raising.[5] Group media revived the original insight of audio-visuals but added a more critical and creative approach to "seeing, hearing, and writing" reality. It tries to bring to consciousness, not the reality of the West, but the present lived realities of the community and the nation. Only then are the group's realities interwoven into the global system.

At the outset, values which are both assumptions and goals are the underpinnings of group media. Foremost is the sense of history: an awareness of the historical processes (e.g., births, growths, and deaths) and conditions, and causal relations surrounding all human realities and events. Secondly, self-reliance, grounded in creative and responsible acts of individuals in community, can improve the quality of human life. Finally, the value of dialogue as a process for change. This includes maximum access to the media and optimum participation by all those involved in the group.

THE GROUP MEDIA PHILOSOPHY

What are the goals of group media? Depending on the lived context, goals may vary and change. When there is poverty and oppression, goals are liberation and self-determination. In the context of formal education using audio-visuals, the goal may be purely educational (e.g. self-actualization). In work, for instance in a cottage industry, the goal is economic. In other words, group media practices cannot be labelled as purely political. This is a very naive perception and understanding of group media.

People as Key Resources in Group Media

Group media give emphasis to people and the community, rather than the technology of modern communication. There is a general tendency for communication to get carried away by changing technology, overlooking the needs of people and the community. The temptation to be fascinated with technology is a normal occurrence in developed or developing countries. Technological determinism is machine-driven instead of person-driven.

The spirit of group media stresses the value of persons, as human beings, not what persons have or can do. A real group media program will avail itself of the research findings in personality development, group dynamics, sociology of community building, interpersonal communications and the like. Group media is not a "cop out" alternative for the disenfranchised, the poor and the oppressed. Group media, by itself, is a viable communication strategy sustained by different academic disciplines.

Group media is more suitable for adult groups. The concept relies much on the collective life experiences of the group as a major resource for interaction. Theoretically, adults have more life experiences. Nevertheless, everyone, including children and adolescents, are experts in their own experiences. These form the building blocks of group media communication. All experiences are valid starting points for group media. What is important is for each member to learn from his original experience and hopefully, become a more enlightened person. This will enable him to achieve his full human potential in the community.

Process as Key Methodology in Group Media

At this point, the methods, processes, and goals of group media have become so intertwined, it is hard to distinguish one from the other. Far from being product-oriented, group media are action-oriented, i.e., from meaningful actions and strategic actions, other experiences and actions can evolve. In Freirean terminology, this action is called "writing or rewriting reality," which is the over-arching goal of group media.

Aside from the context-related goals of group media, there is an umbrella goal: to encourage members of the community to participate and creatively develop their own reality. This development can be measured and its direction changed through dialogue with other members of the group or community dialogue with other groups or communities. Ideally, a small media group is auto-directive and self-reliant.

In brief, group media methodology employs all possible group techniques from the fields of psychology, sociology, education and culture, and communication.[6]

Group media is process-oriented. It is time bound. There are no "instant" effects but always gradual re-awakenings and "sleeper" effects. The process is built on the concept of dialogue: dialogues between persons, between groups and communities, between person and nature, between person and culture or between person and machine. Dialogues take time. Group media will not survive in an "instant" culture.

The test of group media is in the dialogue process. The temptation is always to provide the "answer" instead of allowing the group to work and discover it on their own. Another temptation is to cut the process short by manipulating the directions of the dialogue or by becoming less critical of the experiences under scrutiny. Members and group leaders can become impatient or dishonest with themselves by their silence or laziness (i.e., uncritical stance) and be discouraged by the time involved before "effects" can be felt. Another obstacle to the process is a monologue. A person or a clique controls the dialogue process and prevents other members from participating. The struggle in group media is the struggle against selfish human nature. This is the arena where group media will emerge victorious or suffer being torn limb from limb.

Group media methodology practices the concept of transfer of learning. Ranging from easy to difficult, participants are encouraged to apply in the real world what they have learned in a media group exercise. However, there is no guarantee that an enlightened and successful group media exercise can be replicated in the "real world."

To be effective, the group media system has to be synergistic. This means there is a convergence in the methodology, process, and goals of the group with the communication medium used, the participants, and the environment. Theoretically, any medium can be used for group media. The more suitable medium blends with environment, life experiences of the participants, time-determined goals of the group and dialogue process employed. The convergence of these elements creates new energies to fuel the process of change.

MASS MEDIA AND GROUP MEDIA DEBATE

Some media practitioners raise the question regarding what to use in their communication strategies, mass media or group media. The four historical conditions mentioned earlier forced certain groups to concentrate on group media activities. Without these restrictions, communication theories recommend the use of multiple communication channels (i.e. both mass and group media) to guarantee message redundancy and attention. This insures the first step in the communication process. For effective communication, both mass and group media are necessary and important.

However, if the message is purely informational, e.g. an announcement, then mass media may be appropriate. If the message involves behavior modification, group media may be more effective. Certain messages may need both mass and group media.

When communication effectiveness is the issue, the "either or" situation between mass media and group media becomes irrelevant. Mass media need group media for impact delivery and action response. Group media need mass media for broad coverage and wider impact. Both systems are necessary to achieve effective communication, in theory at least. On the practical level, decisions will be based on resources available and what goals need emphasis.

The Chinese experience uses both mass media and group media.[7] National policies and party politics are disseminated through the mass media, the newspapers and radio in particular. The messages are further displayed in "Dazibao," large poster newspapers or blackboard newspapers in the villages. Then the messages are further discussed in the cells or cadre groups for implementation.

The concept of group media is an essential element for effective communication notwithstanding its historical development. Different forms of group media exist with mass media whenever there is effective communication.

MEASURING GROUP MEDIA EFFECTIVENESS

An outsider, i.e. not a participant of group media, will not be able to fairly judge its effectiveness. If group media practitioners remain faithful to the process, they themselves become the measure of effectiveness.

The role of an outsider is to comment on the consistencies or inconsistencies of the different processes involved in the group media activity. The practitioner should follow the methodology and strive to look for "efficacy" not "effectiveness." Effectiveness tends to look at the end goals only, disregarding the means. Efficacy looks at both the ends and the means as a consistent activity, adjusting or correcting each other in the process of achieving the goal.

GROUP MEDIA IN PHILIPPINE SETTING

In September 1972, the Marcos government declared Martial Law. One of its immediate actions was the closing down of mass media institutions. After some months they were allowed to operate but with strict compliance and censorship by the new dispensation. It was this environment which ushered in group media.

Under Martial Law, media establishments critical of the government were closed down. Leading media men like Joaquin P. Roces and Eugenio Lopez, Jr. were arrested and detained. It was clear that mass media would be controlled solely by the government.

In June 1974, the Catholic Bishops' communication arm, the National Office of Mass Media (NOMM) and the Jesuit Communication apostolate[8] presented a policy paper which endorsed group media in whatever form, as the official means of communication in propagating their mission and goals. The document had an option that whenever permitted or accessible, mass media will be used. The policy was approved in November.

The document further stated that the immediate aim is conscientization, i.e. to make people aware of unjust structures and to lead them to do something about it. The top priority is training in the use and technique of "micro-media:"

> By micro-media we mean those forms of media which are less expensive and within the reach of the greater number of people: cassettes, posters, black and white pictures (photo-language), slides and sound slides, 8 millimeter films, portable video tape recorders, small offset press, rural mimeo press, and live drama.

In the same year, the ETV, the only viable educational television program, closed down due to lack of funds. For ten years, the ETV located at the Ateneo de Manila University campus, was supported by the Ford Foundation.

During the previous year, 1973, the NOMM initiated two major grassroots projects: the rural mimeo press and the blackboard newspaper.[9] The projects were an offshoot of the meetings on the UN celebration of the Population Year. The Pathfinder Fund of Boston, Massachusetts funded both projects.

The rural mimeo press project of the NOMM covered 51 dioceses all over the Philippines. Fifty-one priests and sisters edit 51 newsletters in the dialect. The project supplied each diocese a mimeographing machine and a yearly supply of stencils, ink and newsprint. The project ended in 1976.

The more famous rural mimeo press was *Ang Bandilyo* of Malaybalay, Bukidnon.[10] The mimeo press was attached to the Diocesan radio station and catechetical center. The news writing concept of *Ang Bandilyo* is developmental. No news was final. It was dialogic. As new evidence and information unfolded, the news continued to evolve and was written up in the next weekly edition. *Ang Bandilyo* did not have reporters. Anyone in the parish could be a reporter. All they had to do was write down the piece of news on any sheet of paper, sign it and drop it into the local parish news box. The news was collected, verified and printed. The local bus lines helped distribute the weekly.

The weekly was supplemented by the Diocesan radio station DXBB. The combined effects of the rural mimeo press and the radio station had such a strong influence on the people that the military closed down the radio station, shut down the mimeo press, and confiscated the mimeo machines in November 1976.

The blackboard newspaper project of the NOMM had 25 participants in the small towns of the Visayas and Mindanao, all managed and edited by parish priests. Blackboards were placed in strategic areas of the barrio. The contents of the blackboard ranged from parish activities to prices of rice and corn.

In Bogo, Cebu, Fr. Trinidad Silva edited *The Moalboal Times*.[11] Four huge marine plywood sheets make the main board. Twelve smaller boards are scattered in strategic locations within the poblacion. Twelve others are placed in front of the barrio schools. The editorial staff originally consisted of 13 men with Fr. Silva as editor-in-chief. The rest represented local self-help organizations. They were the news reporters. Every morning, they reproduce from the big board the news for the poblacion. Head teachers going to the barrios hand carry their copies for the barrio blackboards. The boards have a community-building effect. While people read, they begin to discuss the items on the board.

The now defunct National Media Production Center (NMPC), a government office, set up similar projects in 1977 under the name of "Hatid Kabatiran sa Barangay."[12] This project tried to establish rural mimeo press and blackboard newspapers in Rosario and Balayan, Batangas. This early project was a failure. Based on the errors of the past, a new program was initiated called Community Organization Program (COP). With the barangay as a base, the COP program organized drama groups, puppet theater groups, speakers' bureaus, and barangay libraries. As of September 1982, COP had 83 organized blackboard newspapers, 10 community newsletters, 39 aklatan boards, 32 drama groups and 21 speakers bureau groups.

Philippine society has been accustomed to religious folk media. The *pabasa* or *pasyon*, *cenaculo*, *panuluyan* and *santacruzan* are widespread religious practices that are community-based activities. Together with the traditional drama forms like *zarzuela*, *cancionan* and *balagtasan*, the religious folk media provided a rich dramatic heritage for the Filipino. Community theater is a common experience.[13]

The Commission on Population (POPCOM), together with the Institute of Mass Communication (UPIMC) at Diliman, capitalized on this medium to spread the Commission's objectives.[14] Based at the regional POPCOM office, small groups experimented with the different forms of folk media to inform, educate and communicate (IEC) population issues to the public.

The Philippine Educational Theater Association (PETA) is another group working mostly with non-government organizations (NGOs). PETA provides training and education for various groups interested in using the theater as means of development. One major thrust of this group is to develop through the theater a critical view of reality. PETA was training community organizers from both private and public service sectors on how to use theater for community development.

Another group media activity is photolanguage, the use of pictures for development. Like the technique of group dynamics, pictures are used to evoke and provoke dialogue and discussions regarding a chosen theme. After the discussion the group is moved to action by laying out concrete action plans for their community. Posters and picture magazines can also be used.[15] Cassettes[16] and betamax tapes are likewise media for group interaction.

THE FUTURE OF GROUP MEDIA

What is the future of group media? The concept will remain as it exists in local broadcasting media, small CATV and community radio stations. In developing countries, group media as a concept will continue as it does today. If group media development will be affected at all, it will be in the area of how personal computers will change its processes and goals.

In developed countries, the run-away technologies are in the area of computers. They are dramatically affecting the economics of information, i.e., the transformation of information as a major source of livelihood. Watch out for this phenomenon in developing countries. Another technology that can be used by group media, i.e. the personal computer, is in the market. Will computers be synergistic with the group media system: method, process, environment or the participants' experiences? As a technology, will it be strategic for the goals of group media? These are some important questions that will determine the future of group media.

Finally, group media as a concept does not exist for itself. It works with several alternative methodologies, processes and goals. Like all human artifacts, it is a tool that best survives in the hands of the user, should he decide to use it.

REFERENCES

Forum On Group Media, *Group Media Journal*, Vol. IV, Nos. 19-20, December 1985.

Gonzales, Ibarra. *Photolanguage Philippines: A Manual for Facilitators.* Quezon City: Sonolux/Asia, 1981.

Reuter, James, S. J. "The Blackboard Newspaper and the Rural Mimeo Press," Mimeograph, National Office of Mass Media, Manila, 1975.

Notes

[1] See Paulo Freire's *Education for Critical Consciousness*, New York: The Seabury Press, 1973.

[2] A good discussion on the use of the term group media is found in *WACC Journal*, XXIV, 3/1977.

[3] A complete set of instructions and guidelines on this kind of session is found in *Photolanguage Philippines: A Manual for Facilitators*.

[4] D. Jamison and E. McAnany, *Radio for Education and Development*, Beverly Hills: Sage Publication, 1978.

[5] See also P. Freire's *Pedagogy of the Oppressed*, New York: The Seabury Press, 1974.

[6] For a more detailed discussion on group media methodology see *Photolanguage Philippines: A Manual for Facilitators*, Quezon City: Sonolux/Asia, 1981, pp. 76-162.

[7] For a more complete study of the Chinese group media experiences see G. Chu's *Radical Change Through Communication in Mao's China*, Honolulu: The University Press of Hawaii, 1977.

[8] *Media Policy Statement by the Social Communications Apostolate of the Society of Jesus*, November 3, 1974, Manila.

[9] Organizations based at the National Office of Mass Media and are directly supervised by James B. Reuter, S.J., Mimeograph, Manila, 1978.

[10] The following information was based on an interview with the station manager and editor, Fr. Austin Nazareno, S.J. conducted by the author in 1976.

[11] Fr. Trinidad Silva, "A Philippine Version of Village 'Dazibao'," Mimeograph, Manila: National Office of Mass Media, 1979.

[12] T. Atienza, Jr. and T. Asuncion-Reed, "Strengthening Communication Networks Through Community Organization," in F. Rosario-Braid, et. al. (eds.), Communication for Rural Mobilization and Development, Manila: Asian Institute of Journalism, 1984.

[13] A fuller documentation and discussion is found in Sonolux Information, No. 6, September 1982. See also Sonolux Information, No. 11, December 1983.

[14] V. Valbuena, *Philippine Folk Media in Development Communication*, Singapore: AMIC, 1986, pp. 111, 113.

[15] A fuller documentation and discussion on posters as group medium is in Sonolux Information, No. 7, December 1982.

[16] A fuller discussion on the use of cassettes and radio programs is in Sonolux Information, No. 9, July 1983.

Part Six

Adjuncts of Media

No study of the field of communication would be complete without a look into the agencies which are not channels of communication in themselves. They are neither mass media nor mini media, but agencies that support the mass media. For want of a better term we refer to them as adjuncts of mass media.

Chapter XXI discusses advertising agencies and the work they do, while Chapters XXII and XXIII describe the government information service, past and present. Chapter XXIV tells about the exciting work of the news agencies in gathering and disseminating information to all corners of the world 24 hours a day. Finally, Chapters XXV and XXVI deal with the two pillars of the communication profession — communication research and communication education.

Chapter **XXI**

Advertising Today: Profile and Problems

Lutgarda R. Elvinia and Ramon R. Osorio

Advertising is perhaps one of the more stable business sectors in the Philippines today. The advertising industry weathered a floundering economy in 1985 that saw the closing down of a little less than 15 percent of advertising agencies in the country due to bad business. But 1987 augurs better things to come for advertising. What is the Philippine advertising industry and profession like?

PROFILE OF THE INDUSTRY

Number and Size of Advertising Agencies

The 4 A's P or the Association of Accredited Advertising Agencies in the Philippines as of 1985 was composed of 38 advertising agency members (See Appendix A). However, there are around 80 agencies in the country today.

Of the accredited agencies, 76 percent are owned by Filipinos and 24 percent are partly or fully owned by multinationals. But the multinationals account for over 50 percent of the annual national advertising billings. The big 4 are J. Walter Thompson Company (Philippines, Inc.), McCann-Erikson (Philippines), Ace-Compton Advertising, Inc., and SSC & B: Lintas Worldwide Manila.

A Filipino-owned agency, Unit Two Media Corporation, recently merged with Ogilvy and Mather Worldwide, one of the world's largest agencies and the biggest in Southeast Asia,[1] raising the number of mergers from five to six.

Multinationals are big because they have more international resources and connections than wholly Filipino-owned agencies. To correct this imbalance, Filipino agencies want the government to "Filipinize" the industry. But as advertising executive Pedro Teodoro noted, the government has not done anything yet to "Filipinize" the P2 billion advertising industry.[2]

About 88 percent of ad agencies in the Philippines are less than 30 years old. Only five or 12 percent have been in business for more than 30 years. Table 1 indicates that most existing agencies were put up only after World War II, although many of their senior officers were in the business before the war. Of agencies which have been around for about 36-40 years, two are multinationals, one is a partner of a multinational, and one is local.

Advertising agencies do not employ as many persons as other businesses. From Table 2, it can be seen that almost half or 48.72 percent of agencies employ 10-24 persons fulltime. Only 17.95 percent of the agencies hire 25-39 fulltime employees, while 10-26 percent of them have a staff of more than a hundred people. Only J. Walter Thompson, a multinational and one of the largest agencies in the world, employs more than 150 people fulltime.

Table 1. Length of Time in Business of Advertising Agencies

No. of Years*	Frequency	Percent
1 - 5 years	4	10.26
6 - 10	9	23.08
11 - 15	7	17.95
16 - 20	4	10.26
21 - 25	5	12.82
26 - 30	5	12.82
31 - 35	1	2.56
36 - 40	4	10.26
TOTAL	39	100.00

Source: 4A's P Handbook, 1985

Table 2. Number of Full-time Employees in Advertising Agencies

No. of Full-time Employees*	Frequency	Percent
10 - 24 employees	19	48.72
25 - 39	7	17.95
40 - 54	4	10.26
55 - 69	1	2.56
70 - 84	2	5.13
85 - 99	0	0.00
100 - 114	1	2.56
115 - 129	2	5.13
130 - 144	2	5.13
145 - 159	1	2.56
TOTAL	39	100.00

*Source: 4A's P Handbook; 1985

**Percentages were rounded off and may not add up to 100.

Volume of Advertising in Various Media

Despite the slowdown in growth over the years, a study conducted by the AMA (Advertising & Marketing Associates, Inc.), Consolidated Group showed that media advertising expenditures grew remarkably in 1985.

Media advertising spending grew by 40 percent in nominal terms from P1,172.8 million (US $70.3 million) in 1984 to P1,638.8 million (US $87.3 million) in 1985. In real terms, growth was 24 percent.

Growth in 1981-85 closely parallelled the growth of the last two decades. The 15 percent annual growth rate in 1981-85 equaled that of 1970-80 (from P182.5 million to P736.5 million), and was slightly higher than the 13 percent average in 1960-1970 (from P60 million to P182.5 million).

However, in real terms, based on the peso-dollar exchange rate, the annual growth rate of media advertising spending averaged out at -7.0 percent in the 1980s, 2.2 percent in the 1970s and 12.9 percent in the 1960s (See Tables 3 and 4).

Table 3. Advertising Spending per Medium (P Millions) in 1985.

	P	Percent Share
Print	479.5	29%
Radio	322.5	20%
TV	825.5	50%
Others	11.3	1%
TOTAL	P 1,638.8	100%

Table 4. Average Annual Growth Rate: 1981-1985

	1981 ADSPEND (P Million)		GROWTH RATE(%)
	(P)	% SHARE	(P)
Print	372.7	39.9%	6%
Radio	169.5	18.2%	17%
TV	356.3	38.2%	23%
Others	35.0	3.7%	-25%
TOTAL	933.5	100.0%	15%

TV Dominates Ad Spending

Television retained the lion's share of the advertising pie -- a distinction it snatched from print in 1984. Prior to this, print was the premier advertising medium.

In 1980, print captured 45 percent (P328.2 million) of advertising expenditures worth P736.5 million. Four years later, the share of print shrunk to 29.2 percent (P342.3 million of the total P1,172.8 million spent on ads). In 1985, print's share dipped slightly to 29 percent.

In contrast, television advertising increased its share to 46 percent (P543.0 million) in 1984, from 32 percent (P237.1 million) in 1980. In 1985, television's share climbed further to 50 percent.

Major Advertisers

Reports from various media show that the largest advertisers, the top ten in each media category, except print, accounted for more than half of billings in 1985. (See Table 4).

In television, for example, 5 major networks and 12 blocktimers reported that the top ten advertisers accounted for 53 percent (P437.7 million) of total billings of P825.5 million in 1985.

The story is pretty much the same with radio: the top ten advertisers accounted for 54 percent (P174.1 million) worth of gross billings of P322.5 million in 1985. (Table 5).

25.4% Growth in Agency Business for 1985

The billings of 19 advertising agencies, including capitalized fees, increased by 25.4 percent from P1.403 billion in 1983-84 to P1.758 billion in 1984-85. Before that the growth rate in billings in 1982-83 had slipped to 15 percent from 28.5 percent in 1981-82.

Worth noting is the growth rate of 1985's top ten agencies. It averaged 21.8 percent in 1981-1985 compared to the 9.2 percent for medium and small agencies.

The top ten agencies remained virtually unchanged over the last four years. These include - J. Walter Thompson (Phils.), McCann Erikson, Bates-Alcantara (Phils.)[3], Inc., AMA (Advertising & Marketing Associates, Inc.), Consolidated Group, Basic/Foote, Cone & Belding, J. Romero & Associates, Ace-Compton (Saatchi & Saatchi) Advertising, Inc., Hemisphere-Leo Burnett Advertising, Inc., and Atlas Promotions & Marketing Corp.

J. Walter Thompson and McCann-Erikson are wholly-owned subsidiaries of multinationals, Ace Compton-Saatchi & Saatchi, Bates-Alcantara, Hemisphere-Leo Burnett, and Basic/Foote, Cone & Belding are joint ventures. The other four are owned wholly by Filipinos. The six multinational agencies have been among the top ten in the last four years. Data on two other multinational agencies, Aspac & Grey and SSC & B: Lintas Worldwide Manila, are unavailable. It would be interesting to see just how high they would rank.

The top ten agencies' dominance in the market has steadily increased since 1980, when they chalked up a market share of 73 percent. In 1985, they got around 83 percent market share. The six multinational agencies' share was 43 percent in 1981, and 53 percent in 1985.

Advertising Organizations' Role and Function

Fourteen of the 48 advertising agencies organized themselves into the Association of Philippine Advertising Agencies (APAA) in 1956. Pedro E. Teodoro was its first president. The act was prompted by a threat of a proposed tax on agency gross billings. APAA claimed the tax could have wiped out the industry.[4]

Table 5. Top 10 Media Advertisers '85 (Millions)

	Print	Radio	TV	Cinema
Gross Billing	P 479.50	P 322.50	P 825.50	P 6.1
Total Billings of Top 10	158.2 (33%)	174.1 (54%)	437.5 (53%)	3.9 (63%)
Others	321.3 (67%)	148.4 (46%)	388.0 (47%)	2.2 (37%)

	Print	Radio	TV	Cinema
1)	Nestle Philippines	San Miguel Corp.	Phil. Refining Company	Phil. Refining Company
2)	Unilab	Phil. Refining Co.	San Miguel Corporation	Fortune Tobacco Corporation
3)	Phil. Refining Co.	Colgate-Palmolive Phils.	P. & G. P.M.C.	Colgate-Palmolive Phils.
4)	San Miguel Corporation	Fortune Tobacco Corp.	Nestle Philippines	Vibelle Manufacturing Corp.
5)	Colgate-Palmolive Corp.	P. & G. P.M.C.	Colgate-Palmolive Phils.	Jollibee Foods Corporation
6)	Vibelle Mftg. Corp.	Nestle Philippines	Johnsons & Johnsons	La Tondena
7)	California Mftg. Co.	Coca-Cola Bottling	Coca-Cola Bottling	Phil. Gen. Merchandising Corp.
8)	Int'l. Pharmaceuticals	La Suerte	Fortune Tobacco Corp.	La Suerte
9)	Metro Drug	Unilab	Pepsi Cola	Hills Bros.
10)	Philusa	La Tondena	Warner Lambert	Dutch Boy Philippines

On July 7, 1969, the APAA defined an advertising agency as:

> An independent, legitimate and ethical agency which practices the advertising profession free from control by a substantial advertiser or advertisers in order that it may not be prejudiced or restricted in its service to all clients and to the business community, free from control by a medium owner or owners in order that it may give unbiased service to all advertisers. It must not rebate any commission it receives from media to comply with their rate cards and to be able to devote all commissions to the service and development of advertising for the progress of the business community. It must have adequate facilities and employ experienced and able personnel to serve advertisers fairly and efficiently and must have the financial capacity to meet obligations to all concerned.[5]

In line with this definition, the 4 A's P promoted a Code of Ethics for its members to follow.

Other groups - the advertisers, the media, research, suppliers cinema, and outdoor advertising groups also formed their associations.

The advertisers' group, the Philippine Association of National Advertisers (PANA) advocates "Truth in advertising" in its Code of Advertising Ethics and regulates abuses by untruthful advertisers.

There are two media groups - the Kapisanan ng mga Brodkaster sa Pilipinas (KBP) and the Print Media Organization (PRIMO). KBP, now in its 11th year, upgrades broadcast standards by enforcing guidelines for airing programs and by manpower development projects and the accreditation of announcers.

PRIMO is the association of major publications, to which advertising agencies go for accreditation. It helps screen advertisements. It also serves as credit and collection managers. In the Philippine Board of Advertisers (PBA), it takes part in the screening of advertising materials and in the advertising content regulation process.

Another organization is the Market and Opinion Research Society of the Philippines (MORES). It is made up of suppliers and users of research that aim to promote professionalism in research and set the right standards in advertising. For instance, if a claim made by one advertiser is contested by another, MORES steps in and decides which has a better claim. Consequently, the ad may be pulled out in favor of the one proven right.

The cinema group is called the Cinema Advertising Association of the Philippines (CAAP). It is responsible for booking commercials in movie houses. It deals directly with ad agencies and theater owners, among others.

The oldest medium in advertising i.e., billboards, neon signs, even ordinary outdoor signs, is represented by the Outdoor Advertising Association of the Philippines (OAAP) whose members try to police themselves against malpractices like obnoxious street signs, fire or typhoon hazards and the like.

The suppliers of ink, paint, photographic and other materials have banded into the Advertising Suppliers Association of the Philippines (ASAP).

The umbrella organization of all these groups is the Philippine Board of Advertising (PBA) which was set up in May 1974 to forestall government control during martial law. The PBA is a self-regulatory organization. Regulation is based on a Code of Ethics that PBA adopted on April 15, 1975.

In a move to continually improve, update, and upgrade the industry, the PBA formed the Trade Practices and Conduct Committee which "formulates, interprets, implements multi-association agreements related to the practice of the advertising professions."

The committee will soon compile information for a Manual of Advertising Practices on which the review, expansion, and updating of trade agreements will be based.

PROBLEMS FACED BY THE INDUSTRY

Minimal development orientation

Dr. Benjamin V. Lozare of the Philippine Information Agency pointed out some years back that in order for the advertising industry to be perceived as relevant, participative and essential by government, it must complement development efforts in a more coherent, organized and meaningful manner.

To do that, the industry needs to overcome these problems:

- The public, in general, and the government officials, in particular do not understand and appreciate enough the nature, capabilities, and limitations of advertising;
- No effective linkage between the government and the advertising industry;
- No clear government policies on the role of information in the national development strategy; and
- The agencies do not get enough encouragement or incentives for undertaking development-oriented advertising campaigns.

As a result, the government often conveys messages at odds with the industry's advertising campaigns that frequently drown developmental messages.

There is indeed a need for the industry to redirect itself. The first step may well be to understand, study and tackle some problems, among them:

- Not enough professionalism among advertising practitioners;
- Advertising associations are not effective enough;

- Practitioners are hardly aware and know little of national development problems and needs;
- Advertising agencies tend to focus on populations with relatively big purchasing power and not to low income groups.

In development advertising, it is assumed that profit-orientation and development orientation are not conflicting and the advertising cost of development advertising is minimal compared to its benefits. Advertising's power to change society cannot be denied. Using it irresponsibly is indefensible, considering the mass poverty in the country. Thus the only appropriate perspective here is that of social responsibility.

Based on research findings, developmental advertising can:
- Promote values for national development and discourage those that do not; e.g., encourage civic consciousness and discourage having large families;
- Act as catalyst, initiator, and implementor of social change; e.g., encourage citizen-participation in nation building;
- Help focus on and disseminate useful and locally relevant development-oriented information; e.g., providing nutrition information in advertising food products;
- Assist more the non-profit groups doing development work; and
- Promote a climate for development by providing the impetus for business growth, and contributing to public discussion.[6]

Training of Future Advertising Practitioners

The advertising industry seems in need of a program to train young people to become professionals. As the economy shifts from rural to agro-industrial, a developmental approach to training practitioners is made more urgent because:

1. The slump in the demand for local products in foreign markets necessitates the development of local markets;
2. The government is decentralizing development, i.e., from urban to rural;
3. More locally produced goods are flowing into the market;
4. The "cultural imperialism" or "cultural invasion" brought about by foreign mass media has affected some traditional but useful social values;[7]
5. The ever-growing number of Filipinos employed abroad requires information and ideas to preserve their culture;
6. Proposed legislation imposes more stringent rules and regulations for the communication industry, i.e., broadcasting and advertising.

The industry thus will focus not only on selling goods and services, but also on supporting the country's development efforts.

The combination of a liberal arts background and technical skills should progressively lead to "professionalism." The individual must also see himself as a specialist, a recognition that can lead to quality work.

The presence of and the role played by the Asian Institute for the Development of Advertising must be enlarged and supported by both industry and the academe. This calls for strengthening the curricula of schools offering advertising courses and to encourage the exchange of ideas and interaction on a Filipino value-oriented advertising education.[8]

High Cost of Media

The staggering cost of placing ads on TV, radio or print prevents many advertisers from going into supplementary, "non-commercial" advertising. Money for developmental advertising is simply not available.

Need for New and Accurate Assessment of Media Vehicles

Proliferation of newspapers in the post-Marcos era would need accurate audit so that agencies and advertisers would know the best print advertising vehicles. The shift in audience interests toward news commentary programs would generate considerable media buying in this area. Teddy Jurado, president of 4 A's P, notes that these news-commentaries are "a good buy because viewers are currently interested in any political development."[9]

ADVERTISING'S SOCIAL RESPONSIBILITY: QUESTIONS AND CHALLENGES

Is advertising socially responsible?

If we take "social responsibility" to mean the duty to work for the benefit of the socially oppressed, then it would open up tremendously exciting and creative dimensions for advertising. The industry could help these men, women, and children recapture their "sense of human dignity and individual worth."

But certain assumptions must first be understood.

First, the advertising function of a market economy, which sets tastes and values according to its own self-reinforcing criteria.[10]

Second, advertising creates a reality of its own, apart from whatever everyday experience that inevitably becomes part of an individual's personality.[11]

Third, advertising is an agent of choice. As such, it can specify moral context of choice so that the audience decisions could be made with a greater awareness of responsibility.[12]

Studies show that children under 7 years old make up most of the young TV audience. To a child, what is visual is real. They are very susceptible to advertising messages because they cannot yet discriminate the "image" thing from the thing itself.[13]

Clearly then, children at this stage must be protected from their own vulnerability, until such time when they could make their own choices as informed adolescents[14] and discriminating adults.

Even adults make irrational choices. They need adequate information on standards of performance, standards of durability, and standards of safety of competing products in order to make rational choices.[15]

Higher standards could be set in advertising to children, especially food and toy performance claims, and to other neglected or vulnerable groups, like women and poor people.

Footdragging and resistance to this effort come in two ways:

1. The "ostrich principle of resistance," or "the problem doesn't exist." Evasive replies are common tactics.

2. "Too-many-variables" play and we never know how an appliance is used by the consumer. Therefore, it is "impossible" for manufacturers to give assurances about the products.[16]

What consumers would like to be told is how a product typically performs in average use.

To meet this need, responsible manufacturers, advertisers, and consumers assisted by government and non-government agencies, scientists, and other technical people could form a national standards development body. But no public funds need be used. The past regime's excesses in the use of public funds work against this. This is a job that can be initiated and carried out by private groups.

If the consumers do not have the organization or the money, the government may temporarily fill this need by hiring consultants to represent the consumers.

The last concern is sexism.

Sexism in advertising depicts woman as inferior. It is discriminatory, and it degrades and humiliates women.[17] By definition, sexism runs against social responsibility which promotes human dignity and self-worth.[18]

Sexism in advertising is perhaps the most pressing yet largely overlooked issue in the industry, emanating perhaps from the predominance of male decision-makers.[19] While advertisers in other countries attempt to project a more conscious and realistic image of women, Filipino advertisers continue to present the Filipina in the feudal, medieval, and colonial mould. Such an image degrades women who comprise almost 52 percent of the population and about 51 percent of the bread winners in the country.[20]

For instance, Mrs. Corazon C. Aquino's being a female was used as a political issue in the 1986 Presidential election and an attack on her being a female was made through advertisements.

In producing these sexist ads, the advertisers must be taken to task by more responsible and enlightened members of industry. Such sexism perpetuates a stereotyped image of women as weak, dependent, emotional, and irrational. It also clouds and distorts the pressing issues of poverty, unemployment, unequal distribution of income, and social injustice.

Even in development communication, a recent study laments that stereotyped images of women are perpetuated while a male-dominated and male-oriented rural development program is promoted.[21]

"The power to define is the power to control. Communication is power and exclusive access to it is a dangerous unchecked power."[22] Without question, the advertising industry and mass media as conduits of social information and setters of social agenda stand out as some of the most potent transmitters of values and ideas that could bring about the proper changer in the social structure.

Appendix A

ADVERTISING AGENCIES IN THE PHILIPPINES
(4 A's P Membership)

    Able Advertising Agency
*Ace-Compton Advertising, Inc.
    Ad Centrum Advertising, Inc.
    Adformatix, Inc.
    Admakers, Inc.
    Ad Planners & Marketing Counselors, Inc.
    Advertising & Concept Exponents, Inc.
    Advertising & Marketing Associates, Inc.
    Asia Communications Center, Inc.
    Asia-West Marketing Communications, Inc.
**Aspac & Grey
    Avellana & Associates, Inc.
**Basic Advertising, Inc.
Bates-Alcantara (Philippines), Inc., now **Alcantara-DYR
    (Dentsu, Young, & Rubicam)
    Cathprom Advertising, Inc.
    Commerce Advertising Corporation
    Creative Concepts, Inc.
    Design Systemat, Inc.
    General Ads, Inc.
    Great Wall Advertising Philippines, Inc.
**Hemisphere-Leo Burnett, Inc.
    J. Romero & Associates, Inc.
*J. Walter Thompson Company (Phils.), Inc.
    Manprom Advertising Agency
    Marketing & Advertising Counselors
*McCann-Erickson (Philippines), Inc.
**Minds/Kenyon & Eckhardt (Phils.), Inc.
    Nation-Ad Philippines, Inc.
    Pacifica Publicity Bureau, Inc.
    PBS Advertising, Inc.
    Philippine Advertising Counselors, Inc.
    Professional Promotions Group
    Reach Advertising Inc.
***SSC & B: Lintas Worldwide Manila**
    Summit Advertising Corporation

The Marketing & Communications Group
Thrust Ads Corporation
**Unit Two Media Corporation

*Multinational

**Partnership with Multinationals

REFERENCES

*Books and Periodicals

4 A's P Advertising Agency Directory, 1985.
Altschull, J. Herbert. *Agents of Power: The Role of the News Media in Human Affairs*. New York: Annenberg/Longman Communication Books, 198.
Berger, Peter and Luckman, Thomas. *The Social Construction of Reality: A Treatise of the Sociology of Knowledge*. Garden City: Doubleday, 1966.
Bhasin, Kamla and Agarwal, eds. *Women and Media: Analysis, Alternatives, and Action*. Geneva: ISIS (International Women's Information & Communication Service) December, 1984.
Bower, Tom. *The Perceptual World of the Child*. Great Britain: Fontana/Open Books, 1983.
Butler, Matilda and Paisley, William. *Women and the Mass Media: Sourcebook for Research and Action*. New York: Human Science Press, 1980.
Castillo, Gelia T. "The Filipino Woman: Wife, Mother, Worker, and Citizen," in *NSDB-UP Research Illustrated*, Vol. 4, No. 1, January-March 1980.
Crisostomo, Isabelo T. *Modern Advertising for Filipinos*. Quezon City: J. Kriz, 1967.
Halloran, James D. editor. *Mass Media and Socialization*, International Bibliography and Different Perspectives. England: J. A. Kavanagh and Sons Ltd., 1976.
James, Don L. *Youth, Media, and Advertising*. Studies in Marketing No. 15. Austin: University of Texas, 1971.
Lozare, Benjamin V. "The Case for Development Advertising" in *Development Communication and the Asian Imperatives*. Vol. II, Manila: The AFAA, 1980.

Matthews, Bryan, "Brighter Times Ahead for Filipino Advertising," *Asian Advertising and Marketing,* Vol. 7, No. 4, April '86.

Mercado, Orlando and Elizabeth Buck, "Media Imperialism in Philippine Television," *Faculty Research Journal,* Vol.2, March 1982, Maryknoll College.

Mowbray, A. Q. in *Mass Media ana Society* (2nd ed.), Edited by Alan Wells. California: Mayfield Publishing Co., 1975.

"Philippine Board of Advertising: An Update," *Business Day Supplement,* August 23, 1985.

Ward, Scott. "Effects of Television Advertising on Children & Adolescents," *Children and Television* , Ray Brown, ed. California: Sage Publications, Inc. 1976.

Interview

Interview with Mr. Antonio de Joya, June 15, 1986, Makati, Rizal.

Unpublished Paper

Elvinia, Lutgarda Resurreccion. "Advertising for Filipinos," A Proposal for a Textbook Development Project for the AIDA (Asian Institute for the Development of Advertising) and PBA (Philippine Board of Advertising), August, 1982.

Notes

[1] *Philippine Daily Inquirer,* June 24, 1986.

[2] *Manila Bulletin,* June 18, 1986.

[3] Known now as Alcantara DYR (Dentsu, Young, and Rubicam).

[4] Isabelo T. Crisostomo, *Modern Advertising for Filipinos.* Quezon City, J. Kriz, 1967, p. 46.

[5] Ibid, p. 47.

[6] Bejamin V. Lozare, "The Case for Development Advertising" in *Development Communication and the Asian Imperatives,* Vol. II, AFAA, Manila, 1980, p. 66.

[7] Orlando Mercado and Elizabeth Buck, "Media Imperialism in Philippine Television," *Faculty Research Journal,* Maryknoll College, March 1982, pp. 29-35.

[8] Lutgarda R. Elvinia, "Advertising for Filipinos — A Proposal for a Textbook Development Project for the AIDA (Asian Institute for the Development of Advertising) and PBA," Unpublished paper, August 1982, p. 9.

[9] Bryan Matthews, "Brighter Times Ahead for Filipino Advertising," *Asian Advertising and Marketing,* April 1987, pp. 36-37, 50.

[10] Herbert I. Schiller, "Mind Management: Mass Media in the Advanced Individual State," *Mass Media and Society,* Alan Wells, ed., California, Mayfield Publishing Co., 1975, p. 207.

[11] Peter Berger and Thomas Luckmann, *The Social Construction of Reality,* Garden City, Doubleday, 1966, pp. 88-90.

[12] Schiller, p. 207.

[13] Tom Bower, *The Perceptual World of the Child,* Fontana/Open Books, Oxford University Press, 1977, pp. 63-67.

[14] Don L. James, *Youth, Media, and Advertising,* University of Texas, 1971, pp. 101-108; James D. Halloran, ed., *Mass Media and Socialization,* England, J.A. Kavanagh & Sons, Ltd., 1976, pp. 46-52; Scott Ward, "Effects of Television Advertising on Children and Adolescents," *Children and Television,* Ray Brown, ed. California, Sage Publications Inc., 1976, pp. 297-342.

[15] A.Q. Mowbray, "What Consumers Need: Showbiz or Hard Facts?" in *Mass Media and Society,* Allan Wells, ed., California, Mayfield Publishing Co., 1975, pp. 141-145.

[16] Mowbray, pp. 142-143.

[17] Kamla Bhasin and Bina Agarwal, eds. *Women and Media,* Geneva, ISIS, December 1984, pp. 8-18.

[18] J. Herbert Altschull, *Agents of Power*, New York, Annenberg/Longman Communication Books, 1984, pp. 119-123.

[19] Matilda Butler and William Paisley, *Women and the Mass Media*, New York, Human Science Press, 1980, pp. 18-21.

[20] Gelia T. Castillo, "The Filipino Woman: Wife, Mother, Worker and Citizen," Beyond Manila: *Philippine Rural Problems in Perspective*, Canada, IDRC, 1970; NSDB-UP Research Illustrated, Vol. 4, No. 1, January-March 1980, pp. 16-33.

[21] Bhasin and Agarwal, pp. 10-12.

[22] Sen. J.W. Fullbright in 1970, quoted by H.I. Schiller, in *Mass Media and Society*, p. 207.

Chapter XXII

Government Information as Propaganda: The Past

Jose L. Pavia

INTRODUCTION

The 20 years of the Marcos regime saw government information grow from the simple days of issuing press releases to the era of sophisticated, multi-million peso multi-media operation across the archipelago and overseas, principally in the United States.

That public information could develop into a monstrous propaganda machine did not dawn upon the nation until the Aquino assassination in 1983. When the Filipinos saw the monster for the first time, they began to ask what indeed should be the role of a government information service.

What happened between 1983 and February 1986 is now history. Yet the role of a government information service still has to be officially defined even after the Ministry of Information was dismantled in mid-1986 to fulfill President Cory Aquino's campaign promise.

HISTORICAL FLASHBACK

In its desire to reach the people and to tell them of changes and innovations, achievements and progress, the government at the start had set up one form of public information program or another.

In 1947, the Public Information Office (PIO) employed about 40 people under the Office of the President. Johnny Orendain was press secretary to President Manuel A. Roxas. The PIO's objectives were to cover and disseminate information on presidential activities, and to facilitate their coverage by media men.

In 1950, the Philippine Information Service (later renamed Philippine Information Council) was organized. It was under the Office of the President, and sought to provide information to the public. But it was abolished in 1952.

The Council in its brief existence showed how important a systematic information effort was and thus led government communications experts into preparing the blueprint for an organized public information system.

In 1953, the National Media Production Center (NMPC) was established. The NMPC started on a collaborative public information program with other government agencies. Although limited, the program was the government's first attempt at meeting an urgent need - - that of bringing information to and getting feedback from the people in the countryside.

At that time, public information was a novel idea. It lacked direction, planning, and professional manpower.

Duplication of information dissemination marked the early '50s. Public information meant largely issuing of press releases, which tended to be more for publicity than for public information.

In 1958, the NMPC was placed under the Department of General Services. It continued, however, to produce multi-media services for government agencies. In 1969, the NMPC was reverted to the Office of the President. The NMPC was the major public information agency until martial law was proclaimed in 1972.

Public information lacked planning and was carried out in bits and pieces in its early years. There was also an acute shortage of professionally-trained information officers at the time. Thus, for a long time, various government information units worked independently from one another. Undue emphasis was still placed on press releases.

By the '60s, the mass media could have provided the channels for public information. Unfortunately, they were more oriented to profit, and not to development. Without effective channels of communication, the government's information efforts proved anemic.

When martial law was declared on September 21, 1972, the government redefined the rationale for using mass media in its programs to create a New Society. New guidelines on the operation and supervision of mass media were made since the government recognized media's influence on public opinion.

On September 24, 1972, President Marcos, through Presidential Decree No. 1, set up the Department of Public Information (DPI).

The DPI primarily was charged with an overall and integrated government information program. It was to be made an effective instrument of growth and progress. In its organizational structure, DPI had the following units: the Office of the Secretary and its Planning, Financial and Management, Administrative and Technical Services; the Regional Offices; the Bureau of National and Foreign Information (BNFI); the Bureau of Broadcasts; the National Media Production Center (NMPC); and the Bureau of

Standards for Mass Media (abolished in 1976). Essentially, DPI incorporated all major government media such as the NMPC, the Philippine Broadcasting Service (PBS) and the Malacañang Press Office (MPO). Although the integration of government media was brief, it served as a blueprint or a public information setup that was presented anew for presidential approval a decade later.

Francisco S. Tatad, who was press secretary to President Marcos in his second term in 1969, was the first and only DPI secretary. In 1978, the DPI was renamed Ministry of Public Information (MPI) when the form of government changed from presidential to parliamentary.

Tatad then asked President Marcos to revert the Presidential Press Staff (PPS) to the Office of the President, and appoint an official spokesman to head it. He proposed to remain the Minister of Public Information.

But Tatad left the Marcos administration and was replaced by Minister Gregorio S. Cendaña. The MPI under Cendaña focused basically on advertising the President, his wife and the rest of his family. Although Marcos eventually appointed an official spokesman (Adrian Cristobal), the Presidential Press Staff with Deputy Minister Amante Bigonia as its head, remained under MPI. By then, the MPI had become a colossal propaganda machine for the now deposed President and his family.

Cendaña's entry and Tatad's exit put all the government media under one person; if not under one office. Before this, Tatad had control over the MPI and Cendaña had the NMPC. NMPC's presence as typified by MBS Channel 4, the Voice of the Philippines, the multi-colored publications on the Marcoses and fleets of audio-visual vehicles, relegated the MPI to the background. The Cendaña-Tatad rivalry was an example of the Marcos policy of divide-and-rule.

Under Cendaña, the MPI was renamed the Office of Media Affairs (OMA). It was downgraded from a line agency to a support agency on July 28, 1981, a month after President Marcos was reelected. Yet, Cendaña retained his ministerial rank and Cabinet post and the OMA budget trebled in 1982 over the previous year.

With a huge budget on hand, Cendaña restructured and revitalized OMA's bureaus and agencies. All the government information media, including the Bureau of Broadcast's nationwide network, the Philippines News Agency, and the government television, thus competed vigorously with the private media. Cendaña's reinvigorated information offensive was intended to make doubly sure that government messages reached the public. The administration could no longer just presume the private media would cooperate, nor the opposition.

The OMA appeared to have gained the upperhand in the competition despite its setbacks following the Aquino murder. The competition ended when the Marcos government fell in February 1986.

On February 25, a few days after the Aquino government was installed, the Ministry of Information (MOI) replaced the Office of Media Affairs.

The perceived basic functions of the MOI were
- to serve and protect the freedom of all media from editorial interference from any quarter, including the government;
- to provide public relations services for the Philippines, in order to rebuild the country's image abroad; and
- to assist the Office of the President by promoting press relations.

PROFILE OF THE INFORMATION MINISTRY

As the government's information arm, the Office of Media Affairs (OMA) was tasked with formulating and carrying out an integrated information and communication plan to support the national development program. Along this line, it was to disseminate information on state policies, programs, plans and activities designed to make the public understand and actively participate in government activities. Thus, it was authorized to publish newspapers, magazines and other print materials; operate radio and television stations; and maintain non-traditional information networks nationwide.

As a service agency the OMA's guiding tenet was the enhancement of man as a change-agent and beneficiary of development.

The Office of Media Affairs was headed by a Director-General, who sat in the Cabinet as Minister of Information and Press Secretary to the President. Under him was the Bureau of Broadcasts. Under the set-up, Cendaña was also the National Media Production Center's director. Both OMA and NMPC had offices in the 13 regions.

The Philippines News Agency, the government news agency, was under BNFI. The NMPC ran and operated the Maharlika Broadcasting System, the government radio-TV network.

Under a reorganization plan, NMPC was to merge with OMA and the merger would be headed by a Minister. The OMA's line units then would be: a National Information Agency, a Foreign Information Agency, the Philippines News Agency, and a National Media Development Center. A Presidential Information Agency would also be under the Minister's direct supervision.

The new OMA could meet all the government's information requirements through these facilities:

1. The Presidential Press Staff (PPS)

Since 1980, the Presidential Press Staff had been considerably strengthened. A central editorial desk directed multi-media services for the activities of the President.

2. Maharlika Broadcasting System (MBS)

The radio facilities of NMPC and the Bureau of Broadcasts - - made up of 28 stations, five of which are in Metro Manila and one beamed overseas --

were to be integrated into the Maharlika Broadcasting System (MBS), the government's radio-television network. MBS runs three TV stations - - in Metro Manila, Cebu, and Bacolod - - and a relay station in Baguio City. Integration would enable the government radio-TV stations to reach all the major regions effectively.

The MBS radio-TV network, in coordination with the Kapisanan ng mga Brodkaster sa Pilipinas and the PLDT, could air simulcast-hookups and "live" coverages of such events as the Pulong-Pulong (Dialogue with the People) and State-of-the-Nation Address. It could also do remote broadcast coverages of international events hosted by the Philippines.

3. The Philippines News Agency (PNA)

As the official news agency, the PNA operated 17 news bureaus nationwide. It had six foreign correspondents in key U.S. cities. The PNA had news-exchange agreements with ASEAN countries and the 24-member Organization of Asia-Pacific News Agencies (OANA). It also had bilateral news-exchange agreements with ANSA (Italy), Deutsche Press Agentur (West Germany), Agerpress (Romania), Prensa Latina (Cuba) and TASS (USSR).

The domestic and U.S. bureaus and the news agencies of Indonesia, Malaysia and Thailand were linked to Manila by two-way, 24-hour teleprinters. This communication network had been upgraded by memory and video display units under a UNDP-UNESCO-IPDC Assistance Program.

4. Press and Publication Plants

The printing plants of the NMPC and the OMA were to be integrated for optimum use and for upgrading production services. The NMPC had two plants in Quezon City, one on Bohol Avenue and another at the Media Center on Visayas Avenue. A third one was in Malolos, Bulacan. The OMA had printing plants in the Bureau of National and Foreign Information in Metro Manila, in Iloilo City, and in Tacloban City.

5. Regional Offices

The OMA-NMPC regional offices could produce multi-media material on a limited scale. In cooperation with local governments, the new OMA was to maintain 71 provincial development communication offices, and 271 municipal development communication offices equipped with VTR cassettes for showing films and other audio-visual material. A total of 237 community groups were organized nationwide to support the OMA regional personnel working on countryside information. These volunteer groups had 112 audio-visual vans.

6. Film Laboratory

The NMPC film laboratory at the Media Center on Visayas Avenue was a one-stop service facility for film production, from script to screen. The Center had facilities for producing color documentaries, feature films, commercials and film clips in both 16 mm and 35 mm.

7. Community Media

To complement the mass media, OMA-NMPC also used the community media, like community theater, puppet theater, computerized multi-screen slide presentations, photo exhibits, blackboard newspapers and so forth.

8. Videotape Recorder (VTR) Project

In 1983, a VTR Project funded by the Japanese Yen Credit Loan, was launched. In two years, 113 towns received VTR monitor-playback sets to complement communication strategies for the country's 42,000 barangays. In addition, 1,580 sets of TV monitors were programmed to aid priority development programs, including conservation of natural resources; the "Sariling Sikap" program; traditional festivals and rituals; successful entrepreneurs; and the children's program series using the NMPC Puppet Theater.

9. Foreign Information Network

The OMA's Bureau of National and Foreign Information operated four area desks - - the United States, Asia-Pacific, Europe and the Middle East - - and had 11 information attaches posted abroad: in Washington, D.C. New York, Los Angeles, San Francisco, Sacramento, Chicago, Honolulu, London, Canberra, Geneva and Tokyo.

The BNFI had a 24-hour telex link with six U.S. cities: Washington, D. C., Chicago, New York, San Francisco, Los Angeles, and Honolulu.

10. Domestic Information Service (DIS)

In 1983, the OMA organized under the BNFI a Domestic Information Service. DIS produced and syndicated print and broadcast editorial materials on the government's development programs and on current issues of popular interest.

11. International Press Center (IPC)

In 1981, the OMA established under the BNFI the International Press Center. Ideally located at the National Press Club, the IPC catered to the professional needs of visiting and resident foreign journalists.

PERSONNEL AND BUDGET

The OMA had some 5,000 employees, many of whom were contractuals and casuals. Many of them were posted abroad, mostly in the U.S. Civil service requirements, particularly eligibility, led to the distortions in the employee profile in terms of appointments, designations, wages, and promotions. These were a big obstacle in professionalizing the manpower and the career service.

The following table shows the growth of the budget for government information since martial law was proclaimed in 1972.

Table 1. Government Information Budget, 1972-1986

Year	Legislation	Total (In P million)
1986	Batas Pambansa Blg. 879	282
1985	BPB 866	254
1984	BPB 640	248
1983	BPB 230	243
1982**	BPB 131	226
1981	BPB 90	76
1980	BPB 40	31.65
1979	BPB 1	29.77
1978	Presidential Decree 1250	30.79
1977	PD 1050	28.65
1976*	PD 733/904	23.88
1975	PD 503	28.94
1974	PD 233	17.95
1973	Republic Act No. 6551	6.16
1972	House Bill No. 3443	9.52

* BSMM was abolished
**NMPC was integrated into OMA

THRUSTS AND ACTIVITIES

After the 1984 Batasan elections, Cendaña submitted a terminal report on his stewardship of the OMA-NMPC from January 1980 until May 1984.

He told the President ". . All my life I shall remember with pride OMA-NMPC's modest part in the development efforts, the electoral triumphs, the splendid state visits and the successive crises that had engaged the President and his Cabinet these past four years . . . I wish to assure the President that we have been able to build at OMA-NMPC an information community of professional quality, which will continue to serve the Government well, even under a different leadership."

In that report, Cendaña recommended the OMA-NMPC merger to end any duplication of functions. He also proposed assigning an OMA information man in each ministry to harness at the utmost their information resources and capability, and for better coordination. He also recommended mergers of Metro Manila newspapers and broadcast stations in order to rationalize their operations, enhance their viability, and raise overall standards. He considered another priority task was improving political awareness of editors and station managers, and their understanding of the government's objectives, particularly the day-to-day purposes.

Cendaña cited these proposed changes under the new OMA:
- The BNFI will be split into national and foreign bureaus.
- The Information Policy Coordinating Council will coordinate the public information activities of government ministries, agencies, and corporations.
- The Philippines News Agency becomes a separate unit.
- All broadcasting functions will be under the Maharlika Broadcasting System.
- The OMA will be allowed to go into programs that will generate income to pay for supplies and materials, and support services.
- The President may create the Office of Presidential Spokesman that may avail of the OMA's services.

ISSUES AND PROBLEMS

The advent of martial law brought to sharp focus such issues and problems as press freedom and access to information, propaganda and news management.

Central to all issues was press freedom. The government's setting up an information department came in conflict with the Fourth Estate and the advocates of press freedom. The closure of all media facilities in 1972 made the DPI the jailer of press freedom. For indeed, the early years of martial law saw the media as a dog whose leash was held tightly by the government's information arm. The DPI, later known as the MPI and later still the OMA, could do little to rid itself of the stigma.

Access to information typified the double standards the government used. The foreign media had a relatively freer access to news and the information sources. The local press, laboring under censorship and overly cooperative publishers, got the morsels and had to be satisfied with official handouts. Filipino journalists did not take long to become aware that they were second-class practitioners in their country. The consequence was that public information needs could no longer be distinguished from political propaganda.

News management easily evolved when journalistic enterprise was gone and initiative discouraged. The clincher came in the form of fat envelopes government men gave, along with the press release, to journalists. Cartelized journalism was in and the best example was the Malacañang press office. Nobody dared upset the apple cart. Not the mediamen. The cart was safe and it assured the good life. Not the editors who took their cue from the publishers who represented the crony owners. And most certainly not the information minister whose primary task was to make the public accept unquestioningly the government thinking. The crony press thus descended upon the scene very much like the way cronyism settled upon all the vital aspects of the nation's economic and political life.

Many more issues were related, in one way or another, to those already cited.

ASSESSMENT

In the 20 years that Marcos was in power, he himself had conceived, fleshed out, decreed, implemented and orchestrated his own information programs and system which passed for, and became, the government's. It was a classic case of "father knows best" with the family members carrying out the paternal orders happily and without question. The men of Tatad and Cendaña used to refer to Marcos as the supreme editor for it was not unlikely for him to revise, if not dictate, the lead of the day's Palace story.

President Marcos was his own information minister.

Tatad never really got to exercise the information minister's enormous power in a martial law regime. He was cut down to size a few weeks after he became the chief spokesman for the crisis government. The President's relatives and political lieutenants saw to that. And Marcos knew how it was to divide and rule. When Tatad earned his political wings in the 1978 elections, he thought he had the clout. Paradoxically, his clout spelled his doom. The palace intriguers made sure that he would never be a politically-powerful information minister.

Under Cendaña, the government information machinery went into high gear to serve the presidency first and foremost, focusing mainly on political information and propaganda to ensure that the people would unquestioningly swallow the government thinking and message.

In the Marcos experience, the information ministry was never really given the opportunity to perform the role which, ironically, the Marcos regime itself assigned to it. True to form, Marcos, one of the ablest manipulators of men and events, created and operated an information machinery to suit the needs of his New Society and later, his New Republic.

Marcos himself and his 1973 Constitution recognized the people's right to know and to have access to government information so they could benefit from the democratic system and thus, assure themselves of a better life. But the flow of information was not much nor fast enough, was one way, and one track.

The ever growing budget and size of the government information staff were utilized principally for political information and propaganda, concentrated in Metro Manila and in the major cities. The populace hardly got information relevant to them. And neither could they bring their plight to government attention. There were no regular information outlets nor feedback channels. The people could not and were not encouraged to participate in the information system.

The Marcos experience showed that manipulating public information and managing the news bred distrust between the government and the people and resulted in the government's losing credibility. The people saw only propaganda in everything that the government did.

That Marcos controlled (if not owned) all the media bred mediocrity, and caused professional and ethical standards to deteriorate. The stagnation caused media technology to become inadequate and backward. Newspaper readership stayed low at 6.5 million daily in a country of 56 million. Only one out of five households had television sets but 90 percent of TV set owners were urbanites. Three out of four households had a radio set but it would take still another 45 years at current growth rate before every Filipino household could own one. Besides, the mass media served mainly the cities where the market was profitable. The countryside came only as an afterthought. Thus, use and ownership of media remained primarily in the hands of the elite--the rich and the educated.

RECOMMENDATIONS

There is no denying the need for public information exists. For indeed, who will inform the nation and the world about the government, what it has done, is doing, and will do, if not government itself? But the word here is inform - - information, public information. And the need is to satisfy the people's information needs. That is the role an information ministry, agency, office, service or by whatever name it comes, must play. That is it and that is how far the effort should go. If such needs are satisfied, then the government will have done its job.

Government information is news and the government is a major source of news. However, the gathering, writing and distribution of news should not be the government's primary function. These are best left to private media. In cases when the private media do not do it, the government must step in and pioneer in the endeavor. A good example is the Philippines News Service. The government took it over after martial law was declared and renamed it the Philippines News Agency. It was a cooperative of major national newspaper publishers before martial law. The PNA, however, will likely remain a government news agency for some time. The private media cannot yet afford to operate PNA on the scale that it is operated today.

But the government must remove the PNA from the public information system and allow it to operate independently, albeit with subsidy from the government as its single biggest subscriber. There are enough models for this type of arrangement in developing, newly-developed, and even developed countries. Eventually, of course, the PNA has to become a private enterprise.

The role of a government information ministry is in fact the role of the entire government itself.

Chapter XXIII

Government Information As Development Communication: The Present

Delia R. Barcelona and Virgilio M. Gaje

INTRODUCTION

After the February 1986 Revolution, the government information system was overhauled. The new government searched for ways to dismantle the propaganda machine and harness the government information system for rebuilding Philippine society.

GOVERNMENT INFORMATION SYSTEM

Since the Aquino government assumed office, flow of information has been freer. But it still leaves much to be desired because of some barriers.

The media now conveys a variety of opinions. This is a healthy trend. But some media men lack responsibility.

The people are starting to distinguish political from development-oriented public information.

All these point to a need to:

- Adequately meet people's information needs through appropriate laws, policies and programs.
- Set up feedback mechanisms so the people can be heard and have a voice in planning and carrying out national development programs.
- Distinguish political from development-oriented information;
- Promote professionalism and high ethical standards in media;
- Support and encourage the development of rural media; and
- Promote the partnership between the private and public sectors in broadcasting.

Structure

The government information network consists of:

- The Office of the Press Secretary;
- The Philippine Information Agency; and
- The information office in each department or agency of the government.

A Philippine Broadcasting Authority has been proposed to address the unique problems and opportunities in the broadcast industry.

Office of the Press Secretary

The Office of the Press Secretary (OPS) was created under Executive Order No. 92 issued in December 1986. It absorbed the Presidential Press Staff, the Bureau of National Information, Bureau of Broadcasts, and the Maharlika Broadcasting System/Radyo ng Bayan.

The OPS was reorganized on July 25, 1987 through Executive Order No. 297. It is to be the "primary policy, planning, programming, and coordinating entity for the conduct of a relevant and effective information and communication management program that will present the activities, policies and directions of the Presidency and the government."

Thus, the OPS handles the political and other information and media relations of the Office of the President.

OPS is made up of the following:

- Office Proper
- Bureau of Broadcast Services, which was formed out of the Bureau of Broadcasts and Radyo ng Bayan
- News and Information Bureau, which was formed out of the Presidential Press Staff, Philippines News Agency, and the International Press Center
- Bureau of Communications Services, formerly the Bureau of National and Foreign Information
- Presidential Broadcast Staff, formerly RTV Malacañang (directly under the Office Proper)
- People's TV-4 and affiliated stations (under the Office Proper)

Philippine Broadcasting Authority (PBA)

The PBA is a proposed organization to implement media privatization. The Authority is to encourage a partnership between private and public broadcasting and to help develop broadcasting in the country. The PBA will tackle broadcasting industry problems, as distinguished from telecommunication issues. As envisioned, the Authority will encourage self-regulation and concern itself with frequency assignments and assistance to the industry.

Information Offices of Departments/Agencies

Almost all government departments and agencies maintain information offices.

Among those with active information units/facilities are the NEDA-APO Printing Office; AFP Civil Relations Staff; Bureau of Agricultural Extension; Department of Tourism; Commission on Population; Department of Education, Culture and Sports; and National Manpower and Youth Council.

Philippine Information Agency

The Philippine Information Agency was created through Executive Order No. 100 dated December 24, 1986. It absorbed the Office of Media Affairs and the national and regional offices of the National Media Production Center.

PIA is to provide for free flow of accurate, timely and relevant information to assist people in decision-making and in identifying opportunities to improve the quality of life, and enable citizens to participate meaningfully in democratic processes. This means PIA is to handle developmental and general government information.

PIA consists of the following offices:
- Office of the Director
- Research Office
- Information Office
- Institutional Development Office
- Administration and Finance Office
- 13 Regional Offices, 1 Sub-Regional Office
- 48 Information Centers
- National Printing Office, formerly Government Printing Office (directly under the Director)

Thirty-three audio-visual mobile vans extend the outreach of the PIA regional offices and information centers. The 370 Community Development Information Centers in key towns are equipped with television monitors and video players.

Strategies

Decentralization of information outlets

The government thrust at present is to decentralize communication, bring it closer to the people and attune it to their information needs.

Each department or agency will then be responsible for its information program. For instance, the Department of Health will take charge of health information.

Thus, information will be disseminated in tandem with services to be rendered to the people.

This implies the organization of information mechanisms at the grassroots level.

Coordination of information efforts

To prevent various information agencies from working at cross purposes, they need to coordinate with each other. This may be done through an information coordinating council that will consist of representatives from departments and agencies. The council will meet regularly to set policies and directions for government information.

Media development

Developing media is necessary because communication facilities and resources are concentrated in urban centers, to the detriment of rural areas which are most needy of information for personal and community development. It is also necessary because private media are profit-oriented, and cannot be expected to invest much in nonprofit ventures.

Government must therefore initiate developing media for the countryside, involving in it the private media.

Linkage with Private Media/Institutions

Government communication agencies (OPS, PIA, etc.) coordinate with private media through industry organizations, such as:
- Kapisanan ng mga Brodkaster sa Pilipinas
- Publishers Association of the Philippines Inc.
- Public Relations Society of the Philippines
- National Press Club
- Provincial press/media clubs

Coordination and cooperation between government and private media are achieved in at least two areas: Pooled coverages of special events, and exchange agreements on specific government programs, broadcast or published by the private media.

Government communication agencies also maintain links with schools, associations, and international organizations such as UP Los Baños, UP Institute of Mass Communication, Philippine Association of Communication Educators, Asian Mass Communication Research and Information Centre, UNESCO, UNDP, Asia-Pacific Institute for Broadcasting Development, East-West Center, etc.

These organizations may help through scholarship programs, training grants, study tours, technology and funding support, and bilateral research projects.

LESSONS FROM THE PAST

Over-Centralization, Propaganda Orientation

The Marcos regime encouraged and cultivated for 20 years a highly centralized and propaganda-oriented government information system.

This system tended to reinforce rigid and inflexible viewpoints. It was unresponsive to the people's changing communication needs and aspirations. It was also vulnerable to political and ideological manipulation by the top leaders.

Barriers to Free Flow of Information

There were barriers to the free and fast flow of information needed for people to participate meaningfully in democratic processes:

1. Policy barriers

The 1973 Constitution recognized people's right to information on public matters but it was not supported by law, policy, or program.

Basic information policy then focused more on promoting the unquestioning acceptance of government thinking. The communication flow was largely one-way, from government to the people.

2. Organizational barriers

Little distinction was made between political and development-oriented public information. Hence, resources for public information were often used for political purposes. In most instances, political information and/or propaganda crowded out development information.

Seventy percent of government information personnel and resources were concentrated in Metro Manila, thus severely restricting the flow of information in the rural areas.

There were no outlets for government publications and materials.

Inter-agency efforts to coordinate with each other was not effective due to lack of appropriate mechanisms and funding.

People's participation in the planning and conduct of information programs generally was not encouraged.

3. Relationship barriers

The government and the people distrusted each other.

Because government information manipulated the people, it eventually lost its credibility. As a result, people did not believe in public officers disseminating development information.

The relationships between the government and the media did not foster professionalism and ethics.

4. Infrastructural barriers

Media could not fill the people's need for information because of inadequate media reach and distribution.

THE CHALLENGES BEFORE US

A. There is severe information poverty in the country

The combined resources of government and private media are not enough to fill the minimum information requirements.

- Combined circulation of daily newspapers has remained stagnant at about 1.3 million for 14 years. The most optimistic estimates in 1985 showed that only about 22 percent of households would have at least one daily newspaper in a week.
- Radio set ownership in 1985 was 72-77 percent of households. If present rate of growth continues, all households would have a radio set in 2030.
- TV set ownership in January 1985 was between 16-22 percent of households.

The government does not have enough information personnel. Only less than 5,000 or 0.47 percent of the government workforce are in information.

Budget allocation for government information-communication amounts to around P150 million or only 0.19 percent of the 1987 budget. Only P2.50 is spent on communication for every Filipino each year.

Most government agencies, except the Office of the Press Secretary and the Philippine Information Agency, do not have facilities for radio-television production. They usually have only audio-visual and photography equipment. A study conducted by OMA-NMPC in 1984 found out that only eight ministries had in-house printing equipment. Three had complete lines of equipment/facilities for film, audio-visual and special media. These were the Ministry of Agriculture, Ministry of Trade and Industry, and the National Food Authority.

B. Communication in the country is a difficult and complex process

Some 58 million Filipinos comprise roughly 10.4 million households. By year 2000, the population will have reached an estimated 75 million.

Communication is made even more difficult because the country is made up of over 7,000 islands.

Regional, cultural and language barriers pose additional problems. The Aquino government has raised the public's expectations for more and better services which are beyond its ability to cope with. Rising expectations have increased demand for development information.

C. Bureaucratic procedures hamper effective operation of the government information system

Government information operations are hampered by limited budgets; difficulty of hiring better and more creative personnel due to low wages and lack of incentives; and strict accounting procedures which curtail flexibility needed for the effective dissemination of information.

D. Private communication enterprises cannot meet the demands for development information

Private communication enterprises are profit-oriented. They do not go to non-profit ventures. They usually target the moneyed sector of the population, and exclude media-starved or information-poor areas.

LOOKING AHEAD

In a well-developed milieu, the government role in meeting people's information needs is minimal.

In a developing country like the Philippines, however, where the communication channels are not adequate, the government has to take an active role.

The government will also have to keep abreast of new communication technology -- computers, satellites, microwave, optic fiber -- so that it can be used for the people's benefit.

There is danger in government having access to an information network. This is well recognized. The country's experience with the Marcos regime that disseminated self-serving information to entrench itself in power is very recent. But the reestablishment of democracy makes it unlikely for the information system to be so abused again.

To prevent a recurrence of the previous regime's abuses, safeguards must be built into the government information system. They include having a professional corps of information officers whose tenure will not be politically dependent and whose loyalty will be chiefly to the Republic.

But the most effective deterrent will be the citizens' eternal vigilance.

HISTORY OF PHILIPPINE GOVERNMENT INFORMATION SERVICE

June 1, 1953 — National Media Production Center (NMPC) was created to specialize in information/communication.

November 1, 1972 — The Department of Public Information (DPI) was set up through Letter of Implementation No. 12, Presidential Decree No. 1 (Integrated Reorganization Plan) creating the department.

June 1978 — DPI was converted into a Ministry of Public Information (MPI) following the switch to parliamentary form of government.

July 1981 — Attachment of NMPC to MPI through Executive Order No. 708 which reorganized the Office of the President after the Presidential elections of June 1981.

July 1981 — MPI was renamed Office of Media Affairs (OMA) and it was reclassified into a support ministry through E.O. No. 711.

February 26, 1986 — A new Minister of Information was appointed by President Aquino; OMA was renamed the Ministry of Information.

December 12, 1986 — OMA-NMPC was formally abolished by Executive Order No. 85.

December 1986 — The Office of the Press Secretary (OPS) was created through Executive Order No. 92, absorbing some old OMA-NMPC units-Presidential Press Staff, Bureau of National and Foreign Information, Bureau of Broadcasts, and Maharlika Broadcasting System.

December 24, 1986 — The Philippine Information Agency (PIA) was created through Executive Order No. 100, absorbing the central and regional offices of OMA-NMPC.

July 25, 1987 — The Government Printing Office was attached to PIA through Executive Order No. 285, and was renamed National Printing Office.

July 25, 1987 — The OPS was reorganized through Executive Order No. 297.

Chapter XXIV

News Agencies

Adlai J. Amor and
Alexander G. Amor

What are news agencies? These are organisations which gather news and feature stories and send them out to client newspapers.

They may send them through telegraph wires like the Philippines News Agency (thus the term wire service) or like Depthnews, they may mail them out to the client newspapers.

They serve one basic function: to gather news for newspapers, radio stations, television stations, magazines and other media establishments.

They bridge the gap between sources of news and the media establishments by instant transmittal of stories as the news breaks.

Newspapers and radio stations cannot cover the entire country nor the whole world. If they had all the money to spend, perhaps they could do it. But even so, it would still be difficult.

Thus, they have to rely on news agencies to cover the rest of the world - - or just the entire country - - for them. Their reporters can then be assigned to areas not ordinarily covered by news agencies.

Through the use of telegraph facilities, news agencies can immediately transmit stories all over the country in a matter of seconds.

News agencies also serve to link one country to the rest of the world. Without news agencies, people outside of the Philippines may never know what is going on inside the country. Nor would we know what is happening in China, Thailand and our other Asian neighbors.

Some news agencies also provide photos to their client newspapers. Photos accompanying major stories are usually sent by cable or radio while the less urgent ones are sent by air packets.

Working for a news agency is both similar to, and different from, working with newspapers.

A major characteristic in working with news agencies is that there is a deadline every minute.

Stories have been told of young and sometimes brusque reporters. In a press conference involving a slow-speaking foreign dignitary, a reporter requested the dignitary to speak faster so that they could catch their deadlines.

He countered by asking: "When is your deadline?" "My deadline is every minute, sir," one reporter from a news agency said.

This is indeed different from working in newspapers where deadlines are often set at four in the afternoon everyday.

But in news agencies, if a story breaks out at 12 noon, it should ideally hit the wires by 12:01. That fast.

Newspaper reporters and news agency reporters need, however, to be versatile. They must report factually - - and with authority - - on any topic assigned to them. Whether it be the selection of a beauty queen, a presidential election or a golf tournament.

But this may not be true to all news agencies. In most agencies, certain reporters are given special fields to cover. In a sense, they become specialists in that field. It may be in business reporting, science reporting or sports reporting.

Despite this, however, a certain degree of flexibility is still needed.

The writing style is more or less similar: it must be simple. But you will note that stories from conventional news agencies are often more tightly edited and tightly written than stories written by non-wire men.

This is so because news agencies are often limited to a certain number of words and stories that can be transmitted a day. Therefore, they have to discard the non-essentials in favor of saving more space and generating more stories.

News agency editors, however, are freed from the burden of lagging out their stories in a page. But they need to see to it that if an important story breaks, their news agency must break it first to the outside world.

There is, however, a growing tendency for some news agencies to shift from straight-news reporting to providing more of analytical and background articles.

This shift came about as more and more journalists felt that reporting the news should not only be their function. Interpretation should be another important function of modern journalists.

But as this trend continues to generate more interest, newspaper editors are becoming alarmed that news agencies might forget their basic function: gathering news.

A MATTER OF NEWSFLOW

Let us look again at the general flow of news stories from the reporter to the news agency and to the reader.

Imagine yourself as a staff reporter... no, make it a staff correspondent. (It has better ring to it, right?). You work for the Republic News Service, a private cooperative news agency established by independent newspapers.

You wake up one morning a bit groggy after all the beer you had with your colleagues at the National Press Club. Suddenly, you remember you have an important interview at the Department of Education, Culture and Sports.

You dress up, skip breakfast, grab a taxi and arrive just in time for the interview with visiting educators from the People's Republic of China.

Fortunately, they speak comprehensible English. In the course of the interview (other reporters from other news agencies and newspapers are also there), the officials drop a bombshell that they will overhaul the Chinese educational system and adopt the Philippine system.

You get all knotted up. Rapidly, more questions are fielded. (After all, it is not often that Chinese officials drop bombshells on the laps of journalists). When the interview ends the others rush for the telephones.

But since your office was just adjacent to the DECS, you decide to quickly write the story and turn it in:

MANILA (RNS) - - VISITING CHINESE EDUCATORS REVEALED TODAY THAT CHINA WILL OVERHAUL ITS EDUCATIONAL SYSTEM AND ADOPT THE PHILIPPINE SYSTEM....

Three paragraphs... four paragraphs... eight paragraphs... until you've exhausted all the important facts.

You turn it in to your news editor and wait around until he finishes editing your story. He asks some pointed questions for clarification - - but thank goodness (you say to yourself) he did not revise the story.

Your news editor - - who is usually grouchy at this time of the day - - breaks into a wide grin and says: "You'll get a by-line for this."

Immediately, he shoots the story to the editor who goes over it again and releases the story. Ten minutes later, the story is out in the wires - - beating the others by a few minutes.

You feel good, but then you remember that there are other beats to be covered. "You better see your other sources before we get scooped. Or your ass will be on the sling," your editor mildy tells you.

The moment your story hits the newspaper clients of the Republic News Service, it is immediately used by them for their afternoon edition.

The copy editor goes over your story again, beefs it up with some other facts he might have on hand. He passes the story to the editor and then it is laid out.

Your story is printed in the newspaper. A few hours later, the paper hits the streets. Below the front page banner headline is your byline - - your name.

You feel happy. After all, this does not happen often.

So you begin wondering . . . a raise? . . . a promotion? . . .

This illustration might seem to be too simple and too general. That is true.

Underneath all the simplicity in looking at the work of a news agency is actually a very complex organisation involving as many as 100 people for the entire network.

The model cited in the Philippines News Agency more or less applies to most news agencies - - with a few variations here and there.

Other news agencies might have more divisions and more editors. There may be business editors, sports editors, science editors and occasionally, a religion editor.

They are backed up by reporters, stringers and feature writers.

Together, this makes for a team directed by an editor-in-chief. A team that works as one in making sure that the news is delivered fast to the newspapers and to the public. At the same time, maintaining a high quality of work.

INTERNATIONAL NEWS AGENCIES

There are dozens of news agencies operating all over the world. Many are government-owned, but there are also many private and cooperative news agencies.

The Big Ones are of course the Associated Press, Reuters, Agence France Presse and United Press International.

These four international wire services (another name for news agencies, and probably a more appropriate one for these four) are better known to millions of newspapers all over the world. They have existed longer than any other news agencies.

The Associated Press, started in 1848, is the oldest and perhaps the most prestigious. Mark Twain once said: "There are only two forces that can carry light to all corners of the globe - - the sun in the heavens and the Associated Press down here."

It started as a telegraphic relay financed by six major New York dailies. Since then, it has expanded and become a large news cooperative throughout the world.

Client newspapers share the costs of the operations and pay fees according to the size of their newspaper.

The second oldest news agency, Reuters, was established in 1851 with 40 well-trained homing pigeons. These pigeons were trained to relay stock market prices from one city to another due to a 100-mile gap in existing telegraph lines.

The founder, Paul Julius Reuters, was a German-born pioneer in British journalism. He later laid out the groundwork for the vast news agency- - using the telegraph this time.

The United Press Internationsl is the union of the United Press (founded in 1907) and the International News Service in 1958. This is often referred to as "the other guy" by the Associated Press since it started out to provide news to non-AP subscribers.

The Agence France Presse is the descendant of the old French news agency called Havas. AFP was established by the French Resistance fighters during World War II. Today, it has grown to be among the largest international news agencies in the European continent.

These four agencies maintain bureaus here in Manila along with other smaller and lesser-known news agencies. The *Asian Press and Media Directory* (1976) listed over 30 news agencies here in Manila - - either with bureaus, or correspondents or even just stringers.

Even the Hsinhua New China News Agency of the People's Republic of China and Tass News Agency of the USSR have correspondents in the Philippines.

More or less, they have a total of 250 journalists scattered all over the news agencies in Manila. Of the news agencies, UPI has the largest Manila-based staff with around 50 workers.

LOCAL NEWS AGENCY

The sound of typewriters and teleprinters immediately assails one's ears as he enters the offices of the Philippines News Agency.

Throughout the office hangs the pall of acrid cigarette smoke as editors and reporters try to keep calm in the middle of all the tension. Brown desks sag heavily with news copies and files--some of them spilling onto the floor.

The editors sit tensely editing news copies and trying to beat the minute-by-minute deadline. Around the editors are reporters pounding typewriters to finish their stories. Occasionally, an editor would bawl out a reporter and ask some pointed questions.

Today is just a normal working day for the PNA -- typical of the other 364 days of the year.

The Philippines News Agency is the official news agency of the government. It was established in March 1973 following the closure of a private cooperative news agency called Philippine News Service (PNS) when martial law was declared.

But Rony Tiangco, former PNA national news editor and one of the prime movers behind the agency, claimed that there is no connection at all between the PNA and the PNS.

"The PNA was created to serve as an efficient voice of the government and to serve as a model for responsible reporting," he said.

The agency is headed by a general manager. Below him is a managing editor who actually oversees the operations of the news agency.

Under the managing editor are the national news editor, city editor, sports editor, features editor, business editor, international news editor, regional editor, deskmen and reporters.

The PNA has some 80 regular correspondents scattered all over the country and manning the 18 PNA bureaus. Aiding them are more than 100 stringers in various towns and cities. (Generally, correspondents are paid regularly while stringers are paid per story used.)

The PNA used to maintain two correspondents abroad--one in Washington D.C. and another in New York, but they were recalled in 1986.

News materials are gathered by the stringers or correspondents. Sometimes, press releases are sent to the PNA and these are edited into newsworthy pieces.

As soon as the correspondents file their stories, these are sent to the editors for copy reading or rewriting. After the copy is edited, it is submitted to the national news editor who coordinates the movements of all national news. These are then sent to the teleprinters and finally to the PNA subscribers.

The PNA sends as many as 120 stories daily averaging about eight short paragraphs each. For the international news division, about 4,000 words or 20 stories are sent out daily.

These stories are often tightly edited. Nothing but the most essential facts are embedded in the story. This saves time and creates more space for other stories.

The Philippines News Agency supplies a wide variety of stories--from politics to sports, religion, economics, practically the whole gamut.

Essentially, it carries the same stories as other news agencies, but with a particular stress on government activities. "But come to think of it, most stories emanate from the government," a PNA editor said.

The PNA leases its communications channels from a commercial company. It also maintains close working relationships with other news agencies like Reuters and Agence-France Presse whose stories are moved by the PNA to places in the Philippines outside of Metro-Manila.

This explains for tag lines reading PNA/Reuters or PNA/AFP.

The PNA participates in a news exchange program among the four national wire agencies of ASEAN, namely: Bernama of Malaysia, Thailand News Agency, Antara of Indonesia and the Philippines News Agency.

The PNA also has an exchange arrangement with 13 members of the Organization of Pacific and Asian News Agencies (OANA), which consists of: Tass (USSR), Tanjug (Yugoslavia), Kuna (Kuwait), QNA (Quatar News Agency), PTI (Press Trust of India), Yonhap (Korea), Kyodo (Japan), IRNA (Iran), Montsame (Mongolia), APS (Angola), CNA (Cuba), Lankapuvath (Sri Lanka), and KCNA (Indonesia).

The growth of the Philippines News Agency over the last seven years has indeed been impressive. They were, however, initially saddled with various problems.

One of the earliest troubles they had was to establish credibility. Since it is a government agency--and having been created right after the declaration of martial law, people did not tend to believe the agency immediately. There was always a fear that all the news released was government propaganda.

Its main problem today is the lack of qualified people to man the agency. Editors bemoan the lack of young and qualified journalists.

"Schools are not producing qualified people for news agencies or if they are, these are not enough," an editor complained.

Others say that those who are well-qualified to work with news agencies are not working with the PNA or any other news agency.

"News agencies are just not my cup of tea," said a female journalism graduate who now works with a public relations company.

Despite these problems, the PNA has more or less become a government fixture now. "There is even the possibility of becoming only a semi-government agency in the future."

ASIAN NEWS—FEATURE AGENCY

Its beat is Asia, including the Pacific Islands. From the gates of the Imperial Palace in Peking, to the Hindu temples of Afghanistan and to the grass shacks of Fiji.

This region - - where over half the world's five billion population live - - is the coverage of Depthnews, a unique news and feature agency of the Press Foundation of Asia.

Through its stories, the agency tries to capture the pulse of the region, the agonies of its poor, the political trials of its people, the horrors of war and the roaring silence of the vast majority of simple Asians.

This might seem a tall order for a 30-man agency, but not quite really. Nine years after it was organised in September 1969 by leading Asian journalists, Depthnews has earned a name for itself as the pioneer of development journalism.

Depthnews is actually the acronym for Development Economics and Population Themes - - its major areas of coverage. In their rush to meet deadlines, these areas are often overlooked and neglected by the editors as they report the daily events in the country.

Depthnews fills this gap.

The agency maintains six bureaus manned by a dozen journalists all over Asia. Its bureaus are in Bangkok, Hongkong, Tokyo, Jakarta, Kuala Lumpur, New Delhi. The central desk is in Manila. In addition, 18 other journalists serve as Depthnews stringers.

Depthnews is actually four news and features agencies all rolled into one: Depthnews Special, Depthnews Asia, Depthnews Science Service and the various Depthnews national editions.

Depthnews Special - - the original Depthnews of September 1969 - - is a weekly packet of about eight economic and development stories from all over the region. Varying from about 800 to 1,000 words per story, it examines the development and economic trends in Asia today.

Depthnews Asia, started in August 1974, covers the more current news events in the region - - such as the changing political conditions in Asia. DNA touches heavily on political stories but what differentiates it from the ordinary news agencies or wire-services is its in-depth and analytical style.

Depthnews Science Service (DNSS), started in late 1975, aims to encourage science reporting in Asia. What was once considered a "boring beat" has been converted into an exciting field to cover. Science stories are widely defined - - ranging from viroids to wheels and even sorcery.

They are distributed together with Depthnews Special and Depthnews Asia stories.

The Depthnews national editions are written in nine languages: Pilipino, Cebuano, Ilocano, Bahasa Indonesia, Malay, Thai, Korean, Japanese and Hindi.

The stories in these packets are often only of national significance, although they include DNS stories, too.

Depthnews realizes that for development to be meaningful, it must filter down and must be understood by the Asian masses who are more at home with their language than with English.

Through these four services in the Depthnews family, the agency has over 200 clients. They include the *Asian Wall Street Journal, Hongkong Standard, Asian Finance, Rising Times of Nepal* and even such small community newspapers as the *Baguio Midland Courier.*

These newspapers have a combined readership of over 10 million Asians.

Unlike conventional news agencies, Depthnews depends more on stories mailed by its correspondents than the wires. However, it has standing arrangements with Reuters for the use of its facilities to telex stories from Asian capitals to Manila, especially Depthnews Asia stories.

As soon as the stories are received by the central desk, they are edited and then mimeographed. Every week, Depthnews mails out DNS packets and everyday, it mails DNA stories to special client newspapers.

Depthnews sends out an average of 16 stories a week or about 1,000 stories annually — excluding the special stories clients ask it to write.

JOBS FOR JOURNALISTS

And so, you want to work for a news agency?

Many news agency editors complain that they cannot seem to find the right kind of people to man their agencies. Some prefer journalism graduates, plain college graduates or even non-graduates just as long as they can deliver the goods.

There is, however, a growing preference for journalism graduates - - or even English or Pilipino majors. Gone are the days when editors look askance at journalism graduates, grab them by their heads and urge them to un-learn all the things they have been taught in college -- so that they will learn to be good journalists.

However, there are a few exceptional college drop-outs who made it as top journalists in the country today. Some are manning the editorial desks, public information offices - - and even teaching college students how to be good journalists.

But we digress. It is essential for journalists today to have some form of liberal arts education to prepare them for the first jobs that usually come to new journalism graduates: reporters. They must have a broad background because reporters are often asked to cover any story - - be it a science story, a political story, an economic story and even a story on Philippine education.

While it is true that news agency reporters - - like other reporters - - are assigned to specific beats, they are often asked to cover general assignments or to take over the beats of other reporters who might be absent. Thus the need for a broad educational background.

It is perhaps only after being exposed to several beats that one decides to specialize in certain types of reporting. Later in one's career, a journalist might want to be a business reporter, a science reporter, a labor reporter or an education reporter.

So journalists working in news agencies should have a broad educational background.

But more important is the skill or the ability of the journalist to write. What good is one's educational background if he cannot weave a suitable story out of the maze of facts?

News agency reporters often start at the bottom rung with an average salary of P1,500.

But then, there are other fringe benefits reporters get. There are luncheon press conferences where excellent meals are served free.

There are certain government officials who would like to publicise new projects and record harvests. Often, they bring along reporters during their trips - - all expenses paid for, of course.

As one spends more years in the reportorial business, one's salary is increased to as much as P4,000 per month.

Filipino news agency editors usually start from P4,000 to P6,000 per month, depending on one's experience. Some get as high as P8,000 a month.

While news editors get a higher pay than reporters, they are not as mobile as the reporters. But their job is as difficult — even more difficult at times. They must keep a sharp lookout for possible news breaks which reporters (or even they themselves) should follow-up.

Filipino journalists working for foreign news agencies often complain- - and rightly so - - of discrimination in pay scales. Foreigners are often more highly paid than Filipino journalists. In addition, a lot of them get additional allowances like house allowance and cars.

The salary gaps between foreigners and Filipinos should be narrowed. The easiest way to do this of course is to increase the salaries of Filipino journalists.

But no matter. Money as we said, is often secondary in journalism. One goes into the profession with a sense of adventure, not knowing what to find at the end of the tunnel. Young journalists often take comfort in the romantic thought of starving journalists eking out an existence by writing.

But who cares, working for a news agency is an exciting challenge.

Chapter **XXV**

Communication Research: A Status Analysis

Gloria D. Feliciano and Cesar M. Mercado

EARLY BEGINNINGS

The Western-based concept of communication research as a cross-disciplinary area of inquiry was introduced in the country at the turn of the sixties. Professors at the University of the Philippines who had advanced training in journalism in the United States pioneered in the 1960s in conducting studies on the elements of the communication process, i.e., media, messages and media effects on the receivers of messages.[1]

Earlier, John de Young, a visiting sociologist at U.P., studied literacy levels and availability and use of rural communications media, including the village interpersonal network. An information specialist, Marjorie Ravenholt, assessed how much could be understood of the informational materials disseminated in the villages by the National Media Production Center.[2] At the urban level, a practising journalist, Juan Tuvera, did a status analysis of mass communications in public information offices. His study brought to light such problems as: no coordinated planning, proliferation of public information agencies and the lack of professionalism among government information officers. Much earlier, journalists and historians had written about newspapers and other periodicals, and their history, and market analysts had drawn up economic profiles of consumers.[3]

THE SIXTIES

The sixties marked the beginnings of communication research by professionally trained communication researchers. They were highly productive years.

Types of Studies Done

The academic setting provided the rationale for researchers to initially focus on the essential elements of the communication process, namely, sources/producers of messages, the messages themselves, the media/channels and audiences/receivers of messages. Thus, the initial studies during the early 60s could be grouped under the following types:

- studies of communicators/sources of information,
- message studies,
- media studies, and
- studies on audience/receivers of messages.

Initial efforts focused on message studies. They sought to determine the comprehensibility of informational materials by farmers, scientists and scholars, teachers, the academic staff and newspaper readers. Towards the mid-60s researchers' attention shifted from the presentation/style of materials to their content. Thus, various types of specialized reports in the print media were subjected to scrutiny vis-a-vis the subject matter they carried--crime, natural disasters, foreign events, politics and government, racism, movie advertisements and others.[4]

As more money for field work was available, the communication researchers focused their attention on the audiences/recipients of messages. The first audience studies were multi-disciplinary, with communication as one of the components. These were done at the barrio level and dealt with the individual farmer's communication behavior (including readership, listenership and viewership profiles) and the dissemination and use of new information on farm technology. The audience studies had built-in questions which enabled the researchers to establish profiles of communicators or sources of information.[5]

One significant aspect of these studies was its documenting the barrio interpersonal network. This network is a mix of key persons such as the farmer and his wife, the opinion leaders, neighbors, relatives and friends, the extension workers, formal and informal groups composed of farmers or homemakers in the village, the youth and folk media, e.g., songs, dances, verbal jousts and others.[6]

The professionals, as receivers of information, e.g. agriculturists (not extension workers), and college teachers/faculty were also studied. Their feedback, particularly their perceptions, and opinions or both, on a range of topics, including curricular matters and extension work, was solicited. These data were needed for planning development programs that were attuned to their problems and needs.

As communication students gained expertise and skills in research methods, their interests turned toward the study of the sources/producers of messages at the urban level -- writers, editors, broadcasters, movie producers, public relations men, book publishers, and others. Data discussed from these studies, e.g. socio-economic characteristics and communication behavior, became the basis for planning short-term and long-term development programs.

Early research on the communication channels or media was limited to historical studies and investigations which dealt with their organization, structure and control. This was due to the paucity of written records on the media, the lack of trained researchers who could do historical studies on media and the cumbersome nature of the historical research method itself.[7]

Methods and Techniques Used

As a subject-field, communication research is a cross-disciplinary area of inquiry. Print and broadcast journalists, humanists and behaviorists contributed to the growth and development of communication as an academic discipline. As a process, it is concerned with the gathering, analyzing, reporting, and using of data which can lead to a better understanding and solution of communication and communication-related problems.

By design, or method used, or both, studies can be classified into the following: historical studies, case studies, surveys, experiments, content analyses, readability studies and feasibility studies. Historical studies are useful in understanding the origin, growth and development of the communications media in the Philippines. Media studies done in the '60s which utilized the historical method are of three types. One is the purely descriptive study which documents events in chronological order, showing the growth and development of a particular medium such as a newspaper, a radio-television network, a farm magazine, cinema or a folk drama.[8] Statistics used in these studies reinforce text, relating to say, circulation and distribution. They enhance the reports' credibility, all too often, an unintended consequence.

The case study approach is valuable in analyzing a particular communication behavior such as radio listening or television viewing or the diffusion of information from its initial source to its final destination/target. Case studies on the diffusion of agricultural information in four Laguna villages around the mid-60s gave more insights on the factors which either hasten or slow down the acceptance and use of farming innovations.[9] The case study is also useful for generating benchmark data at a small scale before doing a large-scale survey. It is in fact, a useful supplement to surveys.

The survey is admittedly one of the most useful designs in exploring the causes of some phenomena affecting the communication process. It is also useful in determining levels of knowledge, and skills, attitudes and habits of audiences relating to communications media and messages.[10] Researchers in the '60s widely used surveys to get basic information on communicators and audiences. The training programs seemed to favor the survey because it is convenient and manageable, and the trained persons were available to conduct it.

The experiment enables researchers to study the effectiveness of communication activities, among them, the use of radio, or printed material to support classroom lectures, or to compare these media's effectiveness. This is made possible by establishing a relationship between a cause (like radio) and a speculated effect (higher pupils' test scores). The first experiments dealt with ascertaining how effective were black and white illustrations compared with colored ones, and reports written in either technical or semi-technical language compared with those in popular language.[11]

The phrase "old wine in a new bottle" could well apply to content analysis. The method is not new. When people read a publication and interpret it, they, in effect, are doing content analysis. What researchers have done is to widen application and to increase validity and reliability of content analysis.

Researchers developed the readability test in order to make readers, among others, readily understand written work. The test is based on a list of commonly used and understood terms and the use of one or more sources of reading difficulty such as long words, long sentences, modifiers and others. Conventional methods include recall-type tests such as "fill the blanks" or "multiple choice" used in communication arts subjects in the elementary grades.[12]

The feasibility study is sometimes referred to in technical jargon as pre-investment study. It is useful in projecting how viable it will be to set up communications institutions for carrying out new action programs or project or any of their components. This kind of study takes into account how much will be the cost compared with the benefits. An example of this study is setting up a radio station in a community where print media do not exist.[13]

Subject-areas of Inquiry

As may be gleaned from what have been cited, studies done in the '60s focused on the following problems:
- Communication messages can hardly be understood,
- Virtually no benchmark information exists to enable researchers to conduct more complex studies than can be used for policy and planning, especially, to provide guidelines for improving the media industry,
- The physical reach of messages,
- Lack of informational and educational materials for classes,
- Lack of information on the development orientation of media, and
- Limits to press freedom.

Utilization of Research Findings

Communication research in the '60s was problem-oriented in response to:

- Development priorities and needs of an individual or the community,
- Institution-building requirements, such as developing curricula, teaching materials, training programs, etc.,
- Professionalizing the media, particularly print, and
- Solving communication problems, like lessening attrition rate of faculty and staff and whether to abolish the thesis requirement.

The studies, except for university-initiated research, were mostly applied in nature and problem-oriented. Their focus appeared to be on the modern mass media, to the neglect of the more traditional, more interpersonal folk forms in the rural areas. There appeared to have been little room for innovativeness because most of the studies were done in-house rather than in the field. Immediate and direct utilization of research findings, especially those dealing with the press, was assured through the Philippine Press Institute and the then Philippine Press Council.[14]

THE SEVENTIES

Beginning in the 70s, particularly after martial law was declared, studies were focused in these areas:

- Communication support to development programs and projects,
- Cooperative, multi-national studies,
- Policy research for institutional development and support, and
- Multi-sectoral and multi-disciplinary studies.

Communication Support to Development

The accelerated communication effort to support development programs and projects increasingly required large outlays of human, financial and material resources and facilities. Consequently, some administrators of these programs and projects saw the need to study these communication efforts in order to understand better the role they play in carrying out program objectives. They also wanted to know what were their programs' strong and weak points measured in terms of their functions. Lastly, they wanted to assess the impact of their program, in part (the communication aspect) or as a whole. Hence, the developmental-type studies emerged. They dealt with the communication aspects of agrarian reform, population planning, nutrition, drug abuse prevention, civic-action information campaigns, out-of-school programs and projects, use of communications technology for mass education and others.[15]

Population planning was given the most attention by researchers partly because funds were available for it. Studies made much use of analysis and synthesis of existing data, the case approach, the experimental method and the survey. These were mostly evaluative, benchmark and action research. The evaluative studies dealt with how the four elements of the communication process relate to communication problems in the field. Benchmark studies were done on the folk media and on their use to achieve development objectives. The action-research or operations studies were primarily designed to serve decision-makers.[16] A few studies dealt with research methodology and focused on determining how valid and reliable were some research instruments.[17]

Cooperative, Multi-national Studies

The need to pool and conserve scarce resources and facilities in developing, producing and disseminating information and education materials, have led international funding agencies to sponsor multi-national research. Such research minimized the problem of comparing and making compatible communication models and approaches and of making them relevant and applicable to more countries. This type of research has been done and is still being done between countries, regions and continents. For instance, the Philippines has either participated or is participating in the following studies: husband-wife communication in selected Asian countries;[18] studies of media habits, the perception patterns, and the information needs of media audiences across Asia;[19] communication strategies in rural development;[20] the community press in Asia;[21] the flow of TV news in selected Asian countries;[22] and multi-media support to population programs for rural development.[23]

Policy Research and Multi-disciplinary Studies

The increasing government recognition of the importance of research findings as basis for policy, or action, or both, has provided a rationale for policy-oriented studies in communication. Some examples of policy studies in communication are: content analyses of the people's feedback in referendum remark sheets, media monitoring and analyses of media, viz., management of media resources, regulation of media, assessment of public information problems and needs at the office and field levels, and methodological studies. Their results were used for formulating policy and for planning programs and projects for institutional development. For instance, the results of methodological studies have been integrated into the communication research courses, the feedback analyses findings have provided the basis of guidelines for improving the conduct of referenda, and so forth.[24]

Whether to undertake multi-disciplinary and multi-sectoral studies in communication is dictated by such considerations as the economy, the complex nature of development problems and the need to make findings acceptable to larger segments of society. Completed and on-going studies in this area deal with socio-cultural factors affecting urbanization and the use of advanced communications technology in formal and non-formal education.[25]

TRENDS AND DEVELOPMENTS

A second look at the communication studies done in the '60s and '70s point to several trends in these aspects: scope, respondents/subjects, manpower resource, analysis, reporting and others.

Scope

In coverage, communication studies in the Philippines are shifting back to where they started. The early studies were nationwide in scope. However, the succeeding ones became narrower, covering at most a few provinces or villages. The reversion to nationwide studies is due to more research for communication development. In 1974, the University of the Philippines Institute of Mass Communication, in cooperation with the Philippine Council for Agricultural and Resources Research, the Department of Agrarian Reform-Education Services and the University of the Philippines at Los Baños' Agrarian Reform Education Service conducted a nation-wide study on the communication aspect of agrarian reform.[26] A year later, the UP-IMC, in cooperation with the Commission on Population and the United Nations Fund for Population Activities conducted a survey of communication "infrastructures" in the 13 regions of the country.[27] The results were used in planning the Information, Education and Communication (IEC) strategy of the POPCOM. Supported by the same agencies, UP-IMC also studied five mobile or "traveling" experiments in strategic areas in the country.[28]

Respondents/Subjects

Since the Philippines is largely rural, majority of the research are expected to have rural respondents. The nationwide studies mentioned earlier had such respondents. In general, university research is an exception. In the schools, many communication studies have students as respondents. Students are the most available subjects.

Manpower Resource

The main sources of research manpower are the schools offering communication degrees. Heading the list of research institutions are the UP-IMC in Diliman and the Department of Development Communication of UP at Los Baños. Most communication studies available today come from them. The next three schools which are doing research are the Department of

Communication, Ateneo de Manila University, the School of Communication at Silliman University, and the Faculty of Arts and Letters at the University of Santo Tomas. Other schools, which have the manpower to conduct communication research are the Lyceum of the Philippines School of Journalism, Maryknoll College Department of Communication Arts, Centro Escolar University, Philippine Women's University, St. Paul's College, San Beda College, Pamantasan ng Maynila and Far Eastern University.[29]

Government information agencies such as the defunct Department of Public Information and the National Media Production Center have, in the '70s, increased their research capability. Other development-oriented agencies likewise have begun doing communication studies to support their programs and projects.[30]

One of the private agencies which has contributed much to audience research in the Philippines is the Philippine Mass Communication Research Society (PMCRS), a Metro Manila based research outfit. Some advertising agencies have also established core research staff for their media work.

Method of Analysis

The percentage and some measures of central tendency and the chi-square are the statistical methods of analysis commonly used in communication studies in the Philippines. Because they are sufficient to meet the objectives of these studies, they are widely used by researchers. The analysis of variance (ANOVA) is the most widely used statistical tool in experiments. It is useful in determining the comparative effectiveness of the various media and media approaches.

Reporting

A hindrance to using research is the late reporting of results. The usual practice is to complete the entire study before reporting to planners, implementors and the general public. Reporting piece-meal the finished portions appears to have solved the problem. Newspapers have also shown increasing interest in reporting research results.

One noteworthy development in reporting communication studies is the printing of a monograph on "Communication and Adoption in Rural Development."[31] This monograph is a project of the U.P. Community Development Research Council, the UP-IMC, and the Department of Agriculture. It analyzes all communication studies in the Philippines from 1955 to 1972 and is written in very simple language. Seven thousand copies of this monograph were distributed to provincial agriculturists and extension workers. It has gone through a reprinting.

OTHER DEVELOPMENTS

In the past, communication research in the Philippines tended to follow the trend in the more advanced countries. However, from their experience in studying development projects, they soon recognized the limitations of Western research methods when used in developing countries like the Philippines.[32] Thus, a growing divergence is now evident between communication research in the Philippines and the more advanced countries.

One point of divergence lies in the research orientation, in general. In the more developed countries, communication research is becoming more theory-oriented. In the Philippines, as in other developing countries, communication studies have tended to be more problem-oriented. This is understandable. In the more developed countries, many communication theories, most of them at the micro level, need to be tested. In the developing countries, many communication problems related to development projects are at the macro level, which Western theories cannot adequately explain. It appears that the proper approach to communication research in the country is to build models based on field situations, then test them in the field to refine them and make them more valid.

Another point of divergence is on the research design. While research in the developed countries is inclined towards the laboratory experiment, the trend in the Philippines is towards action-research or operations studies. It appears that research in the developed countries will become more quantitative, whereas studies in the Philippines are bound to strike a happy balance between the quantitative and qualitative approaches. It would seem that in development the communication process is as important as the effect. Communication research in the country recognizes the importance of this philosophy.

SOME PROBLEMS AND PROSPECTS

The problems in communication research today can be categorized into three:

- lack of support from administration or management,
- inadequate resources and facilities, and as has been pointed out,
- imbalance, which favors action research.

These problems are interrelated, interdependent and overlapping.

The administration's or management's lack of support is due, in part, to their lack of knowledge about the nature and value of communication research to development policy, planning and implementation of programs and projects. This results partly in the second problem cited, i.e. inadequate resources and facilities -- physical, material, financial -- to do communication research. Exceptions are when communication researchers themselves become fund-raisers for their own research projects or when new policy is contemplated for which no adequate rationale exists.

The emphasis on action-research or operations studies, to the neglect of basic research (studies that will contribute to theory or model-building, development of research methods, techniques and tools and of indicators or measures of media development), is also partly due to the first two problems. Basic research is expensive in terms of time, funds and effort. Moreover, the results do not lend themselves directly and immediately to creating an "impact" that would impress administration or management.

But there is room for optimism: more students now are becoming genuinely interested in pursuing a formal course in communication research.[33] More researchers are being promoted to administrators or managers. There are now more opportunities for communication research-trained graduates to fill in research positions or positions in development planning. There are also more funding agencies open to including a communication component in a social or behavioral research project. The prospects are many and bright and the challenge is great. It is up to the communication researchers to take advantage of the prospects and respond to the challenge.

Notes

[1] Gloria D. Feliciano and Crispulo J. Icban, "Communication Research," in *Philippine Mass Media in Perspective,* Gloria D. Feliciano and Crispulo J. Icban (eds.), 1987 pp. 249-282.

[2] The agency referred to is the National Media Production Center. The overall objective of the National Media Production Center is to "facilitate national development through the production of development information communication. It also aims to contribute to the growth of communication research in the country." From *Public Information: Issues and Facts.* Studies submitted by the Institute of Mass Communication Working Group to the *Ad Hoc* Presidential Committee on Information Policies. Page 68.

[3] Gloria D. Feliciano, "An overview of Communication Research in Asia: Status, Problems and Needs," in No. 6, Papers of the East-West Communication Institute, 1973, pp. 1-20.

[4] Emilinda V. de Jesus, "Mass Communication in the Philippines," in *Asian Mass Communication Bibliography No. 4,* 1976, pp. 1-280, Singapore.

[5] Gloria D. Feliciano, "The Farm and Home Development Project: An Evaluation," in the Study Series Number Thirty of the Community Development Research Council, 1968 pp. 1-364.

[6] Alicia M. L. Coseteng and Gemma A. Nemenzo, "Folk Media in the Philippines," Monographs of the UP/IMC/POPCOM/UNFPA Population Communication Project, 1975

[7] Gloria D. Feliciano, "An Overview of Communication Research in Asia: Status, Problems and Needs," in No. 6 Papers of the East-West Communication Institute, 1973, pp. 1-20.

[8] _____, Ankanahalli Shanmugam and Kazuhiko Goto, *Manual of Research for Developing Countries,* U.P. Institute of Mass Communication, Diliman, Quezon City, 1969.

[9] _____, "Diffusion of Agricultural Information in Four Laguna Barrios: Some Emerging Patterns," Paper presented at the IRRI Seminar, June 10, 1965 (mimeographed).

[10] _____, "A Manual of Research in Family Planning Communication," a project of the Division of Development and Application of Communication, UNESCO, Paris.

[11] Cesar M. Mercado, Gloria D. Feliciano and Thomas G. Flores, "The Relative Effectiveness of Four Types of Extension Publications," in the *Philippine Agriculturist,* Vol. XLIV, No. 10, March 1966, pp. 833-843.

Ely D. Gomez, *Relative Effectiveness of Four Types of Informational Materials to PACD Adult Classes in Some Laguna Barrios.* UP College of Agriculture, November 1984 (Unpublished Master's Thesis).

[12] Modern Readability tests corresponding to these conventional methods include the "Cloze Procedure."

[13] These types of studies were neglected due to the lack of qualified researchers in what has been described as a new field -- media economics. There appears to be a need between communication specialists and economists -to collaborate in this type of studies.

[14] The Philippine Press Institute at that time ran a monthly newsletter, *Press Forum* which was the venue of communication research reports written in popularized form.

[15] EDPITAF, *A Handbook on Broadcasting in the Philippines,* PIS-CTE, 1976, pp. 150-151.

Cesar M. Mercado et. al., "Communication Study on Agrarian Reform," in UP/IMC/PCARR/DAR-ARES/UPLB-ARI, September 10, 1976.

Project Documents, UP-IMC/POPCOM/UNFPA Family Planning Communication Program, Institute of Mass Communication, University of the Philippines, 1972-1976.

Reynaldo V. Guioguio, et. al., *A Study of the Communication Factors Related to Drug Abuse Prevention Education in Selected Communities in the Philippines.* UP-IMC, September 1977.

[16] Alice M. L. Coseteng and Gemma A. Nemenzo, *Folk Media in the Philippines,* Monograph, Institute of Mass Communication, University of the Philippines, Quezon City, 1977.
  Cesar M. Mercado, et. al., Program Support Operations Research, UP-IMC/POPCOM/UNFPA, Institute of Mass Communication, University of the Philippines, 1977.

[17] Herminia M. Alfonso, et. al., *AKAP Instruments in Family Planning: A Compilation* (September 1975).
  _____, *Comparative Study of KAP Instruments in Family Planning, 1975.*

[18] Benjamin V. Lozare, et. al., *A Comparative Study on Communication and Related Factors Affecting Husband-Wife Communication and the Practice of Family Planning in Japan, India, the Philippines and Singapore* (1973).

[19] Reynaldo V. Guioguio, *A Study on the Mass Media Habits of Urban Residents in Metropolitan Manila,* a masteral thesis co-sponsored by the UP Institute of Mass Communication Information and Research Center, 1975.

[20] Cesar M. Mercado, *Communication in Agricultural Extension,* July, 1975.
  _____, *Field Strategies for Introducing Change,* August 1975.
  _____, *Development Communication,* October 1975.

[21] Asian Rural Press Project sponsored by the Asian Mass Communication Research and Information Centre, Singapore and jointly undertaken with the Institute of Mass Communication, University of the Philippines (on-going research).

[22] Gloria D. Feliciano, et. al., *The Flow of TV News in Selected Asian Countries* (on-going research).

[23] UP-IMC/POPCOM/UNFPA Population Communication Project, Institute of Mass Communication, University of the Philippines (Quezon City, 1977.

[24] UP-COMELEC Analysis of the February 1975 Referendum Remark Sheets (1975).
  UP-COMELEC Analysis of the October 1976 Referendum Remark Sheets (1976-1977).

[25] Gloria D. Feliciano, et. al., *Possibilities on the Use of Satellites for Education and Communication* (Background paper prepared for the workshop on Communications Technology for Education in the Philippines, El Grande Hotel, Paranaque, July 20-26, 1975).

[26] Cesar M. Mercado, *Communication in Agricultural Extension,* 1975.

[27] UP-IMC/POPCOM/UNFPA Population Communication Project, Institute of Mass Communication, University of the Philippines (Quezon City, 1977).

[28] Cesar M. Mercado, et. al., *Traveling Experiments in Population Communication,* UP-IMC/POPCOM/UNFPA Population Communication Project, Monograph Series No. 10 (Quezon City, 1977).

[29] Cesar M. Mercado, "The Status and Needs of Communication Research in the Philippines," Benchmark Information PCAR First National Agriculture System Research Congress, UP at Los Baños Campus, Los Baños, Laguna, February 12-17, 1973.

[30] These agencies include the Communication Foundation for Asia and the Population Center Foundation.

[31] Cesar M. Mercado, *Communication and Adoption in Rural Development,* UP-CDRC/UP-IMC/DA, 1976.

[32] Gloria D. Feliciano, "The Limits of Western Research Methods," Institute of Mass Communication, University of the Philippines, Quezon City, 1965.

[33] This is based on the experience of the Institute of Mass Communication, University of the Philippines at Quezon City which instituted a communication research curriculum in its undergraduate program in 1975.

Chapter **XXVI**

Communication Education: An Overview

Crispin C. Maslog

I f there is one word perhaps that can best describe Philippine communication education in the past decade and a half, it is growth.

When we made our first survey of communication schools in 1970-71, we were able to identify only 13 institutions offering degree programs in journalism or communication. Today, 16 years later, there are at least 42, a better than three-fold increase (See Appendix A).[1]

One interesting feature of this growth is the emergence of communication school chains, as in newspaper chains. The first group one notices from Appendix A is the Ateneo chain -- Ateneo de Davao, Ateneo de Naga, Ateneo de Manila, Ateneo de Zamboanga and Xavier University in Cagayan de Oro. Then there is the St. Paul's group -- St. Paul's Iloilo, St. Paul's Manila and St. Paul's Quezon City, all offering communication degrees. The biggest chain, of all, however, is the U.P. group -- U.P. Diliman IMC, UP Los Baños DevCom, UP Los Baños ComArts, UP Baguio, UP Cebu, UP Tacloban and UP Visayas in Iloilo. Seven units in all offering communication at U.P.

Another interesting thing about this growth, in numbers, is that it is towards the provinces, away from the Metro Manila area. In 1970-71, there were only two institutions in the province offering degree programs in journalism and communication -- the School of Journalism and Communication at Silliman and the Department of Agricultural Communication at the College of Agriculture in Los Baños. Today, a decade and half later, there are 23 -- 12 in the Visayas, 7 in Luzon and 4 in Mindanao. The majority of communication schools now, therefore, are in the provinces (Table 1).

Table 1. Geographical Distribution of Communication Schools.

Distribution	No. of Schools[2]	Percent
Metro Manila	19	45.24
Luzon	7	16.67
Visayas	12	28.57
Mindanao	4	9.52
TOTAL	42	100.00

HISTORICAL BACKGROUND

Of the communication departments or programs, two date back to the 1950s or earlier--Far Eastern University's Department of Communication, which was started in 1956, and the University of Santo Tomas' Bachelor of Literature in Journalism program, which started in 1936. The majority of them were established in the two decades between 1960 and 1980. This was the period of greatest growth. If we look at the 1980s, however, we see that six communication programs or departments have already been started and we are still in the mid-80s. It seems that the period of growth is still continuing (Table 2).

Table 2. Year Communication Schools/Programs Started.

Year	No. of Schools	Percent
1959 and before	2	4.76
1960-1969	12	28.57
1970-1979	13	30.95
1980 and later	6	14.29
No data available	9	21.43
TOTAL	42	100.00

The University of Santo Tomas can lay claim to having the oldest continuing communication program if we trace the origins of its present communication offerings to its earlier journalism program. In 1936 the University of Santo Tomas established a journalism major within the Faculty of Philosophy and Letters, offering the degree of Bachelor of Literature in Journalism (Litt.B.).

The Faculty of Philosophy and Letters itself was established by U.S.T. in 1898. In 1964, however, it was merged, amidst much protestations from students and alumni, with the College of Liberal Arts under the new Faculty of Arts and Letters, which now offers the degrees A.B. in Journalism and A.B. in Communication Arts.

It might be mentioned in passing that some of the brightest names in Philippine journalism and letters today have come from U.S.T.--Francisco Tatad, Vic Maliwanag, Jaime M. Flores, Rolando Tinio, Jesus Peralta, Ofelia Alcantara, Bienvenido Lumbera, Wilfredo Nolledo, Juan Gatbonton, Julie Yap Daza, Olaf Giron, Eric Giron and Ben Rodriguez, among the post-war graduates we know.

While U.S.T. has the oldest continuing journalism program, it was the University of the Philippines that set up the first journalism courses in the country in 1919, when Dean Conrado Benitez asked an American, Walter Wilgus, to come and develop a journalism curriculum in the university. The journalism course did not last long, however, because the U.P. President displeased a legislator who eliminated the U.P. budget for journalism.

Some of the other earlier attempts at journalism courses were made by Philippine Christian College, Philippine Women's University and De La Salle College. These programs came and went--and some came back again. Journalism education was revived at the University of the Philippines under the English department which offered a bachelor of philosophy or bachelor of arts degree for journalism majors. In 1965, U.P. established the Institute of Mass Communication, which now offers the A.B., M.A. and Ph.D. degrees in communication.

Lyceum-University established a School of Journalism in 1952, offering two degrees--an A.B. and a B.S. in journalism. Later this was phased out and a Mass Communication Department was established under the College of Arts and Sciences in 1984.

The beginning of the UP Los Baños development communication program date back to 1954, when the Office of Extension and Publications was established under the College of Agriculture. It was not until 1962, however, that the major in agricultural information was started, under the Department of Agricultural Information. In 1974, it was renamed Department of Development Communication, to become the first school to offer a bachelor's degree in development communication.

GENERAL PROFILE

Of the 42 schools, 36 are offering undergraduate degree programs only, 2 graduate programs only and 4 are offering both undergraduate and graduate programs. The Asian Institute of Journalism in Manila and Central Luzon State University in Muñoz, Nueva Ecija offer graduate degrees only, at the master's level (Table 3).

Pamantasan ng Lungsod ng Maynila, Philippine Women's University, U.P. Diliman and U.P. Los Baños offer both undergraduate and graduate programs. U.P. Diliman and U.P. Los Baños offer Ph.D. programs in communication, the first and so far the only such programs, in Asia. Of the two Ph.D. programs, the one at U.P. Los Baños came earlier, in 1977. U.P. Diliman started its Ph.D. program in 1982.

Table 3. Levels of Communication Program Offerings.

Level	No. of Schools	Percent
Undergraduate only	36	85.71
Graduate only[3]	2	4.76
Undergraduate and graduate programs[4]	4	9.53
Total	42	100.00

Of the 40 undergraduate schools, 30 offer a Bachelor of Arts degree in communication, by far the great majority. Five offer a Bachelor of Science degree, while four offer various versions of the Bachelor of Communication degree. These are the Bachelor in Broadcast Communication, Bachelor in Business Journalism, Bachelor of Mass Communication and Bachelor in Communication Arts (Table 4).

Table 4. Undergraduate Degrees Offered

Degree Offered	No. of Schools	Percent
Bachelor's degrees	4	10.00
Bachelor of Arts	30	75.00
Bachelor of Science	5	12.00
No. data available	1	2.50
Total	40[5]	100.00

The five schools offering the Bachelor of Science degree are U.P. Los Baños, Visayas State College of Agriculture, University of Southern Mindanao, U.P. College Tacloban and Xavier University. They are all offering B.S. in Development Communication, which indicates their science orientation compared to the other communication programs.

One way of looking at the various undergraduate programs is to classify them into generalist or specialist. A communications program is defined as generalist if it has no major or if the major field covers a broad area of communication like mass communication, communication arts or development communication. The generalist programs require their students to take all the courses in the curriculum, in effect making them jacks of all trades. The majority of the programs, 24 (or 60 percent) are generalist oriented, while 15 (37 percent) are specialist (Table 5). A communication program is specialist if the major field covers a more specific area of communication (e.g. community broadcasting, development journalism, radio and TV broadcasting, speech communication, theater arts, writing, etc.).

Table 5. Nature of Undergraduate Communication Programs in Schools.

Nature	No. of Schools/ Depts./Programs	Percent
Generalist	24	60.00
Specialist	15	37.50
No data available	1	2.50
Total	40	100.00

In the 42 schools there are 21 different majors being offered, from advertising to theater arts. The most common major is mass communication, which probably is a misnomer, because the field is so broad that one becomes a generalist in this field. Twenty of the 42 schools, however, refer to this as their major offering. The next most popular major is radio broadcasting (9), followed by journalism (6), development communication/journalism (6), and communication arts (5), which again is a broad field. The broadcasting major comes under various nomenclatures, i.e., broadcast (1), broadcast communication (3), community broadcasting (4) and rural broadcasting (1). One interesting development is the growing popularity of development communication (4) and development journalism (2) as a major (Table 6).

Another sign of growth in Philippine communication education is the bourgeoning enrolment. In the 26 undergraduate schools included from which data was available, the enrolment totalled 5,037 in 1984-85. If we estimate the enrolment of the remaining 14 schools not included in the survey at 50 per school, we would have a total of 700 more students.

The biggest enrolment was in Far Eastern University, with 1,460 students in its mass communication and speech and drama programs. The second biggest enrolment was in U.P. Institute of Mass Communication, 476. This did not include its graduate students. If we put together the two departments at U.P. Los Baños (185 for Development Communication and 115 for Communication Arts), U.P. Los Baños would rank third in enrolment at 300 students.

Table 6. Undergraduate Major Fields Offered in Communication Schools.

Major Field	No. of Schools Offering	Percent
Advertising and Public Relations	1	1.61
Broadcast/Broadcasting (Broadcast Communication, Community Broadcasting, Rural Broadcasting)	9	14.52
Communication	2	3.23
Communication Arts	5	8.06
Communication Research	1	1.61
Development Communication/Journalism	6	9.68
Educational Communication	2	3.23
Film and Audio-visual Communication	1	1.61
Journalism	6	9.68
Mass Communications	20	32.26
Mass Com-Journalism	1	1.61
Radio and TV Broadcasting	1	1.61
Speech Communication	2	3.23
Speech and Drama	1	1.61
Theater Arts	2	3.23
Writing	1	1.61
No data available	1	1.61
TOTAL	62[6]	100.00

One interesting fact about these enrolment figures is that 76 percent of the students were female. This is most likely because the field has expanded from journalism and radio to communication in its broadest sense. Today one finds graduates of communication schools not only in newspaper offices and radio stations, as in the past, but also in advertising agencies, government information offices, communication research and planning offices, and agricultural extension agencies, among many others.

To teach these 5,000 or so communication students, there were 330 members of the faculty in these 28 schools (both graduate and undergraduate) from which data was available. U.P. IMC at Diliman had the biggest complement of full time teachers at 52, followed by U.P. Los Baños with 43 (if we combine Development Communication's 27 and Communication Arts'

16). U.P. Visayas had the third largest group of 30 teachers, but this perhaps is deceiving because this was the faculty of the Division of Humanities under which the communications program operates. U.P. Tacloban had the smallest faculty at 3.

U.P. Tacloban, incidentally, also had the least number of students, 13. Outside of U.P. Tacloban, one notes that it is the state universities that can afford more full time faculty.

Out of the 330 faculty members, 169 were part time while 161 were full time. Again, one notes that the state universities are the ones with more full time faculty, while the private institutions make do with part time faculty.

In terms of full time faculty only, UPLB's Development Communication had the most number of Ph.D.'s (8) followed by U.P. IMC (6). AIJ had a big staff of Ph.D.'s (9), but they are all part time, except one, the executive dean herself.

IMPRESSIONS AND QUESTIONS

1. There has been a tremendous increase in the number of schools offering communication training programs in the past decade and a half. The question is whether unrestrained growth is necessarily desirable. Are we getting too fat, and do we need the slimming down exercise? Are there enough jobs for our 5,000 or so students when they graduate in the next four years?

If we are growing, are we growing in the right direction? Or, to put it another way, are we growing in the right places? To put it still another way, are we too crowded with communication schools in Manila, and is there still room for expansion in the provinces, in view of the need of communicators for rural development? Is there a need for us to develop our own areas of strength, so that our programs complement each other rather than compete?

2. In the private schools there are more part time than full time teachers. Does this fact affect the quality of the teaching and eventually the quality of the students we graduate? What can we do about this problem?

3. With the exception of a few of the state universities, there are few Ph.D. or even M.S. level faculty for communication in these schools. Is there a need for graduate level training in communication for would-be teachers?

4. Philippine communication schools/programs offer a great variety of majors. The 42 included in this survey offer about 21 majors ranging from advertising to writing. Are these the majors we should be offering, and are they relevant to the needs of our people and our country?

5. The majority of our communication schools offer programs with generalist rather than specialist orientations. Is this, indeed, the right thing to do--prepare our students for a wide variety of situations in the outside world, rather than equip them with specific skills?

6. The majority of our communication curricula are arts-oriented rather than science-oriented. This is because journalism and mass communication grew out of English departments. With the growing importance of science and technology in today's world, however, is there a need to reexamine this situation and change the emphasis?

7. In relation to mass communication, the question has been asked with more frequency and sense of urgency in recent years: for whom is mass communication? A national study in India a couple of years ago substantiated the claim that the mass media in that country benefit the rich and the powerful rather than the masses. Should it be any different in the Philippines? If not, are we then training communicators who will only contribute to widening the gap between the rich and the poor? Communication and communication education for what? For whom?

These are questions that are difficult to answer and there are no ready answers for them. But by asking the questions, we hope to define the problems and begin the search for answers.

Notes

[1] The data in Appendix A and the tables in this paper are based on replies to a questionnaire and catalogues from the communication schools. The survey was conducted by the Philippine Association of Communication Educators in 1984-85.

[2] The University of the Philippines at Los Baños (UPLB), which offers B.S. DevCom and A.B. Com Arts, is counted as two separate schools.

[3] Asian Institute of Journalism (AIJ) and Central Luzon State University (CLSU) offer graduate communication programs only.

[4] Pamantasan ng Lungsod ng Maynila, Philippine Women's University, U.P. Diliman, and U.P. Los Baños (DevCom Dept.) offer both undergraduate and graduate programs in communication.

[5] Excludes AIJ and CLSU which offer graduate communication programs only.

[6] Some schools offer more than one major field.

Appendix A

Philippine Schools/Departments/Programs of Communication and Degrees Offered

School/University	Mother Unit	School/Department/Program	Year Dept. Started	Degrees Offered	Year Degree Offered	Major	Minor
1. Angeles City University Foundation	College of Arts & Sciences	Dept. of Mass Communication		AB Mass Communication		Journalism	
2. Asian Institute of Journalism			1980	Diplomate in Journalism Master in Media Management	1980		
3. Assumption College	College of Arts & Sciences	Dept. of Mass Communication	1969	AB		Mass Communication	Journalism Media Production Arts Advertising & Public Relations
4. Ateneo de Davao University		Humanities Division		AB	1977	Communication	
5. Ateneo de Naga University		Dept. of English & Development Communication		AB		Development Communication	
6. Ateneo de Manila University	College of Arts & Sciences	Dept. of Communication.	1966	AB	1966	Communication	

377

7. Ateneo de Zamboanga University	Liberal Arts Division	Dept. of Mass Communication	1978-1979	AB	Mass Communication
8. Cebu State College					
9. Central Luzon State University	Institute of Graduate Studies			MS MPS	Development Communication Development Communication
			1982 1982		
10. Centro Escolar University	College of Arts & Sciences		1969	AB in Mass Communication	Journalism Broadcasting
11. De La Salle University	College of Liberal Arts	Language & Literature Dept. Dept. of Communication Arts	1974 1982	AB	Communication Arts
12. Divine Word University of Tacloban		English/Mass Communication Dept.	1981	AB	Mass Communication
13. Far Eastern University	Institute of Arts & Sciences	Dept. of Communication	1956	AB	Mass Communication Speech & Drama
14. La Salle College (Bacolod)				AB	Mass Communication
15. Lyceum of the Philippines	College of Arts & Sciences	Mass Communication Dept.		AB	Mass Communication
16. Maryknoll College		Communication Arts Dept.	1965	AB	Communication Arts
17. New Era College	Institute of Arts & Sciences		1981	AB	Mass Communication

18. Pamantasan ng Lungsod ng Maynila		Dept. of Languages & Mass Communication	1969	Bachelor of Mass Communication MA	1969 1973	Communication
19. Philippine Women's University	College of Arts & Sciences	Communication Arts Dept.	1960	AB MA	1960 1984	Communication Arts Communication Arts
20. Polytechnic University of the Philippines	College of Arts & Sciences	Dept. of Communication	1977	Bachelor in Broadcast Communication Bachelor in Business Journalism		
21. Silliman University		School of Communication	1966	Bachelor of Journalism Bachelor of Mass Communication	1967-1970 1978-present	Community Journalism Community Broadcasting Advertising/ Public Relations Religious Communication Arts
22. St. Joseph's College				AB		Mass Communication
23. St. Louis University	College of Human Sciences	Communication Arts Dept.	1968	AB in Communication	1979	Broadcasting Journalism Advertising/ Public Relations Mass Communication
24. St. Paul's College (Iloilo)			1979	AB		
25. St. Paul's College (Manila)	College of Liberal Arts	Communication Arts Dept.		AB		Communication Arts

26. St. Paul's College (Quezon City)	Liberal Arts Program	1968	AB	1968-1969	Mass Communication
27. St. Scholastica's College (Manila)	School of Liberal Arts		AB		Mass Communication
28. St. Theresa's College (Cebu)	Cebu Area for Mass Communication	1977	AB		Mass Communication
29. Trinity College	College of Arts & Sciences	1977	AB	1977	Mass Communication
30. University of Negros Oc Occidental-Recoletos	College of Arts & Sciences	1976	AB	1976 1983	Mass Communication Journalism Radio & TV Broadcasting Advertising/Public Relations
31. U.P. Diliman	Institute of Mass Communication	1965	AB in Communication	1964-65 1966-67 1975-76 1984-85	Journalism Broadcast Communication Communication Research Film and Audio Visual Com.
			MA in Communication	1975-76 1975-76 1975-76	Journalism Broadcast Communication Communication Research
			Ph.D. in Communication	1982	

32. U.P. at Los Baños	College of Agriculture	Dept. of Agricultural Communication	1962	BSA	1962	Agricultural Communication
		Dept. of Development Communication	1974	BS in Development Communication	1974	Development Journalism Community Broadcasting Educational Communication
	UPLB Graduate School	Dept. of Development Communication		MS in Development Communication	1973	Development Journalism Community Broadcasting Educational Communication
				Ph.D. in Development Communication	1977	General Development Communication
33. U.P. at Los Baños	College of Arts & Sciences	Dept. of Humanities		AB Communication Arts	1974	Speech Communication Theater Arts Writing
34. U.P. College Baguio	Division of Humanities	Discipline of Mass Communication	1982	AB Mass Communication	1982	Journalism Broadcast Communication

35. U.P. College Cebu	Profession Program Undergraduate Studies Division	1976	Bachelor in Com. Arts	Broadcast Communication Journalism
36. U.P. College Tacloban	Dept. of Development Communication	1976	BS in Development Communication	1976-77 Development Journalism Community Broadcasting Rural Broadcasting
37. U.P. Visayas	Division of Humanities	1976	AB	1976 Comparative Literature 1984-85 Broadcast Communication
38. University of Santo Tomas	Faculty of Philosophy & Letters		Litt. B.	1936 Communication Arts
	Faculty of Arts & Letters	1964	AB	1964 Communication Arts Journalism
39. University of Southern Mindanao	Dept. of Development Communication	1980	BS in Development Communication	Development Journalism Community Broadcasting Educational Communication

40. Visayas State College of Agriculture	College of Agriculture	Dept. of Development Communication	1977	BS in Development Communication	Community Broadcasting / Development Journalism
41. West Visayas State College	School of Arts & Sciences	Division of Mass Communication	1965	AB	Mass Communication
42. Xavier University	College of Agriculture		1976	BSA	Development Communication
	College of Arts & Sciences		1979	AB	Development Communication

Epilogue

This epilogue needs to be said. There were other things about the life of this book which need to be said—how it came to be, and how it carries our hopes that those who shall be reading it shall, at some future time, add their own insights to those which are already contained here.

This book got its major impetus from the 1984 and 1985 PACE conferences in UP Los Baños.

During these conferences, PACE felt that one of the more urgent needs of communication schools throughout the country was a basic text on communication.

We also agreed that a core curriculum for mass communication schools had to be designed in the light of new developments in Philippine communication. We presented this as a model communication curriculum for the Department of Education, Culture and Sports to use as a standard for Philippine schools.

But obviously, before the formal approval of any curriculum from the Department, a prior step would have to be addressed: an updated textbook which would introduce the student to the field of Philippine communication.

The 1986 PACE Conference was held at Tagaytay after the EDSA Revolution and the main chapters of this book are the outcome of that conference.

While it will be difficult to catalogue the contribution of individuals who in one way or another helped in making this book we feel it is proper to at least acknowledge the role of PACE, as an organization, in its making. PACE has not only been the driving spirit behind this book, but also a potent and significant influence on communication in this country today.

PACE believes that this book is a significant one. Thorough. Well edited. A much-needed update on communication after the long sleep of death during the time of the Dictator.

We recall an excitement, an electricity which was generated in all participants during that 1984 conference at UPLB, when the keynote speaker, Fr. Joaquin Bernas, S.J., reminded us about the call to vigilance issued by Philip of Macedon during the time of the Peloponnesian wars. And how suddenly in 1985 our Orly Mercado, resplendent in his moment of triumph, became for us an occasion for new hope in what the media, media education, and the men and women in communication media can do for the society of the post EDSA Revolution.

With this book, we acknowledge that new spirit, that new hope which rose in our hearts when, during those moments PACE found a new meaning in our work in communication education and decided to chart the new directions we must take, if we are to do something for our country in the Cory era.

We hope that this book may be better appreciated by its readers if they realize that it is part of a communal effort of PACE to situate for our students the new-found freedoms we enjoy in the Philippines today.

Alberto V. Ampil, S.J., at Xavier
PACE Vice President
September 24, 1988